An Introduction to the Ancient World

Integrating the results of scholarly work from the past decade, the authors of *An Introduction to the Ancient World: Second Edition*, De Blois and Van der Spek, have fully updated and revised all sixteen chapters of this best-selling introductory textbook. It is unique in covering the history and culture of the ancient Near East, Greece and Rome within the framework of a short narrative history of events and offers an easily readable, integrated overview for students of history, classics, archaeology and philosophy, whether at college, at undergraduate level or among the wider reading public.

Focusing mainly on the social, political and cultural processes which have influenced later western civilizations, this revised second edition offers a completely new section on early Christianity and more specific information on the religions, economies, societies of the ancient Near East. There is extended coverage of Greek, Macedonian and Near Eastern history of the fourth to second centuries BC and the history of the Late Roman Republic. The consequences of Julius Caesar's violent death are covered in more detail, as are the history and society of Imperial Rome.

Benefits and features of this new edition:

- Comprehensive: covers 3,000 years of ancient history and provides the basis for a typical one-semester course
- Lavishly illustrated: contains maps, line drawings and plates to support and supplement the text, with updated captions.
- Clearly and concisely written: written by two established and respected university teachers with thirty years' experience in the subject areas.
- Well-organized: traces the broad outline of political history but also concentrates on particular topics
- User-friendly: includes chapter menus, an extensive and expanded bibliography organised by subject area and three appendices, an improved introduction and the addition of an epilogue.

Lukas de Blois is Professor of Ancient History at the University of Nijmegen, the Netherlands, and specialises in Roman and Greek history and ancient historiography. **Robartus van der Spek** is Professor of Ancient History at the Free University of Amsterdam, and specialises in the history of the ancient Near East.

AN INTRODUCTION TO THE ANCIENT WORLD

L. de Blois and
R.J. van der Spek

Translated from the
Dutch by Susan Mellor

 Routledge
Taylor & Francis Group

LONDON AND NEW YORK

First published in 1983 by Uitgeveri Coutino b.v.

First published in English in 1997
by Routledge

Second edition published 2008
by Routledge
2 Park Square, Milton Park, Abingdon, Oxon. OX14 4RN

Simultaneously published in the USA and Canada
by Routledge
270 Madison Ave., New York, NY 10016

Reprinted 2009, 2010 (twice)

Routledge is an imprint of the Taylor & Francis Group, an informa business

© 1997 and 2008 L. de Blois and R.J. van der Spek

Designed by Keystroke
Typeset in Amasis and Avenir by Swales & Willis, Exeter, Devon
Printed and bound by TJ International Ltd, Padstow, Cornwall.

British Library Cataloguing in Publication Data
A catalogue record for this book is available from the British Library

Library of Congress Cataloging in Publication Data
A catalog record for this book has been requested

ISBN10: 0–415–45826–9 (hbk)
ISBN10: 0–415–45827–7 (pbk)
ISBN10: 0–203–89312–8 (ebk)

ISBN13: 978–0–415–45826–9 (hbk)
ISBN13: 978–0–415–45827–6 (pbk)
ISBN13: 978–0–203–89312–8 (ebk)

CONTENTS

ILLUSTRATIONS

MAPS

FIGURES

PREFACE TO THE NEW EDITION

This "Introduction to the Ancient World" is a thoroughly revised and expanded edition of the book with the same title that appeared in 1997. Like its predecessor it is still a short survey of the history of the ancient Near East, Greece, and Rome that can be used in courses of ancient history, but also in broader kinds of teaching, such as courses focusing on (ancient) culture and society, at different levels of education.

In selecting the material for the first edition we employed three basic criteria. First of all, we decided to discuss phenomena of a general historical interest that also played a role in other historical periods, such as social structures, the urge for expansion, the development of government, political theories, division of power, social conflicts, production methods, and religions. Our second criterion was the effects of such factors in later Western civilization. Where possible, we discussed issues that were to become important in Europe and the New World in later times. Our third criterion was the discussed topics' place in a continuous historical context. We believe that if your aim is to write a book providing a brief introduction to a particular period in history there is no sense in discussing topics without considering how they relate to one another, and placing them in the wider context of historical development. That is the reason why this book contains a survey of the entire history of ancient Egypt, Western Asia, Greece, and Rome.

A revised edition is a consequence of progress in scholarly work. In the years since the publication of the first edition our understanding of the ancient world has been enhanced by new archaeological finds and texts, but it has also changed, because scholarly interests have changed. Today's scholars are more interested in matters such as mentality and spiritual life, and are less preoccupied with socioeconomic processes. Any book is the product of its time, and the twenty-first century approaches the ancient world in a different way than the twentieth. This is why the book has been so thoroughly revised. Our aim to provide a brief introduction to the ancient world has remained unchanged, but we felt that some topics should now be given more attention, and that we should here and there provide more event-based history. We have also rewritten large parts on the basis of commonly accepted new insights.

L. de Blois has written the chapter on the Greeks in the Classical period (Chapter 10), the chapters on Roman history (Chapters 12–16), and Appendices 1–3. R. J. van der Spek is the author of the parts on the Near East, Greece in the Archaic period, and Hellenism (Chapters 1–9 and 11 and the Epilogue of Chapter 16 on the end of the ancient world). All the chapters were the object of mutual comment and discussion.

Over the years many scholars have given us invaluable advice and have saved us from errors and thereby improved the book. We are very grateful to them. The authors of this book are of course responsible for the text of the book as it now is, including interpretations and any remaining errors.

L. de Blois and R. J. van der Spek
Nijmegen/Amsterdam, January 2008

INTRODUCTION

The ancient history covered in this book is the history of the cradle of European civilization. Since the voyages of discovery of the sixteenth century and especially since the colonial imperialism of the nineteenth and twentieth centuries, this civilization has spread across the whole world; its roots, however, lie in the countries surrounding the Mediterranean, in particular in the cultural centers of the ancient Near East and in those of the ancient Greeks and Romans. It is in those areas that, between 3500 BC and AD 500, many of the distinctive features of modern Western culture originated. Christianity, for example, evolved from Judaism in Palestine and acquired its philosophical accoutrements and organizational structure in the Roman empire; Islam has borrowed a lot from Jewish, Christian, and Greek traditions; present-day Western philosophy is firmly rooted in Greek schools of thought; many current legal systems are largely based on Roman law; education in the Greek and Latin literary culture is still provided at secondary schools today. Other elements of modern Western culture that originated in the Mediterranean are architecture and the visual arts, literature, and also science, which evolved from Greek ways of thinking.

All this does not mean to imply that the ancient world is interesting for these reasons alone. Antiquity is an integral part of human history, fascinating in its own right. Ancient history, moreover, offers us a wonderful opportunity for comparative research. Numerous processes, phenomena, and relations that we find important in more recent historical periods actually occurred in analogous forms in antiquity, too. Phenomena of all times and all places first manifested themselves in the Mediterranean in antiquity: this area witnessed the emergence of states and cities and of their governments, social stratification, the development of decision processes, the origins of expansion and its effects on social relationships and modes of thought, the interaction of different cultures (acculturation and integration processes), and developments in religion and philosophy. They are all very similar to what we have witnessed in recent times, and yet at the same time quite different.

Neither does ancient history being the history of the cradle of European civilization imply that antiquity still exists today. Antiquity is literally a thing of the past, like youth in an old man. It is the difficult task of historians to recreate a reliable account of those bygone days. Like all other sciences, history is constantly in motion. The interpretation of the past presented by this book's authors is a product of two authors writing in the early twenty-first century, strongly influenced by present-day standards. So this antiquity differs from the antiquity of almost twenty years ago, when the first edition of this book was published.

Our knowledge of ancient history is partly based on what has come down to us through the ages—information that was passed on from generation to generation, from antiquity to the present day. Numerous works of classical historians, poets, orators, philosophers, and scientists have been preserved because they were copied over and over again until ultimately the invention of printing made them accessible to a wider public. Of course, quite a few other ancient works have not survived the ravages of time. One important "filter" should be mentioned here. A good deal of ancient philosophical and scientific heritage has come down to us via the Arabs, who based a large part of their lavish literary and scientific output in the Middle Ages on ancient— mostly Greek—works. They of course added their own interpretations, and that had a profound influence on Western thought.

Another major source of information on ancient times is the evidence that has been recovered in excavations or has come to light in other ways. Such evidence includes inscriptions (texts engraved in stone or some other durable material), papyri (letters, receipts, poems and other pieces of writing on a type of paper that was made from Egyptian papyrus reed), clay tablets, and coins (bearing representations and legends). Papyri have been found almost exclusively in Egypt, where they have been preserved by the dry desert sand. Houses, public buildings, temples, fortifications, and other structures and such objects as ornaments, weapons, and household goods can also tell us much about the past.

For the history of the ancient Near East in particular we have to rely on evidence of the latter kind, that is, finds recovered for example in excavations. The same incidentally holds for the history of the Celts and Germanic peoples. In the ancient Near East the process of passing down knowledge from one generation to the next came to an end in the first centuries of the Christian era, when the languages and scripts that had been employed for that purpose went out of use. Until the nineteenth century, when large-scale excavations and the deciphering of some ancient written languages opened up a wealth of new information, our knowledge of the ancient Near East was limited to what could be inferred from references in the Bible and in the works of Greek and Roman authors.

But finds have also greatly increased our understanding of Greek and Roman history. Valuable information has been obtained in specialist studies of different categories of finds, such as epigraphy (the study of inscriptions), numismatics (coins), papyrology (manuscripts written on papyri), and archaeology (material remains, architecture, town planning, painting, sculpture, etc.).

History is preceded by prehistory—the period for which we have no written evidence and for knowledge of which we are consequently entirely dependent on material remains. Archaeologists have divided prehistory into three distinct periods on the basis of the different durable materials that were used for the manufacture of objects in those times. These three periods are the Stone Age, the Bronze Age, and the Iron Age. The dates of these ages differ from region to region. The span of this chronological system in fact extends into historical times in some parts of the world, for example in the ancient Near East, where the Iron Age started around 1200 BC, some two thousand years after the development of writing. The beginning of historical times also differs from one region to another. The Apennine peninsula, for example, entered history more than two thousand years later than Egypt. The mere fact that writing was introduced in a particular area in a particular period does not always mean that we have a wealth of written evidence for that area and period. Much of the written evidence that has been preserved is poorly legible or provides only limited information, being, say, nothing more than part of a palace's administration of a particular year.

In antiquity itself, information was by no means equally distributed among the different classes and groups of the various societies. There were no newspapers or any other mass media. The lower social classes were dependent on the shreds of information that they picked up in the streets and village squares, from transients and passers-by, and they were readily impressed by rumours. They were, moreover, insufficiently educated to be able to critically assess the information that reached them. The notables and the people who traveled to foreign regions, such as merchants and seafarers, were better informed. They maintained relations of guest-friendship with people in other towns and other regions, with whom they also corresponded. Letters and news were exchanged via merchants and other travelers.

Throughout this book, frequent use is made of the terms "Indo-European" and "Semitic." The reason for this is that it is common practice to classify and name ancient peoples on the basis of the languages they spoke. The Semitic languages are closely related to one another and the same holds for the different branches of the Indo-European family of languages. Hebrew, Aramaic, Akkadian, and Arabic are all Semitic languages. The Indo-European languages include Greek, Latin (the language spoken by the Romans), Persian and the Celtic and Germanic languages. The terms "Semitic" and "Indo-European" have little to do with race or nation.

To conclude, a few remarks on chronological systems. Nowadays, we are accustomed to a uniform chronological system that is known and used all over the world, but things were different in antiquity. In ancient times, each people had its own chronological system, based on the reigns of kings, the terms of office of high officials, or important events. In Athens, for example, time was reckoned on the basis of the terms of office of the archons (the town's chief magistrates), while historians sometimes used olympiads—the intervals between the Olympic Games, which were held every four years. Events in Athens were said to have taken place in such-and-such an olympiad or during the term of office of this or that archon. The system used in Rome was based on the terms of office of the two consuls (the two chief magistrates in the Roman republic). The same system continued to be used in the imperial age, when the consuls had less power, having become subordinate to the emperor.

Another problem concerns present-day reconstructions of ancient chronologies. Thanks to information on methods used to reckon time in antiquity, such as those described above, we are often able to establish relative chronologies for certain periods without too much difficulty. Archaeologists likewise usually succeed in reconstructing relative chronologies by dating finds in relation to the distinct layers from which they are recovered. New buildings were in bygone days often built on top of the ruins of collapsed older structures, so layers further removed from the present-day surface are generally older than those higher up. Far more difficult—sometimes even impossible—is to date events or the time of an object's production in absolute terms, i.e., in dates relating to our chronology. Fortunately we do have some keys to help us. The most important are references in ancient texts to astronomical phenomena such as solar eclipses, the 14C method, and dendrochronology. The 14C method yields a rough estimate of the age of

FAMILIES OF LANGUAGES

Semitic languages

Old Akkadian ⎫
Babylonian ⎬ = Akkadian
Assyrian   ⎭

Amorite

Aramaic and Chaldean

Canaanite and Phoenician

Hebrew

Arabic

Egyptian ⎫
Ethiopian ⎭ partly Hamitic = African family of languages

Indo-European languages

Sanskrit

Hittite

Aryan or Iranian languages: Median, Persian, and Parthian

Greek

Latin and the languages derived from it:
Italian, Spanish, French, and Romanian

Slavic languages
Russian, Polish, Serbian, Croatian, Czech, Slovak, and Bulgarian

Celtic
languages of Celts, Galatians in Asia Minor, Britons and Celtiberians in Spain; now: Breton, Welsh, and Irish Gaelic

Germanic languages
languages of the Frisians, Franks, Saxons, Batavians, Angles and Goths

Armenian

Languages of unknown families

Sumerian

Hurrian and Urartian

Kassite

Elamite

dead organic matter by measuring the decrease in radioactive radiation in the organic matter and the amount of time this will have involved. Dendrochronology is based on long sequences of growth rings in old tree wood, established on the basis of the knowledge that the widths of tree rings show the same annual deviations over large areas due to the climatic conditions in the years in question. In spite of these methods a lot of uncertainty often remains. Sometimes the available information is too scanty or it is unclear which solar eclipse a particular text refers to. The problems of course increase the further back in time we go. Many events in the third and second millennia BC, not to mention earlier ones, can only be dated approximately. The exact dates of some events in later periods of ancient history are also uncertain. Interpretations of the chronologies of Western Asia and Egypt between c. 2000 and 1300 in particular are constantly changing, resulting in differences of some 50 to 100 years in some cases. No consensus has yet been reached. So the dates given for this period on the following pages are rough estimates and where possible rounded figures.

PART I THE ANCIENT NEAR EAST

1 THE ORIGINS OF THE CIVILIZATIONS OF EGYPT AND MESOPOTAMIA

On the banks of the rivers Euphrates and Tigris in Mesopotamia (largely what is now Iraq) and the Nile in Egypt emerged civilizations that were to have a profound influence on the history of the eastern half of the Mediterranean. The rise of these civilizations, just before 3000 BC, was characterized by increasing urbanization, the birth of states, and the invention of writing. These civilizations did not appear out of the blue, of course; their foundations had been laid over a period that spanned several hundreds of thousands of years. Archaeologists have divided this long period, which is called the Stone Age, into an Old, Middle, and New Stone Age on the basis of changes in the stone implements that were produced during that period. In the Old and Middle Stone Ages people lived off what they happened to come across, off the animals they hunted, and the plants they gathered. They followed their prey into new areas and were hence constantly on the move. By the end of the Middle Stone Age (c. 10,000 BC), man had improved his tools to such an extent that he was able to make more efficient use of the natural resources. That meant that some groups of people could remain in one area for a longer period of time, sheltered from the elements in primitive huts or caves. The next step in man's development was the transition to an entirely new way of life characterized by a greater control of nature: man started to cultivate the cereals which he had until then always gathered as wild plants, and domesticated the animals which he had hunted in the past. This transition took place at different times in different parts of the world, but it is believed that it occurred in the Near East first. The process really got under way around the beginning of the New Stone Age, or Neolithic, as this period, characterized by the use of ground stone tools, is also called. Being of such tremendous importance for the further development of civilization, this transformation is often referred to as the "Neolithic revolution," although the whole process actually took thousands of years and the first signs of the fundamental changes that were to take place had already appeared long before the Neolithic.

Two different kinds of agriculture are distinguished: rainfall agriculture and irrigation agriculture. A prerequisite for rainfall agriculture is an annual precipitation of at least 250 mm. So this form of agriculture could be practiced only in Iran, northern Iraq, northern Syria, and the coastal Mediterranean. Egypt and southern Mesopotamia had to rely on irrigation agriculture. Areas that are dependent on rainfall agriculture are very vulnerable. A slight decrease in rainfall will immediately lead to a food crisis and a more protracted change in climate will have major social and political consequences.

"Irrigation" is understood to include both natural and artificial irrigation. The best conditions for agriculture based on natural irrigation were to be found in Egypt. Every year, the Nile flooded the land before the sowing season (between July and September). The Egyptians could then sow their crops in the damp soil when the river receded. In Mesopotamia the land was less regularly flooded, the floods moreover occurring earlier in the year—from February until April, i.e., just before harvesting time. This meant that the occupants of that region had to practice artificial irrigation. Irrigation agriculture was far more productive than rainfall agriculture, enabling crop yield ratios of at least 15:1, often indeed a lot higher. We get a good impression of how high such ratios are when we compare them with later figures for Greece, Italy, and medieval Europe, where the average ratio was about 4/5:1 and a good ratio was 7/10:1 (e.g., in Campania in Italy). Another reason why crop yields were higher in Mesopotamia is that people in that area used a sowing plow (see Figure 1.1).

The development of agriculture was of fundamental importance for the further history of mankind. It meant that more people could remain settled in one particular area for a longer period of time and that more people could concentrate their attention on activities other than food production. People consequently started to specialize in all kinds of crafts and became carpenters, tanners, scribes (at least after the invention of the art of writing, around 3400 BC) and metalworkers (after around 3000 BC, when man discovered how to exploit and smelt copper ore and produce bronze, an alloy of copper and tin). A civil service and a priesthood emerged (and the associated institutions: the state and the temple). Some of the villages that had originated at the beginning of the Neolithic began to resemble fortified cities; Jericho, for example, had already evolved into a city by around 7000 BC and there were several cities in Asia Minor and Syria. The largest and most influential cities, however, were those that arose on the banks of the major rivers of Egypt and Mesopotamia in the fourth millennium BC. It was there, along those rivers, that the largest quantities of food could be produced and the largest numbers of people could live together.

FIGURE 1.1   Sowing plow; impression of a cylinder seal (2nd millennium BC)

Notes. With this instrument plowing and sowing could be combined. The central figure is pouring seed into a chute, which guides it directly into the furrow. This minimized the loss of seed, enabling a prolific harvest.

The core of a Mesopotamian city was the temple, the abode of the state deity, whose needs had to be provided for by the community. Those temples grew into powerful organizations that owned vast estates; they engaged in a wide range of activities, including agriculture, stock breeding, and various crafts, for which they employed a large staff.

It was the requirements of this temple economy that led to the invention of writing, some time between 3400 and 3200 BC. The Mesopotamian script is known as the "cuneiform" script— so called after the wedge-shaped appearance of the impressions of which the later characters of that script were composed. The hieroglyphic script of the Egyptians was developed around the same time as the cuneiform script.

At first, the cuneiform and hieroglyphic scripts were both partly pictographic (with each word being represented by a picture) and partly ideographic (with each word being represented by a symbol). Later on, the signs came to stand for sounds (syllables), too. The Egyptian script only rendered consonants, vowels being ignored. Both the Mesopotamian and the Egyptian script remained highly complex forms of writing and were used only by small groups of specially trained professional scribes.

In antiquity, the presence of cities did not lead to contrasts between the urban and rural populations of the kind known to us from later times. In most of the cities the majority of the inhabitants were peasants, who left the city to work on their land every morning and returned in the evening. In the ancient Near East, a far greater and far more important contrast than that between city dwellers and country folk was that between the sedentary and the nomadic way of life. This contrast was closely associated with a major difference in subsistence patterns. Agriculturalists led a sedentary life; they remained settled in one area because they had to till their land and look after their crops. Herders were nomads; they constantly moved around from one place to another in search of fresh pastures for their animals. However, there was not always such a clear-cut difference between the two. Primitive agriculturalists sometimes remained in one area for only a short period of time, to then move on again a few years later, when they had exhausted the soil. Some herders moved around within a relatively small area, for example from summer pastures to winter pastures. This seasonal migration is called "transhumance." The transhumant nomads liked to remain in the vicinity of the settlements of the agriculturalists, with whom they could then exchange products. Occasionally a group of (semi)nomads would adopt a partly or entirely sedentary way of life and take control of a city. There were also wealthy landowners who owned herds besides land and employed herders to pasture their animals, sometimes at considerable distances from their dwellings. Throughout the entire history of the ancient Near East the representatives of these two opposed ways of life were constantly flung between feelings of hatred and friendship towards one another—hatred because the sedentary peoples were afraid of being plundered by the (semi)nomads, and friendship because the two groups were dependent on one another for the exchange of products. The contrast between the two different ways of life became a popular theme in the literature of this area. It forms the basis of the Biblical story of the shepherd Abel who was murdered by the agriculturalist Cain.

The geographical conditions of Egypt and Mesopotamia were very similar in some respects: both areas were dependent on river water due to the almost total absence of rain, and both were poor in various important resources, such as metals and timber. In other respects, however, they were totally different. Conditions for agriculture, for example, were more favourable in Egypt

FIGURE 1.2 Clay tablet from Jebel Aruda, Syria, length 9.2 cm, c. 3400–3200 BC.

Notes. The tablet shows a number (372?) and impressions made by a cylinder seal. A cylinder seal was made of some hard material in which a design was carved in mirror image. When the seal was rolled over soft clay, the design was impressed in the clay. The impressed clay tablets served to identify the owner (private person, temple, palace) of the objects to which they were attached. Clay tablets developed from the custom of keeping records of goods (or cattle) by enclosing clay tokens in a sealed clay envelope. The clay envelope had to be broken when the quantities of the goods were to be checked. Later the number of tokens, representing the quantity of goods, was indicated on the outside of the envelope. In a following stage, the tokens were altogether omitted: the envelope became a solid clay tablet indicating a number. Later clay tablets show numbers and marks representing the goods. This is how the first script originated. At an even later stage, the marks were also used to indicate a sound or a syllable. The same system of numbers encountered on this tablet, which came to light in an excavation conducted by a team of archaeologists from Leiden (the Netherlands) in Syria, is also known from Mesopotamia and southwest Iran (Elam). This points to the existence of intensive trade contacts that embraced the whole of Western Asia by the fourth millennium BC already. This is confirmed by the recurrent motifs that are observable on earthenware all over this region.

than in Mesopotamia. As already mentioned above, the Nile flooded the land before the sowing season, the Euphrates and Tigris not until later in the year. Whereas the Egyptians could sow their crops in the fertile deposits left behind by the receding river, the Mesopotamians had to go to great efforts to conduct the water to their fields via canals. The water of the Nile was, moreover, of a better quality; that of the Euphrates and the Tigris contained harmful salts, which became mixed with the groundwater. The groundwater level of the low-lying, flat land was very high and

MAP 1.1 Rainfall in the Near East

Notes: In the areas with less than 250 mm rainfall no crops can be grown without irrigation. In the areas to the south of the 100-mm limit too little grows to allow stock-keeping.

the salts migrated to the surface of the land via capillary cracks in the clay. Protracted irrigation without sufficient drainage could ultimately make the soil unfit for cultivation owing to complete salinization. That this indeed happened can be inferred from the crops that were cultivated: in southern Mesopotamia the amount of barley cultivated gradually increased, whereas the amount of wheat decreased. The reason for this is that barley is more resistant to salt. Egypt, on the contrary, is believed to have grown more wheat than barley throughout antiquity.

Another important difference between Egypt and Mesopotamia concerns the surrounding areas. In Egypt the transition from arable land to desert sand was so abrupt that it was possible to stand—literally—with one foot in a green field and the other in the dry desert sand. In Mesopotamia the transition from fertile to less fertile land was more gradual. Secondly, being totally surrounded by uninhabitable deserts, Egypt was far less accessible than Mesopotamia, and consequently far more isolated from the outside world. This difference had major political consequences: whereas the history of Egypt is fairly stable and static, with relatively little interference from outside, that of Mesopotamia is characterized by constant invasions of foreign peoples, many of whom assumed control and founded new empires. Nevertheless, a considerable degree of continuity was preserved in Mesopotamia too, as most of the newcomers adapted themselves to the original occupants' cultural traditions.

2 THE THIRD MILLENNIUM

THE EARLY BRONZE AGE

Egypt, the Old Kingdom (c. 2600–c. 2150)

The history of ancient Egypt is divided into periods in two different ways, namely on the basis of "dynasties" and on the basis of "kingdoms." The division based on dynasties was devised by the Egyptian priest Manetho, who wrote a history of Egypt in Greek in the third century BC, in which he divided the chronology of Egypt between thirty dynasties or royal houses. The division into three "kingdoms" is modern. These kingdoms comprise periods in which Egypt enjoyed great prosperity and political unity. They alternate with "intermediate periods" of decline and political fragmentation. In the intermediate periods Egypt was not ruled by a single king, but by several local governors who had acquired independence in their own provinces. In those periods several dynasties were consequently in power at the same time—a fact that escaped Manetho, who arranged all the dynasties in successive order.

The three kingdoms are the Old Kingdom (c. 2600–c. 2150), the Middle Kingdom (c. 2000–c. 1800), and the New Kingdom (c. 1550–c. 1100). The last period distinguished in the history of ancient Egypt is called the Late Period. In that period (from c. 750 BC until—in fact—AD 1922) the country was frequently ruled by foreign dynasties or was incorporated in other powerful empires.

As can be inferred from the above dates, the third millennium comprises the Old Kingdom and a preceding period in which Egypt was united into a single realm, which is known as the "Early Dynastic Period" (c. 3000–2600; first and second dynasties). It is in this Early Dynastic Period that the Egyptian hieroglyphic script was invented. In spite of the fact that Egypt was unified under one ruler in this period, the whole history of this country was to remain characterized by a distinction between Lower Egypt, which comprised the Nile Delta, and Upper Egypt, which embraced the area to the south of the Delta up to the First Cataract (rapid). The king was called the "Lord of the Two Lands," the pharaohs wore double crowns and there was a double administrative system. This duality was in keeping with the Egyptian belief that only things that consisted of two parts were complete.

It was the kings of the Old Kingdom who commissioned the construction of the pyramids, for which the Egyptians are famous all over the world. These monumental tombs testify to the tremendous power of the kings of this period and their strong hold over manpower and material resources. The pyramids were built near Memphis, the capital of ancient Egypt.

The peasants were summoned to work on these ambitious building projects in the periods that the land was flooded. Their readiness to make this great effort is understandable when we consider that kingship was regarded as a divine institution. The works of tens of thousands of people, the pyramids are clear testimonies of the great organizational capacity of the early Egyptian state. The largest monuments were built during the fourth dynasty (c. 2500); they are all of stone. The younger pyramids, which were built from mudbrick, are smaller.

FIGURE 2.1
The crowns of Egypt

Notes. 1 The white crown of Upper Egypt; 2 The red crown of Lower Egypt; 3 The double crown.

1

2

3

FIGURE 2.2   The pyramids of Kings Cheops, Chephren, and Mycerinus near Giza, fourth dynasty

Notes. The fertile Egyptian land is visible in the foreground. The pyramids in the background are in the desert. The transition from fertile land to desert sand is still as abrupt as it was in antiquity.

The Old Kingdom lasted for five centuries. By the end of that period the provincial governors had become so powerful that the pharaoh was no longer able to sustain his central authority. The provincial governors had been granted land as a form of "salary" and this land had been passed on from father to son, along with the office. As a result, the pharaoh had gradually lost his hold on his officials. We now also know that the area flooded by the Nile gradually decreased towards the end of the Old Kingdom. Around the same time, reports of famine started to appear. That is probably the reason why the Egyptians started practicing artificial irrigation, in order to be able to make the most efficient use of the scarcer water.

Mesopotamia, Sumer, and Akkad

The third millennium also saw the rise of another great civilization in the Near East—that of Mesopotamia. The foundations for this civilization had been laid in the fourth millennium already, but it was the Sumerians and the Akkadians who brought it to fruition in the third millennium. Of these two peoples, the Sumerians were the most important. Exactly when they arrived in Mesopotamia and whether it is they who deserve the credit for the invention of writing and the construction of the first cities in southern Mesopotamia we do not know. What we do know is that they are the people who made those cities great; they also made extensive use of the art of writing for keeping accounts in their temples and palaces and for composing religious and literary texts. Sculpture, architecture, religious imagery, literary styles, and views on kingship, law, and society were all developed by the Sumerians (Early Dynastic Period, c. 2900–2300 BC).

The Sumerians also laid the groundwork for various sciences, including arithmetic, astronomy, botany and medicine. In their schools, the Sumerians learned their complex script by memorizing all kinds of texts. Lists of technical terms in numerous different fields have been preserved. The lists of the different professions practiced in those days provide a fair amount of insight into the development of specialization enabled by the major economic improvements brought about by the introduction of irrigation agriculture (see p. 10). Vestiges of the sexagesimal system of Sumerian arithmetic are still observable in our division of the hour into sixty minutes and of the circle into 360 degrees. The Sumerians passed on their culture from one generation to the next, over many centuries, but also over vast areas, across the whole of the ancient Near East. Their cuneiform script was adopted in regions as far away as southwest Iran (Elam) and even Syria (Ebla), where the Sumerian language was learned and Sumerian texts were studied in schools modeled on those of the Sumerians. That way the cultural history of Western Asia became infused with the Sumerian civilization.

And yet the Sumerians never really showed any imperialistic tendencies; they never aspired to gain control over large parts of Western Asia. Instead, they continued to live in modest city states. At first, life in those city states revolved entirely around the temple, led by a priest-ruler, but later on a dichotomy gradually emerged, resulting in a secular ruler whose duties included leadership in war operating independently alongside a high priest. This marked the birth of kingship, and beside the temple arose a palace, with its own bureaucracy, estates, and workshops. Now and then, a king of such a city would capture a few other cities. The Sumerians of later ages regarded kingship as a matter of course, as something that had come down from heaven in the very beginning.

For three thousand years the palace and the temple remained the two most powerful organizations in Mesopotamia. Throughout that period those organizations constantly intruded into one another's sphere of influence. Sometimes they would dispute territory or quarrel about the autonomy of the temples; at other times, however, they would be of help to one another. The kings, who were regarded as the representatives of the deities, would for example frequently commission and support the construction of temples.

The Akkadians are so called after Akkad, the city that became the center of an empire around 2300 BC. Founded by King Sargon, this empire embraced the whole of Mesopotamia and extended all the way into Asia Minor (see Map 2.1). Akkadians were Semites, that is, speakers of a Semitic language. This group of languages nowadays includes Arabic and Hebrew. The "Akkadians" were already living in Mesopotamia at the beginning of the third millennium (mainly in an area a short distance to the north of the territory occupied by the Sumerians), but it was only when they started using the cuneiform script for their own language, Old Akkadian, that they began to stand out as a distinct group. The Akkadians borrowed much from the Sumerians, including their script, their religious imagery, scientific principles, and literary styles. But their culture also contained elements of their own because they continued to worship their own deities (which were, however, identified with Sumerian gods) and to use their own language. The Akkadians built a large and powerful empire; Sargon's successors even claimed hegemony over the entire world, calling themselves "King of the Four Quarters of the World"; they also had themselves deified. But they were unable

MAP 2.1 The ancient Near East in the third millennium BC

to prevent the local revolts and invasions of tribes from the east that were ultimately to cause the downfall of their empire.

The collapse of the Akkadian empire was followed by the revival of several Sumerian cities, which is referred to as the "Sumerian renaissance" (*c.* 2100–2000). The kings of Ur, known as the "Third Dynasty of Ur," founded another great empire in Mesopotamia. Thanks to the discovery of some 100,000 clay tablets, part of the palace's administration, we are relatively well informed about this empire. These tablets show that the palace had eclipsed the temple and had acquired complete control over the economy.

The empire of Ur was also overthrown by invaders, this time from the West, namely the Amorites. The Amorites, a tribe of nomads who spoke Western Semitic languages, were attracted to Mesopotamia by the region's fertile river valleys. They caused much havoc among the occupants of those valleys, whose fields they pillaged. They also cut off the cities' grain supplies. Local officials took advantage of this situation to sever their ties with Ur and established their own independent dynasties. Some scholars argue that climate change was an important factor in this period, too, with progressively drier conditions increasing pressure of the steppe nomads on the river valleys. This would imply that the crises that occurred in Egypt and Mesopotamia at the end of the third millennium were caused by the same climatic phenomenon.

FIGURE 2.3 The Ziqqurat of Ur, Third Dynasty, *c.* 2100 BC

Notes. Such stepped temple towers were built from the end of the third millennium until into the third century BC. They evolved from the temples on platforms known from late prehistoric times. The temple of Ur was dedicated to the Sumerian moon-god Nanna, who was called Sin in Akkadian.

Epilogue

The third millennium BC ended with a period of great confusion and stagnation in the two most important cultural centers of the Near East: Egypt and Mesopotamia. Nevertheless, a firm basis had been created on which later generations could continue the work begun by their predecessors. For example, Egyptian painting, relief carving, and freestanding sculpture had already acquired their distinctive features, which were to remain essentially unchanged for many centuries.

Although Sumerian died out as a spoken language, it continued to be used as a written language for religious and scholarly purposes, while Akkadian became the spoken language in Mesopotamia and the international language for correspondence and administration. Akkadian also started to be used increasingly for literary texts, too. The Sumero-Akkadian culture consequently continued to exert a powerful influence. Traces of that influence are indeed observable throughout the entire history of the Near East right up to the Hellenistic period.

3 THE SECOND MILLENNIUM

THE MIDDLE BRONZE AGE (c. 2000–c. 1600)

Egypt, the Middle Kingdom (c. 2000–c. 1800) and the Second Intermediate Period (c. 1800–c. 1550)

Shortly before 2000 BC, a dynasty of provincial governors in Thebes (the eleventh) restored unity in Egypt and made Thebes the capital of the new unified realm. The most powerful kings of the Middle Kingdom were those of the twelfth dynasty. They led military campaigns into the Levant without, however, succeeding in gaining permanent control over that area. It is in the reports of those campaigns that we find the earliest mention of the towns of Jerusalem and Shechem. In their campaigns in the south the Egyptians were more successful: there they managed to extend their sway over Nubia (the Sudan) up to the Third Cataract. The kings of the twelfth dynasty are also renowned for their exploits in their home country: they brought the Fayyûm oasis into cultivation and made that area fit to become the center of their government. During their reigns, pyramids and temples for the dead arose in the Fayyûm. The kings of the twelfth dynasty also put an end to succession problems by choosing one of their sons as their successors and appointing him co-regent during their lives; that son then succeeded his father after the latter's death.

The Middle Kingdom was the golden age of Egyptian culture, especially literature. It was the period in which hieroglyphs acquired their ideal shape and literary works gained an exemplary quality, making them "classics."

Around 1800 the power of the kings started to decline again and unity was lost. There came an end to the campaigns and fewer building projects were launched. These developments mark the beginning of the "Second Intermediate Period" (c. 1800–1550), the period in which Egypt came to be ruled by foreigners: the Hyksos. These people, who probably came from the Levant, settled in the Nile Delta (something similar had previously happened in Mesopotamia, where a tribe of Amorites had settled). After some time, the Hyksos gained control over the Delta and established their own dynasties. Other local rulers were forced to acknowledge the suzerainty of the Hyksos dynasty.

MAP 3.1
Ancient Egypt, 3000–525 BC

Mesopotamia, the Old Assyrian and Old Babylonian empires

In Mesopotamia, the early second millennium saw the birth of two nations that were to dominate the history of that region for the following fifteen hundred years: Assyria and Babylonia. Oddly enough, much of the credit for these nations' rise to power is due to a foreign people, namely the aforementioned Amorites, who had settled in Mesopotamia around the end of the third millennium (see p. 18). This infiltration of a semi-nomadic people into an area with a highly developed culture, followed by the newcomers' assumption of power in that area, is an example of a phenomenon that took place several times throughout the history of the ancient Near East. The Amorites gained control over Assur, Babylon, and Mari (see Map 3.2), but they did not entirely relinquish their nomadic way of life. The titles assumed by some of the Amorite rulers clearly reflect their somewhat hybrid position. They would call themselves "King of the city of X, chief of tribe Y." The Amorites did not succeed in supplanting the Sumero-Akkadian culture entirely on their own. Sumerian and Akkadian remained the written languages (the latter now comprising two variants: Assyrian and Babylonian) and the cuneiform script continued to be used. After some time, Amorite went out of use as a spoken language, too.

- - - - - Old Assyrian Empire (c. 1800)

············ Old Babylonian Empire (c. 1750)

- ---- -·- Old Hittite kingdom

MAP 3.2 The Old Assyrian and Old Babylonian empires

Northern Mesopotamia, the Old Assyrian empire (c. 2000–c. 1760)

The city of Assur had already existed in the early third millennium, under the dominion of the empires of Akkad and Ur, successively. It gained independence around 2000 BC. The city's profitable trade, with cities in Asia Minor and elsewhere where the Assyrians acquired trading districts (see p. 55), brought it to great wealth and prominence. A recession around 1800 was followed by a new period of prosperity in the eighteenth century, when the Amorite Shamshi-Adad I seized the throne. He extended his sway over northern Mesopotamia and put his son on the throne in Mari. With Shamshi-Adad I, kingship acquired a more absolute character.

Southern Mesopotamia, the Old Babylonian empire (c. 1800–c. 1600)

In the eighteenth century, Babylon, which had until then been a fairly insignificant city, acquired strong political power, which it was to retain for many centuries. Even in periods of political weakness it continued to exert an influence on Mesopotamian culture. Many of the kings who captured Babylon in later times respected the Babylonians' gods and traditions and acknowledged the city's special status. The foundations of Babylonian culture were laid by the Amorite king Hammurabi (eighteenth century; the exact dates are a matter of debate), who during his reign conquered almost the whole of Mesopotamia, including Assyria. Hammurabi is most renowned for his code of law (see Figure 3.1), which is a valuable source of information on the

FIGURE 3.1 The Code of Hammurabi of Babylon, *c.* 1750 BC. Height 2.25 m

Notes. Basalt stele found in Susa, the capital of the Elamite empire. The stele was apparently taken to Susa as war booty by plundering Elamites. Seated on the throne is the sun-god Shamash, who was also the god of justice, because the rays of the sun expose the evil practices that cannot bear the light of day. He is recognizable as the sun-god by the rays at his shoulders. Hammurabi is standing in front of the throne. The text contains a prologue, laws, and an epilogue. In the prologue Hammurabi introduces himself as the king whom the gods have appointed to ensure the maintenance of justice. In the epilogue he states that he has made the laws "to prevent the strong from oppressing the weak and to see that justice is done to widows and orphans." The stele advises those who have suffered injustice to refer to the code of law. Finally, future kings who do not comply with these laws are threatened with the curse of the gods.

social structure of this period. This law code (discussed in greater detail in relation to Figure 3.1 and on p. 59) became one of the standard works read at Babylonian schools and as such it had a profound and lasting influence. Written in a monumental cuneiform script, the ancient Babylonian dialect became exemplary for later Mesopotamian writing—also in Assyria—and thus "classical."

The glory of the Old Babylonian empire was short-lived: the empire began to crumble under Hammurabi's successors, the kings gradually losing their military power and authority. Shortly after 1600 Babylon was even taken by a king of the Hittite kingdom that had emerged in the eastern part of Asia Minor (see Map 3.2 and p. 29), who led a plundering expedition into Mesopotamia. Having sacked Babylon, he returned to his native country. The Old Babylonian empire never recovered from this blow and proved too weak to defend itself against a new wave of invaders, the Kassites from the Iranian mountains. Once again Mesopotamia came under foreign dominion. These newcomers were also to adapt themselves to the original occupants' traditions (see p. 27).

THE LATE BRONZE AGE (c. 1600–c. 1200)

The "concert of powers"

The four centuries between 1600 and 1200 were characterized by a more or less stable balance of a group of great powers which maintained contacts with one another through the regular exchange of embassies and letters. The situation was somewhat reminiscent of the nineteenth-century "European concert of powers." The powers in the late Bronze Age were Egypt (the New Kingdom), Mitanni, the Hittite empire, Assyria and Babylonia. This is also the period of the flourishing of what are known as the Minoan civilization of Crete and the Mycenaean civilization of the Greek mainland (see pp. 29–31). Other important centers of power in this period were the highly developed city states of Syria and Palestine, which had lost nothing of their former glory. They included Byblos, Tyre, and Sidon. A little further north was the city of Ugarit, where excavations have brought to light much of great interest, such as Sumerian and Akkadian clay tablets, but also tablets inscribed in a phonetic cuneiform script of thirty signs in the city's own language. The areas between these states were still traversed by many different nomadic and seminomadic tribes (see Map 3.3).

The power of all these states, from the largest to the smallest, was based on a new invention which spread across the entire Near East at a formidable rate around 1600: the war chariot, a fast, two-wheeled vehicle that was drawn by horses. These chariots were owned by a privileged, aristocratic elite that was awarded land in exchange for its services. Without large contingents of chariot warriors it was virtually impossible for a state to safeguard its authority, and many of the small states lost their independence and were reduced to satellite states of the great powers (see Chapter 7).

············ Egyptian, Hittite, Babylonian and Assyrian spheres of influence
c. 1250 (after the battle at Kadesh)

- - - - - Mitannian sphere of influence c. 1370

MAP 3.3 The ancient Near East, 1600–1200 BC

Egypt, the New Kingdom (c. 1550–1100)

Once again it was a dynasty of Theban rulers who restored unity in Egypt. The last king of this dynasty, the seventeenth according to Manetho, shook off the yoke of the last king of the Hyksos dynasty, the fifteenth(!) according to Manetho, and set about evicting the Hyksos. His work was completed by his brother, who is regarded as the founder of the eighteenth dynasty (these historical facts aptly illustrate the defects of Manetho's system).

The eighteenth dynasty (c. 1550–c. 1300 BC) is probably the most famous in the whole of Egyptian history. Its kings, who were referred to by the title of "pharaoh" (literally: "great house" = "palace"), immediately set about building up an empire. Their campaigns took them to the Euphrates in Syria and deep into Nubia. The best-known pharaoh of this dynasty is Thutmose III (c. 1450).

Nubia was of particular interest to Egypt because of its gold, the word "Nubia" meaning "land of gold." It was governed by a viceroy (who was referred to as the "King's son") and stood under fairly direct control of Egypt. Egyptian influence prevailed in Nubia in cultural terms, too. Egyptian temples were erected and Egyptian artistic conventions, religious practices, and written culture were adopted. In Palestine and Syria, Egypt exerted less direct control. The kings of the city states in those areas retained their authority, but had to admit Egyptian troops and controllers into their territories. Those regions were only marginally influenced by Egyptian culture. Egyptian cultural influence was in fact largely restricted to coastal cities like Byblos, Tyre, and Ugarit, which had already been conducting trade with Egypt for a long time.

FIGURE 3.2 Coronation of Queen Hatshepsut by Horus, the falcon-headed sky-god, and Thoth, the ibis-headed scribe of the gods

Notes. Hatshepsut was one of the few female pharaohs. The step-mother and aunt of Thutmose III, she was also his regent because at the time of the untimely death of her husband (and half-brother) Thutmose II, Thutmose III, the son of one of her husband's minor wives, was still under-age. Thutmose III married one of Hatshepsut's daughters, so she was also his mother-in-law. From the beginning of the New Kingdom onwards, Egyptian pretenders to the throne strove to boost the legitimacy of their claim by marrying the daughter of the ruling pharaoh's principal wife. This led to many marriages between brothers and (half-)sisters. Hatshepsut, not satisfied to rule as a regent, had herself officially crowned as pharaoh. She made a peaceful expedition to Punt (the east coast of Africa), and brought back a range of exotic plants and animals to Egypt. On Hatshepsut's death, Thutmose III assumed control. He totally renounced his former regent, refused to acknowledge her kingship and had her figure chiselled out of all representations, including this wall painting. Thutmose led many military campaigns into Palestine and Syria, beyond the Euphrates and into Nubia in the south.

The most extraordinary pharaoh was without doubt Akhenaten (*c.* 1350). He attempted to transform the Egyptian polytheism into a religion based on the worship of only one god, the sun god Aten. All other cults were suppressed, especially that of the Theban god Amon, whose name was expunged from all records. Akhenaten even transferred the capital from Thebes to a new site, which he called Akhetaten (present-day El-Amarna). During this period of religious reforms changes took place in the nature of Egyptian art, too. The former fairly stereotyped art with its rigid conventions gave way to a freer mode of expression. Figures were given more individual traits and compositions became less formal. The Egyptian convention of portraying faces, hips, and legs in profile and eyes and shoulders in frontal view was however retained. While engrossed in his religious pursuits, Akhenaten neglected his administrative duties. The city states in Syria and Palestine, which were suffering increasing harassment from nomadic and semi-nomadic tribes, began to take matters into their own hands. Akhenaten sent very few or no troops

FIGURE 3.3 Akhenaten, Nefertiti, and their daughters

Notes. The sun disk Aten with the blessing hands is visible in the middle. The rays on the far left and far right bear the symbol of life ("ankh"). Such informal scenes are quite uncommon in Egyptian relief sculpture.

to assert his authority. His successor, the well-known Tutankhamun, who had a poor constitution and met with an early death, reverted to the old Egyptian traditions and made Memphis the capital of his realm. The eighteenth dynasty came to an end when three generals successively seized the throne.

Egypt managed to recover its unity once more, in the thirteenth century. That was largely thanks to the efforts of Ramses II (1279–1212) of the nineteenth dynasty, one of Egypt's most ambitious builders. He is the pharaoh who commissioned the construction of the temple at Abu Simbel, which, in the late 1950s, Unesco saved from the rising water of the reservoir at the Assuan Dam.

Babylonia and Assyria

Shortly after the fall of the Old Babylonian empire, around 1600, a tribe of eastern invaders, the Kassites, assumed control in Babylon. They governed Mesopotamia for over four centuries. The Kassites adjusted themselves to the Babylonian culture, which was essentially the product of the merging of the former Sumerian and Akkadian civilizations. Their temples and their artistic styles

FIGURE 3.4   Ramses II in the battle at Kadesh against the Hittites, 1275 BC

Notes. Ramses II on his war chariot in the battle at Kadesh against the Hittites (1275 BC). The king is the only warrior shown riding his chariot alone (incidentally with the reins at his hips, which would have been impossible in practice). All the other chariots are driven by separate charioteers. The illustration emphasizes the king's superhuman capacities (see p. 49).

were entirely Babylonian in character; Sumerian and Akkadian continued to be used as written languages. That way, continuity was maintained.

The Assyrian empire was weak at first. Its kings were effectively subject to the kings of its northwestern neighbor Mitanni, but they acquired independence when the latter empire was overthrown by the Hittites shortly after 1350. This ushered in a new period in Mesopotamia's history, in which the region was governed by two medium-sized states, Assyria and Babylonia, in a more or less stable balance of power which was to last until the eighth century BC.

Mitanni

Mitanni was a state situated between the upper reaches of the Euphrates and the Tigris. Its occupants were Hurrians or Khurrites (the biblical "Horites"), who had lived in that area since the third millennium and had over the centuries gradually spread towards Asia Minor and Syria and Palestine. That meant that Hurrians were also to be found outside Mitanni, for example in the Hittite empire. Although Hurrian (which was written in the cuneiform script) was used for official documents in Mitanni and the Hurrians worshipped their own deities, several Indo-Aryan elements are discernable in Mitannian culture. Some treaties, for example, mention Indian gods and some of the Mitannian kings had Indo-Aryan names.

The Hittite empire

From time immemorial peoples with urban civilizations whose origins are unknown to us had been living in Asia Minor. The language of the people who settled in central Anatolia at the beginning of the second millennium includes distinct Indo-European elements. These people we call the "Hittites." Around 1700 BC their kingdom, the Old Hittite kingdom, rose to power, extending its sway over Syria. One of the Hittite kings even penetrated into Babylon shortly after 1600 (see p. 24). However, due to internal power struggles, the Hittite kingdom gradually became weaker and lost its conquered territory. King Suppiluliumas managed to restore Hittite power around 1340 and established what is known as the Hittite new kingdom or empire. He subjected powerful cities in Syria and Asia Minor and settled accounts with his neighbors, the Hurrians in Mitanni, where he installed a puppet on the throne. The Hittites' custom was to conclude peace treaties with the kings they defeated, who were usually allowed to remain on their thrones (what are known as "vassal-rulers" or "client-kings"). Large numbers of such treaties have been recovered in excavations in the Hittite capital.

Hittite culture is greatly indebted to Mesopotamian civilization. The Hittites adopted the cuneiform script and used the Akkadian language for certain kinds of texts, such as the afore-mentioned treaties. These treaties invoke Mesopotamian gods. Several works of Mesopotamian literature, including the Epic of Gilgamesh, were translated into the Hittite language. But other influences are observable, too. Religious texts, for example, were written in ancient non-Hittite languages. Hurrian influences are also evident, especially after the reign of Suppiluliumas. Teshup, the Hurrian god of thunder, even became one of the principal deities of the Hittite empire.

Crete and Mycenae

It was in the second millennium, too, that the cultures of Crete and Mycenae reached their greatest heights, after a development that can be traced back to the third millennium BC. In modern literature the culture of Crete is referred to as "Minoan" (after the island's legendary King Minos), and that of the Greek mainland as "Helladic" (after "Hellas," the Greek word for Greece) or Mycenaean (after the fortified palace Mycenae on the Peloponnese in Greece).

The most important city on Crete was Knossos. Two striking aspects of this city are that it was not fortified and that its wall paintings, in marked contrast with those of the Near East, depicted predominantly peaceful scenes. The frescoes show motifs drawn from local plant and animal life and scenes of open-air religious ceremonies and remarkably few military feats. Such frescoes have also been found on the island of Thera, which acquired its typical crescent shape following a volcanic eruption.

The palace was the center of an economic system comparable with that of the Third Dynasty of Ur or that of the New Kingdom of Egypt. Such an economic system is described in greater detail on page 53. A syllabic script, known as Linear A, was developed for the palace's administration. As this script has not yet been deciphered, we know very little about the people who used it or the language they spoke. The source of Crete's prosperity is less of a mystery to us: the island owed its wealth largely to its flourishing trade. Cretan ships transported goods all over the Mediterranean, calling in at ports in regions including Egypt, Syria and Palestine, the Aegean islands, Cyprus, and Greece.

Around 1450 an expedition of warriors from Mycenae conquered Crete. Many settlements on the island were destroyed, but Knossos was spared and became the most influential city. New frescoes, warriors' burials containing lavish bronze grave goods and many Egyptian imports testify to the city's newly acquired wealth. The large palace with its many rooms (see Figure 3.5) must have presented an awesome aspect, because later Greeks referred to it as "King Minos' Labyrinth."

Since about 2700 BC a civilization had been taking shape on the Greek mainland that was in many respects comparable with that of Crete. It is believed that a people speaking a Greek (i.e., Indo-European) language settled in Greece around 2000 BC.

Shortly after 1600 several of their urban centres (Mycenae, Pylos, Tiryns) developed into flourishing cities. The entire civilization then acquired an indisputably more military character. At first these cities were also unfortified, but between 1400 and 1300 their palaces started to be surrounded by imposing defenses. In these fortified palaces the kings ruled together with an elite of charioteers, who were awarded land in exchange for their services and whose horses were

FIGURE 3.5 The throne room at the palace at Knossos (partly reconstructed)

paid for by the state. Although there is little evidence to suggest that any one of the cities ever gained control over the whole of Greece, or even over the Peloponnese, traces of destruction indicate that they waged wars on one another.

The Greek mainlanders borrowed the Cretan writing system from their neighbors, and adapted it for their own, Greek, language. The resultant script is known as Linear B. When the Greeks crossed over to Crete around 1450 they introduced this Linear B there, too.

International relations

Thanks to the discovery of an archive of clay tablets at Akhetaten (= El-Amarna) in Egypt we are fairly well informed about the international relations of this period. This archive contained several letters that the kings of the great powers wrote to the Egyptian pharaoh, but the majority of the letters were written by the kings of the city states in Palestine and Syria, which were under Egyptian domination. These letters are clay tablets inscribed in the Babylonian cuneiform script. In those days Babylonian was the language of international relations. Besides this archive various other letters have survived from this period.

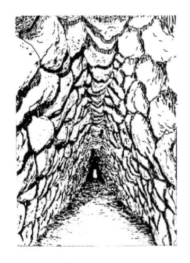

FIGURE 3.6a
Fortifications at Hattusas, the
capital of the Hittite empire

FIGURE 3.6b
Fortifications at Tiryns, near Mycenae

Notes. Note the remarkable similarity in architecture. Large blocks of stone were fitted together without mortar, like the pieces in a jigsaw puzzle. The arches are false; they do not form a closed span. Greeks of later ages were greatly impressed by the size of the blocks of stone. They used the term "Cyclopean" to describe such masonry. Cyclops were giants in Greek mythology who had only one eye, above the nose.

Another important source of information on international relations are the Hittite treaties that have been preserved in large numbers. Some of these treaties are on unequal terms, between the Hittite king and his vassals, the rulers of the Hittite satellite states (see pp. 29 and 60–2); others, between the kings of the great powers, are on equal terms. It is clear that great pains were taken to ensure that the terms of the latter treaties were reciprocal.

The annals celebrating the king's valiant deeds, which those same kings had inscribed on clay tablets, the walls of temples, and other surfaces, constitute a third source of information.

Together, these three sources have greatly increased our understanding of the diplomatic relations of those days. Friendly relations were maintained via the regular exchange of messengers, letters, and gifts and through political marriages. Many close alliances were formed for fear of a mutual enemy or because former enemies came to realize that they had nothing to gain by continuing hostilities. During its campaigns of conquest, Egypt, for example, came into conflict with Mitanni, but the two powers made peace with one another in the fourteenth century, when the Hittite empire started to pose a serious threat. However, this was to be of no avail to Mitanni, for it was rendered powerless by Suppiluliumas (1344–1322). The Western half was turned into a Hittite vassal state and the eastern part came under Assyrian control. For a long time the Egyptians and the Hittites disputed Syria. Egypt's power over its territories in the Levant weakened under the reformer pharaoh, Akhenaten. Some vassals defected to the Hittite king, others claimed authority as independent rulers (see also p. 26). Pharaoh Ramses II (1279–1212) of the nineteenth dynasty set about recovering Egypt's lost territory and was quite successful in his campaigns until the Hittites brought him to a halt in the battle at Kadesh (1275). The ensuing status quo resulted in a peace treaty (1259) between Ramses II and Hattusilis III, which has survived in an Egyptian version, carved in the walls of a temple near Thebes, and a Babylonian variant, inscribed in a clay tablet that was found in Hattusas. Peace lasted until the fall of the Hittite empire around 1200.

4   THE FIRST MILLENNIUM

THE EARLY IRON AGE (*c.* 1200–*c.* 750 BC)

Disruption and Recovery

Around 1200 BC the entire Near East was faced with a drastic political and social upheaval. The concert of powers and their satellite states were overthrown. The Hittite empire disappeared, though a few Neo-Hittite city states arose in northern Syria and southern Asia Minor. Egypt lost its position of power in the Levant and Nubia. The Cretan and Mycenaean civilizations likewise came to an end. The cities of Ugarit and Emar in Syria were destroyed, never to be rebuilt. Assyria and Babylonia saw their power undermined, but managed to survive as medium-sized territorial states in northern and southern Iraq.

Empires come and go throughout history, but a disruption involving so many states all at the same time is surprising. This blow is often attributed to pressure from migrating peoples. Assyria and Babylonia were confronted with invasions of Aramaic and Chaldean tribes from the steppes and deserts between Palestine and Mesopotamia, which they had great difficulty repelling. The Aramaic invaders settled in large parts of Syria and southern Mesopotamia, the Chaldeans favoring the area around the Persian Gulf. The consequences of the attacks of a group of invaders known as the "Sea Peoples" seem to have been even more disastrous. The name "Sea Peoples" we owe to an Egyptian source. The annals of Ramses III (1184–1152) tell us how this Egyptian king defeated peoples "from the countries of the sea" in the Nile Delta. The peoples are described as a threat to the Hittite empire, Cyprus and Syria. Letters found at Ugarit also refer to a threat from the sea. Some of the Sea Peoples are mentioned by name in the Egyptian inscriptions. The best known are the Philistines, who settled in the southwestern part of the region that was called Palestine after them. But a lot remains unclear. The Egyptian annals, for example, may be propagandistic; the origins of the Sea Peoples remain unknown and it is uncertain whether they were indeed responsible for the downfall of Mycenae and the Hittite empire. Also unclear is what may have caused such a mass migration of peoples. One possibility—for which we indeed have evidence—is that drought and hunger forced the nomadic steppe occupants to invade the fertile river valleys. In areas with only just sufficient precipitation to allow agriculture (250 mm per year; see Map 1.1 on p. 13) even a slight fluctuation in climate will have drastic consequences. The climate became cooler and wetter again in the eighth century.

The twelfth century is a great turning-point in history in another respect, too: it also marks the beginning of the Iron Age. Iron had been known throughout the entire second millennium, in particular in Asia Minor, but the products that were made from this metal, such as knives, were then still considered luxury goods. After 1200, however, iron started to be used on a large scale and that is why historians and archaeologists have fixed the transition from the Bronze Age to the Iron Age around 1200 BC.

Egypt, the Third Intermediate Period (c. 1100–715 BC)

As mentioned above, Egypt lost its conquered territories in Syria and Palestine and also those in Nubia. It was not able to preserve unity in its heartland either, as is apparent for example from the fact that Amon's high priest in Thebes set himself up as a semi-independent ruler. Libyans infiltrated the Delta and the Fayyûm region and founded settlements there. Between 950 and 730 Egypt was even ruled by dynasties of Libyan pharaohs. Egypt did make some attempts to recover its lost territory in Palestine. One of the kings of a Libyan dynasty managed to penetrate into Jerusalem, the capital of the newly emerged kingdom of Judah (c. 935 BC). He robbed the temple, but failed to establish permanent Egyptian authority in Judah.

In what is known as the Late Kingdom (715–332) Egypt was almost constantly ruled by foreign powers and managed to regain its independence for short periods only. The first to take control, around 730, was the Nubian kingdom centered around Napata, which had broken away from Egypt around 1100, without, however, distancing itself from Egyptian culture (see p. 25 and Map 3.1). Later on, Egypt was to be incorporated into other powerful empires that emerged in Western Asia, namely those of Assyria (between 671 and 655) and Persia (525–404 and 343–332). They will be discussed below.

Syria and the Phoenicians

Small states took advantage of the weakening of the great powers to reassert their independence. Among the states that succeeded in regaining their autonomy in this period are the city states of Syria, in several of which groups of foreigners had settled. Some, for example Karkemish, were ruled by Hittite kings; they are known as Neo-Hittite kingdoms. Other cities passed under Aramaean rule. One of those cities is Damascus, which became the center of a fairly large territorial Aramaean state, referred to as Aram in the Bible.

The original occupants of the ports to the west of the Lebanon Mountains, including Byblos, Tyre, and Sidon, were not driven out by foreigners. This region is usually referred to by the Greek term "Phoenicia." The Phoenicians, however, called themselves Canaanites. The Phoenician towns recovered from the blows inflicted by the Sea Peoples reasonably quickly and developed into independent city states ruled by a king and a council of elders. It was quite some time before they were forced to acknowledge the supremacy of a great power. Now that they no longer had to compete with Crete and Mycenae they evolved into the most powerful trading cities in the ancient Near East.

The Phoenicians were of paramount importance for Western civilization: it is they who passed on the culture of the ancient Near East to Europe and it is via them that the Greeks first came into contact with the Near East. In this period, in which overseas trade by Greeks was still virtually non-existent, the Phoenicians exported Near Eastern products to Greece and other regions in the West.

The influence of the Phoenicians spread across the Mediterranean in a different manner, too—in the form of colonies that the Phoenicians started to found on Cyprus and in North Africa, Sicily, and southern Spain in the tenth century BC. These colonies, many of which were founded as trading posts, grew into independent cities. The best-known Phoenician colony is Carthage in North Africa, which was founded by colonists from Tyre in the ninth or eighth century BC. Carthage was later to become a great autonomous power (see pp. 142–4).

The most important Phoenician contribution to civilization is undoubtedly the invention of the alphabet. The Phoenician alphabet differed from the other writing systems hitherto used in that, instead of a sign for each syllable, it comprised only signs for consonants. With its total of only twenty-two signs, as opposed to the more than 600 signs of the cuneiform script, it was accessible to a much wider public. In Mesopotamia and Egypt the art of writing had been known only to a small group of specially trained scribes. Another great difference with respect to the cuneiform script is that the new alphabet was written on papyrus or leather. Unfortunately, however, both those materials are highly perishable and little written evidence relating to Phoenician history has consequently been preserved. The earliest written texts of the peoples who first adopted the Phoenician script, the Aramaeans and the Israelites, have not survived either.

Israel

The reason why we are nevertheless reasonably well informed about the Israelites is that they conscientiously copied the works of their richly varied literature over and over again to preserve them for future generations. These works, which comprise poetry, histories, laws, and wisdom literature, constitute the books of the Hebrew Bible or Old Testament, the basis of the Jewish religion and, together with the New Testament, also that of Christianity (see pp. 261–4). They have survived to this day because these religions, unlike all the others of the ancient Near East, never became extinct. A great problem for historians is that the texts were not written down in the form in which they have been preserved until relatively late, that is, during the Babylonian exile, around 550 BC or even later (see p. 40). Moreover, they are very much colored by the message they contain: the people of Israel must worship only their own god Yahweh (YHWH), live according to His standards and laws, and not venerate other deities. This faith would bring people God's blessing, whereas worshipping other deities would bring on Divine Wrath. The latter was taken to explain the Babylonian captivity. This was no easy message in a world in which all peoples were accustomed to worshipping many gods.

The earliest history of Israel is particularly difficult for us to reconstruct. The Israelites claim to have descended from Abraham, who left Mesopotamia to live in Canaan (Palestine). There he lived the life of a nomad herder. Famine drove Abraham's grandson Jacob and his twelve sons into Egypt, where the Israelites increased tremendously in number. The pharaoh, however, forced them to work hard for him; they had to help build two new cities in the Delta: Pithom and Raamses. The book of Exodus tells us how the Israelites escaped from Egypt, led by Moses, and how, after a long journey through the desert, they arrived in Canaan (Palestine). The book of Joshua recounts how, after Moses' death, the Israelites captured and/or destroyed the Canaanite cities under Joshua's leadership and took possession of the land. Theologians and historians have avidly searched for mention of these events in other sources, but all that they have managed to verify is that Ramses II built Pithom and Raamses and that his successor Merneptah met with "the people of Israel" during a campaign in Palestine. Archaeological research has likewise failed to produce evidence of a single mass invasion of Palestine. Over the years, scholars have spent rivers of ink hypothesizing about the problem of how the people of Israel penetrated into the city states of Canaan and managed to acquire control over many of them. One possibility is that all this took place in a process of gradual infiltration, comparable with that of the establishment of Aramaean states in Syria around the same time.

Whatever the case may be, the Israelites faced a precarious future, in which they were to put up many a struggle against the cities of Canaan and later groups of settlers. The Philistines proved particularly formidable opponents, as they had iron weapons whereas the Israelites were still fighting with weapons of bronze. The Israelites lived in fairly disorganized communities scattered across Palestine. In times of war they would sometimes unite under the leadership of "judges" (cf. the book of that name in the Bible). The fierce battles, in particular that against the Philistines, aroused a desire for a king who would be able to lead the Israelites in battle single-handed. The first of their kings was Saul. He did not succeed in establishing a dynasty, for after his death David, who had served under the Philistines as well as under Saul, ousted Saul's family and ascended the throne himself (c. 1000 BC). David conquered Jerusalem for the Israelites and made that city the capital of his kingdom. According to the Bible, he then turned Israel into a fairly powerful territorial state (Map 4.1). David was succeeded by his son, Solomon, who had a temple for the God of Israel built in Jerusalem. It is difficult to verify this information through sources outside the Bible or archaeological evidence, though we do have a ninth-century Aramaic inscription referring to "the house of David."

After Solomon's death, his kingdom broke up into two parts—though it is actually questionable whether it can be said to have been truly unified before then; there had always been strong contrasts between the north and the south. Many Israelites were not (yet) prepared to pay the costs required for a well-organized kingdom. Solomon's son retained leadership over the southern half of the kingdom only: that became the kingdom of Judah, in whose capital, Jerusalem, David's descendants remained in control for several centuries. The northern half of the kingdom elected a different king, who founded a new, separate kingdom called Israel. Israel was to have a less stable government. Different dynasties followed one another in rapid succession. The kingdom also had to settle many border conflicts with Aram (Damascus). In the ninth century it acquired a new capital, Samaria.

Israel and Judah were politically insignificant states. In the eighth century both kingdoms were reduced to vassal states of a new state rising to power in the Levant: Assyria.

THE WESTERN ASIATIC EMPIRES (c. 750 BC–AD 651)

The Neo-Assyrian empire

Assyria held out reasonably well during the difficult times after 1200. The empire continued to be ruled by a king and the army was organized with increasing efficiency in the battles against

——————   The kingdoms of Israel and Judah, c. 850

-- --- --·   The kingdom of David, c. 1000

Orontes

Karkar

Byblos

PHOENICIANS

Sidon

Damascus

Tyre
Dan

ARAM

Akko

Megiddo

ISRAEL

Samaria

Sheckem

Jordan

Bethel

Jericho

PHILISTINES

Jerusalem

Ashkelon

JUDAH

Lachis
Hebron

Gaza

Beersheba

MOAB

EDOM

Elath

MAP 4.1
The kingdoms of Israel
and Judah, c. 850 BC

The kingdom of David c. 1000 BC,
according to the Bible. Its size
and significance are a matter of
contention.

the Aramaeans. Military innovations (the use of cavalry, the perfecting of siege engines) made the army powerful enough to make raids into distant regions, some as far away as the Mediterranean coast. But it was some time yet before the Assyrians managed to obtain permanent control over large areas.

The first who succeeded in doing so was Tiglath-Pileser III (745–727) and his reign is therefore held to mark the beginning of the Neo-Assyrian empire. The Assyrian kings secured the loyalty of more and more vassal rulers and transformed vassal states into provinces, which

FIGURE 4.1 The Assyrian army attacks a town

Notes. Note the diversity of the Assyrian forces: visible are archers, lancers, swordsmen, and siege instruments. In one of the siege instruments a figure is reading out a text, probably in Aramaic because he is holding a piece of papyrus or leather instead of a clay tablet. He is probably proclaiming some propagandistic text or terms of surrender.

they put under the authority of Assyrian governors (see pp. 60–2). A case in point is Samaria, the capital of Israel, which Sargon II (722–705) placed under Assyrian governorship after his predecessor had captured it in 722. The Assyrians' custom when capturing a city was to deport the city's population and replace it by foreigners. This is what happened in Samaria, too. Judah managed to retain its status as a vassal state.

The Assyrians are notorious for their deportation policy. They frequently deported large parts of a rebellious population as a means of punishment. Many of the people who were deported from their homelands were forced to help build or expand the capitals of the Assyrian empire; for Assyria, being sparsely populated, was always in great need of specialized craftsmen. Other deportees were incorporated in Assyria's standing army, which the Assyrian kings had formed at the end of the eighth century. The largest numbers of people, allegedly some hundreds of thousands, were deported by Tiglath-Pileser III and his immediate successors. The masses of foreigners, many of whom spoke Aramaic, who were consequently imported into Assyria caused the Assyrian heartland to lose its Assyrian character. The Babylonian-Assyrian language was gradually replaced by Aramaic, which presented the advantage that it was written in a much simpler script—an alphabet.

Babylonia also lost its independence. The Assyrians had always more or less spared Babylonia out of respect for its traditions, setting themselves up as protectors of the Babylonian culture against the uncouth Chaldeans, who harassed the Babylonians from their home country along the Persian Gulf. However, when a Chaldean king usurped the Babylonian throne, Tiglath-Pileser intervened and annexed Babylonia (729 BC). Instead of reducing it to a vassal state or a province, he ascended the throne himself, after conducting the traditional Babylonian rituals. The Assyrians' respect for the culture of the Babylonians was based on the ties of language, script, religion, and literature and the mercantile relations that had united these two peoples for so many centuries.

Ashurbanipal (669–631), the last of the great Assyrian kings, ordered his officials to search for ancient Babylonian texts and bring them to the capital, Nineveh, where they were to be copied and stored in archives. It is in that city that the best-known version of the Epic of Gilgamesh was found. Other Assyrian kings did not share Ashurbanipal's respect for the Babylonian culture. In 689, after a period of poor relations with the Babylonians, who felt they were not being granted their due privileges, Sennacherib (705–681) razed Babylon to the ground.

At its greatest expanse, the Assyrian empire also included Egypt (671–655), which it had incorporated after the Egyptians had encouraged the Palestinians to revolt against the Assyrians during the reign of the Nubian dynasty. The Assyrians were unable to reduce Egypt to a province, but they did succeed in turning several Egyptian provincial governors into Assyrian vassal rulers. One of those rulers, Psammetichus I (664–610), threw off the Assyrian yoke around 655. That was the prelude to a new revival of Egyptian influence, which was to last about a century. The new dynasty is called the Saite dynasty (the twenty-sixth, 664–525), after the new capital, Sais. In their efforts to bring the old Egyptian culture back to life, the Saite kings emulated the former traditions of the Old Kingdom. This period is therefore also referred to as the "Saite Renaissance." It was in this period, too, that contacts between Egypt and Greece intensified. Greek mercenaries served in the Egyptian army and Psammetichus allowed the Greeks to establish a trading post at Naukratis (see p. 70).

The loss of Egypt heralded Assyria's downfall. The Assyrian kings slowly lost their hold over their vassal states in Palestine, including Judah. Things really started to go wrong after the death of Ashurbanipal (631). The stability of the Assyrian empire was strongly dependent on the king's capacities. Many of the frequent changes of power that followed Ashurbanipal's death gave rise to revolts. The final blow was the result of a combination of factors: three pretenders fighting one another for accession to the throne within Assyria, the outbreak of a revolt in southern Babylonia, whose governor, Nabopolassar, claimed control of Babylon, and the emergence of a serious foreign threat: the Medes in the East. Nabopolassar joined forces with the Medes and together they overthrew Assyria. Between 614 and 609 they captured and almost completely destroyed all of Assyria's capitals. On the country's ruins they then laid the foundations for two new empires: the Median empire to the east of the Tigris, with Ecbatana as its capital, and the Neo-Babylonian empire, whose capital was Babylon, to the west (see Map 4.2). Egypt temporarily occupied Palestine, only to lose it to the Babylonians shortly after.

The Neo-Babylonian empire

The Neo-Babylonian empire is often referred to as the "Chaldean empire" because the new dynasty is assumed to have been Chaldean in origin and because Babylonians are often referred to as "Chaldeans" in Jewish, Greek, and Roman texts. Nabopolassar, the founder of the new dynasty, may have come from the south, where many Chaldeans lived, but the kings were never called "Chaldean" in contemporary Babylonian texts. There were not that many differences between the Babylonians and the Chaldeans because the Chaldeans had been greatly influenced by Babylonian traditions for quite some time. They had long ago exchanged their nomadic way of life for a sedentary existence, they worshipped Babylonian gods, and bore Babylonian names. In the Neo-Babylonian empire, official inscriptions, religious texts, letters, and contracts were written in cuneiform script. The Babylonians, however, would never have referred to themselves as "Chaldean"; the word "Chaldean" had negative connotations in Assyrian and Babylonian texts. But in the eyes of outsiders the terms "Chaldean" and "Babylonian" increasingly took on the same

Median empire *c.* 660

Neo-Babylon empire of the Chaldeans *c.* 560

Lydian kingdom *c.* 560

·············· Assyrian empire *c.* 660

MAP 4.2   The Near East in the seventh and sixth centuries BC

meaning and they frequently confused the two. Jews, Greeks, and Romans often called Babylonians "Chaldeans" and they even used the term "Chaldeans" to refer to Babylonian priests, diviners, and astrologers, as if it were a technical term. Meanwhile, however, the gradual replacement of Babylonian by Aramaic (possibly related to Chaldean) as both the spoken and the written language continued. This process, which had started in the Neo-Assyrian period, is difficult for us to follow because most Aramaic texts were written on papyrus or parchment, of which only very little has survived.

The Neo-Babylonian empire was actually founded by Nebuchadnezzar II (605–562), the king known to us from the Old Testament. Nebuchadnezzar was a great builder; he was largely responsible for the erection of the palace, the town walls, and the temple tower of Babylon. It was he who turned Babylon into the metropolis that made such a profound impression on people all over the world, in particular the Jews. Over the years he conquered Syria and Palestine. His successes made Judah a vassal state. Later on, when the king of Judah revolted against him, Nebuchadnezzar reduced the kingdom of Judah to a province. According to the tradition established by his predecessors, he then deported its population to Babylonia (what is referred to as "the Babylonian Exile" in the Bible, 586 BC).

This period was of great importance for the history of the Jews (= "Judeans"). They were allowed to remain with their families, living in their own communities in Babylonia. It was in this period that they wrote down large parts of their traditions. By continuing to adhere to their own religion, the Jews managed to preserve their identity.

FIGURE 4.2 The Ishtar Gate of Babylon built by Nebuchadnezzar II (605–562), rebuilt in the Pergamum Museum in Berlin

Notes. The gate and the walls flanking the entrance were built of blue glazed bricks. Marduk, the god of Babylon, was paraded through this gate to the New Year's house, which lay outside the town, on the day of the New Year's Festival (early April).

The last Babylonian king, Nabonidus, was an intriguing figure. He was a fervent worshipper of the moon god Sin of Harran and neglected the cult of Marduk, the supreme god of Babylon. He went to live in the Arab desert for a while and left the government of his kingdom to his son, Belshazzar. His behavior was the cause of great discontent in Babylon, making that town an easy prey to the new power that emerged in the East: Persia.

The Persian or Achaemenid empire

The Persian empire evolved from that of the Medes. The Medes and Persians had settled in the Iranian highlands in the ninth century. They spoke closely related "Iranian" (Indo-European) languages. In the sixth century the Medes extended their sway over a large territory stretching from Iran into Asia Minor (see Map 4.2). We know very little about how their empire was organized, but it is believed that it lacked a powerful centralized administration.

Around 550 BC, the Persian Cyrus (who is called Koresh in the Bible), a vassal ruler in the Median empire, captured the Median capital Ecbatana and assumed control over the empire, which is from that date onwards referred to as the "Persian empire." As the Medes continued to play an important part in that empire it is sometimes also called the empire of the Medes and Persians. The Jews and the Greeks often used the word "Medes" when referring to Persians.

- - - - - Frontiers during the reign of Darius I *c.* 490

·············· The 'Royal Road' of Darius I

MAP 4.3 The Persian empire, 593–331 BC

Cyrus built up an empire of vast proportions. The first of his conquests was Asia Minor, which he took after defeating Lydia (whose capital was Sardis) in the western part of Asia Minor in 547 or a few years later. The Greeks in particular were well acquainted with Lydia, as that kingdom had annexed their cities along the western coast of Asia Minor in the sixth century. Lydia's king, Croesus, was and—still is—legendary for his proverbial wealth. His wealth was, however, of no avail to him in his battle against Cyrus.

Next, Cyrus turned his attention to Babylonia. The Babylonians, who were disappointed with their rulers Nabonidus and Belshazzar, hoped that Cyrus would prove to be a better king. Cyrus took advantage of this in his propaganda. He indeed showed respect for Babylon and its traditions. He did not destroy Babylon and allowed the worship of Marduk to continue. In this respect Cyrus was, however, behaving in very much the same way as the majority of the Assyrian kings of the past.

He was also well-loved by the Jews, who were then living in Babylon in exile; they believed that he had been sent to them by God. After he had conquered Babylon, Cyrus allowed the Jews to return to Judah and to rebuild their temple in Jerusalem. Many Jews made grateful use of this opportunity and in Judah they founded a more or less autonomous temple state ruled by the high priest and a governor, usually a Jew, who was appointed by the Persians. Other Jews remained in Babylonia, where they remained faithful to their religious customs. This community survived into the twentieth century.

Cyrus' behavior towards Babylon and the Jews earned him the reputation of a very mild, tolerant ruler, which he still has today. However, when seen in a wider context, his behavior was in fact not very different from that of other rulers of the ancient Near East. Like them, he too

FIGURE 4.3a Human-headed winged bull, palace of Sargon II at Dur-Sharrukin, *c.* 707 BC

Notes. Such giant bulls were placed at the entrances to Assyrian palaces. These divine beings protected the entrance from evil powers.

FIGURE 4.3b Human-headed winged bull, palace of Xerxes in Persepolis

Notes. A clear example of the Persians' imitation of Assyrian art.

adapted his approach to the circumstances, treating some subject peoples with clemency, others with severity.

Cyrus' final campaign took him to the River Indus in the East, where he was killed in battle. Cambyses (530–522), his son, incorporated Egypt into his empire (525) and put an end to the sway of the Saite dynasty (see p. 39).

Darius I (522–486) was the great organizer of that empire. Before he ascended the throne, the empire had consisted of a number of super-provinces or "satrapies." One of those satrapies was the former Neo-Babylonian empire (see Map 4.2). Darius reorganized his empire, creating some twenty smaller satrapies. Each satrapy had to pay a fixed tax. The satrapies were ruled by governors or "satraps." In periods of weak central authority some of those satraps managed to acquire a good deal of power and set themselves up as semi-independent rulers. The kings tried to stop this process by having their satraps' activities checked by secret informers—the "king's eyes and ears" (an expression that is incidentally only found in Greek texts). The commanders of the satrapy's army contingents were in principle also directly responsible to the king.

Under Darius' successor, Xerxes (486–465), a revolt broke out in Babylonia, where Babylonian kings had remained in power for some time. Babylon suffered some damage in the suppression of that revolt and Xerxes replaced the greater part of the ruling elite of the temples, which nevertheless continued to function.

We will meet Darius and Xerxes again in the part on Greek history, in the discussion of their— failed—attempts to subject Greece. In the fourth century the Persians made a fresh attempt to undermine Greek power, this time via a divide-and-rule policy. Many Greeks crossed over to Persia in that century, most in order to serve in the Persian army as mercenaries.

The Persian empire was essentially a continuation of the former Mesopotamian empires. Its administrative organization—and its art, too—owed much to Mesopotamian traditions. However, Persian art also betrays influences of the civilizations of other subject peoples, such as elements borrowed from Greek culture. Like their predecessors, the Persian rulers usually respected the religious customs of the peoples they subjected. In some respects, however, the Persians adhered to their own customs and traditions. Persis remained the main center of their authority; it is there that Darius I and Xerxes built their new capital Persepolis alongside the other capital, Susa, which was once the capital of Elam (southwestern Iran). They also continued to worship their own, Persian, gods. Of profound influence was the Persian prophet Zarathustra (Zoroaster in Greek), to whom we will return in the chapter on the religions of the Near East. Whether the kings of Persia also ranked among Zoroaster's followers we do not know.

For two centuries the Persians ruled over the whole of the ancient Near East. Around 330, however, a new power, this time from the West, made a forceful entry onto the political stage of Western Asia and Egypt: Macedonia, under the leadership of Alexander the Great.

The Hellenistic kingdoms

Alexander's conquest of the Persian empire brought the ancient Near East, for the first time in its history, under the dominion of a foreign people from a different world, with an advanced civilization of their own. After Alexander's death, his empire broke up into a number of smaller kingdoms ruled by dynasties founded by his generals. The greater part of Western Asia came under the control of the "Seleucids." Egypt became the kingdom of the "Ptolemies." The area comprising southern Syria and Palestine (including Judah) was a bone of contention between the Seleucid and the Ptolemaic kingdoms (see Map 11.2 on p. 123). These kingdoms will be discussed later, after we have considered the history of the Greeks up to the reign of Alexander— from which time onwards the history of Greece and that of the Near East are inextricably linked. Two general comments can already be made at this point, however. First of all, in organizational terms, the kingdoms that were formed after Alexander were very much like their predecessors, and, secondly, in spite of the fact that the new rulers did not embrace the cultural traditions of Western Asia and Egypt as the foreign conquerors of the past had done, the civilizations of those areas nevertheless lived on under the Greek-Macedonian domination.

The Parthian or Arsacid empire

The civilizations of the ancient Near East were in fact to outlive the Hellenistic kingdoms. In 141 BC, after a long struggle, Mesopotamia fell to the Iranian Parthians, who from that time onwards controlled what are now Iran and Iraq, from Pakistan to the Euphrates. Babylonia faced hard times, characterized by numerous internal wars and Arab raids that led to economic problems (price increases, impoverishment). Even so, various Babylonian traditions (cuneiform script, cults, astronomy) survived and Assur saw a revival of the cult of the god Ashur with an Aramaic liturgy. The Parthian empire lasted until AD 226.

The Neo-Persian or Sasanid empire

The next empire into which Mesopotamia was to be incorporated, from AD 226 until *c.* 636, was the Neo-Persian (also known as Sasanid or Sasanian) empire. The politics of this empire's Sasanid kings caused the ultimate downfall of Babylonian civilization. The empire was greatly influenced by the Iranian traditions of the Persian empire. The worship of Zoroaster was now openly promoted above all other cults. Formerly prosperous cities such as Hatra, Assur, and Dura-Europos were destroyed. These empires will be discussed in greater detail on pp. 137 and 268.

The Roman empire

The Romans also appeared on the political scene in the Near East. In 64–63 BC they occupied and annexed Syria, the last remaining part of the Seleucid kingdom. The Egyptian kingdom of the Ptolemies succumbed to the Romans in 30 BC. The written traditions, temple architecture, artistic conventions, and cult practices of Egyptian civilization survived for several centuries under the Roman dominion. We will return to this matter on p. 138. See also pp. 198 and 205.

The Arabs

The Sasanid and Roman empires (after AD 395 the Eastern Roman or Byzantine empire: see p. 292) ruled over the ancient Near East until the seventh century (see Map 16.1, p. 278), when, after the death of the prophet Muhammad, the Arabs brought about great changes. In the seventh century they conquered an area comprising almost the whole of Western Asia and northern Africa. The Islamic religion that they established there has held sway over that area to this very day. They reduced the Eastern Roman empire to an insignificant territorial state and in 651 they put an end to the Neo-Persian empire.

5 RELIGION

POLYTHEISM

Most religions of the ancient Near East were polytheistic, which means that many different gods were worshipped. This belief in many gods was associated with the people's world view. They believed that each force of nature represented a divine power. The cosmos had originated when primeval gods had risen from a divine primeval sea. They had given birth to new gods and that process had repeated itself for many generations. These gods were personifications of cosmic phenomena like the sky, air, earth, sun, moon, stars, etc. In Mesopotamia, in particular, this cosmos was believed to be unstable. Monstrous forces tried to destroy the gods. It was up to a young, strong god to defeat those forces; for this he was rewarded with supreme power over the other gods and the mortals on earth. This theme is expressed in, for example, the Babylonian creation story featuring Marduk, and in the creation story of the Hurrians revolving around Teshup, the god of thunder. Myths (stories of gods) explaining natural phenomena and the origin of the world are distinctive features of the religions of the ancient Near East.

The annual death and rebirth of the vegetation was also explained in myths. The death of the cereal grain, out of which grew the cornstalk, was associated with the death of a god (Osiris in Egypt), while the vegetation's stagnated growth during the hot, dry period of the year was attributed to the fact that a god spent part of the year in the underworld (in Mesopotamia that god was the Sumerian Dumuzi, corrupted to Tammuz in the Hebrew Bible; in Ugarit it was Aliyan Baal). The wives or sisters of those gods mourned over their loss and went in search of them (Isis, Ishtar, and Anath, respectively).

Every city and—usually—every state had its own supreme god, who was venerated in specific rites. In the Sumerian city of Nippur that god was Enlil, who was also regarded as the governor of the whole world (imperialistic kings therefore strove to conquer Nippur, so that Enlil would grant them control over the world). The supreme god of Babylon was Marduk, the Assyrians venerated Ashur, and the Egyptians worshipped the sun god Ra in the period of the Old Kingdom and the Theban god Amon, who was also identified with Ra as Amon-Ra, during the Middle and Late Kingdoms. The chief god of a city that was made a capital usually also became the state god and the supreme god of the pantheon. That god then stood at the top of a theological system

FIGURE 5.1   The cosmos: papyrus of Paser, twenty-first dynasty, *c.* 1000 BC, showing Egyptian gods

Notes. Nut, the sky-goddess, is shown standing on her hands and feet. Geb, the earth-god, is reclining beneath her and Shu, the air-god, is supporting (the goddess of) the sky. The birds next to Shu represent the soul of the deceased or that of the sun-god. The sun is sailing across the sky in a boat. The top scene shows the deceased's activities in the underworld.

FIGURE 5.2
The Egyptian god Osiris,
the "Lord of Eternity"

Notes. In the primeval age Osiris was the king of Egypt. He was killed by Seth. Isis, the sister and wife of Osiris, managed to conceive a son, Horus, by having intercourse with her husband's corpse. Horus avenged his father's death by killing Seth and he then became the king of Egypt. Osiris became the king of the underworld. The pharaoh was the reincarnation of Horus in life and became Osiris when he died.

From the fifth dynasty onwards the king was also believed to be the son of the sun-god Ra. There are two Horuses in Egyptian religion: the falcon sky-god and the younger Horus, the son of Osiris, who is represented as a child sucking his finger, to indicate his tender age.

Osiris was also compared to a cereal grain, which must die in order to be able to germinate.

FIGURE 5.3

The Phoenician god Baal riding a lion: relief from the ninth century BC

Notes. It was very common to represent gods riding on animals in the Levant. The crown that Baal is wearing is derived from that of Osiris. The symbols of the moon (crescent) and the winged sun are visible above the god's head.

which defined the ties of kinship between the supreme god and the gods of other cities. However, these systems rarely had a fixed order and there were no dogmas determined by any religious or political authority.

Polytheistic religions are flexible and readily accept foreign gods into their pantheons, either as new gods or through identification with existing gods.

At a very early stage already, the gods were represented as anthropomorphic beings, that is, in the form of human beings. They were also endowed with human characteristics. In Egypt the gods were also portrayed as animals or as hybrid creatures, part beast and part man, which greatly astonished other peoples, in particular the Greeks and Romans, who regarded them with contempt.

The gods were worshipped to obtain their favor and to ensure that they would maintain world order and the fertility of the land. The worshippers served the gods meals, via offerings, and performed all kinds of rituals during which myths were recited. Worship was a state affair, but people also venerated their favorite gods privately.

The king played an important part in religious activities. Some kings, like the kings of Early Dynastic Uruk, Assyria, and Egypt, served a double function, as the king and the high priest. But even the kings who were not themselves high priests regarded themselves as the supreme god's principal servants; as such they were responsible for ensuring that the will of the gods was done. Their main task was to win the gods' favor. To that end they built temples for the gods and took part in all kinds of rituals. Sumerian texts, for example, mention rituals involving a sacred marriage in which the king had intercourse with the city god's high priestess to secure the fertility of the land and a good harvest. The kings of Babylon had to participate in the New Year's Festival, on which occasion they were temporarily divested of their authority. They had to avow that they had committed no crimes against the Babylonians and had to promise that they would respect the Babylonians' privileges. After that, they were restored to their power for another year. During this festival, which lasted for several days, the Babylonian epic of creation was recited, to reassert Marduk's triumph over the powers of chaos. In spite of their leading roles in religious affairs, the kings of Western Asia were hardly ever considered divine. Only the kings of Akkad, the Third Dynasty of Ur and the Greek-Macedonian Seleucid dynasty had themselves deified. The Hittite kings were believed to become gods after their deaths. In Egypt, kingship was regarded as a divine institution. The king was believed to be the incarnation of the sky god Horus and the son of the sun god Ra. The people looked to him to secure the fertility of their land and for the regular flooding of the Nile. Statues of the king were venerated in cults. As a person, the king was, however, an ordinary being, with human characteristics, who prayed to the gods and was not on a par with the Egyptian deities. In Egypt, too, religion was a state affair and the king played a leading part in religious rites and in the temple's administration. More than in Mesopotamia, the kings had superhuman qualities. Their official utterings counted as words of a god.

Private persons also prayed to the gods, but much less is known about such individual forms of worship. Many private persons had their own patron gods, who mediated on their behalf with other—sometimes more powerful—gods.

Human beings could find out what the gods had in store for them by, for example, studying the stars, the livers of sacrificed animals, or the flight of birds. Before venturing on important undertakings, kings would consult priests who specialized in these forms of divination. The "Chaldean" astrologers (see p. 134) acquired great fame in the Greco-Roman world.

Egyptians and Mesopotamians held entirely different views on life after death. The Egyptians believed that life would continue under the same pleasant conditions as on earth, provided that the body remained intact. They therefore took great pains to preserve the bodies of the deceased by embalming ("mummifying") them. To the Mesopotamians, life after death was a bleak prospect: the deceased went to a dismal area inside the earth, where an unpleasant time awaited them. This we know from the Epic of Gilgamesh.

The Epic of Gilgamesh is one of the earliest masterpieces of world literature. It was composed by Sin-leqi-unninni in Babylonia some time between the thirteenth and the eleventh century BC. It is written in Babylonian cuneiform script and comprises around 3000 lines on eleven clay tablets (the series also includes a twelfth tablet bearing a translation of a Sumerian poem about Gilgamesh). The greater part of the text was found in the library of the Assyrian king Ashurbanipal (668–631 BC), who tried to collect all Sumerian and Babylonian literature. But some parts were found in other Assyrian cities, in Babylon and Uruk. The youngest fragment, from Babylon, dates from 130 BC, i.e., from the time when the city was under Parthian control. This shows how tremendously popular the epic was.

The epic recounts the adventures of Gilgamesh, the king of Uruk (c. 2750 BC), who sets out to seek immortality. Gilgamesh is a tyrannical king who allows no woman to marry as a virgin. The gods therefore create a monstrous being, Enkidu, intended to bring him into line. Gilgamesh and Enkidu fight one another, but become friends after their struggle. The epic tells us how they plan to acquire eternal fame by defeating the demon Humbaba in the Cedar Forest in Lebanon, in which endeavor they succeed. When Enkidu dies, Gilgamesh, inconsolable, is again faced with the inevitability of death. He resumes his search for eternal life and his quest takes him to the very edge of the earth, beyond the Waters of Death. There he meets Utanapishtim, who has survived the great flood and been granted immortality by the gods. The adventures of Utanapishtim, written on the eleventh tablet, caused a stir in the nineteenth century, when these texts were discovered, because the Babylonian flood myth shows close parallels with the story of the deluge in the book of Genesis in the Bible. Utanapishtim, however, disappoints Gilgamesh: the gods made humans mortal, and there is no escaping death. Back in Uruk, Gilgamesh has only the city's walls, which he built, to grant him eternal fame.

In what is classed as its standard version, the Epic of Gilgamesh is not an original creation, without any background. It is based on a collection of Sumerian epics about Gilgamesh that were already in circulation in the third millennium. They were probably passed down orally, recited by bards at the kings' courts. The epics were written down at the time of king Shulgi of Ur (Third Dynasty), who also created a library. They were taught at the schools for scribes in Babylonia, but also in such distant places as Hattusas (Boğazköy) in what is now Turkey, where fragments of Hittite translations have been found, Ugarit in Syria, and Megiddo in Israel. There were also separate Sumerian and Babylonian epics of the great flood.

HENOTHEISM AND MONOTHEISM

Polytheism is not the only form of religion. Sometimes people placed all their confidence in one of the gods of a pantheon and regarded all the other gods, whose existence they nevertheless did not doubt, as powerless beings. This form of religion, which is known as henotheism or monolatry, was to be found in early Israel. Some Assyrian and Egyptian texts also show signs of henotheism. One step further is monotheism. Monotheists worship only one god and deny the existence of other gods; they will generally not tolerate the worship of other gods either. The world view of a monotheistic religion is consequently very different from that of a polytheistic religion. The cosmos is not believed to be governed by a multitude of divine powers. The sky, earth, sun, and moon are not gods; there is only one god, who has created the universe and his creation is material. Monotheism was very rare in antiquity.

A frequently discussed problem is whether the cult established by the Egyptian pharaoh Akhenaten (see p. 26) (c. 1350 BC) was monotheistic. This pharaoh made the sun god Aten his patron god and tried to suppress the cult of the former supreme god, Amon. He had all representations and every mention of Amon removed where possible and changed his own name, Amenophis or Amenhotep (meaning "Amon has mercy") into Akhenaten ("agreeable to Aten"). The other gods he neglected altogether. In some places he even had the word "gods" expunged. Aten was represented as the disk of the sun with rays ending in blessing hands—a form of portrayal that differed markedly from the usual, according to which the gods were represented as human beings, animals, or a combination of the two. Aten was one aspect of the sun god Ra, who was represented as a human being crowned by a solar disk. So the name of Ra was still acceptable. The king himself was now truly divine and claimed to be the sole intermediary between Aten and his people. In Akhenaten's cult Aten was the supreme deity; he was the creator and benefactor of the world. As we do not know whether Akhenaten actually denied the existence of other gods, it is difficult to say whether his cult was monotheistic or henotheistic. Akhenaten's views were too revolutionary for most Egyptians, whose traditional world view, based on a multitude of gods, it totally upset. As his world view also excluded Osiris, who played such an important part in the cult of the dead, his reforms did not catch on and after his death the Egyptians quickly reverted to their old traditions.

FIGURE 5.4 The Judgment of the Dead: illustration from the book of the dead of Tahurit, twenty-first dynasty, *c.* 1000 BC

Notes. From right to left: Osiris, the king and supreme judge of the underworld, bearing the insignia of a king; Maat, the goddess of cosmic order, truth, and justice, recognizable by the feather on her head; the ibis-headed Thoth, the scribe of the gods and the moon-god, accompanies the deceased into the presence of Osiris; the falcon-headed Horus keeps an eye on the balance's plummet; the dead woman Tahurit. The left pan of the balance, with an urn containing the heart of the deceased, and the right pan, with a figurine representing Maat, must be in balance. If they are out of balance, the deceased will be torn up by the monster at the bottom of the scene and will die a second death: total destruction. This illustration, in which the pans are shown in balance, was intended to magically prevent this. Note the Egyptian custom of portraying human beings with the face, hips, and feet in profile and the eyes and shoulders in frontal view.

Far more successful was the monotheistic religion professed by the people of Israel, or rather by a small, zealous group of adherents who for many centuries fought stubbornly for the exclusive worship of YHWH (Yahweh), the God of Israel, while most of their fellow Israelites and most of the kings of Israel and Judah also worshipped other gods besides YHWH. It was to that same end, to propagate the exclusive belief in one God, that the books of the Old Testament were written (see pp. 35 and 40). By adhering to this tradition, the Jews who returned from their exile and those who spread across the world in later times managed to preserve their identity, even though (excluding one brief intermittent period) they were to remain deprived of their national autonomy, which they lost at the time of the Babylonian Exile, until 1948.

The Persian religion preached by the sixth-century prophet Zarathustra (Zoroaster in Greek, *c.* 1000 BC) approached monotheism to some extent. This religion is known to us from sacred texts called Avesta, the oldest hymns (Gathas) of which go back to the tenth century BC. Younger parts originated in the fifth century or later and were written down in the Sasanid era. Zarathustra taught his followers that the world was governed by two principles: Good and Evil. The former was represented by the Persian supreme god Ahura Mazda (Oromasdes), the latter by the evil spirit Angra Mainyu or Ahriman. Both were assisted by divine helpers ("angels and devils"). Human beings partook of the struggle between the two by following one of them. Zarathustra's teachings ("Zoroastrianism") were not immediately accepted in Persia; on the contrary, they met with a good deal of opposition. From time immemorial, the Persians had worshipped many other gods besides their supreme god Ahura Mazda, of whom Anahita (the goddess of the waters that bring fertility) and Mithras (the god of light and truth) were the most important. Whether the Achaemenid kings were Zoroastrians is not certain. It is thought that Zoroastrianism became an influential, state-supported religion only in the Neo-Persian empire (cf. pp. 268–9). So here, too, the renunciation of polytheism proved a difficult step. The arrival of Islam in Persia in the seventh century AD soon pushed Zoroastrianism into the background. Nevertheless, about 600,000 adherents of this religion are still to be found in Iran today. Among them are also the "Parsees" of India.

6 ECONOMY AND SOCIETY

AGRICULTURAL ECONOMY, LAND TENURE

Throughout the whole history of the ancient Near East, agriculture formed the basis of the economy. Crop cultivation and animal husbandry were the main subsistence activities. Landed property was the principal form of wealth. Merchants, too, eagerly invested their profits in land. In the ancient Near East the temple and the palace were the chief landowners, but at all times there were also private landowners. In Sumer, the principal landowner was originally the temple, which was also the administrative center of the city in which it stood. At some point, however, a separate leader (the king) emerged from the temple administration and established himself in a palace with his own landed property. The palace and the temple were never entirely independent of one another: it was the king who built the temples and the king also participated in important rituals (see pp. 48–9). He supervised the management of the temple land, which earned him income. Temples in captured areas were often ransacked. In Egypt there were also temple estates and palace estates, but it was often difficult to distinguish between the two because the temple was in fact a state enterprise managed by the king. In periods of weak central authority the temples sometimes acquired independence.

"Redistribution economy"

Everywhere in the ancient Near East (including Crete and Mycenae) the economy revolved around the vast palace and temple households. The Near Eastern economy was different from the classical Greek and Roman economy in that respect. Egypt had what is known as a redistribution economy, controlled by the palace. Via taxes, the state collected the population's farming surpluses, which it then redistributed in the form of allowances for priests and officials, wages for the builders of the royal tombs, gifts for temples, members of the royal household, and the harem, etc. At the very bottom of this system was the Egyptian farmer, who had to support himself with the products of his own plot of land; he could augment his livelihood via barter.

The economy of the Mesopotamian temple and palace domains was based on a similar redistribution system. In early dynastic Sumer the temple was the chief landowner. Part of the land was exploited by the temple's own staff, part was granted to the people employed by the temple, and part was leased. The people employed by the temple were paid in food rations, too. Besides farms, the temple domains also included workshops where specialized craftsmen worked. Over the ages, the palace gradually became more important; by the time of the Third Dynasty of Ur (c. 2100–2000) the state dominated the entire economy, including that of the temples. The clay tablets on which the records of the numerous local offices and depots were kept show that the state concerned itself with all fields of the economy.

After the collapse of the Third Dynasty of Ur there were more options for private land tenure, but the palace and the temple nevertheless remained the principal landowners until the Parthian period (around the beginning of the Christian era).

Means of payment

In societies without coined money, like those of the ancient Near East, plots of land and food rations were important means of remuneration. High-ranking officials were often granted vast estates for their sustenance. The palace also used land as a means for paying soldiers for military service, for example in the Old Babylonian period. When those soldiers then set out on campaigns, they would lease their land. The land granted to soldiers was not exempt from taxation. A similar system existed in the Assyrian, Persian, and Seleucid empires and in pharaonic and Ptolemaic Egypt. After the introduction of the war chariot (c. 1600), charioteers were granted extra large plots of land; their horses and chariots were also provided by the state—a custom that was later to be adopted in Mycenaean Greece (see p. 24) and Rome (see p. 147), too.

For traders, the possibility of using fixed means of payment and units of account is of great importance. Pure barter involves many practical drawbacks. Grain, silver, gold, tin, and copper have at one time or another all served as means of payment, in fixed units of weight. Units of weight of those materials were also used to express the value of goods. Over the ages, units of particular weights of silver (in Mesopotamia) and copper (in Egypt) gradually evolved into proper means of payment. In the eighth and seventh centuries, the kings of Syria, Assyria, and Lydia started to provide lumps of precious metal of a fixed weight with badges. They are regarded as the first coins. They were, however, exclusively intended for use in social and political spheres (gift exchange). It was not until over a century later that coins acquired a commercial function, initially in the Greek world. In the Near East, money in coin was introduced only in the Persian era, in particular during the reign of Darius I, when coins started to be used on a limited scale in the western parts of the empire. In those early days a coin's value was still largely dependent on its silver content and its weight.

TRADE

The fact that the economy was based on agriculture does not mean that there was no need for trade. Egypt and Mesopotamia lacked important resources like timber, copper, and tin. Excavations have demonstrated the existence of trade contacts spanning long distances, from Asia Minor to Iran, already in pre- and proto-historic times.

However, throughout antiquity, trade was fraught with great dangers, especially trade via land, owing to the poor and slow means of transport and the risk of robbery. Goods intended for trade had to be light, non-perishable and costly if they were to yield profits. Large volumes of goods (such as grain) could only be efficiently transported by ship. It was too expensive to transport grain over long distances by land because the draught and pack animals (mules) that were used for that purpose were slow and had to be fed, which implied extra costs.

In view of the great risks and investments involved in trade, and as the products that were transported were usually costly, it is not surprising that the majority of the earliest commercial enterprises were commissioned and "financed" by the wealthiest institutions—the temple and the palace. That does not imply that the merchants were employed by the temple or the palace. We know that in the Old Babylonian empire, merchants managed a treasury jointly with the palace, in which both had deposited silver as opening capital. Thanks to the discovery of an archive of some 18,000 clay tablets at Kanesh in Asia Minor (Kültepe, Turkey), we are also well informed about ancient Assyrian trade. Although the Assyrians had no political power in Kanesh there was a trading quarter populated by Assyrian merchants in that city. The Assyrian government concluded commercial treaties with the rulers of Kanesh. Even in those early days (c. 1900 BC) customs were in use that were quite similar to modern banking practices. For example, people were already using transferable acknowledgements of debt payable to bearer. Archives of private enterprises that specialized in trade, lease activities, the granting of loans, and the exploitation of land have survived from the Neo-Babylonian and Persian eras. The Phoenician cities maintained trade contacts with countries in other parts of the Mediterranean.

SOCIAL ORGANIZATION

All the societies of the ancient Near East were stratified, that is, a distinction was made between different groups of people on the basis of birth, wealth, and status. Almost everywhere the king was at the top of the social hierarchy. Under the king were groups of high- and lower-ranking officials who enjoyed the emoluments associated with their offices. In some periods, only the members of a social elite were admitted to the administrative posts, but in times when the king enjoyed powerful authority, persons who were not members of that elite were sometimes also appointed to those posts.

The ordinary population consisted of groups that differed from one another in terms of wealth or in the kinds of work they did. From the earliest written sources we know that families and private persons owned transferable land, and that in those early days there was already a considerable range of widely varying professions. It is not so easy to classify the population on the basis of social position. What complicates the picture is that one person could simultaneously own private land, exploit a plot of land that the palace had granted him as a fief in exchange for military service, and additionally lease land from a private person. Whether a person owned land or leased it from another tells us little about that person's status.

Finally, there was also a distinction between free men and slaves. Freedom was a relative concept in the ancient Near East because political freedom was restricted by the king's power. There were, however, councils, and citizens of respected ancient cities such as Babylon, Nippur, and Assur made sure they enjoyed the privileges to which they were entitled. There were, moreover, different forms of dependence which are difficult for us to distinguish, but there was also a group of people who can be termed slaves proper. That group can be further subdivided on the basis of the different kinds of slavery that existed in those days. The kind of slaves who were treated as merchandise enjoyed the least freedom ('chattel slaves'). That category consisted of people who had been made slaves after being taken captive in wars or in raids. They were consequently usually foreigners. Some people were reduced to slavery by debts; this is known as debt bondage or bonded labor. A debtor who was unable to pay his debts became his creditor's property for a certain period of time or for the rest of his life. Those slaves usually enjoyed more rights and their position was legally defined. Hammurabi's famous law code (c. 1750 BC) restricted the term of debt slavery to three years; the laws of the Israelites to a maximum of six years. However, not everyone abided by those laws (cf. slavery in Athens, p. 85, and in Rome, p. 156). Some parents sold their children as slaves, especially to the temples. That was one way in which poor people could ensure a livelihood for their children.

Slaves were used for all kinds of tasks, varying from estate management to work in the mines. Many performed household duties. At no point in the history of the ancient Near East, however, did slavery assume the importance it was later to have in classical Greece and Rome.

The prisoners of war who were not killed were often forced to work in the temples or palaces. Their status could then vary from that of a household slave to that of a kind of tenant farmer or craftsman, who was granted land and/or food rations for his sustenance. Landowners, temples, and palaces preferably employed free tenants to till their land. Even if they had slaves, they would often grant them lease contracts for the tilling of their land. Large domains sometimes included entire villages. Their occupants were not slaves—they were not transferable merchandise—but they were not free to do as they pleased either. From Assyrian and Seleucid sources we know that any people living on a plot of land that was sold to a new owner were included in the sale agreement. Small-time landowners tilled their land themselves or with the help of their families; they couldn't afford slaves. We must, however, beware of lapsing into sweeping generalizations and underestimating the importance of slaves. Wealthy families in Babylon in the Neo-Babylonian and Achaemenid eras often possessed several dozen slaves. Documents from the archives of the Egibi family of merchants in Babylon covering the years from 606 until 482 BC refer to more than 200 privately owned slaves.

From the law code formulated by Hammurabi (c. 1750/1700 BC) we know that not everyone was equal before the law. Punishments varied from severe to quite light, depending on whether the offence in question had been committed against a court official, a common subject, or a slave. This is known as class justice.

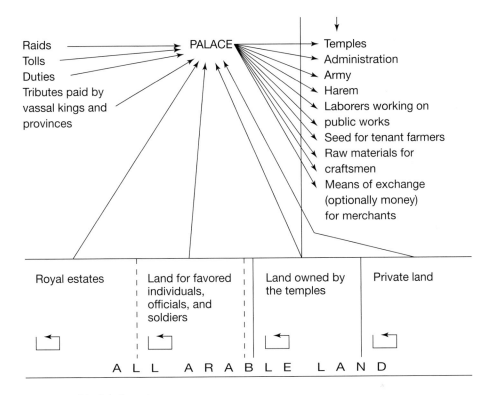

FIGURE 6.1   Model of a palace economy

Figure 6.1 gives an impression of how a palace economy functioned. This of course varied from one state to another and from one period to another owing to variations in political conditions. For a start, the relationship between the temple and the palace was always a delicate affair. Sometimes the temple enjoyed a high degree of independence, for example at the beginning of the Early Dynastic period in Sumer; at other times, such as during the reigns of the kings of the Third Dynasty of Ur and in the Neo-Babylonian and Persian periods, the temple's activities were entirely controlled by the palace. In Egypt the pharaoh was the high priest and the ultimate authority of all of the temples; the temple was in fact a state enterprise. There were also differences in the ratios of landed property. In Early Dynastic Sumer, for example, the greater part of the land seems to have belonged to the temple; by the time of the reigns of the kings of Akkad and the Third Dynasty of Ur the state had apparently gained control over a larger proportion of the land, whereas a substantial part of the arable land was held in private tenure in the Old Babylonian period. We have no exact data on the different ratios. What also varied were the payments made by the palace. Sometimes the palace would grant the people it employed plots of land for their sustenance; at other times it would favor payment in the form of food rations.

In actual fact, the domains of the kings, temples, and private persons constituted individual centers of small-scale redistribution economies aiming at autarky.

As for the tolls and duties, they did not always have to be paid: sometimes the king would grant certain temples, officials, or private persons (for example the inhabitants of privileged cities) exemption from taxation.

Note: The symbol ⌐┘ denotes produce that remained at the domain for its occupants' consumption.

FIGURE 6.2 Labor force

7 GOVERNMENT

KINGSHIP

Throughout almost the entire history of the ancient Near East, kingship was the normal form of government. Peoples who were not ruled by kings were considered barbaric. According to Mesopotamian tradition, kingship, like other expressions of human civilization, had come down to earth from heaven.

The main functions of the king were those of military commander, supreme judicial authority, and high priest. Most kings accompanied their armies to the battlefield in person. Some scholars maintain that kingship came into being with the appointment of the first military commander.

The king also administered justice, either in person or via judges who pronounced legal decisions on his behalf. Many codes of law set up by Near Eastern kings have survived. The best known is that of Hammurabi, but we also have codes of law from Ur (c. 2100 BC), Assyria, and the Hittite empire. The laws of Israel laid down in the Old Testament are different in that they were not formulated by kings, but by priests.

Most of these law codes are casuistically formulated: an introductory clause starting with "when" describes a case (*casus*), an offence, while the main clause stipulates the punishment. From this we can infer that these codes of law are actually written reports of legal decisions—a form of case law. The Roman legal system also included this form of law.

The king's function in religious practices has already been discussed in Chapter 5, on religion.

Most kings had absolute power, but in some periods the king had to consider the opinions of councils of elders and/or free citizens. This is believed to have been the case in Early Dynastic Sumer, in Assyria before the Amorite *coup d'etat* in 1800, in the old Hittite kingdom, and in some Phoenician cities. In the cities there were in particular councils of elders and/or free citizens with local, predominantly legal powers. A typical phenomenon is that the checks to the king's authority decreased as his kingdom expanded.

THE ADMINISTRATIVE MACHINERY

In administrative matters the king was assisted by officials, who were usually paid in land for their services. That land frequently became hereditary property—a development that implied a serious threat to the king as it gave his officials the means and opportunity to act on their own authority (e.g., as happened at the end of the Old Kingdom in Egypt). Assyrian kings successfully minimized the risk of this taking place by rigorously dismissing high officials and reclaiming their land and by appointing eunuchs as their officials.

The administration of a large empire, that is, a state including vast foreign territories over which it has acquired supremacy, involved special problems. A distinction can be made between an empire's heartland and its peripheries—the regions brought under the heartland's sway. In the ancient Near East the latter regions were usually governed as either vassal states or provinces. When a state was made a vassal state its king was allowed to remain in power, provided that he promised to give allegiance to the king who had defeated him, renounce foreign politics, and pay tribute. The kings of the Hittite empire transformed many subject states into vassal states (see p. 29) and so did the kings of Mitanni, Egypt (its possessions in Syria and Palestine), and those of the Neo-Assyrian empire. However, if a vassal ruler rose against the king or failed to pay the due tributes or if a newly appointed vassal ruler proved disloyal, the king would reduce that ruler's territory to a province and place it under the authority of a governor whom he himself appointed.

The practice of reducing vassal states to provinces became increasingly common after the reign of the Assyrian king Tiglath-Pileser III (745–727) and was continued in the Neo-Babylonian, Persian, and Hellenistic empires. It had, however, been applied much earlier already: the kings of the empires of Akkad (c. 2300 BC) and Ur (c. 2100) had already appointed officials to act as governors of the regions they conquered. Well-organized empires, such as the Neo-Assyrian and Persian empires, appointed stationary or itinerant inspectors who were to keep a close watch on the governors' activities and report anything out of the ordinary to the central authority.

Sometimes provinces would come to form such integral parts of the empire that the distinction between the heartland and the peripheral districts became blurred. This could happen, for example, when provinces were treated in the same manner as the heartland, and a uniform culture embracing the whole of the empire was created. The history of the Roman empire presents excellent examples of such a development (see pp. 234 and 272). In the Near East this development was greatly encouraged by the mass deportations that generally took place whenever a state was transformed into a province. It was usually the top layers of a society and the craftsmen who were deported on those occasions. They were granted land in the heartland or in the newly annexed provinces. Some were enrolled in the army; they were then granted land in exchange for their services. The deportees were relatively loyal towards their new ruler, out of gratitude for their newly acquired position and because of the vulnerability of that position— for the original population viewed the arrival of these newcomers with disfavor. Some deportees were less fortunate. They were set to work on major building projects in the capitals or were presented to temples or private persons as slaves. The Neo-Assyrian king Tiglath-Pileser III and his immediate successors are particularly notorious for their mass deportations. The later Assyrian kings made less use of this policy; the numbers of people who were deported from their homelands

FIGURE 7.1 Part of the black obelisk of Shalmaneser III, king of Assyria 869–824 BC

Notes. King Jehu of Israel lies prostrate at the feet of Shalmaneser and offers him tribute. The cuneiform text reads: "Tribute of Jehu (Ia-ú-a), the son of Omri (Hu-um-ri-i)."

Omri founded a dynasty in Israel, but Jehu did not belong to that dynasty. The expression literally means "Jehu of Omri-country." Countries were often described in this manner. The relief clearly reflects the relation between the king, represented as a large figure, and a vassal ruler, shown as a smaller figure.

also gradually decreased. However, deportation continued to be used as a means of oppression until the Hellenistic period. In the Neo-Babylonian, Persian, Seleucid, and Parthian empires, the deportees managed to retain their identity for quite some time. Some communities even had their own governments; there were for example self-governing communities of Egyptians, Syrians, Phrygians, Lydians, and, in particular, Jews. From time to time groups of exiles were allowed to return to their home countries. The best documented example is the return of the Jews from their exile during the Persian era.

One of the main motivations for expansion was undoubtedly the lure of riches in the form of booty and tributes. Lists of spoils taken in raids and tributes make up large parts of the royal inscriptions, especially those of the Assyrian kings. Exemption from taxation was a great privilege. The Assyrian kings granted this privilege to a few cities that were important in a religious respect such as Assur, Babylon, and Nippur. In the Persian empire the heartland, Persis, was exempt from some taxes. Some important trading centers, such as the Phoenician cities, were allowed a fairly high degree of autonomy because the large imperialistic states realized that it was in their own interest, too, that those cities continued to thrive. In the first place, they would benefit from those cities' wealth via the taxes they imposed, and, secondly, goods that were of importance to them, too, were imported via those cities. When the Phoenician cities were incorporated in the Persian empire they became important bases for the Persian fleet. A king who violated the—often time-honored—privileges of such cities was bound to meet with difficulties. The practice of granting the heartland exemption from direct taxation where possible remained customary throughout the whole history of the ancient world. It was also applied in Athens (p. 95) and Rome (p. 176).

THE ARMY

Wars evolved from minor skirmishes concerning territorial issues and raids aimed at securing means of support into organized expeditions with the objective of permanent occupation of the invaded territory. The size of the army increased accordingly. For a long time war was a seasonal affair. The ordinary, peasant population was called up to fight in a war and the best time for a campaign was the early summer, just after harvesting time. This was also a favorable time as far as logistics, the availability of grain and water, and temperatures (not yet too high) were concerned. Over the ages, the army gradually evolved into an institution. Of great importance with respect to this development was the introduction, around the end of the Late Bronze Age (1600–1200), of the custom of awarding soldiers land and supporting an elite of charioteers. From the end of the eighth century, the Assyrians had a standing army that enabled them to engage in warfare all the year round, although they continued to levy troops from the farming population on a seasonal basis, too. In the Persian empire more and more use started to be made of mercenaries besides native soldiers. Large empires were unable to levy sufficient troops from the dominant population and so the subject peoples had to supply contingents to reinforce the army. A final noteworthy phenomenon is that military innovations such as the war chariot spread fast, and were quickly adopted in all the regions where they were introduced.

PART II THE GREEK WORLD

8 THE EARLY IRON AGE (c. 1200–c. 750 BC)
"The Dark Ages"

DISRUPTION AND RECOVERY

The fall of Mycenaean civilization (c. 1200, see p. 33) had far-reaching consequences. The strictly organized palace economy collapsed completely and was never to re-emerge. The Linear B script that had been used for the palaces' administration passed into oblivion; the Greeks of later centuries used a totally different form of writing. Linear B was rediscovered only at the end of the nineteenth century, when tablets inscribed with the script came to light in excavations. The meaning of the tablets was, however, to remain a mystery for several more years, awaiting the deciphering of the script in 1952. The palaces that had been so influential in the centuries preceding the fall were destroyed, never to be rebuilt, though cities such as Knossos on Crete and Tiryns on the Peloponnese remained occupied. Many Greeks fled to the west coast of Asia Minor. This movement of people is also known as the "Ionian migration." The Greeks who settled in Ionia were later to contribute greatly to the revival of Greek culture. The population of Greece itself shrank and its once so splendid material culture became severely impoverished. The Early Iron Age is also the time of the invasion of the Dorians, who settled in the Peloponnese, on Crete and in the southwest of Asia Minor.

We are poorly informed about the social structure in the dark ages. Most of what we do know has been inferred from archaeological evidence and the "Iliad" and the "Odyssey," the great epic works that are attributed to the poet Homer. The "Iliad" describes an episode from the war that a group of Greek kings (among whom was Agamemnon of Mycenae) waged against the city of Troy—or Ilion, as it was also known—in northwest Asia Minor. The "Odyssey" tells the story of the adventures of Odysseus, the king of the island of Ithaca, on his journey home after the destruction of Troy. These epics are based on ancient tales that were recited by bards at the courts of kings and noblemen. Whether both epics were written by the same author is a matter of debate. We actually know nothing about Homer. It is now usually assumed that the "Iliad" was written around 700 and the "Odyssey" a few decades later, but the issue is still debated.

The Trojan War was assumed to have taken place at the height of Mycenae's wealth and power, but the society described by Homer bears very little resemblance to the society known to us from the Linear B tablets; it is, instead, substantially a reflection of the world in Homer's own time and preceding centuries. In Homeric society a king was not a leader in a palace economy associated with an extensive city life, but a wealthy landowner who was the *primus inter pares*, the first among equals, in times of war. His peers were the heads of large agricultural households. All military power rested with these nobles, because they could afford to arm themselves. They would ride out to battlefields on horseback or by chariot, to then descend to fight their opponents in individual duels. The rest of the population played a much smaller part in military affairs. In the epics, cities, nonetheless, play an important role, suggesting that their author(s) was (were) familiar with the emerging Greek city state (see Chapter 9).

The values of this aristocracy had a profound influence on Greek mentality. The nobles were expected to protect their households, and they therefore had to show themselves to be strong, able-bodied men. The competitive element inherent in this ideology also found expression in games. Well known, for example, are the Olympic Games which were organized for the first time in 776 BC.

Owing to the absence of contemporary written evidence and the impoverished material culture, this period—especially the part from 1100 until 900—is referred to as "the dark ages." In the past few years our understanding of this period has, however, increased, largely thanks to information obtained in excavations. From Lefkandi on the island of Euboea we now know a fine example of a large house measuring about 45 × 10 meters and dating from the tenth/ninth century, which must have belonged to a local aristocrat of the kind described above. We now also know that this elite maintained contacts with other areas, especially in the eastern Mediterranean. The island of Cyprus seems to have held a key position in these contacts. When the Phoenicians settled on this island in the ninth century they encountered Greeks who had been living there since the Mycenaean era. The Greeks on Cyprus were still speaking their old Mycenaean dialect and continued to do so. They also had their own script.

9 THE ARCHAIC PERIOD (c. 750–c. 500 BC)

INTRODUCTION

The eighth century BC saw the first of a series of important changes which marked out a new course in the history of the civilization of Greece. What was to follow was not a revival of the former Mycenaean culture but the emergence of an entirely new culture, with a character all of its own. The individual character of this culture does not imply that Greece was at this time an isolated area, cut off from contacts with the outside world. The Archaic period in Greece coincides with the era of the great empires of Western Asia with their age-old cultures—the Neo-Assyrian, Neo-Babylonian, and Persian empires, all of which lay fairly close to Greece. It was in the Archaic period, too, that the Greek trading post Naukratis was established in Egypt (c. 650 BC) and that the Greeks in Asia Minor came into contact with Lydia and Phrygia. In this same period the Greek cities in Asia Minor were to come under Persian control, when Cyrus conquered that area in 547 BC (see p. 42). Sea-borne trade was in these days in the hands of the Phoenicians, who traded their goods in Greece, too. From 900 onwards Greeks called in at ports along the Phoenecian coast (Tyrus, Al Mina) and on Cyprus. Seen against this background, it is not surprising that Greek religion, art, science, and material culture betray various Eastern influences.

As mentioned above, the Archaic period was a time of new developments and great changes—cultural changes, but also demographic, economic, social, and military changes. These developments and changes, which were all closely related and influenced one another, were ultimately to bring about the peculiarly Greek types of society of the succeeding, Classical period.

DEMOGRAPHIC AND ECONOMIC CHANGES

Archaeological research has shown that the eighth century in Greece was characterized by a broad recovery of settlements and material culture, reflected by a certain monumentalization in construction. Huts evolved into houses, wooden temples were replaced by stone structures, and villages grew into towns, which were surrounded by walls. There is more large-scale evidence of a distinct elite, for example in the burial practices. This suggests an increase in population.

The growth in question was probably a gradual development, spanning the period from the tenth to the fifth century, rather than the explosive expansion in the eighth century hitherto often assumed on the basis of a substantial increase in the number of burials found. But, especially in a primitive economy, even a gradual increase in populations meant that more mouths had to be fed and that necessitated great changes in farming practices. Waste land was brought under cultivation and the range of crops was expanded. This led to a gradual decline in stock-keeping.

Some Greeks took to the sea, hoping to make a living through piracy or trade. Noteworthy in this context is that whereas in Homer's works seafaring traders are still all Phoenicians, the slightly younger poet Hesiod already mentions overseas trade contacts maintained by Greeks (such as his own father). This does incidentally not necessarily imply a historical development: Homer's world is that of idealized large-landowning heroes—later Greeks (and Romans, too) also saw commerce as an inferior enterprise—whereas Hesiod's work is a much closer representation of everyday life.

A third consequence of the growth in population was the development of cities, as a result of the fusion of expanding villages. These cities were ideal outlets for the landowners' increased agricultural produce. It was via these cities, too, that the luxury goods from the Near East which were coveted by the wealthy elite were imported into Greece. Many noblemen consequently took up residence in the cities.

The *polis*

The eighth century is also the century of the birth of the *polis*. A *polis* was a community with its own political organization; the word "political" is in fact derived from *polis*. The term *polis* is usually translated as "city state" because a city was generally the key element of a *polis*. A *polis* was in principle always a city with its surrounding land, but more important than the city were the "citizens," the *politai*. Greek authors more often speak of "the Athenians" than of "Athens." In Greek texts the word *polis* incidentally by no means always has this specific "political" meaning, but may simply stand for a "city," even a non-Greek city.

A typical *polis* comprised a relatively small territory with an administrative center, usually urban, which contained the chief sanctuary and a meeting place, the *agora*, where the magistrates and the people assembled when decisions were to be taken. Later on the *agora* came to serve as a marketplace, too. The town usually contained a fortified hill (*akropolis*), on which the occupants could take refuge in times of danger.

The *polis* was governed by officials with specific responsibilities, such as military leadership, jurisdiction, or the supervision of religious practices, who were appointed in some kind of election. This does not mean that all the *poleis* had the same form of government. What they did have in common was that only very few were ruled by kings (Sparta was one of the few *poleis* where kingship was not abolished). In most *poleis* the noble landowners monopolized the political offices. We refer to them as "noble" because they claimed their privileges by reason of birth; such a constitution is called an aristocracy (see the box below). The strong emphasis on high birth was probably connected with the increased importance of land tenure. In the ancient world, ownership of land was often justified by family claims to ancestral land. In Greece this led to an outlook revolving around an *oikos* (household comprising parents, children, grandchildren, and sometimes also dependent farmers and slaves), which preferably belonged to an important lineage that could boast descent from a famous ancestor.

The *polis* was of supreme importance to its occupants, who gradually became true *polis* citizens (*politai*). The status of *polis* citizen came to be more important than that of the member of a clan.

A principal concern of all *poleis* was "freedom and autonomy"—the freedom from domination by a great power or by another *polis*, which implied autonomy, that is, the possibility of making one's own laws.

The Greeks regarded life in a *polis* as the most ideal and most humane form of existence. The idea of being incorporated in a large empire was intolerable to them and they did everything within their power to prevent the risk of that ever happening. Even so, it did happen quite often. Until 479 the *poleis* in Asia Minor formed part of the Persian empire. After that date they were confronted with Athenian imperialism. After 338 almost all *poleis* came under foreign

---

DIFFERENT FORMS OF GOVERNMENT

Monarchy

"Sole rule." The rule of a single, usually hereditary, king with a legitimate claim to power.

Tyranny

"The rule of a tyrant." A tyrant is an autocratic ruler who has seized control without having a legitimate claim to that control.

Aristocracy

"Rule of the best" (Greek: *aristoi*). The "best" are usually understood to be the members of noble families. In an aristocracy, birth is hence the criterion for power.

Oligarchy

"Rule of a few" (Greek: *oligoi*). The rule of a small group of—mostly rich—politicians, who do not necessarily have to be of noble birth.

Timocracy

Forms of government in which property criteria are the qualifications for access to the administrative offices.

Democracy

Rule of the *demos*—the (male) population with citizen rights. In a democracy the public assembly has decisive power.

control—first Macedonian and later Roman (see pp. 101 and 172). They did try to preserve their autonomy in local affairs where possible and their efforts were often quite successful.

The *polis* was not the dominant political unit in the whole of Greece. In less-developed areas, tribal structures prevailed in the form of so-called *ethnē* (plural of *ethnos*, which literally means "nation"): groups of small communities that joined forces in special circumstances, in particular in military operations. Sometimes cities were formed within these *ethnē*, which later developed into *poleis*. Ancient Greece never achieved political union. The Greeks did, however, feel united by their common language (even though it included various dialects, such as Doric in Sparta and the southwest of Asia Minor, and Ionic in Athens and the western part of Asia Minor), by their worship of the same gods, and by their communal traditions, such as the Olympic Games which were organized at Olympia in honor of Zeus, the supreme god of the Greek pantheon.

The Greek world showed a marked resemblance to Phoenicia, whose towns were also independent, autonomous city states and whose occupants likewise shared a common language and religion. The Greeks in fact borrowed much from the Phoenicians, including their alphabet and many of their artistic motifs. They may well have got the idea of living together in *poleis* from the Phoenicians, too. Something else in which the Phoenicians showed the Greeks the way was colonization. The settlements that the Phoenicians founded in the western Mediterranean (see p. 35) served as good examples to the Greeks in their search for new trade contacts and areas to live.

Colonization

The period from the eighth until the sixth century was the time of the second Greek expansion (the first having taken place around 1100): the well-known Greek colonization. There are very few Mediterranean and Black Sea coasts where the Greeks didn't found colonies. Different theories have been put forward to explain this colonizing movement. Some associate the phenomenon with the problems caused by the growth of the population. Others see it as a solution to internal conflicts within the elite of a certain Greek city and an opportunity for a threatened group to create a new existence for itself. It must also have been partly caused by the fact that more and more Greeks were venturing onto the sea, following the example set by the Phoenicians. The very fact of the foundation of the Greek colonies presupposes a certain amount of experience in trade and shipping and knowledge of the geography of the Mediterranean. It is therefore believed that the first of the Greeks' overseas settlements were established for commercial reasons. Such a settlement is known as an *emporion*; well-known examples are Al Mina in Syria, Naukratis in Egypt, and possibly also Pithecusae on the island of Ischia in the Gulf of Naples. The majority of the colonies were, however, agricultural settlements, founded in fertile areas and occupied by farmers, That's why so many colonies were founded along the shores of the Black Sea, in Sicily, and southern Italy. The latter two areas in fact attracted so many Greek settlers that they were collectively known as *Magna Graecia* ("Greater Greece") in antiquity. Large, flourishing Greek cities arose in those areas, some of which are still important towns today, preserving the relics of their glorious past. Impressive remains of Greek architecture can be admired for example in Syracuse, Agrigento, and Paestum (Poseidonia; see Map 9.1b).

■ Direct influence of
  Greek culture

▢ Also influenced by
  the Greeks

MAP 9.1a   Influence of Greek culture in the Archaic and Classical periods, c. 600–330 BC

Note. During the Greek colonizing movement Greeks spread over large parts of the Mediterranean and many peoples came into contact with Greek civilization.

- • Greek mother cities
- · Greek colonies
- ★ Phoenician mother cities
- ☆ Phoenician colonies
- □ Carthaginian colonies

MAP 9.1b   Greek and Phoenician colonization

The term "colonization" is actually misleading. A Greek colony (*apoikia*) was not a foreign territory governed by the city that founded the colony, but a new, independent *polis*, which was bound to its mother city only by moral and religious ties. It is hence not surprising that the Greek colonists, in their search for suitable locations for these independent *poleis*, steered clear of areas containing well-organized states, such as the Levant, Egypt, and Etruscan Italy (see p. 141). The settlements that the Greeks did establish in the latter areas, such as Naukratis in Egypt and Al Mina in Syria, were not independent *poleis*. The colonizing expeditions to some areas such as southern Italy were incidentally small-scale enterprises at first, with the colonists living side by side with the native population. Only in the sixth century did some of these colonies grow into cities proper, with a predominantly Greek population.

Although most colonies were not founded for commercial reasons, they did encourage trade. Trade was very important for the Greeks as it enabled them to obtain grain, which was in short supply in Greece, from areas where it grew in great abundance. Corinth imported most of her grain from her colonies in Sicily, while Athens, which founded only very few colonies, obtained her grain mainly from the regions surrounding the Black Sea. Once food could be imported from overseas, the impulse to further colonization slackened. The Greeks' quest for new land came to an end almost completely around 550 BC, when their colonization campaigns met with increasing opposition from the Persians, Carthaginians, and Etruscans.

The waste land that was brought under cultivation in Greece was used to grow new crops, mainly olives. Sealed in earthenware vessels, the products of these crops, i.e., mostly olive oil, could be exported. Trade greatly boosted industry in the cities: ships had to be built and earthenware vessels had to be produced to enable the transport of the new products. The young *poleis* also vied with each other in building bigger and bigger temples. All this activity implied a good deal of extra work for those not involved in agriculture. It did not, however, lead to a contrast between an urban and a rural population. Most city-dwellers were farmers whose land lay outside the town. They left the town every morning to till their fields or they had a member of their families, a slave, or a tenant do the work for them. Throughout the whole history of the ancient world there were only very few cities that were dependent on imports from regions with surplus grain because the majority of their inhabitants were not engaged in agriculture. This was the case only in extremely large cities such as Athens in the fifth century, Alexandria (Egypt), and Antioch (Syria) in the Hellenistic period (see pp. 102, 120, and 127) and Rome and a few other cities in the Roman empire around the beginning of the Christian era.

SOCIAL CHANGES

The economic and demographic developments described above had social consequences, too. In the first place, they led to the emergence of a group of *nouveaux riches*—people who managed to make a fortune in one way or another. Some grew rich through trade; they would often invest their profits in land. Others had the foresight to start growing the new crops and products in the relatively infertile soil of their land. Those crops were more profitable per unit of land.

For the old-fashioned small farmers struggling to remain self-sufficient, however, things became increasingly difficult. Their family property had to be split up amongst their children with every new generation, and as the population expanded the lots became smaller and smaller until they were ultimately too small to support a farmer and his family. The small farmers were, moreover, unable to switch to the new crops: olive trees do not bear fruit for the first few years after they have been planted and the farmers did not have the necessary resources to tide themselves over the years without income. Nor did they have any surplus land on which they could have grown other crops besides cereals. Many small farmers had to take out loans as they did not produce sufficient surplus grain to sow their next crop. But as their crops didn't become any bigger and they nevertheless had to repay their loans, most of them were reduced to debt bondage, having secured their loans on their person as was customary in those days.

Military changes

In the "dark ages" only the noble elite had engaged in warfare (see p. 66). This changed in the course of the Archaic period, when the *nouveaux riches* and well-to-do farmers could also afford to equip themselves with armor. That armor comprised a helmet, a breast plate, greaves, a spear, and a shield. The latter, which was in this period attached to the (left) arm at two points—at the hand and the elbow—was of particular importance. The soldiers were called "hoplites" after *hoplon*, the Greek word for this shield. Most of the hoplites did not possess a horse, but that was no disadvantage in a battle, as the horsemen always descended from their horses to fight. The hoplites did not fight in single combat as the nobles had done, but in a formation in close array known as a *phalanx*. The hoplites had to ensure that their ranks remained closed so that the unprotected right sides of their bodies were covered by their neighbors' shields. This called for a strong sense of solidarity (*cf.* Figure 10.5a, p. 97). At first the hoplites came from the richest social classes, but after some time the middle classes began to supply hoplites, too. In Sparta this began in the seventh century, in Athens at the end of the sixth century.

Wars in the Archaic period were nothing more than small-scale border conflicts. As the main objective was usually plunder, they were over after one or two clashes. Sometimes there were long periods without any actual fighting in wars between *poleis*.

CULTURAL CHANGES

It was in the Archaic period, too, that the foundations for Greece's great cultural achievements were laid. Greek painting, architecture and sculpture, the literary genres, religious imagery and cult practices, and Greek philosophy all have their roots in the Archaic period. It is in these cultural achievements that Greece's indebtedness to the Near East is particularly evident.

The alphabet

A first major cultural asset that originated in the Near East is the alphabet, which the Greeks borrowed from the Phoenicians in the tenth or ninth century BC. The exact date is not certain: the earliest surviving Greek characters date from the early eighth century (see p. 35). The Greeks, however, introduced an important innovation: they adapted this alphabet, which consisted exclusively of consonants and included a few characters that could in certain circumstances indicate vowels, for their own language by using some of the existing characters exclusively for vowels and adding a number of new characters. The resultant alphabet proved extremely efficient. After only a few minor modifications it was adopted by the Etruscans and later also the Romans, who ultimately passed it down to us. Today, the Latin version of that same alphabet is still used for writing in numerous different languages all over the world. For what purpose the alphabet was introduced into Greece is not entirely certain. It may well be that the Phoenicians were the people with whom the Greeks first came into contact when they ventured overseas in search of trade, and that the alphabet was introduced for business purposes.

Literature

Whatever the reason for the introduction of the alphabet may have been, the oldest pieces of Greek writing known to us are literary texts. These texts were, however, not intended to be read by a wide public; they were written down so that they could be memorized and recited. That is why the oldest texts are all in verse, whether they are epics, like the works of Homer and Hesiod, political pamphlets, such as those of Solon (see p. 84), or the works of the earliest philosophers (see p. 80).

Homer was of tremendous importance to the Greeks. His epics, the "Iliad" (approximately 15,600 lines) and the "Odyssey" (approximately 12,000 lines; see also p. 65), were regarded as a kind of Bible. The study of those epics was a compulsory part of Greek education until well into the Hellenistic era. The world that is described in these works is that of the nobility in the dark ages and the early Archaic period (insofar as his poetry describes a clearly identifiable era and not some idealized past). Homer's representation of the competitive mentality of the nobles and his portrayals of the gods as superior anthropomorphic beings with the same mentality as the aristocracy had a profound influence on Greek thought and religion.

Homer's work is strongly reminiscent of the Epic of Gilgamesh (see pp. 49–50). In both cases we are dealing with major epics based on stories that were after a long oral (and in the case of the Epic of Gilgamesh also written) tradition collected in a single composition. In both cases the works are set in a mythical past with a historical element and feature heroic deeds, adventurous journeys, and eternal fame. And in both cases there are direct contacts between gods and humans. All three epics remained tremendously popular for many centuries and were taught in schools.

Thanks to Hesiod we know something about the lower classes of early Greek society. His epos "Works and Days" presents a picture of contemporary farming practices and describes the harshness of a farming existence. In this work we also learn about the injustice that the farmers suffered at the hands of the nobles, whose bribery and extortion Hesiod criticizes. In his "Theogony" Hesiod systematized the legends about the gods of the Greek pantheon (see p. 79, for a further discussion). Greek literature after Homer is characterized by a trend toward greater individualism. Whereas we know nothing whatsoever about the man who wrote the "Iliad" and the "Odyssey," the later author Hesiod already tells us something about his personal circumstances. But it was not until the seventh century that Greek poetry began to strike a truly personal note, with short lyrical poems conveying the poet's deepest feelings. That is also when the first Greek love lyrics were written. Other poems express views on society, varying from criticism of the aristocratic way of life to fear of the aristocracy losing its power. A striking difference with respect to the ancient Near East, where literature (including the Old Testament) and art were usually anonymously produced, is that Greek authors of literary works—and works of art, too—made their names known, presenting themselves as artists.

The visual arts

Our knowledge of Greek painting is almost entirely restricted to vase painting. The Mycenaean art of fresco painting disappeared within a very short time in the dark ages. The ninth century saw the birth of a new style of vase painting in Athens, characterized by zigzags and swastikas, to which stylized human figures were later added (see Figure 9.1a). The mythical creatures and plants of the style that began to take shape in Corinth around 725 BC betray affinities with the art of the East. Yellow is the predominant color of this style, which is known as the Orientalizing style (see Figure 9.1b). In the sixth century Athenian vase painters started to decorate their vases with figures painted in black silhouette. This "black-figure" style was later superseded by the "red-figure" style. The Attic vases depicting scenes from Greek mythology and everyday life were distributed over a very wide area. Thousands of these vases can still be admired in museums today (see Figures 9.1c and 9.1d).

FIGURE 9.1b Corinthian oil flask, c. 615 BC; Orientalizing style

Notes. Note the sphinx. Winged mythical creatures, part man and part beast, were common motifs all over the ancient Near East. A well-known example is the large sphinx near the pyramids of Giza in Egypt. The sphinx was also represented in Phoenicia. See also the winged bull colossi of Assyria and Persia shown on p. 43.

FIGURE 9.1a Drinking beaker in the Geometric style that was found in the "Kerameikos," Athens' cemetery: eighth century BC

FIGURE 9.1c Panathenaic amphora, *c.* 510 BC; black-figure style

Notes. The scene represents a running contest. Filled with olive oil, this amphora was one of the prizes that could be won at the Panathenaic Games.

FIGURE 9.1d (*right*) Oil flask from Athens, *c.* 465 BC; red-figure style

The poses of the free-standing statues that have survived from the Archaic period suggest that the earliest Greek sculpture owed much to the art of Egypt (see Figures 9.2a and 9.2b). However, it did not take the Greeks long to shake off these influences and develop an entirely original style of their own.

Architecture

Greek architecture also acquired many of its distinctive features in the Archaic period. The most impressive buildings were the temples, which, being the dwellings of the gods (and of their statues), were modeled on the dwellings of mortals. The most conspicuous aspect of their plans is the lavish use of Doric, Ionic, and—from the fourth century onwards—Corinthian columns (see Figures 9.3a–9.3c). The best preserved Greek temples are to be found in southern Italy and Sicily (see Figure 10.13, p. 117).

Religion

Greek religion had much in common with ancient Near Eastern religion (*cf.* p. 46). In the first place it was a polytheistic religion. The gods, especially after Homer had described them in

FIGURE 9.2a
Egyptian sculpture of a nude male: Old
Kingdom, fifth dynasty, *c*. 2400 BC; from
a private grave at Saqqara

FIGURE 9.2b
Archaic sculpture of a young man
(*kouros*): probably sixth century
BC (*c*. 530)

Notes. Greek Archaic sculpture was clearly modeled on Egyptian examples. But whereas Egyptian sculpture remained virtually unchanged from the Old Kingdom until the Late Period, Greek sculpture underwent important developments, towards a more realistic representation of stances. See p. 97 for the sculpture of the Classical period and p. 131 for that of the Hellenistic era.

FIGURE 9.3b
Ionic order

FIGURE 9.3a   Doric order

Notes. a. tympanum; b. frieze; c. triglyphs; d. metope; e. architrave; f. capital.
The differences between the three orders are most apparent in the capital;
g. column; h. fluting; i. stylobate; j. volute; k. base; l. acanthus scrolls.

The Doric order originated in Greece, probably in the seventh century BC.
A well-preserved Doric temple is to be found at Paestum in southern Italy.
The Parthenon in Athens (fifth century) is another example of a Doric
structure. The Ionic order was developed in Ionia (Asia Minor) and the
Aegean islands, but was also used in Greece, for example for the little temple
of Athena Nike on the acropolis in Athens. The Corinthian order is a little
younger (end of the fifth century).

Greek architecture was widely imitated by the Romans. It had a profound
influence on European architecture of later centuries, in particular that of the
Renaissance (sixteenth century) and that of Classicism (end of the eighteenth
century) and Neo-Classicism (end of the nineteenth century).

FIGURE 9.3c
Corinthian order

his epics, were seen as anthropomorphic beings; there was no official dogma; rites played an important part in establishing a good relationship with the gods; each city (*polis*) had its own patron god or—very often—goddess, whose temple stood on the *akropolis*, where the *polis'* religious ceremonies took place. The Greeks' views on death and the after-life showed close similarities with the Mesopotamian notion of a shadowy, somber underworld, where more or less the same dire fate awaited all the souls of the deceased. Of a somewhat different nature was the movement in Greek religion known as Orphism. The term "Orphism" comes from a collection of Orphic literature ascribed to the mythical singer Orpheus, the son of Apollo. This mystery religion was based on the assumption that the body and the soul were separate entities. The soul was believed to be imprisoned within the body, from which it could free itself after death, via reincarnation, asceticism, and purification rites. This principle of the disunion of body and soul— and the resultant depreciation of the body—had a profound influence on the philosophers Pythagoras (*c.* 530) and Plato (*c.* 429–347), and eventually became an important doctrine in Christianity, too.

The belief in a blissful life after death, at least for the initiates of the secret religious rites, held a central place in the mystic cult of the corn goddess Demeter at Eleusis (Demeter means "mother earth"; she was already worshiped in the Mycenaean period). This cult celebrated the release of Persephone, Demeter's daughter, from Hades (the underworld), where she was imprisoned for one third of the year. Her rebirth symbolized the sprouting of the ear of corn from the dying corn grain. A similar belief was associated with the death of Osiris in Egypt (see p. 47). A different natural phenomenon, the death of nature during the dry season, was symbolized in the cult of Adonis, a god of Phoenician origin (see pp. 46–8). "Adon," meaning "Lord," was the term used by the Phoenicians to address their god Baal.

The Greek pantheon, whose gods featured in Greek myths and in sculpture and were worshiped in the official *polis* religion in the major temples, was essentially Homer's creation. Homer had represented the pantheon as a sublimated aristocratic society. His gods were formidable, beautiful, strong, immortal men and women with both the good and the bad qualities of mortals. In the Trojan War they assisted heroes in both camps. The best-known gods were, first of all, the supreme god Zeus, the god of thunder, who resided on Mount Olympus in northern Greece together with the other gods. His main sanctuary was at Olympia in the Peloponnese, where the Olympic Games were held in his honor every four years. He was the patron god of justice and law. His wife was Hera, the patroness of marriage. Zeus had a daughter, Athena, the goddess of war and the arts and crafts, who was worshiped in Athens in particular. Apollo was the god of light, order, and reason. His oracle at Delphi attracted many people, and also *poleis*, who would ask him for advice before undertaking any action. Dionysus was the passionate god of wine, intoxication, and the wild forces in nature. Sometimes the gods had sexual intercourse with mortals. Heracles (Roman Hercules) was born out of such a union between Zeus and a mortal. He was venerated for his strength and his courageous Twelve Labors, with which he made the world a better place for mortals.

Our knowledge of the legends on the origins of the Greek gods we owe to Hesiod's "Theogony," which has notable analogies in Mesopotamian, Phoenician, and Hurrian-Hittite succession models. The legends of these models explain how the supreme god—Marduk, Baal, and Teshup, respectively (Zeus in the Greek pantheon)—acquired his supremacy in struggles with the primordial deities (see p. 46). As no such genealogy is to be found in Homer it is most likely that Hesiod got the idea of recounting the history of the deities from Eastern examples, with which he may have become acquainted in the Greek settlement of Al Mina in Syria.

There were, however, also marked differences between the religious world of the Greeks and that of the ancient Near East. In the first place, the Greek temples never played such a central part in economic, cultural and administrative affairs as did, for example, the Sumerian temples. Nor did the Greek temples have large estates or a priesthood with the power to manipulate politics. The Greek myths that have come down to us did not originate in the temples either. Homer and Hesiod were laymen, who gave their personal interpretations of the gods on their own authority, although they do claim to have been inspired by the "Muses," the daughters of Zeus and Mnemosyne, who presided over the arts and literature. The Greek temples did, however, contain many valuable goods, because many people would donate gifts to the gods. Temples were important pawnshops and their treasures were emergency reserves for the *poleis*.

Philosophy

Natural philosophy and physical science arose in the seventh century BC in Ionia in Asia Minor (at the periphery of the Eastern world) and in the Greek colonies in the west (southern Italy and Sicily). Some original minds in those areas no longer accepted the explanations for physical phenomena given in the myths (see p. 46). Instead, they tried to fathom the nature of the primal substance from which everything (such as earth, water, fire, and air) had evolved and to analyze processes in the natural world via logical reasoning. Very little of what these early philosophers commited to writing has come down to us. We would probably find their ideas rather naive today. They are, however, important in that they represent the first steps towards a new, rational way of analyzing and explaining natural phenomena, which was to become the basis of Western scientific thought.

These thinkers did not repudiate the deities of their religion, but simply placed their findings alongside the traditional religious beliefs or tried to combine their ideas with the ancient myths. This approach brought the philosopher Xenophanes (sixth century) to a monotheistic (see p. 50), logically reasoned theology. Xenophanes believed that the gods of the myths were only helpers and different embodiments of the one supreme god. He criticized Homer's accounts of the gods' deeds, which he considered quite ribald. This view was to find increasing support among later Greeks and Romans, especially their elites. It was only in the fifth century that a few philosophers approached a theology that denied the existence of the gods of the Greek pantheon. Anaxagoras (c. 500–c. 428) and Democritus (c. 460–c. 370) believed that everything ultimately consisted of indivisible parts, which Democritus called "atoms." Anaxagoras maintained that the movement of those parts was controlled by a divine spirit, the mover of the cosmos; whether Democritus shared that opinion we do not know. Anaxagoras, then, came quite close to a mechanical, materialistic conception of the universe.

The most renowned philosopher in the West was Pythagoras. He was born on the island of Samos, but emigrated to Croton in southern Italy at the end of the sixth century. He believed that the cosmos was logically composed of seven spheres according to certain numerical ratios; the lowest sphere was that of the earth. Knowledge of numbers and measures (mathematics) was the key to understanding the cosmos and nature. Pythagoras' belief that the human soul, which he saw as a separate entity, was imprisoned in a body at birth and moved on to another body after death, was inspired by Orphism.

Pythagoras was not only interested in studying order in nature; he also aspired to create order in the Greek cities in southern Italy. His followers, the Pythagoreans, developed a political philosophy which they attempted to implement in practice. Some Greek cities in southern Italy, such as Tarentum (present-day Taranto) in the fourth century BC, were indeed ruled by Pythagoreans for some time. They believed that the business of government was best left to wise, philosophically trained experts. The well-known Athenian philosopher Plato (see p. 114) counted several Pythagoreans among his friends.

POLITICAL CHANGES

The economic, social, and military changes brought about political changes, too. The Archaic period saw the rise of new forms of government and of what was to become one of the most important legacies of the ancient world: Greek political thought. The gradual crumbling of the economic and military basis on which the power of the nobility was founded ultimately led to the fall of the aristocracy in most *poleis*. This process started with demands for:

1   written legislation that would put an end to the aristocracy's arbitrary rule by laying down regulations (that is at least what the literary tradition tells us; according to surviving legal texts the primary aim was to regulate power relations within the aristocracy);
2   admission to the offices (this was demanded by the non-aristocratic wealthy citizens; they were in a position to make this demand because they had military power as hoplites);
3   cancellation of debts, abolition of debt bondage and redistribution of land (demanded by the impoverished farmers and debt bondsmen).

Tyranny

Almost everywhere in Greece the fall of the aristocracy went hand in hand with the appearance of tyranny. The Greeks borrowed the word *tyrannos* from one of the languages of Asia Minor. It was originally used for an autocrat who had seized absolute control to which he was not officially entitled. A king could also become a "tyrant," by assuming powers that transcended those of a *primus-inter-pares* king. This happened for example in Argos. The Greek tyrants were almost all members of aristocratic families who had come into conflict with other nobles and somehow managed to seize power. Exactly how they succeeded in their endeavors is in many cases unclear to us. A case in point concerns Corinth. After several decades under the sway of the Bacchiad family a fairly insignificant member of that family called Cypselus (*c.* 657–625) assumed sole control in the city.

Originally, "tyranny" was a fairly neutral term. We have both positive and negative accounts of tyrants' acts. But as the situation was humiliating for both the old aristocracy and the emerging elite not belonging to the tyrant's supporters, a tyrant—and especially his successor—would usually soon lose support. "Tyrannical" then acquired a pejorative meaning. Very few city states were ruled by tyrants for longer than two generations. Their form of government was then replaced by an oligarchy or a democracy.

Sparta

In Sparta the hoplites put an end to the rule of the aristocracy. Sparta had already evolved into a hoplite state *par excellence* in the seventh century. Nevertheless, Sparta—unlike other Greek states—did not institute a tyranny but maintained hereditary kingship.

To be able to understand this we must first consider the unique composition of the population of the Spartan *polis*. Sparta was dominated by a group of Dorians who had subjected the city's native population during the dark ages. Of these Dorians, who were referred to by the Homeric term "Lacedaemonians," the occupants of Sparta, or Spartiates, enjoyed full civil rights, whereas the occupants of the villages around Sparta, the *perioikoi*, had only local autonomy. The subject population of the area ruled by Sparta (Laconia) had no rights whatsoever; they were called "helots." The helots belonged to the state and are therefore also referred to as "state slaves." Their land had been split up and assigned to individual Spartiates, for whom they had to till that land. The Spartiates themselves did not work, but spent their entire lives in military training.

Like Athens, Sparta founded hardly any colonies. Instead, she stilled her hunger for land by conquering Messenia in two wars, between 700 and 600 BC. The Spartiates reduced the inhabitants of Messenia, who were also Dorians, to helots. This, however, meant that they then faced the difficult task of having to control a group of people who outnumbered them. This, and the constant threat of the fairly powerful Dorian neighbor state of Argos, with which the Spartiates were frequently at war over the hegemony of the Peloponnese, induced them to devote their full attention to military training. Spartan boys were taken from their mothers at the tender age of seven. From then onwards they were raised by the state. They were rigorosly trained in the endurance of hardship and were turned into tough, strong men. When they reached manhood they joined a mess, whose members ate, trained, slept, and fought together. Each Spartiate had to pay a contribution to his mess.

The Spartiates were hence entirely dependent on a powerful militia for the preservation of their privileged position. As the aristocracy had not been very successful in the wars against Messenia and Argos, the hoplites had been able to get their own way in Sparta at a very early stage. Sparta's reforms are attributed to the law-giver Lycurgus, a man about whom nothing is known with any certainty. It is generally assumed that he introduced his political reforms in the seventh century.

After Lycurgus, the Spartiates were referred to as *homoioi*, or "equals." This equality referred to their equal position in the hoplite *phalanx* and to their equal vote in the *apella*, the assembly to which only they had access. They may also have been assigned equal lots of land with groups of helots in Laconia, and later Messenia. But in other respects the Spartiates were not entirely equal. For example, in addition to their assigned land they also owned private lots of land, and those lots differed in size. What also led to inequality was that some Spartiates neglected their farms by failing to keep their helots under strict control. Others on the contrary made a fortune from bribes, taxes, and booty obtained abroad. Another popular way of becoming rich was by marrying an heiress of a well-to-do Spartan family that had produced no sons. These wealthy Spartiates forced up the contributions to the messes until the poorer ones could no longer afford to pay them. They were then reduced to the status of second-class citizens.

Sparta's public assembly never evolved into a truly democratic body. The real power was in the hands of the *gerousia*, a council of elders of at least sixty years of age who were chosen for life by the assembly. The readiness with which the assembly accepted the *gerousia*'s supremacy is understandable in a state in which military discipline was more highly esteemed than a critical mind. Sparta's two kings (for whom the age requirement of course did not apply) also ranked among the *gerousia*'s thirty members. To return to the question of why kingship was retained in Sparta: as the two co-regent kings, who belonged to different royal families, balanced one another, there was never any risk of the kingship becoming very powerful. The kings' sole task was to command the army in wartime. In later times an additional magistracy was created alongside the monarchy. This was held by five "ephors" (*ephoroi* = overseers), who were chosen annually by the *apella*. They were responsible for the city's day-to-day administration. The creation of this additional magistracy probably helped to prevent calls for further democratic reforms because the ephors, who were supposed to represent the citizens' interests, counterbalanced the kings.

In the ancient world the Spartan constitution was highly esteemed for being a "mixed constitution," comprising a monarchy (two kings), an aristocracy (the *gerousia*), and a democracy (the *apella* and the ephors). The strict Spartan lifestyle, which appeared to be the key to the city's success, was also greatly admired. In the sixth and the early fifth centuries BC Sparta was indisputably the most powerful city state in Greece.

Sparta was anxious to corroborate her hegemony in the Peloponnese but did not like the idea of doing so by conquering more cities and then having to control even more helots. In the mid-sixth century she solved this problem by creating the Peloponnesian League, in which she united most city states in the Peloponnese, including Corinth, under her leadership. Argos did not join this league. Outside Greece, Sparta established relations with Lydia and Egypt, which were then both in conflict with Persia (see pp. 42–3). With this act Sparta showed herself to be hostile towards tyranny, for Persia's custom was to rule over conquered Greek city states by placing local pro-Persian tyrants in control. The Greek cities in Asia Minor (Ionia) were governed by such tyrants.

Many contemporary and later admirers praised Sparta as an exemplary state, in spite of the fact that the city could boast virtually no cultural achievements whatsoever, as she had devoted all her attention to military training and had avoided contacts with the outside world. Indeed, Sparta always remained more of a village than a city.

Athens

Athens underwent a unique development that culminated in the famous Athenian democracy. It is this democracy that made Athens the bearer of Greek culture *par excellence*. Athens, in contrast to Sparta, was for some time ruled by tyrants.

Athens had remained inhabited after the fall of Mycenaean civilization and was not affected by the Dorian invasion. The development of the geometric pottery style around 900 marked the beginning of a period of great prosperity and cultural achievement. By *c.* 850 trade contacts had been established with Al Mina in Syria. Around 730, however, Athens' progress came to a temporary standstill while other city states, such as Corinth, began to flourish. The growth of her population did not induce Athens to found colonies. Apparently Attica was large enough to accommodate the greater part of the increased population. Some peasant families, however, must have met with difficulties when the family property became too small to be divided amongst the next generation.

Athens was ruled by an aristocracy. Kingship had been abolished fairly smoothly some time during the dark ages and the king had been replaced by three, later nine, archons, who exercised the former king's functions of army commander, high priest, and supreme judge. Only the members of the old-established aristocratic families (*eupatridai*—families with noble fathers) were eligible for these functions. After their one-year's term of office they became members of the council of nobles, the Areopagus or "Council of the Hill of Ares," so called after the place where they held their assemblies. The Areopagus had considerable effective political power.

However, in Athens, too, the position of the aristocracy was undermined by the economic, social, and military changes outlined above. Around 632 BC, one Cylon tried to make himself tyrant, but his attempt was unsuccessful because the aristocracy could then still rely on sufficient support. Some ten years later, however, the aristocrats' unrestrained power suffered its first blow when Draco codified the prevailing customary law. He put an end to blood feuds. But as his law code did not entail any true reforms the feelings of discontent remained.

These conditions were conducive to tyranny, but in 594 Athens averted that danger for some time by granting an archon, Solon, special powers to settle the conflicts between the nobility and the rest of the population. Solon had to find solutions for the dissatisfaction of two groups. The first comprised the wealthy citizens who demanded a share in the political power from which they had hitherto been excluded because they did not belong to the nobility. The second group consisted of the peasants who had fallen into debt and now demanded the cancelation of their debts and a redistribution of land. Solon belonged to a noble family of moderate means. He had spent some years of his life earning his own living by engaging in overseas trade. Around 600 he had participated in the conquest of the island of Salamis from the neighboring city of Megara. Because of all this he was highly respected by all classes.

Solon's first step was to divide the Athenian citizens (*politai*) into four property classes. The first two classes (the *pentakosiomedimnoi* ['500 bushel men'] and the *hippeis* ['knights']) comprised the wealthiest nobles and the nobles one level below them plus the *nouveaux riches*. The third class consisted of the small landowners, the *zeugitai*. The *thétes* ("hired laborers"), who had very little or no property, constituted the fourth class. It should be borne in mind that this classification applied to Athenian citizens only. Apart from Athenian citizens, Athens' population also included metics (*metoikoi*), or resident aliens, many of whom had lived in Athens for several generations already. They were free, but did not enjoy civil rights. There were also slaves in Athens. In Solon's system the two highest classes had access to the office of archon. The three highest classes were allowed to serve on a newly created Council of Four Hundred (whose establishment was a blow to the Council of the Areopagus). All four were admitted to the general assemblies (it was not all that common for people without landed property to be admitted to assemblies in Greece). Solon, then, replaced birth by wealth as the criterion for political influence.

Although reduced, the aristocracy's power was not yet broken. Most of the rich were still nobles and retained their prestige at a local level. They still had a function in jurisdiction too.

For the impoverished farmers and debt bondsmen Solon proclaimed the *seisachtheia*, the "shaking off of burdens": he canceled all their debts, freed debt bondsmen, bought back Athenians who had been sold as slaves abroad, and forbade Athenian citizens to offer their own person as security in obtaining loans. There were in those days also Athenian citizens who were known as *hektēmoroi*—"sixth parters." They had to give one-sixth of the produce of their land to a nobleman. We do not know the origin of this obligation. Some believe it was some form of payment of debts, while others regard it as payment for protection by the nobleman. Whatever the case may be, Solon also abolished the status of the *hektēmoroi*.

Solon's measures had far-reaching consequences. From then onwards, Athenian citizens could no longer become slaves to other Athenians. However, that did not mean the end of slavery, for Athenian landowners and proprietors of craft centers simply purchased foreign slaves whenever they needed more labor. Athenians—like many other Greeks—regarded wage labor as a form of slavery. There was in their eyes only a marginal difference between selling one's labor and selling one's person. And as they made every effort to avoid having to do such demeaning work themselves, a major part of the need for labor had to be met by slaves.

Solon also took measures to secure sufficient food supplies. He forbade the export of grain and encouraged farmers to grow olive trees, whose product—olive oil—could be exported. It was indeed under Solon that the associated industry of pottery production started to flourish in Athens (black-figure painting: see p. 75).

Another of Solon's reforms involved the replacement of Draco's law code by a new code and the establishment of the *hēliaia*, the people's (jury) court. Every year, a list was drawn up of six thousand citizens, from among whom a certain number of jurors (often five hundred and one) would then be chosen by lot to pass judgment in a particular case.

There is one important demand which Solon did not satisfy, namely that for a redistribution of land, which he considered too radical. In conceding to cancel all debts, Solon was actually tackling the problems' symptoms instead of their causes. For some farmers his measures were satisfactory (*hektēmoroi* were not necessarily small farmers and they now became independent landed farmers), but they did not solve the problems of farmers with insufficient land. Furthermore, as those farmers and their families were now forbidden to secure loans on their person, it had become virtually impossible for them to borrow money. Many of them no longer managed to make ends meet and moved to the city of Athens.

Peisistratus, a scion of a noble family of modest means, took advantage of the discontent among the poor in Athens and the small farmers in Attica. With their support, he seized power and made himself tyrant. Peisistratus remained in control for only one year (561) after this first attempt, but in 546 he made a more successful bid for power. Having built up considerable resources by exploiting gold mines in Thrace he was able to hire a good bodyguard, with which he defeated the aristocrats and their supporters. The members of this bodyguard, who came from the lower classes, he armed as hoplites. Peisistratus did not abolish Solon's constitution, but he did make sure that things went the way he wanted them to. He reduced the power of the aristocracy even further by making men who were not aristocrats hoplites and instituting a system of traveling judges, which meant that the common people were no longer exclusively at the mercy of noblemen in local disputes. He even showed the population that the aristocrats were not as omnipotent as they seemed by banning many nobles and confiscating their property; that property he used to help small farmers switch to cultivating more profitable crops, in particular olives. He also embellished the city of Athens. He promoted national religious festivals, the *Panathenaia*, in honor of Athena, Athens' patron goddess, and the *Dionysia*, in honor of Dionysus. His aim in all this was to strengthen the bonds between the population and their *polis* at the expense of local ties and aristocratic traditions.

Whether Peisistratus organized land distributions we do not know. It is not very likely that he did, because contemporary authors descended from noble families would not have remained silent about such a burning issue, for the land owned by the elite would have been at stake.

But even if he did not distribute land, Peisistratus did improve conditions for the common people. The commissions for the construction of new temples and the increased industrial activity provided the necessary employment. The small farmers in Attica benefited greatly from his relief measures. It was thanks to Solon and Peisistratus that the majority of the Athenian citizens were able to support themselves as small farmers in the Classical period.

FIGURE 9.4 The sanctuary of the god Apollo at Delphi

Notes. This temple was a sanctuary for all the Greeks. The Delphic oracle of the god Apollo was very famous. If a Greek was anxious to find out whether an undertaking would be successful, he would visit this temple, ask the god a question and present a gift (or make a vow). The priests then brought a prophetess into a state of ecstasy and listened carefully to her utterings. They believed that the god would convey his answer via her pronouncements. They translated the god's answer into poetic—usually ambiguous—formulas, which they passed on to the person seeking advice. Greek cities would often consult the Delphic oracle on the eve of important enterprises, for example before founding a colony or before introducing political reforms. The priests of Delphi consequently had considerable political influence in the Greek world and even in adjacent areas, for example Asia Minor.

After his death (528), Peisistratus was succeeded by his sons, Hippias and Hipparchus. As elsewhere, the tyranny did not outlast this second generation. In 514 Hipparchus was killed by Harmodius and Aristogeiton following a private feud. Although this murder was actually of little consequence, the murderers were celebrated as heroes—"tyrannicides"—in literature and sculpture.

In 510 the aristocrats collectively put an end to the tyranny with the support of Sparta, which shared their hostility towards tyrants (see p. 83). Hippias fled to the Persian empire.

As was customary after the abolition of a tyranny, a struggle then broke out between rival members of the aristocracy. In 508 Cleisthenes, a member of the Alcmaeonid family—in those days the leading aristocratic family in Athens—emerged triumphant from this struggle. He owed his success to the fact that he had allied himself with the common citizen people, the *demos*. The consequence of this was that he had to grant the *demos* a share in political power, to which end he had to curtail the aristocracy's power even further. This made Cleisthenes the founder of the famous Athenian democracy. He made the *demos* of male citizens the backbone of the government and the army, which now became a citizen army of hoplites.

Cleisthenes divided the territory of the Athenian *polis* (that is, Attica) into ten "tribes" (Greek: *phylai*) or districts. Each of these tribes consisted of three *trittyes* (a coastal *trittys*, an inland *trittys*, and an urban *trittys*). The smallest unit was the deme (Greek: *dēmos*, not to be confused with *dēmos* = citizen body), a village or parish, of which there were 139 (see Map 9.2). This division became the foundation of the Athenian polity. Fifty men from each tribe were granted seats in the Council of Five Hundred (*boulē*). A list of candidates was set up for each tribe, from among whom the fifty were chosen by lot. In Athens, drawing lots was considered the most democratic procedure, for elections involved the risks of demagogy or of popular leaders becoming too powerful. The members of the Council of Five Hundred were appointed for one year. It was not permitted to sit on the Council more than twice, and not in consecutive years. This meant that many Athenian citizens had an opportunity to become members of the Council and gain political experience.

The Council was responsible for day-to-day administration and for preparing the agenda and decisions for the public assembly (*ekklēsia*). The public assembly consisted of all the male citizens of the *polis of* Athens, collectively the *dēmos* (hence *dēmokratia* = rule of the [male] citizen body). The bills forwarded by the *boulē* were by no means binding. The public assembly had the right of amendment and the right to accept strongly deviating proposals or to reject a proposal altogether. The public assembly voted by call and took the final decisions. All this made Athens a "demo-cracy": the *dēmos* took decisions of policy (that is, the male citizens—women, metics, and slaves had no share in the decision process).

Cleisthenes' system meant a blow to the aristocrats, who still enjoyed considerable power on a local level. The boundaries dividing the tribes, *trittyes*, and demes cut right across the noble families' spheres of influence. The deme was moreover a small-scale democracy, with its own chosen administrators, council, and public assembly. All the inhabitants of the deme were equal and they all had ample opportunity to gain administrative experience on a local level. Nevertheless, the nobles still had considerable prestige and often managed to get themselves appointed to the important offices. But they too had to abide by the rules of the democracy. Moreover, until 461, the Council of the Areopagus still exercised some control over local administration, although we

MAP 9.2 Cleisthenes' division of Attica into *trittyes*

Notes. Each tribe comprised an urban, a coastal, and an inland *trittys*. So each tribe consisted of three *trittyes*. Some historians have taken the fact that the *trittyes* were all situated along the main roads to the center of Athens to imply that they were created specifically to facilitate the mobilization of citizens: the recruits from the individual *trittyes* would have been able to quickly make their way to Athens when an army was to be formed.

do not know exactly how much power it had. As this council consisted of ex-archons, there were still many aristocrats among its members. The archons were still the highest magistrates and they were still chosen from the highest two property classes of Solon's class system, which had not been abolished. Although the *nouveaux riches* now also qualified for the archonship, it was usually members of the old aristocratic families who were appointed to this office. The archonship lost much of its former esteem in 487 BC, when it was decided to appoint archons by drawing lots. The prestige of the office of *stratēgos*, or general, on the other hand, increased, because the ten generals who commanded the army and the fleet continued to be elected from among the most suitable candidates. They could be re-elected any number of times after their one-year term of office. The generals were to acquire considerable political power after 487 (see p. 107).

The last measure that Cleisthenes is believed to have introduced is "ostracism." Once a year, the public assembly was asked whether there was any need for an ostracism. If there was, those present at the next meeting had to write the name of a person they considered a threat to the state on a potsherd. The person whose name occurred on most sherds was then banned for ten years. However, he did retain possession of his property. Several politicians fell victim to this practice in the fifth century. Some managed to regain their prominent position after returning from their exile, but for most it meant the end of their careers.

10 THE CLASSICAL PERIOD (c. 500–c. 330 BC)

THE PERSIAN WARS

Around the middle of the sixth century BC the expanding Persian empire reached the western coast of Asia Minor. In 547 or a few years later, the Persian king, Cyrus the Great (559–530), conquered Lydia and, in so doing, gained control over the Greek cities on the western coast of Asia Minor, which the Lydians had captured shortly before then (see p. 42). In most of these cities the Persians selected local aristocrats who were favorably disposed toward them and appointed them as tyrants. They were to govern the cities under the supervision of the Persian satraps (see p. 43).

In 499 BC the Greeks of Asia Minor tried to depose their tyrants and break away from the Persians. But their attempts were unsuccessful: in 495–494 the Persians squashed their revolt in a series of battles on land and at sea. Shortly after, in 492, the Persian king Darius I (522–486) set out on an expedition to punish Athens, which had sent a small fleet to assist the rebels. The Persians sailed across the Mediterranean and landed at Marathon in Attica (Map 10.1), where they were defeated by the Athenian hoplites under the command of Miltiades (490). This battle won Athens fame throughout the entire Greek world. In spite of her fifty-year-old hostility towards Persia (p. 83) and her reputation as the strongest military power in Greece, Sparta did not take part in the Ionian revolt or in the battles of 490.

Ten years later, in 480, Darius' successor, Xerxes, resumed the hostilities. In the belief that the only way of securing his control over the west of Asia Minor was by subjugating the free Greeks of the Greek mainland, he set out to Greece with a large army and a fleet. The army marched along the coast so that it could be provisioned by the fleet sailing alongside it (see Map 10.2). Most Greek states had in the meantime united in a league which was led by Sparta, but in which Athens also had much influence. In 483 Athens had followed the *strategos* Themistocles' advice and had begun to create a large navy. In that year, a fresh rich vein of silver had been discovered in the mining area of Laurium in southern Attica (see Map 10.3). The profits of this silver were not divided among the citizens as some Athenians had wished, but were spent on building warships of a new, fast, and more maneuverable type known as "triremes" (Figure 10.1). Some Athenians, especially among the higher classes, failed to see the need for a strong navy.

MAP 10.1   Persian campaigns against the Greeks, 492–479 BC

Notes. The Persian expedition of 492 failed due to heavy weather, that of 490 passed straight across the sea, and that of 480 again, as in 492, comprised an army marching along coastal roads and a fleet sailing alongside it, so that the ships could supply the land forces with provisions. The army that the Persians composed for their expedition of 480 was very large by contemporary standards (approx. 80,000 men according to a reliable estimate). As transport by land was slow and of insufficient capacity for such a large army, provisions had to be supplied by sea. Greece was relatively poor in resources, so some provisions had to be supplied from the Persian hinterland. When the Persian fleet was defeated off Salamis (480), the Persian army, which stayed behind in Greece, had to be reduced in size. That made it easier for the Greeks to defeat the Persian land forces, too, in 479.

MAP 10.2 Greece on the eve of the Peloponnesian War

In their opinion, the battle at Marathon had shown that an army of hoplites was all that was required to defeat the Persians. What they were probably afraid of was that the poorest citizens (the thetes), who would row the ships, would acquire more military importance and hence a dominant position in the Athenian democracy. Themistocles did not share this opinion. He believed that a powerful navy was vital for Athens, in particular in view of the city's heavy reliance on the import of grain (see p. 95): only with a powerful navy would Athens be able to repel the Persians and secure her trade routes against Greek rivals at sea.

In 480, along the coastal road near Thermopylae and in the adjacent bay of Artemisium (see Map 10.1), the Greeks made an unsuccessful attempt to stop the Persians advancing by land and sea. The naval battle was important, too, because if the Greeks were to defeat the Persian navy, it would no longer be able to provision the large Persian army via its ships. Throughout antiquity, transport by land was slower and more difficult. The Spartan king Leonidas and three hundred Spartan hoplites attempted to hold up the Persian land forces at the pass at Thermopylae for as long as possible and fought themselves to death, but in doing so they did succeed in covering

MAP 10.3
Attica at the time of
the Peloponnesian War,
431–404 BC

Notes. Sparta's allies are under-
lined. Laurium: silver mines.

Decelea: the fortress that the
Spartans occupied in 413 on
Alcibiades' advice. From there
they could cut off access to the
mines of Laurium, obstruct all
agricultural activities in Attica,
and keep a close watch on
Athens. x = fortifications or
battlefields

FIGURE 10.1 Athenian warship (trireme)

Notes. The ship's most dangerous weapon was its ram (right). Such a ship was usually manned by 100 to 150 or
even more rowers, 10 to 20 marines (hoplites), and a few seamen (steersman, captain, sailors).

The Athenian fleets sometimes included transport ships bearing soldiers, weapons, and horses, which enabled
them to sail to their destination and then fight the enemy both on land and at sea.

the retreat of the Greek army and navy. The Athenians evacuated their city and took their cattle
along with them to the island of Salamis opposite Athens. Xerxes ordered the abandoned city to
be destroyed, but his navy was defeated by the Athenians and their allies in the bay of Salamis.
Xerxes was now no longer in a position to swiftly subject Greece and was forced to reduce the
Persian army, which remained in Greece, as he was unable to secure adequate provisions.
One year later (479) the Greeks, under the command of the Spartan regent Pausanias, defeated
the Persian army at Plataeae. The Persians retreated from Greece and the fighting shifted to the
west coast of Asia Minor, where the Athenian fleet liberated the Greek cities from the Persians—

a fact which the latter refused to acknowledge until 449, when the hostilities came to an end. The battles against the Persian army and navy were to appeal to Greek imagination for many centuries. In Europe they later came to represent the triumph of the free Greek states over Asia, thanks to which Greek culture, the source of Western civilization, was saved from suffocation by Eastern despotism.

SPARTA AND ATHENS AFTER 479 BC

After 479 Sparta left the command of the battle against the Persians to Athens. The Spartans had no fleet to speak of and the theater of war, the west coast of Asia Minor, lay overseas. The Spartans, moreover, didn't like the idea of having large forces fighting battles far away from home for long periods of time because they were constantly fearful lest the helots should rise against them. A helot revolt did indeed break out in Messenia in 464 BC, after a severe earthquake, and it took the Spartans almost four years—and a great deal of effort—to suppress it. In 462/1 Sparta desperately appealed to Athens for help, but when the Athenian general Cimon, who sympathized with Sparta, arrived with his troops he was sent back home again. The Athenians responded to this rebuff by waging war on Sparta and her allies from 461 until 446. For twelve years (461–449) both Persia and Sparta were Athens' enemies. Sparta, however, had by this time entered a period of stagnation. The class of Spartiate full citizens had dwindled as a consequence of a fall in birthrate and the degradation of impoverished Spartiates to second-class citizens (see p. 83). The privileged Spartiates had come to represent an even smaller minority amongst the other Spartans, the *perioikoi* and the helots.

THE DELIAN LEAGUE (477–404 BC)

In 477 Athens founded her own league against Persia: the Delian League. Most Greek islands, the Greeks on the west coast of Asia Minor, and some other Greek cities joined this league. Only a few large islands supplied ships and soldiers; most member states contributed money to the league's treasury (kept on the island of Delos), which largely financed the league's fleet and army. In the fifth century the league became an instrument of Athens' power politics, especially after 460, when Pericles gained control of the city. Although the Delian League had originally been founded for a specific purpose—the battle against the Persians—it was not dissolved in 449, when the hostilities against the Persians came to an end. The league's territory (Map 10.2) had in fact become Athenian territory. Allies who wished to secede from the League were forced to remain members and to continue to pay the tributes. Athens started to interfere in her allies' internal affairs; she meddled in their legal and financial matters and brought friendly democratic governments to power in several member states. The Athenians also established a network of colonies (cleruchies) at various strategic points (usually islands) in the league territory. These colonies were not new, independent city states as the colonies of the Archaic period had been, but were regarded as additions to the Athenian *polis*; the colonists kept their Athenian citizenship. In actual fact, these colonies were Athens' military bases. This form of colonization led to an increase in the number of Athenian hoplites. Most of the colonists were citizens without property (thetes), for whom this was a way of obtaining land and rising to a higher property class, that is, that of the *zeugitai*. This was to Athens' benefit, for it was the *zeugitai* who provided the lion's share of both the heavy infantry and the naval forces. The thetes who became *zeugitai* could no longer be used as rowers, but that was no problem for Athens, because the city could recruit plenty of rowers and sailors from among volunteers from the league member states. Most of those volunteers were lured by the pay and the prospect of booty, though some may have wished to join the navy for idealistic reasons, for many of the poor citizens of the member states of the Delian League were great admirers of the Athenian democracy. Almost all of the states that wanted to resign from the League and deserted Athens were led by oligarchic regimes. In the course of the fifth century a polarity emerged in Greece: Greeks in favor of a democracy supported Athens while those with an oligarchic disposition (usually the rich) sympathized with Sparta.

Athenian leaders in the fifth century

In the fifth century Athens was led by a number of admirable statesmen who knew how to address the public assembly and who were also competent army and fleet commanders: Themistocles (*c.* 490–470), Cimon (*c.* 470–461), and Pericles (460–429). They were all members of the aristocratic elite but their loyalty was with the democracy. The Athenian citizens elected them generals time and time again.

Themistocles and Pericles realized that their objective, which was for Athens to acquire hegemony over the whole of Greece, would ultimately bring them into conflict with Sparta. They therefore built long walls around Athens and her port, Piraeus (see Figure 10.2). The idea was that the Athenians would then be able to import everything they needed via the sea, while Sparta's land forces idly besieged the city, because the Athenian fleet still retained the supremacy over the seas surrounding Greece that it had acquired in the Persian wars. The policies of Themistocles and Pericles were characterized by expansionism in external affairs and a trend towards democracy in internal affairs (see p. 107). The more conservative Cimon wanted to avoid conflicts with Sparta, but he lost his popularity and was ostracized when a war broke out between Athens and Sparta in 461 (p. 93).

FIGURE 10.2 The "long walls" between Athens and Piraeus

Notes. As can be seen in this figure, Piraeus was a newly built city, with a regular layout, whereas Athens was an "organically" grown city.

Athens' aim in that war was to extend her influence over central Greece and the Peloponnesian coast opposite Attica. At the same time, the Athenians supported the Egyptians' revolt against Persia (c. 455). All this proved too much: in 454 Athens suffered a crushing defeat in Egypt and in 446 the city found herself forced to conclude a compromise peace agreement with Sparta and abandon her ambition to extend her sway over central Greece. By this time the Greeks had already made peace with the Persians (in 449).

After their failure in Egypt (454) the Athenians, allegedly out of fear of a Persian expedition to Delos, transferred the league treasury from Delos to Athens and assumed control over the league's financial affairs.

The years between 446 and 431 marked a summit in Athens' history in terms of the growth of her power, her prosperity, and her cultural achievements. This greatly alarmed Sparta, which had managed to recover somewhat from the blows inflicted on her and was still the unrivalled supreme power in the Peloponnese. Other Greek states also viewed Athens' success with growing anxiety. They began to look to Sparta to defend the autonomy of the Greek city states against Athens' imperialistic tendencies. Most Greek city states that were not members of the Delian League were moreover ruled by aristocratic or oligarchic leaders, who dreaded the spread of democracy.

Athens' state income

Athens' power politics and her magnificent achievements in the visual arts, architecture, and literature rested on a sound financial basis. The city had a regular income consisting of her allies' tributes, which were paid into the League treasury, but of which Athens was the main beneficiary, the profits of the exploitation of the silver mines at Laurium, and the tolls and harbor dues that were levied at Piraeus. On top of this there were the head taxes and market dues paid by foreigners who worked in Athens and Piraeus (the metics). Those taxes and the harbor dues brought in large sums of money, because after the Persian wars Athens had become the most important market and commercial center in Greece. Large numbers of Ionians and other Greeks had settled in Athens as merchants and craftsmen. Athens had in fact inherited the trade and industry of the Ionian cities that had suffered such hard blows in the Ionian revolt and the Persian wars.

Athenian citizens were not required to pay direct taxes on a regular basis. Taxation was imposed only incidentally, in times of financial emergency. Wealthy citizens were occasionally expected to equip a warship or to finance a building project or a theatrical performance. These financial services to the state were called "liturgies." In the fifth century Athens also derived revenues from the gold mines in Thrace (see Map 10.2). Thrace also yielded the timber for Athens' ships.

Another—indirect—source of financial benefit was Athens' powerful political position. Thanks to her large navy, Athens could virtually monopolize the trade with the cereal-producing areas in southern Russia, and could consequently keep grain prices low within the city. Athens managed to retain this advantageous position until the end of the fourth century BC, when the loss of the city's naval power spelled the beginning of hard times for Athens' poor.

THE GREAT PELOPONNESIAN WAR (431–404 BC)

After a short period of peace (446–431), a new war broke out between Athens and Sparta in 431, when Athens came into conflict with Sparta's maritime allies, Corinth and Megara. This war was far more intensive than the previous one (461–446). The Greek historian Thucydides, who described this conflict, was of the opinion that the Peloponnesian War (431–404) was the fiercest war ever fought in Greek history. The Athenians and the Spartans both rallied their allies behind them. Most of the Greek states that had hitherto remained neutral now took sides with Sparta (see Map 10.2).

In the past, wars between Greek city states had been minor skirmishes and plunderings, with only one or two pitched battles, after which peace had been made. In the Peloponnesian War, however, the entire Greek world, from Ionia in the east to Sicily in the west, was engaged in constant fighting involving large land and naval forces.

Pericles entered the war well prepared. He had created a treasury of 6,000 talents (see Appendix 2, p. 300) and had developed a long-term strategy. His aim was to launch a series of brief attacks on Sparta from the sea and to entice the Spartans into a vain attempt to besiege Athens and Piraeus, which would use up all their resources and exhaust their men. To that end he concentrated the population of Attica within the long walls surrounding those cities. Pericles had no faith in pitched battles on land because Sparta still had the best hoplites in the whole of Greece and, as she had so many allies, her troops would also vastly outnumber those of Athens. Sparta's weakness was her war fund: the city could not afford to finance a protracted war.

Athens suffered several major setbacks during the war. Her leader, Pericles, died in 429 and between 429 and 427 a severe plague killed about one-third of the city's population. Moreover, Athens did not adhere strictly to Pericles' plans and launched several risky expeditions after all. Nonetheless, in spite of all this, the city held its own in the first stage of the war (431–421). In 421 Athens concluded a peace treaty on reasonable terms. Athens' enemies had not succeeded in breaking the city's power.

However, due to a combination of factors, Athens lost the second stage of the war (413–404). One of these factors was the loss of the best part of the city's army and navy in

FIGURE 10.3 Pericles (c. 495–429) wearing the helmet of a heavily armed soldier (hoplite)

a reckless and totally vain attempt to gain control of Sicily. Between 415 and 413 Syracuse, which was at that time the most densely populated Greek city after Athens, defeated the Athenians with the help of Sparta. The aristocratic demagogue Alcibiades had persuaded Athens' assembly to embark on this enterprise, but he himself defected to Sparta when grave scandals in his private life made it impossible for him to remain in Athens. He advised the Spartans to establish a

FIGURE 10.5a   A hoplite

FIGURE 10.4
Pallas Athena, the patron deity of the city of Athens

Notes. Roman copy of a Classical Greek sculpture. Athena was the goddess of science and the arts and crafts, but also of warfare, which is why she is here represented with a helmet and a spear.

FIGURE 10.5b   A lightly armed Greek soldier

permanent military base in Attica, to help Syracuse and to open up relations with Persia. Sparta followed his advice and in 413 the war flared up again, opening the second phase of the Peloponnesian War.

The Spartans occupied fort Decelea (Greek: Dekeleia) in Attica (see Map 10.3), from where they obstructed agriculture all over Attica and prevented access to the silver mines at Laurium. Thousands of slaves escaped and Athens was cut off from major food supplies and sources of income. Persia sided with Sparta and gave the Spartans the means they needed to build up a strong fleet. This induced many of Athens' allies to defect to Sparta. At first, the Athenians managed to win some battles at sea under the leadership of Alcibiades, who had returned to Athens again after private conflicts with Spartan rulers and Persian satraps. In 405 however, the Athenian fleet was decisively defeated by the Spartan Lysander off Aigospotamoi in the Dardanelles (see Map 10.2). In 404, lack of food forced Athens to surrender.

Athens had suffered severe losses. It is believed that the number of adult male citizens in Athens decreased from about 35,000 to about 21,000 between 432 and 400. The Delian League was dissolved, the long walls were pulled down, and a pro-Spartan oligarchic government was installed in Athens, which began a reign of terror. That government was not to last long though, for after only one year it was overthrown and a democratic regime was restored. The Spartans resigned themselves to this shift in power.

THE YEARS BETWEEN 404 AND 336 BC

In the years after 404 no Greek state was powerful enough to unite the whole of Greece under its leadership. Between 404 and 338 coalition wars kept flaring up between Sparta, which still led the Peloponnesian League, Thebes, which was steadily acquiring considerable power and led a league of city states in Boeotia (see Map 10.4), and Athens, which had managed to recover surprisingly rapidly from the devastating defeat she had suffered in 404. Athens had not lost all her maritime power, and was still the most important market town, the most densely populated city, and the leading cultural center in Greece.

Sparta found herself faced with an increasing shortage of Spartiates. It is believed that by 371 Sparta counted no more than about two thousand Spartiates, as opposed to at least 20,000 adult male helots—and that is a low estimate of the number of helots.

The Persians had meanwhile started to stir up dissension between the Greek *poleis* and leagues to prevent the risk of them uniting and then turning on Persia—something which they greatly feared because they had begun to lag behind the Greeks in military tactics and experience. The Persians' interference in Greece can be split into two phases: in the first half of the fifth century they launched attacks on the Greeks, but between 413 and 340 they reverted to divide-and-conquer tactics and tried to play the Greek states off against one another by constantly subsidizing different states.

The following example illustrates their strategy. In what is known as the Corinthian War (395–386), the Persians first supported Athens and some of Sparta's defected allies (Corinth, Thebes) because Sparta had prevented the Persians from reasserting their authority over the west coast of Asia Minor after 404. Around 394, the Persians granted Athens financial support to restore

MAP 10.4   Greece c. 360 BC, just before the rise of Macedonia

her fleet and rebuild the long walls but, when Athens consequently threatened to become too powerful, the Persians helped Sparta instead. In 386 the Persian king, acting as an arbitrator, dictated the terms of the peace between Sparta and Athens; this is therefore known as the "King's Peace." Athens' rebuilding program was checked; Sparta was to remain the most powerful state in Greece and the Persians were to regain control over the Greek cities along the west coast of Asia Minor.

The Second Athenian League (377–355)

But Sparta's hegemony was soon to be challenged again. In 377, while Thebes was also acquiring considerable military power, Athens established the Second Athenian League, in which she united her anti-Spartan allies. This league was dominated less by Athens than the first league had been.

The allies were not required to pay tributes to the federal treasury, they retained their autonomy in internal affairs and they had a say in the League's foreign politics in the League's own assembly. This League was to have a short life. When, after 362, Athens began to show imperialistic tendencies and started to plant colonies of Athenian citizens (cleruchies) in the League territory, her chief allies revolted (357–355) and the League collapsed.

Social and military changes

A new development in all these wars was the increasing use that was made of mercenaries, of whom there was no lack anywhere in Greece. In the Peloponnese in particular, many impoverished peasants became the victims of the concentration of land in the hands of the wealthy. There was little that could be done to stop this process in the oligarchic states in that region, for the wealthy landowners were also the rulers of the states and only citizens above a certain property qualifi-cation had political power; the mass of poor citizens didn't have full citizen rights in those states. Moreover, it may well be that the peaceful conditions that Sparta had been maintaining in the Peloponnese since about 546 BC had led to over-population. It was incidentally not only landless farmers' sons who became mercenaries; men driven into exile would likewise often join the army—as their property was usually confiscated at the time of their exile, they needed a livelihood.

The year 371 marked a turning point in the coalition wars between Thebes, Sparta, Athens, and their allies. In that year the Theban Epaminondas, a genius in military tactics, destroyed the Spartan army at Leuctra (see Map 10.4). He then marched on to the Peloponnese, where he freed the helots in Messenia (but not those in Laconia) and dissolved the Peloponnesian League. Sparta lost over half of her citizens with full citizen rights, her League, which had been her main weapon for almost two centuries, and one of her principal helot territories. The city was reduced to a second-class power of no more than regional importance. This led to a series of interstate wars and revolutions in the Peloponnese. The poor citizens demanded land reforms, cancellations of debts, and less oligarchic governments. The revolutions gradually spread to central Greece, leaving a flow of exiles and destitute drifters in their wake. For many of those people the only chance of earning a living was by hiring themselves out as mercenaries. This led to a massive outpouring of thousands of Greeks crossing the Aegean Sea to enlist in the Persian army. Thebes and Athens were unable to fill the vacuum left by Sparta. Thebes' power had depended too heavily on the skills of one outstanding statesman and general, Epaminondas. When, in 362, he was killed at Mantineia, in the battle against the Spartans and the Athenians who had sided with Sparta out of fear for Thebes' rising power, Thebes soon lost her commanding position.

The rise of Macedonia

After 360 it was Macedonia that benefited from the discord between the Greek states. Until then, Macedonia had always been a backwater, where the social and economic conditions of Homeric times (p. 65) still more or less prevailed. The land was governed by a king, who was the highest ranking member of a landed aristocracy. The nobles ruled over the subordinate, dependent farmers on their estates in a paternalistic manner. The farmers provided the infantry; the aristocrats themselves constituted the cavalry. Macedonia lay at the very periphery of the

Greek world. Although the Macedonians spoke a northwestern Greek dialect, the Greeks did not regard them as Greek, and they were not allowed to participate in the Olympic Games. Only the royal family was classed as Greek because it was assumed that it descended from Argos.

Philip II (359–336): the end of the Classical period in Greek history

The Macedonian king, Philip II (359–336), modernized his army after the Theban model and took possession of the Thracian gold mines, which had been exploited by Athens in the fifth century (see p. 95). Philip was a great admirer of Greek culture and his aim was to use his army and his newly acquired gold to extend his sway over the whole of Greece. In a series of skillfully planned military campaigns and diplomatic maneuvers he managed to turn the dissension in Greece to his own advantage. Between 342 and 338 the Athenians and the Thebans attempted to stop him, but he defeated their armies in 338 BC, in the decisive battle at Chaeronea (see Map 10.4).

Philip tried to set up a form of government that would be acceptable to the Greeks and, in 337, all the Greek states with the exception of Sparta accepted his proposal to create a new league together with Macedonia. This was the "League of Corinth." The member states did not have to pay tributes. Under the terms of the agreement they were to enjoy full freedom and autonomy in their internal affairs and there were to be no more interstate wars or revolutions. Philip's intention was probably to lead the League in an attack on Persia and to conquer Asia Minor, but before he was able to set about realizing his plans he was killed in 336, following a private quarrel.

Historians have all along seen the year 338 as a major turning point in Greek history, marking the end of the era of the free, autonomous city states. The contemporary Greeks, however, did not all see things that way: opinions regarding Greece's future differed, even among the Athenians, Philip's greatest enemies. For example, the well-known Athenian orator and politician Demosthenes (384–322 BC), who fiercely opposed Philip, wanted Athens to remain entirely independent and to retain all her power. The orator and publicist Isocrates (436–338), on the other hand, saw the unification of all the Greeks

FIGURE 10.6 Demosthenes (384–322 BC)

Notes. Having risen to power as a legal orator in Athens, Demosthenes became one of Athens' leading politicians around 356. His speeches have remained renowned into our times, in particular the speeches in which he expressed his anxiety about the rise of Philip II and urged the Athenians to defend their freedom, autonomy, and power.

under a powerful leader as an effective answer to the endless succession of revolutions and wars between states. In his opinion, the conquest of Asia Minor, followed by a large-scale establishment of Greek colonies in that region, would solve many problems in Greece. He therefore urged the Greek states to join forces in an attack on Persia. In actual fact, the Greeks had already started migrating to Asia. Thousands of Greek mercenaries were enlisting in the Persian army and trade with the East was also intensifying. This trade was conducted via the Greek cities on the west coast of Asia Minor, which had passed under Persian control again in 386. These phenomena foreshadowed what was to follow in the next stage in Greece's history, the Hellenistic era (p. 127).

THE ATHENIAN POPULATION IN THE FIFTH AND FOURTH CENTURIES BC

In the fifth century BC Athens became the economic and cultural center of Greece and the most densely populated city in the Greek world. It is believed that by about 432 the city counted some 35,000 adult male citizens, between 20,000 and 30,000 or even more adult male slaves, and between 10,000 and 15,000 adult male metics (free non-Athenians who lived and worked in Athens and Piraeus). Many Greeks, especially from Ionia, which was threatened by Persia, and from Athens' allied cities, took up permanent residence in Athens and Piraeus. Moreover, vast numbers of slaves were imported into Attica. These slaves had widely differing backgrounds. Some were captives and deportees from hostile regions, such as the Persian part of Asia Minor. Others were offered for sale by slave traders: punished offenders, abandoned children who had been raised by slave traders, and victims of piracy, banditry, and war in different parts of the surrounding world.

The metics

The metics enjoyed personal freedom, but had no Athenian citizen rights. They had no vote in the assembly and were not allowed to take a matter to court themselves, at least not in the fifth century (in the fourth century they were granted this right). The metics had to pay fixed direct taxes (see p. 95) and were liable to service in the Athenian army. They were not usually allowed to possess land in Attica; only very rarely was a metic granted the right to own land, as a reward for services rendered to the city state. Most metics were craftsmen, sailors or day laborers, but some were wealthy doctors, bankers, merchants, or architects, who participated actively in Athens' economic and cultural life.

The slaves

In Athens, slaves worked alongside free citizens and non-citizens in agriculture and transport, housekeeping, and skilled trades. Large concentrations of slaves were to be found in important workshops and trading centers, in dockyards, and in the mines of Laurium, where some ten thousand slaves are thought to have worked around 432. When slaves bought their freedom or others bought it for them, or when they were released from slavery, they acquired a status that resembled that of the metics. In some cases they were forced to continue to perform the tasks they had carried out as slaves. A free man or woman could purchase the freedom of a slave he or she wished to marry. Some slaves were bought free by usurers, who would then force the freed slave to repay them, sometimes at high interest rates. It was probably also possible for a master to redeem a slave, after which the former slave would pay back the sum his master had paid for his freedom (optionally in instalments) with money earned through hard work. Sometimes a master would grant a well-educated slave permission to earn the money needed to purchase his freedom by carrying out extra, paid tasks for others besides the work his master required him to do.

The slaves of Attica were less given to revolt than the helots of Sparta. Coming as they did from various regions in and around Greece, and even from further away, they had virtually no sense of any common interest. Moreover, the status of the different kinds of slaves in Attica differed and so did the way in which they were treated by their masters. Domestic slaves, such as private teachers and secretaries, and the slaves who managed shops and farms were better off than many poor, free citizens, while the slaves of small farmers and craftsmen were regarded almost as members of their master's family. For the slaves who worked in the quarries and the mines, however, conditions were far from rosy.

The helots of Laconia and Messenia, who lived together in villages, constituted homogeneous national groups; they were all ruthlessly oppressed. The Laconian helots are believed to have descended from the pre-Dorian population of that region (see p. 65).

The presence of so many metics and slaves meant that Athens could mobilize a large proportion of her civilian population for years on end in times of war; the metics and slaves could then take over the tasks of the mobilized men and life at home could continue as usual. Even in times of peace, Athens kept a standing fleet of up to sixty warships. A warship of the trireme type was manned with a crew of around 120–150, of whom about twenty were marines and sailors; the others were rowers (thetes and volunteers from elsewhere). Unlike the Romans in the late republic and the imperial age, the Athenians were not generous with their citizen rights and privileges, which included the ownership of land within the *polis.*

Women in Athens and Sparta

Athenian society was a male society. Enjoying virtually no political rights, Athenian women were citizens up to a point only. They had no share in political decision making or jurisdiction, they were not allowed to appear in court themselves, and their property was managed by their husbands, their fathers, a brother, or some other male member of their families. Women belonging to Athenian citizen families were much sought-after as partners for Athenian citizens: since 451/0 only children born from such a relationship were legally entitled to Athenian citizen rights by birth. Women from Athenian citizen families did, however, play important parts in the public worship of the gods and other religious tasks. Married women in Athens lived mostly indoors, where they performed their daily tasks. Those tasks were in fact quite plentiful, for in those days many products were still made at home and a large part of the children's education and most medical care were provided at home. Athenian married women rarely went outdoors unchaperoned. The marriageable age for a female was fourteen to fifteen. For men it varied more; most men married when they were between twenty and thirty-five.

FIGURE 10.7 The Athenian Acropolis, the city's religious center

Notes. At the bottom of the picture are the porches of the Propylaea, which provided access to the Parthenon (the temple of Athena; upper right) and the Erechtheum (the sanctuary where sacred relics from the time of the city's foundation were kept; upper left).

Key to figure 10.7 (opposite))

1. Hadrian's library; 2. Roman *agora*; 3. the Tower of the Winds; 4. the Erechtheum; 5. Mycenaean stairway; 6. old temple of Athena?; 7. the Parthenon; 8. the temple of Rome and Augustus; 9. the site of the *temenos* of Zeus Polieus; 10. Themistocles' wall; 11. Cimon's wall; 12. Acropolis museum; 13. Pheidias' workshop?; 14. foundation trenches of retaining walls predating the construction of the Parthenon; 15. Chalkotheke; 16. *temenos* of Athena Ergane; 17. *temenos* of Artemis Brauronia; 18. place where the statue of Athena Promachos stood; 19. temple of Athena Nike; 20. the Propylaea; 21. base that supported the statue of Agrippa; 22. Beule gate, third century AD; 23. cave of the Furies; 24. Areopagus; 25. site of the Aigeion; 26. place where the statue of Aphrodite Pandemos stood; 27. Odeum of Herodes Atticus; 28. Stoa of Eumenes (or Roman?); 29. site of the *temenos* of Aphrodite; 30. site of the *temenos* of Themis; 31. old Asklepieion; 32. later Asklepieion; 33. Thrasyllus monument and Corinthian columns; 34. Odeum of Pericles; 35. theater of Dionysus; 36. temples of Dionysus; 37. monument commemorating Nicias.

FIGURE 10.7 *continued*

There was one group of women in Athens who were less restricted in their movements: the *hetairai*, who were something of a cross between a courtesan and a female companion. Some of those women were well educated and cultivated; they were often to be found in the company of the Athenian statesmen.

In most other Greek cities a woman's life will have been very much like that in Athens, except in Sparta, where the wives of the Spartiates lived a different existence. As the male members of the families lived in messes and spent most of their time in military training, their wives were able to move about freely and had a very attenuated family life. Spartan women received good athletic training, just like the men. The idea was that they would then give birth to better warriors.

FIGURE 10.8

A Greek private house

Notes. 1. entrance; 2. *aule* (inner court); 3. front porch; 4. *megaron* (a hall reserved for men); 5. bedrooms; 6. *exedra* (an open alcove); other rooms: living rooms and rooms for servants. Only wealthy Greeks owned houses like this.

FIGURE 10.9

Fragment of the so-called Ludovisi Throne, originally from the Greek town of Locri in southern Italy. The fragment was found close to Villa Ludovisi in Rome in 1887. The girl appears to be a *hierodoulos* (temple slave) of Aphrodite, goddess of love and fertility.

FURTHER DEVELOPMENT OF THE ATHENIAN DEMOCRACY

In the fifth century BC the Athenian democracy was further expanded. In 487 Themistocles' proposal for a new system for selecting archons was accepted: the criterion that the archons were to belong to the two highest property classes (see p. 84) was retained, only now they were to be chosen by lot. From this point onwards the office of archon was frequently held by citizens who, besides their wealth, had nothing on which to pride themselves. The archons consequently came to lose much of their influence in administrative affairs to the generals, for they (and also the treasurers) were still elected by the public assembly for their outstanding talents. Almost all the Athenian rulers of the fifth century were generals, who were elected over and over again, until they died (Pericles in 429) or fell into disgrace and were ostracized (Themistocles in 470, Cimon in 461; see p. 88).

The Council of the Areopagus in 462/1

In 462/1 the power of the Council of the Areopagus, the most conservative bastion in Athens, was drastically curtailed. After the conservative general Cimon had marched his hoplite forces to the Peloponnese to help Sparta in her struggle against the helots (see p. 93), the democratic rulers Ephialtes and Pericles saw to it that the Areopagus lost all its political power. From then onwards this council served only as a court of law for capital crimes. The supervision and control of legislation and the magistrates were transferred to the Council of Five Hundred, the assembly, and the popular law courts. To facilitate this control, the magistrates were required to give account of their actions at the end of their term of office.

This shift in power spelled Cimon's downfall and the defeat of the conservatives, who wished to spare Sparta and found the democracy too radical.

Pericles

Pericles was the most influential politician in Athens after 460. Under his leadership Athens introduced a system of state pay for state service that enabled poor citizens to play a part in decision making and administrative matters. In the second half of the fifth century, citizens were granted a small allowance (about half a day's wages) for sitting on the Council of Five Hundred and on the juries of the law courts. From 399 onwards those who attended the public assemblies were also paid for their time. On national feast days, such as feasts in honor of the gods that were intended for the entire *polis* community, the citizens were paid lump sums. As all this implied considerable extra expenses, Athens stiffened the qualifications for citizenship: from Pericles' time onwards only those Athenians whose father and mother were both Athenians were granted full citizen rights.

During Pericles' time and the following century the public assembly, the body that took the decisions in the Athenian democracy (p. 87), convened at least forty times a year. The site where these meetings were held, Mount Pnyx in the center of Athens, had room for about six thousand persons at most. The citizens who had farms in Attica probably didn't attend the meetings that often. It is generally assumed that the public assembly was dominated by inhabitants of Athens herself, who could afford to miss a day's work on a regular basis. The allowances that were handed out from 399 onwards seem to have done little to change this situation.

The democracy and the fleet

The effect of the introduction of the system of state pay for state service and the shifts in political power in 462/1 was that poor citizens acquired more influence in jurisdiction, decision making, and the executive. At the same time, the poor citizens were also acquiring more military importance, for it was they who provided most of the sailors and rowers for the war fleet. On one occasion, in 411, the Athenian fleet saved the democracy. That year, a group of oligarchs took advantage of the sense of despair that had pervaded Athens since the disaster on Sicily and the resumption of the Peloponnesian War (see p. 97). Large parts of Athens' population blamed the democratic government for the blows that the city had suffered and a moderate oligarchic government was instituted. However, in the end the fleet, which was stationed off Samos, threatened to sail to Athens to restore the democracy by force. Daunted by this threat, the Athenian rulers then reverted to the democratic system of before 411.

Old and new politicians

Until 429, all of Athens' rulers were still members of the aristocracy. The nobles were at a great advantage in terms of property (and the income they derived from it in the form of revenues and interest), spare time, educational background, and experience. Moreover, the fact that they belonged to the old, respected families appealed to the voters, even in the democratic system. They were supported by citizens from all ranks of society, whose loyalty they secured by granting them services, different forms of patronage, or charity. The poor were dependent on the wealthy for charity, the small shopkeepers for their patronage. The aristocrats were also supported by their political friends among the higher classes and by influential financiers. Their splendor and their liturgies (p. 95) greatly impressed the masses. Thanks to their numerous contacts and networks outside Athens they were also better informed.

However, in the last decades of the fifth century and in the fourth century Athens was from time to time led by politicians of a different stamp. After Pericles' death, there were no leaders who were good generals and admirals and who were at the same time capable of managing financial affairs and manipulating the public assembly. The leading Athenian politicians after 429 were either good military men, good public speakers, or good financiers, but these qualities were never combined in a single ruler. Because of their different backgrounds and different attitudes, these politicians frequently came into conflict with one another. Most were still members of the aristocratic families, but some were entrepreneurs, such as Cleon, a manufacturer of leather goods and a gifted orator, who molded Athens' assembly to his will between 429 and 422. A radical democrat, he was very much against concluding a compromise peace treaty with Sparta. Contemporary authors, who were usually aristocrats themselves or associated themselves with the aristocracy, used the derogatory term "demagogues" to describe this type of non-aristocratic politician. Lacking the aristocracy's traditional means of power, these politicians had to exploit their debating skills to persuade the people at large to accept their viewpoints.

The stability of the Athenian democracy

The stability of the Athenian democracy in the Classical period caused much amazement among both contemporary and later observers. But in actual fact there was not that much cause for wonder. By the Classical period the democratic regime had firmly taken root among the Athenian population. It had already proven tremendously successful before 431. The control of the Council of Five Hundred and the popular law courts over the officials with executive powers was well arranged; under normal conditions, officials with oligarchic inclinations had no chance of changing the constitution.

The shared history of warfare and the privileges which distinguished the Athenians from their allies, the metics, and the slaves had created strong feelings of solidarity among the Athenian citizens of all classes. These bonds were moreover strengthened by the Athenians' great pride in their city's outstanding literary and artistic achievements. Written speeches that have come down to us from this period praise Athens' military and cultural fame as if it were the merit of the *polis* as a whole, of the collective Athenian *demos*.

Some modern historians relate the stability of the Athenian democracy to Athens' imperialistic tendencies. This imperialism offered the nobles great opportunities for winning fame and yielded substantial material benefits for many social groups. The thetes could earn money and obtain booty by joining the navy, poor peasants were granted land in Athens' colonies, and hundreds of educated Athenians acquired good positions in administration, jurisdiction, and banking in the league territory—at least in the fifth century. Athens' powerful position in the trade to the Black Sea moreover ensured cheap grain (see p. 95). These material advantages may explain why the poor citizens never persuaded the assembly to distribute the property and land of the aristocracy and why they left intact the wide gulf that separated them from the wealthy Athenians. In the Athenian democracy there was no equality in terms of property or income, only equality before the law, in the application of the law, and in most political rights of the adult male citizens. The adherents of the above theory maintain that it was because of these conditions, and the fact that they could continue to hold the highest offices, that the rich accepted the democracy and were prepared to make themselves useful to the entire *demos* through their administrative activities and liturgies.

The presence of large numbers of slaves is also often put forward to explain the success of the Athenian democracy. The democracy demanded a high level of participation from the citizens: forty assemblies a year, every year five hundred new members for the *boule*, and large jury courts. All this, it is argued, was possible only because there were so many slaves to do all the work while the citizens spent their time in deliberation. On the other hand, the extent of slavery in Athens is a matter of contention. It is far from certain whether common small farmers and craftsmen will have had the means to keep slaves.

Criticism of the Athenian democracy

But not everybody admired the Athenian democracy. From the mid-fifth century onwards, oligarchically minded authors criticized the democracy for giving the poor the opportunity to tyrannize the wealthy and sensible citizens, and for granting the ignorant masses far too much power. In the fourth century the criticism intensified. Many nobles held the democracy responsible for the blows that Athens had suffered since 431; they claimed that the assembly, under the influence of demagogues, had pursued a whimsical zigzag course that had ultimately led to Athens' defeat in 404. They saw how in their own times differences of opinion between generals, financiers, and orators were resulting in confused and inconsistent policies. Moreover, it was the rich and the nobles who had to pay the poll taxes that were regularly imposed to cover the many deficits that occurred after 404, when Athens lost her tribute reserve, and the damage caused in the war in Attica after 413 (see p. 98), which had to be repaired on top of the city's usual expenses. On various occasions in the fourth century, Athens sent a fleet out on an expedition without giving it sufficient money, forcing the crew to resort to piracy.

ATHENS AS THE CENTER OF GREEK CULTURE IN THE CLASSICAL PERIOD

Later generations of Greeks and cultured Europeans from around AD 1500 onwards saw the period between 480 and 338 as the Classical era, the heyday of Greek civilization. In those hundred and fifty years, Athens was the unrivalled center of Greek culture and the school of Greece. The city acted as a magnet for the most talented artists and scholars from all over the Greek world, in particular from Ionia, which had been the center of Greek civilization in the Archaic period and was now threatened by the Persians. In Athens, everyone was free to say, write, or produce whatever they liked, providing that certain religious taboos were respected: no one could deny the existence of the gods or insult one of Athens' state gods with impunity.

Another important reason why so many artists flocked to Athens was that it was a relatively wealthy city. Both the state and private persons granted artists commissions and spent large sums of money on major religious festivals (liturgies).

The presence of so many talented, creative Greeks from all corners of the world fostered fruitful exchanges before a wide public, which saw and heard so much that it was able to make critical judgments. A remarkably large proportion of the Athenian population could read to some extent.

This favorable combination of factors (talent, money, freedom, and an interested, critical public) created an ideal environment for major achievements in the fields of architecture, the visual arts, literature, and philosophy. During Pericles' reign, Athens was lavishly embellished—partly with the money of the Delian League—with temples, statues, and colonnades, and important literary genres were developed.

Attic drama

Attic drama (tragedy and comedy) is believed to have evolved from the traditional alternate singing of a choir and its leader during the processions that formed part of the celebrations held in honor of Dionysus, the god of wine, intoxication, ecstasy, and the wild forces in nature. The Athenian tyrants of the second half of the sixth century had promoted the cult of Dionysus because it was not connected with any of the old aristocratic families (see p. 86). Like the Panathenaea, the major celebrations of Athens' town goddess Athena, this cult belonged to the *polis* as a whole.

FIGURE 10.10   Schematic representation of the development of the theater

Notes. 1. *orchestra* surrounded by the seats for the audience; 2. the area intended for the audience (*theatron*) was separated from the *orchestra*; a *skene* (= stage) was added behind the *orchestra* to serve as a background; 3. the *skene* (which began to play an increasingly important part as a stagehouse for the dramatic action) was raised and made deeper; 4. the Roman theater: the area reserved for the audience (*cavea*) was semicircular, the actors' stage extending over almost the entire width of the diameter; 5. one of the best preserved ancient Greek theaters is that at Epidaurus. Every year this theater, which can seat 14,000 persons, attracts flocks of visitors from all over the world who come to see the ancient tragedies brought back to life at the Epidavros festival.

The democratic government that succeeded the tyrants was also favorably disposed towards such cults.

Most tragedies focused on the relations between mortals and the gods—for example, on conflicts between man-made laws and divine ordinance, or between man's aspirations and his destiny as ordained by the gods. These and other subjects were usually derived from the same ancient legends and myths that had previously inspired the epic poets of the Archaic period (see p. 74). Popular themes were the adventures of Oedipus, who killed his father and married his mother without knowing who they were, and the dilemma of Orestes. Orestes was the son of Agamemnon, the commander of the Greeks in their battle against Troy. He felt it was his duty to avenge the death of his father, who had been killed by his wife Clytemnestra when he returned from Troy. But by killing Clytemnestra, Orestes would be committing matricide, which was ethically unacceptable. The best-known tragedians were Aeschylus (525–455), who wrote the *Oresteia* trilogy and *The Persians* (about Xerxes' defeat at Salamis), Sophocles (495–406; his works include *Oedipus Tyrannus* and *Electra* = Orestes' sister), and Euripides (a younger contemporary of Sophocles). Quite a few of Euripides' works have survived. Among those works is the *Bacchae*, about the triumph of ecstatic Dionysiac rites.

In the fifth century, when they first made their appearance, comedies were rather like political cabaret, presented in the form of a play. The best-known representative of this genre is Aristophanes. In 411, during the Peloponnesian War, he wrote the *Lysistrata*, in which women withhold sex from their husbands in an attempt to persuade them to make peace. Aristophanes is thought to have died in 386. Comedies lost their political element in the fourth century and evolved more into a form of bourgeois entertainment referred to as "new comedy." The best-known exponent of this genre is Menander.

The choir played parts in both tragedies and comedies. Its singing was accompanied by music and dancing. The performances, which were held in open-air theaters, were financed by wealthy citizens and metics. Contests were held during the Dionysian celebrations, in which plays written by different poets competed for a prize, awarded by a jury. Around the end of the fifth century, repeat performances started to be organized of the most popular plays. In this way Attic drama rapidly spread across the whole Greek world.

Philosophy

In Classical Athens, philosophers did not focus on nature alone; man and his intellectual capacities, his behavior and his state and society all became objects of philosophical speculation.

The sophists

In the second half of the fifth century and in the early fourth century, itinerant teachers started to give paid lessons in rhetoric. Eloquence in speech and writing was a great advantage in the democratic organs, in the law courts, and at all kinds of celebrations and other public events. The teachers of rhetoric were called sophists. Athens became one of the most important centers of their activities. There, the teachers found a wealthy public for whom eloquence was of the greatest importance. The sophists' lessons gave rich young men who could afford to pay for this form of education an extra advantage over others.

Besides providing lessons in rhetoric, the sophists also reflected on such matters as state and society, language, and standards of human behavior. To these fields they tried to apply the rational, logical way of thinking of natural philosophy. Some sophists can be said to have been pioneers in grammar and linguistics. Radical sophists maintained that laws and rules were mere man-made conventions and agreements; they were not to be seen as absolute or divine.

Rhetorical education

In the fourth century BC, a special system was developed for rhetorical education. This system gradually spread over the whole Greek world. Between the ages of eight and twelve, the children of the elite were taught how to read, write, and figure in their own homes or at their teachers' homes. In the next three years of their lives they learned all about the authors of Classical Greek literature, after which a rhetorician trained them in the art of oratory. Rhetoricians taught their pupils in schools; they did not travel around like the sophists. The best-known rhetorician of fourth-

FIGURE 10.11   Scene showing a Greek school represented on a vase

century Athens is Isocrates, whom we have already come across above (see pp. 101–2). These forms of education cost money and were hence not accessible to the poor. The Greek upper classes who had received a grounding in rhetoric developed a cultured, elitist, spoken and written language. This language, and their cultural background distinguished them from the poor and from parvenus who had money, but had not enjoyed a good education.

In the fourth century, rhetoric had an increasing influence on all kinds of prose writing and even on drama. At the same time, literature acquired a certain bourgeois element. Whereas fifth-century authors had derived many of their themes from heroic epics, which were steeped in the standards and values of the old aristocracy, authors in the fourth century started to focus on issues like education, standards of human behavior, and other aspects of bourgeois ethics. All this was taking place around the time that the aristocracy's political influence was declining. As we have already seen above, in the Athenian democracy the nobles gradually lost their monopoly of power to talented orators and military and financial experts who were no longer all members of the aristocracy.

Socrates and Plato

The sophists' chief opponents were the Athenians Socrates (469–399) and his most gifted pupil, Plato (429–347). Socrates was of the opinion that laws were rooted in absolute moral standards, which he attempted to discover by asking people for the definitions and exact meanings of concepts like wisdom, piety, courage, etc. Ironically, the Athenians, who were suspicious of all his questioning, regarded him as the worst sophist. In 399 a popular law court condemned him to drink poison because, it was felt, he was "corrupting the young." Socrates did not write down anything himself, but we do know something about his ideas from the works of his pupils Plato and Xenophon, an Athenian aristocrat who is best known for his historical writing and his military achievements.

Plato tried to solve Socrates' problem. He believed that all things on earth were imperfect approximations to prototypes and forms that existed in a higher sphere, the sphere of *ideai* (unfortunately this term is often erroneously translated as "ideas"). For example, all tables on earth were embodiments of the *idea* table in that higher sphere and could for that reason be called tables. Plato believed that the human soul existed before birth, when it had knowledge of the *ideai*.

FIGURE 10.12 Socrates (469–399)

Notes. The son of a sculptor or a mason, Socrates was originally a middle-class craftsman. On several occasions he fought as a hoplite in the Athenian army. He appears to have died a poor man. As a young man he was interested in natural philosophy, but later he focused more on ethics and the definition of concepts. Unlike some sophists, he believed that laws had absolute power. He took an active part in the political life in his city. In 406 he presided over the assembly which, in a rowdy meeting, condemned various admirals to death. Although they had that year won a major sea battle against the Spartans (near the Arginusae islands), those admirals had failed to save the many Athenians who had fallen overboard in a rising storm.

At birth, the soul was incarcerated in a mortal body and it lost most of its knowledge of the *ideai*. Only by thoroughly studying every aspect of reality, starting with a foundation course in mathematics, could man slowly regain his soul's former knowledge and experience. For Plato, the highest form was the form of the good, which is sometimes synonymous with god. Plato's ideal state was a sober agricultural *polis* with a limited, fixed number of citizens who were grouped into three classes: governing philosophers, guardians, and workers. The philosophers had to undergo a thorough training to learn as much as possible about the *ideai* and acquire expertise in administration and jurisdiction. Such men would then have both the most appropriate moral background and the required skills to provide the best form of government conceivable. As the guardians' task was to defend the state, they had to be trained in military tactics and morale. The workers had to provide for the material needs of the two higher classes and produce whatever the community required; they were to have no political power. It was best if the philosophers had no private property and no families. There would then be no risk of them being tempted to further their private interests at the state's expense. The positions of the two higher classes were not to be hereditary: each generation would have to select the most suitable candidates for the offices of philosopher and guardian.

In 367 and 361 the Syracusan tyrant Dionysius II (367–357) invited Plato to visit him in Sicily. But he was disappointed with Plato's advice and sent the philosopher home again on both occasions.

Around 390 Plato founded the Academy, a school in which he discussed his theories with pupils and other interested parties. This school was to remain a center of Platonic philosophy until AD 529. Plato's followers were later also referred to as academics.

Aristotle (384–322)

Plato's most brilliant pupil was Aristotle (384–322). He did not believe in Plato's world of *ideai*, but thought that all things on earth could be logically grouped into species and categories by analyzing their inherent properties and qualities. Aristotle was a universal scholar. He wrote about formal logic (i.e., the art of reasoning in a logical and coherent manner), nature, the supernatural, poetry, prose, ethics, and political science. Aristotle's political ideal was a state in which virtue and competence in all aspects of human activity would be the standards of government and citizen life: a higher form of aristocracy (*aristos* = the best).

For the particular situation of his own time, he found a *polis* with a mixed constitution (combining monarchic, aristocratic, and democratic elements) the most desirable. This constitution was to be acceptable to the population at large and was to steer a middle course between the unhealthy extremes of tyranny and the arbitrary rule of the masses. In Aristotle's opinion the presence of a powerful middle group was important for a state's stability. The assembly was to convene only rarely and was to allow itself to be led and advised by a group of trained experts. If there could be no mixed constitution, then a democracy was more preferable than a tyranny or an oligarchy. Aristotle maintained that all citizens were capable of participating in administrative matters. The sum of the expertise of all individuals was important for good government. A democracy could make use of the expertise of all the citizens, which was better than the collective expertise of a small group or the expertise of a single leader, as in an oligarchy or a tyranny.

Aristotle also established a school: the Lyceum. In those days the words "Academy" and "Lyceum" referred to buildings or locations in Athens or Attica.

Historical writing

Herodotus

The fifth century BC also saw the birth of historical writing. The "father of history" was Herodotus. It is assumed that he lived from *c.* 485 until 425 and came from Halicarnassus, in the southwestern-most corner of Asia Minor. He spent part of his life in Athens and died as a citizen of the Athenian colony Thurii in southern Italy. He wrote "The Histories" about the Greco-Persian wars (the conflict between Europe and Asia) and the events that led up to them and about the customs, traditions, and histories of many different peoples and states in Asia and Greece. Instead of recounting myths like Homer had done, he tried to write down accurate accounts, based on interviews and critically assessed information. His work actually evolved out of the Ionian tradition of geography and ethnology: already in the Archaic period Ionian merchants had shown a keen interest in learning more about the lands and the peoples they visited on their travels.

Thucydides

The Athenian Thucydides lived from around 460 until 400 or a few years later and wrote a history of the Peloponnesian War. Whereas Herodotus had taken a wide view of contemporary and past events, Thucydides narrowed the scope of history to the fields of politics and warfare. He was the first to make a fundamental distinction between cause and occasion, for example in his analysis of the outbreak of the Peloponnesian War. He also tried to explain backgrounds and underlying motives in speeches that he put into the mouths of his protagonists. Thucydides concentrated on the history of his own time. Other Greek historians were later to follow his example.

Rhetorical historical writing

After Thucydides, historical writing came to feel the influence of rhetorical education (p. 112). From the fourth century BC until the end of antiquity, the historical works that were written in both Greek and Roman cultural circles were phrased in the language that the elite learned at the schools of rhetoric. This was a language full of all kinds of stylistic motifs, dramatic effects, and moralizing clichés, which was also used for show speeches and other forms of rhetorical prose. Good historians, however, used this language to describe events as they had actually happened. They did not revert to writing florid, inaccurate folk tales and heroic legends, which, nonetheless, continued to exist alongside historical works throughout the whole of antiquity. Important events were immortalized both in historical works phrased in affected rhetorical prose, which were read by a small literate circle of political experts, and in folk tales.

THE GREEKS IN THE WESTERN MEDITERRANEAN

The city states that the Greeks had founded along the coasts of southern Italy, Sicily, and southern Gaul (see Maps 9.1a and 9.1b) in the colonization period (750–550) had risen to great prosperity.

The remains of imposing temples and other buildings that can still be admired along those coasts today bear witness to the material wealth of these cities in the sixth and fifth centuries BC. This wealth was largely the consequence of the fertile soils and the favorable locations of the sites that the colonists had selected for their settlements. Thanks to the good transport possibilities of those sites, the surplus agricultural produce could be easily exported. In the course of the sixth century the Greeks' colonization in the west came to an end. The trading city Carthage, which was a colony itself founded by the Phoenician city of Tyre, rose to power and kept the Greeks out of northern Africa, southern Spain, Sardinia, and the western point of Sicily. The Etruscans, then the best organized and most highly developed people in Italy, held a powerful position in central Italy, the Po valley and Campania. Together with the Carthaginians, they frustrated the Greeks' attempts to found colonies on Corsica around 545.

The tension intensified around the beginning of the fifth century. In 480 (the year of Salamis) the Carthaginians attempted to gain control over all Sicily, but the Syracusan tyrant Gelon (485–478) routed them at Himera. He then turned Syracuse into the most powerful Greek *polis* in the west, and the most densely populated Greek city after Athens, by transferring parts of the

FIGURE 10.13 The temple of Hera at Poseidonia or Paestum, fifth century BC

Notes. Paestum (along the western coast of southern Italy, to the south of Naples) was a colony founded (*c.* 600 BC) by Sybaris, which had in turn been founded by Achaea, a region in the north of the Peloponnese (Sybaris lay at the northwestern corner of the Gulf of Taranto in southern Italy. It was founded *c.* 720 BC and was destroyed by the neighboring city of Croton *c.* 510 BC). Around 390 BC the Greeks living at Poseidonia were overpowered by Italians from the hinterland. From then onwards Poseidonia was an Italian city. In 273 the Romans turned it into a Latin colony (p. 151) and called it Paestum.

populations of Greek cities all over Sicily to Syracuse. His brother, Hieron I, who succeeded him, destroyed the Etruscan navy in 474 in the great naval battle off Cumae (a Greek city near Naples).

That marked the beginning of the gradual decline of the power of the Etruscans, who were from then onwards no longer a threat to the Greek city states. However, a new danger was emerging in southern Italy, where groups of Greeks were absorbed by the tribes surrounding them and the remaining Greek city states were regularly threatened by the tribes living in their hinterlands. Between 282 and 270 the Greek city states all gradually came under Roman control. A few lying closer to Rome, such as Neapolis (now Naples), had come under Roman sway earlier, shortly after the mid-fourth century. After 270 Rome controlled the whole of Italy, including the Greek *poleis*.

Around the middle of the fifth century Sicily was the seat of constant battles between Syracuse and the native tribes in the interior of Sicily. Between 415 and 413 Athens attempted to gain hegemony over Sicily (see pp. 96–7). A few years later, in 409, the first of what was to be an endless series of wars broke out. The contenders were the Sicilian Greeks, led by Syracuse, and the Carthaginians. These wars were to continue, with the odd breathing space, until the third century BC and were not to end until Rome conquered the whole of Sicily (241 BC; see p. 168).

The constant wars had important consequences for the internal relations within the Greek cities. Syracuse, for example, was ruled by a democratic government for only a very short period, from 466 until 405. For almost the whole of the rest of the Classical period that city was governed by tyrants. Time and time again successful generals managed to seize control and make themselves tyrants. They relied on the support of their mercenaries and the poor citizens, who hoped that the new ruler would reward them with revolutionary measures such as land distributions and the cancellation of debts.

In the fourth century the strong enemy pressure compelled the Greeks to reorganize into larger units so that they would be better able to defend themselves. They had the choice of two options: they could organize a league of autonomous *poleis* or they could bind cities together in a territorial monarchy with a large Greek city serving as a fortified center. The tyrants Gelon and Hieron I had already tried out the latter option (see above), but their family had lost its political power in 466. The Syracusan tyrant Dionysius I (405–367) made a new attempt. He captured the eastern half of Sicily and the southwestern part of the Italian mainland and abolished numerous Greek city states. The populations of those states he transferred to Syracuse and he settled mercenaries in the emptied cities and in a series of newly founded cities, which belonged to Syracuse. However, those efforts brought him, and later Syracusan tyrants with similar ambitions, into conflict with the Greek occupants of the city states, who fought stubbornly to preserve their autonomy. This situation came to an end in the third century BC, when all the Greek city states in southern Italy and Sicily passed under Roman control.

The Greeks in the western Mediterranean made original, important contributions to Greek literature, philosophy, art, and architecture. It is they who first brought the peoples of Italy, Gaul, and Spain into contact with Greek civilization. In so doing they paved the way for the large-scale assimilation of Greek culture by the Romans, Gauls, and other Western Europeans that was to take place later.

11 THE HELLENISTIC WORLD (c. 330–c. 30 BC)

INTRODUCTION

Alexander, who became king of Macedonia in 336, took up the plans his murdered father, Philip II, had been unable to realize and brought them to a successful conclusion (see p. 101). As we will see below, he conquered the entire Persian empire. His conquests ushered in a new phase in the history of Greece as well as that of the ancient Near East. That phase is called the "Hellenistic age." In the present chapter we will restrict ourselves to the period of the Greco-Macedonian domination over the aforementioned regions. In the second and first centuries BC the Greco-Macedonian kingdoms fell one by one to the Roman and Parthian empires. However, that did not spell the end for what is known as "Hellenistic culture." In the following sections we will try to outline what "Hellenism" embraces.

ALEXANDER THE GREAT

In 334, after quelling a revolt of Greek city states, Alexander and his experienced Macedonian army, enlarged with contingents from the League of Corinth, sailed across to Asia Minor, where he combined his forces with Macedonian troops that had already been sent there by his father, Philip. This brought his army to a total of 43,000 soldiers and 5500 cavalrymen. In Asia Minor he routed an army of the Persian satrap and in so doing conquered the Greek cities along the west coast of Asia Minor. He then turned his attention to the Phoenician cities, where the Persian fleet was based, because he feared that the fleet might attack Greece during his absence. However, on his way toward those cities he first had to defeat the Persian land forces, which were commanded by Darius III. In the ensuing battle, at Issus (333 BC), it was ironically the Greek mercenaries serving in the Persian army (see p. 102) who offered him the fiercest resistance (see Map 11.1).

As for the Phoenician cities, the conquest of Tyre in particular proved a time-consuming enterprise: the siege of that city was to last no less than seven months. Next, Alexander marched along the coast to Egypt, where the Egyptians, resenting the Persian regime, welcomed him

MAP 11.1 Alexander's empire

with open arms. During a visit to the oracle of Amon (Ammon in Greek) he was greeted as a pharaoh—in other words, as the son of the Egyptian god Amon, whom the Greeks identified with their supreme god Zeus. This made a deep impression on Alexander, who subsequently started to behave like a king of divine birth. He called himself the son of Zeus Ammon. Of great importance was his foundation of Alexandria, the city that was later to become Egypt's capital.

After this interlude in Egypt, Alexander advanced to the heart of the Persian empire. At Gaugamela (see Map 11.1), he once again defeated the Persian land forces (1 October 331 BC). He had himself crowned with a diadem as the "king of Asia" and from then onwards a diadem came to symbolize Hellenistic kingship. Babylon, Susa, and Persepolis offered him no resistance whatsoever. In Persepolis he confiscated the well-stocked Persian treasury and ordered the palace to be burned down as retribution for the destruction of Athens in 480. Within only a few months Alexander continued his campaign. The eastern satrapies did put up a fight, but they too were all defeated. Alexander showed his goodwill towards the subjugated population by marrying Rhoxane, a local princess. At the Indus river he defeated an Indian ruler, Porus. But by then his soldiers had had enough of all the fighting and they refused to march on any further. In 324 Alexander yielded to his men and returned to Babylon. One year later (11 June 323 BC), at the age of almost 33, he died after a brief illness.

FIGURE 11.1 Maquette of the city of Pergamum, one of the most important foci of Greek culture in the Hellenistic era

Notes. The city formed the center of a small, but efficiently governed kingdom in the northwest of Asia Minor, which had shaken off the yoke of the Seleucids at the beginning of the third century BC (*c.* 260 BC). The kings of Pergamum had to fight many a battle against the Celts (Galatians), who invaded the Greek world in 279 and settled in central Anatolia. Pergamum had libraries, schools of rhetoric, and a famous temple of Asklepios (Aesculapius), the god of healing, where thousands of sick came to be cured. The city had developed from a fortress around 300 BC. Between 215 and 133 BC Pergamum was a loyal ally of Rome. In 188, after defeating the Seleucid king Antiochus III (who reigned from 222 until 187 BC), the Romans expanded the kingdom of Pergamum to the Taurus Mountains. In 133 BC the last king of the Pergamene royal house of the Attalids, Attalus III, bequeathed his kingdom to Rome because he had no children who could have succeeded him. This shows that the Hellenistic kings regarded their kingdoms as their private property.

Alexander saw himself as the legitimate successor of the Persian kings and started to behave accordingly. He tried to adopt the Persian court ceremonial, which included kneeling before the king as an attitude of respect, but to the Greeks and Macedonians this was totally unacceptable. They were accustomed to kneeling only before their gods and saw their king as the first among equals. As far as the administration of his empire was concerned, Alexander left many matters unchanged and adapted to local traditions. Taxes continued to be paid in the same manner as in the past. Alexander allowed several Persian satraps to retain their authority, because he considered their Persian administrative experience to be of vital importance. His officers had to accept this. Alexander even forced his officers to take Persian wives.

But in some respects Alexander distanced himself from Persia. He called himself the king of Asia, not Persia. He ordered the palace at Persepolis to be burned down and took up residence in Nebuchadnezzar's palace in Babylon. As he intended to make Babylon his main residence, he ordered the rebuilding of the temple tower—an act that would have befitted a true Babylonian king. His empire was to be a worthy successor of the Asian empires. These plans turned Macedonia, formerly the heartland of his empire, into a backwater. All this brought Alexander into conflict with his generals, who were greatly displeased by this turn of events.

FROM ALEXANDER TO THE ROMAN CONQUEST

After Alexander's death, the lack of a suitable successor almost immediately led to the break-up of his empire into smaller states. An army assembly at Babylon appointed Alexander's feeble-minded half-brother Philip Arrhidaeus to the throne and decided that if Rhoxane, who was then expecting a child, should bear a son, that son would be made joint king. The effective power, however, came to rest with the Macedonian generals, who divided the power at conferences and above all on the battlefields. Power in Asia first of all fell to Antigonus the One-Eyed, who was granted the title of "*stratēgos* ['general'] of Asia." His main rivals were Seleucus, the satrap of Babylonia, and Ptolemy, the satrap of Egypt. Seleucus was forced to flee from his satrapy in 316 and sought refuge at Ptolemy's court, but in 311 he managed to return to Babylon, where he proclaimed himself the *stratēgos* of Asia. Antigonus succeeded in retaining his power in the Levant and Asia Minor for some time. He set himself up as the patron and liberator of Greek cities—a propaganda slogan that was to be borrowed by many—even Roman—leaders after him.

The official kings, Philip Arrhidaeus and Alexander IV, were killed in 317 and 310, respectively, and the fiction of Alexander's family's kingship came to an end when the main pretenders assumed the title of king in 306 and 305. The struggle meanwhile continued. In 301 Antigonus was defeated at Ipsus in Asia Minor by a coalition that included Seleucus, while Ptolemy "helped" by occupying Palestine and southern Syria. Antigonus died at the age of 81.

The outcome of these "wars of the *diadochoi* [successors]" was the dissolution of Alexander's empire. The most important of the kingdoms that were then formed are the Ptolemaic kingdom (Egypt), founded by Ptolemy I (323–283), the Seleucid kingdom (Asia), founded by Seleucus I (311–280), and the Antigonid kingdom (Macedonia), which from 276 onwards was ruled by Antigonus Gonatas (277/6–239), one of the descendants of Antigonus the One-Eyed. Besides Egypt, the Ptolemies controlled Cyrene, Cyprus, Palestine (until 200), and some Greek islands. The Seleucids held sway over the greater part of western Asia and after 200 also Palestine. They had no authority in the northern and eastern parts of Asia Minor.

Later on, a few smaller kingdoms were formed alongside these large kingdoms, largely at the expense of the Seleucid kingdom. They included the kingdoms of Pergamum, ruled by the Attalids (early third century), Bactria, governed by Greek colonists, Parthia, which was ruled by Indo-Iranian invaders and became quite powerful, ultimately seizing power in Mesopotamia from the Seleucids in 141 BC (see pp. 44 and 137), and the Maccabean kingdom of the Jews (see p. 136). All these kingdoms are shown on Map 11.2.

Macedonia: the Antigonid kingdom

Macedonia, the old heartland of Alexander's empire, was a much coveted apple of discord and remained the seat of battle of the *diadochoi* for longer than any other area. Only in 277/6 did

MAP 11.2   The Hellenistic kingdoms, c. 200 BC

Antigonus Gonatas, a grandson of Antigonus the One-Eyed, succeed in establishing a stable dynasty that was to survive for more than a hundred years. The Antigonid dynasty had the advantage of being native and being able to build on its own, native traditions. Since the battle at Chaeronea (338), Macedonia had a powerful position in Greece, strengthened by political alliances with the Corinthian League (see p. 101) and garrisons at Athens and elsewhere, but the Antigonids were in their power politics constantly thwarted by Ptolemies and Seleucids, by leagues of states emerging in Greece, and by aggressive tribes from the north. One of those tribes proved too formidable an enemy. That was the tribe of the Galatians—Celtic people who in 279 marched straight across Macedonia, penetrating deep into central Greece. After spending a year at Delphi they crossed over to Asia Minor, where they forced the Seleucids and Attalids into fierce military action. They ultimately settled in central Asia Minor.

The Antigonids' most persistent opposition came from the far west—from Rome, which intervened in the Greek hornets' nest at the request of Greek city states. In four wars (215–201, 200–196, 171–168, and 149–146 BC) the Romans curtailed the Greek and Macedonian power. In 196 they declared the Greek cities "free and autonomous," in 168 they defeated the last Antigonid king and divided Macedonia into four republics, and in 148 they reduced Macedonia to a Roman province. Two years later the Romans subjected Greece, which they put under the supervision of the governor of Macedonia (see p. 174). In the next century some other Hellenistic kingdoms were likewise to become Roman provinces.

FIGURE 11.2 The Great Altar of Zeus of Pergamum, built to commemorate Pergamum's successes against the Galatians

Notes. The sculptures include scenes showing battles between gods and other beings, symbolizing the battle against the Galatians.

Athens and Sparta

On the whole, rebellions against Macedonia were rather unsuccessful. That also holds for the uprising that was provoked by the Athenian orator Demosthenes after Alexander's death. After suppressing this rebellion, the Macedonians installed a garrison in Athens and changed the city's constitution: from then onwards only people above a certain property qualification were to enjoy citizenship. This spelled the end of the Athenian democracy in the original sense (321 BC). Athens' days as an important participant in international politics were over. The city did succeed in throwing off the Macedonian yoke and restoring the democracy a few times after that, but each time she had to call in help from outside. In Athens, self-government never meant much more than local government, and like elsewhere the polity became increasingly oligarchic, as a result of which "democracy" came to stand for "republic." After quelling a revolt, the Romans established a timocratic oligarchy in Athens in 86 BC.

Sparta's influence had also declined; the city had become a mere shadow of the great power she had once been, although she had managed to hold her own outside the League of Corinth. The number of Spartiates had decreased to 700, 600 of whom were poverty-stricken. The attempts of King Agis IV (244–241) and King Cleomenes III (236–222) to increase the number of Spartiates by raising *perioikoi* to the status of Spartiates had failed. What's more, they had led to a wave of revolts in southern and central Greece. To create the extra citizen holdings required to expand the privileged class, these kings had redivided the land—and that had inspired Greeks in other regions to demand the same. In 222 the Macedonians defeated Cleomenes at Sellasia, a short distance to the north of Sparta, and in so doing put an end to his aspirations.

Leagues of states in Greece

The Aetolian and Achaean leagues were more successful at maintaining their independence. These leagues had been formed in regions where the *ethnos* was the dominant political unit (see p. 70). They differed from leagues like the Delian League and the Peloponnesian League in that they were not led by a single *polis*. They were actually "federations." The citizens of those federations enjoyed double citizen rights, as inhabitants of their *polis* and as members of their league. But these leagues were also unable to prevent the intervention of the great powers in their affairs. In fact, they even invited great powers such as the Seleucid kingdom and Rome to mediate in quarrels between individual league members. In the end they all succumbed to the supreme power of Rome.

Asia: the Seleucid kingdom

The Seleucid kingdom was the largest of the Hellenistic kingdoms, comprising almost the whole of Asia from present-day Turkey to Afghanistan, except for Palestine and southern Syria, which belonged to Egypt. In some respects it was a continuation of the Persian empire under a Macedonian dynasty. The division into satrapies remained unchanged. The empire's heartland was, however, not Persia, but Babylonia. Seleucus I founded a new residence there shortly after 305: Seleucia-on-the-Tigris. In northern Syria he created a second heartland by establishing four new cities. One of those cities was Antioch-on-the-Orontes, which evolved into a metropolis that was to retain its leading position even in the Roman era. The city still exists today: Antakya in Turkey.

The Seleucid kingdom was a very disparate realm, containing a wide variety of peoples and cultures, so its fragmentation was a constant menace. Although many Greeks and Macedonians settled there, in particular in Seleucia and Antioch, only the Greeks in the west of Asia Minor were autochthonous and the dynasty remained foreign. Even so, the kingdom managed to survive more or less unscathed for some 170 years thanks to an efficiently organized government and a powerful army financed by levies from wealthy areas such as Babylonia, Syria, and Asia Minor. Antiochus III the Great (222–187) made a successful attempt to reinforce the kingdom. He gave a repeat performance of Alexander's campaign to India and in 200 BC he wrested control of southern Syria and Palestine from Egypt. But like Xerxes and Seleucus I before him he overplayed his hand in attempting to intervene in Greece. His ambition brought him into conflict with Rome (191–188). The Romans defeated him at Thermopylae in Greece and at Magnesia in Asia Minor. The terms of the peace treaty forced him to surrender his territories in Asia Minor to Rome's ally Pergamum and to pay a tribute of 15,000 talents (see Appendix 2). The Seleucid treasury was to suffer the consequences of this burden for twelve years, as the sum was to be paid in instalments. The loss of Asia Minor was not the mortal blow to the Seleucid kingdom. Antiochus IV Epiphanes (175–164) even managed to conquer Egypt (169–168). But he was not to enjoy his new acquisition for very long. Fearing a confrontation with the Romans, who in 168 had revealed their great might to the East by putting an end to Antigonid Macedonia, he surrendered it. Antiochus IV was also the king who quelled the revolt of the Jews (see p. 136). After his death, in 164 BC, the Seleucid kingdom rapidly weakened owing to dynastic struggles stirred up by the Romans. The now inevitable mortal blow was the loss of Mesopotamia, which in 141 fell to a new kingdom rising to power: that of the Parthians (see p. 44). By that time, the Seleucid kingdom had shrunk from its former glory as "Asia" to little more than "Syria." In 64 the Romans took over control and reduced the Seleucid kingdom to the province of Syria (see p. 198).

Egypt: the Ptolemaic kingdom

The Ptolemaic kingdom (Egypt) flourished under Ptolemy I (323–283) and Ptolemy II (282–246). Alexandria became a large, wealthy city and an important center of science and culture. In the second century its strength was sapped by dynastic struggles, the loss of Palestine and enclaves in Syria (200), and growing unrest among the indigenous Egyptian population. In the second and, especially, the first century the Romans interfered increasingly in Egypt's affairs. In 30 BC Egypt lost its independence. The last queen of the Ptolemaic dynasty, Cleopatra VII, committed suicide when Egypt was captured by Octavian, who was later to become the Emperor Augustus (see pp. 205 and 210).

Especially under its first three kings, the Ptolemaic kingdom was well organized and built on the old pharaonic institutions. We know a lot about this kingdom from the many papyri surviving from those days. Most are in Greek, but quite a few are written in an Egyptian italic script known as "Demotic." They tell us that the state was governed almost as a company, with a close-knit bureaucracy, especially for tax matters. The new capital, Alexandria, grew into a veritable metropolis—a center of economic and cultural prosperity.

THE GOVERNMENT AND THE CITIES OF THE HELLENISTIC KINGDOMS

It is often maintained that in the Hellenistic era large monarchies took the place of the small independent city states (*poleis*) of the Classical period. This is only partly true. The Hellenistic monarchies lay in areas where such states had flourished for centuries already, namely in Egypt, Western Asia, and Macedonia. Greece remained the country of the city states. But the city states had by no means all been free and autonomous before then; many had been dominated by Athens or Sparta. Moreover, large monarchies had annexed Greek *poleis* or had dominated them already through dexterous politics before the reign of Alexander the Great. Lydia and Persia had annexed the *poleis* along the west coast of Asia Minor. The politics of the city states on the Greek mainland had been overshadowed by the Persians' interference from the Peloponnesian War onwards. Sparta had for example been assisted by the Persians in that war and in 386 the Persian king had dictated the terms of the "King's Peace." Later on it was the Macedonians who interfered in Greek politics. Their intervention had resulted in the League of Corinth, led by the king of Macedonia.

All the same, the Hellenistic era also witnessed important new developments. In the first place, the city states were now no longer able to play powerful roles in international politics as Sparta and Athens had done in the fifth century. Secondly, the protagonists in Greek politics were no longer the city states but the leagues (see p. 125). A third new development was the establishment of new Greek cities all over the Near East. This development actually started with Alexander the Great, who founded many cities under the name of Alexandria from Egypt to what is now Afghanistan (Kandahar = Alexandria). The Seleucid rulers also established many new cities, which they gave Macedonian dynastic names, such as Seleucia-on-the-Tigris and Antioch-on-the-Orontes (see Map 11.2).

Some cities evolved from the colonies of soldiers and veterans which the Seleucids planted at several locations, such as Dura-Europos on the Euphrates in Syria. In Egypt the soldiers were granted plots of land at locations scattered across the kingdom rather than in colonies. This is one of the reasons why no more Greek cities arose in Egypt after Alexandria, Naukratis, and Ptolemais. The new cities were populated with Greek emigrants, Greek veterans, but also Oriental natives. Some of those cities became very large and attracted flocks of new immigrants. Alexandria evolved into a cosmopolitan center of many different peoples—Greeks, Egyptians, Jews, and Syrians. Alexandria, Antioch, and Seleucia grew into cities with hundreds of thousands of inhabitants.

Both the old and the new Greek cities enjoyed a special position within the various kingdoms. The kings set themselves up as the champions of the "freedom and autonomy" of the Greek cities. The cities were allowed to govern themselves with their own chosen magistrates, a council, and an assembly, as befitted a *polis*. Every city had its own territory, where the citizens owned arable land, which was often tilled by native dependent farmers. Some of the cities were exempt from taxation. But of course they were not truly independent—usually a royal governor kept an eye on things. In principle, only Greeks and Macedonians were granted citizen rights; the non-Greek occupants enjoyed a certain degree of autonomy in their own ethnic organizations (*politeumata*). We mustn't lump all these cities together, though. The degree to which they underwent Greek influences differed considerably. The cities of Asia Minor, for example, had already been influenced by the presence of the Greeks for quite a while by the time the cities further east began to emerge; the former were consequently far more Hellenized than the latter. The relationship between Greeks and non-Greeks is still a poorly understood historical issue.

Besides the Greek cities there were still of course the ancient Near Eastern cities: Memphis, Thebes, Babylon, Uruk, Susa, Jerusalem, and the Phoenician and Syrian cities. The kings' attitudes towards these cities were somewhat ambivalent. On the one hand they allowed the cities to retain both local autonomy (although they would often appoint a Greek or native governor to supervise their administration) and many of their local customs. The Near Eastern cities could for instance continue to administer justice and draw up contracts according to their native practices. In addition, they were not banned from rebuilding or embellishing their temples. They were also allowed to possess land, just like the Greek cities. On the other hand, however, the ancient Near Eastern cities were no longer able to claim a significant place in political and economic activity. Not one of the cities was made a capital. Many of the new capitals were founded near the ancient Near Eastern cities and were partly populated with people transported from those cities. Seleucia-on-the-Tigris, for example, was populated with deportees from Babylon, which was also deprived of part of its territory.

In time, Greek communities emerged in several of the Near Eastern cities and some of the cities also acquired a Greek signature. They were then usually given a new, dynastic name and the gymnasia, theaters, and temples based on Greek models that arose within them gave them a decidedly Greek touch (gymnasia were schools for sports and military training originally; they later evolved into centers of Greek literary culture, but physical training and sports remained important). Susa for example became Seleucia-on-the-Eulaeus. This did not necessarily imply a total transformation into a Greek city. Thanks to several hundred texts written in cuneiform script and some Greek inscriptions we are reasonably well informed about the situation in Babylon. Under Antiochus IV a Greek community with its own institutions was established there. The cuneiform texts speak of *politai* (citizens) who assembled in the theater (whose remains have also been excavated) and a council of elders. There was a gymnasium and a school of philosophy. This Greek community is attested into the first centuries of the Christian era, by which time the Parthians had long assumed power in Babylon. It may well have included Hellenized Babylonians. The native institutions meanwhile continued to exist alongside the Greek ones. The temple, led by a temple head and a temple council with its own meeting place, continued its activities. The temple council served as a kind of town government for the Babylonians. In both Greek and Near Eastern cities royal governors usually kept an eye on what was going on.

Although the large states were all monarchies, their governments were not all the same. In Macedonia the king was still traditionally the first among his noble peers and was still appointed by an army assembly. In effect, however, kingship assumed an increasingly absolute character in all the states. In the Near East and Egypt the king had been an absolute monarch from the very beginning and that did not change. A great difference with respect to Macedonia was that in Asia and Egypt the ruler was not a native. Alexander the Great had planned to involve the native population more in administrative and military affairs. He had intended to make a Near Eastern city, Babylon, the main royal residence of his empire and to admit Persians to the office of satrap. His successors, however, did not support this policy; they relied on Greeks and Macedonians where possible. When the great immigration of Greeks came to an end, the Hellenistic kings became increasingly dependent on native Orientals. Many of those natives had by then, however, become Hellenized to varying degrees. Ptolemy IV was to make use of native soldiers to a large extent. He deployed mainly Egyptian troops in his attempts to keep the Seleucid king Antiochus III out of Palestine. The victory of Raphia in 217 BC was won with their assistance. This greatly boosted the Egyptians' self-confidence.

The appearance of a new ruling elite in the Near East had little effect on the social structures in that area; it was only the upper layer that changed. In organizational terms, the Seleucid kingdom was very much like the Persian empire, while the Ptolemaic kingdom was in many respects a continuation of the Egyptian kingdom of the pharaohs. A noteworthy phenomenon was the ruler cult, to which we will return later in this chapter.

ECONOMY AND SOCIETY

Greece

The problems that Greece had experienced in the fourth century (see p. 100) continued in the Hellenistic era. The gulf between the haves and the have-nots widened, the poorer population continued to make demands for land reforms and the cancellation of debts, and the cities continued to be torn apart by social conflicts. The oligarchic governments of several city states were overthrown in bloody revolts and the rich were robbed. These uprisings were too radical and their triumphs were consequently short-lived; time and time again the oligarchs managed to return to power. In many cities only persons of above a certain property qualification enjoyed citizen rights and were entitled to sit on the councils.

When Greece came under Roman domination the Roman rulers supported the ruling elite because they found a small oligarchy easier to control than an unpredictable democracy. For many of the poor, one of the few remaining ways of earning a living was by hiring themselves out as mercenaries in the armies of the great Hellenistic kingdoms; that way they stood a chance of being allowed to settle in a veteran colony. The populations of the cities in Greece consequently decreased even further. Cities such as Athens and Corinth lost their positions as leading trade centers to newly emerged powerful cities like Alexandria in Egypt and Antioch in Syria, and to Rhodes.

The Near East

The conquests of Alexander the Great did not bring about any great economic or social changes in the Near East. The Egyptian economy remained a redistribution economy. Thanks to the many Greek papyri that have survived from the Hellenistic era we are better informed about the Egyptian economy of this period. The state controlled all agricultural activity by determining what crops were to be sown and providing the seed for those crops. Products were processed in state enterprises; private retail traders had to charge consumers set prices for their products. The chief aim of Ptolemaic politics was to fill the treasury with precious metals by imposing high taxes and customs dues and exporting grain and other products. The high taxes made things very difficult for the peasants. Some no longer managed to make ends meet and fled from their land. Things were to become even worse in the Roman period.

In the Seleucid kingdom, too, economic conditions remained virtually unchanged. The land remained in the hands of the palace, the temples, and private landowners. Most of the work was done by the native peasant population. We don't know much about their social status. Many were bound to the land they tilled: if that land was sold, they were included in the transaction. They had to work for the person or institution that owned the land, that is, the king, a temple, a private landowner, or a citizen. A king would sometimes grant favored private individuals large plots of land with entire villages on them. We know virtually nothing about small landowners. Slavery, which was such an important factor in Greek economy, was of much less significance in the Near East, because Near Eastern societies had from the outset always included a large dependent element and so there was no great demand for slaves. There may well have been a demand for slaves in the industrial cities where many Greeks settled. Many of the people who were taken captive in the numerous wars were sold into slavery. Sometimes their families managed to purchase their freedom before they were taken to the slave markets, but most ended up as slaves in Rome (see p. 180) or in other slave-importing states.

Trade intensified in the Hellenistic era because more money became available. Alexander had put the large quantities of gold stored in the Persian treasuries into circulation and the government's investments in armies and fleets, new cities, and building projects boosted industry.

Trade from Egypt and Western Asia to India, via the Red Sea and the Persian Gulf, intensified. India supplied mainly pepper, southern Arabia incense.

The many wars had an ambivalent effect on the economy. On the one hand the fighting caused a lot of damage. The Babylonian astronomical diaries tell us that grain prices soared between *c.* 324 and 300. That's because Babylonia was a constant seat of battle of the *diadochoi*. Inflation, moreover, increased substantially when the Persian gold was brought into circulation. Babylonia was affected less by all this after 300, by which time the Seleucid kingdom was firmly established and the wars were taking place at the periphery of the kingdom. It was only with the arrival of the Parthians that the fighting moved back into Babylonia, resulting in permanent instability and high prices.

On the other hand the wars implied great wealth for the victors. Income from taxes and booty enabled many cities to expand and flourish, in particular the capitals Seleucia, Antioch, and Alexandria. And the wealth in turn attracted trade and industry.

CULTURAL ASPECTS

General

The Greek cities played an important part in spreading Greek culture across the Near East. Tens of thousands of Greeks flocked to those cities, taking their language, their religion, their educational systems, and their traditions along with them. School masters, rhetoricians and teachers of grammar, literature, geometry, the theory of music, and other subjects settled in all of the Greek cities. The wealthy citizens employed private teachers to teach their children the literary culture of the elite. Children also received physical education. Many cities organized athletic contests modeled on the Olympic Games. Athletics started to be practiced as a profession—a development that was to intensify in the Roman period. All these aspects of Greek culture were taught and practiced in the gymnasia. Every self-respecting city also had a theater, besides temples and offices for the city's administration.

Similar Greek buildings soon arose in the Near Eastern cities, too. The notables in those cities learned the Greek language and adopted Greek customs to varying extents. We must, however, bear in mind that it was mainly the upper classes in these Near Eastern cities that underwent this "Hellenizing" influence; beneath this thin Greek veneer the original culture lived on. In Babylonia, for example, chronicles, astronomical diaries, horoscopes, and contracts continued to be written in the cuneiform script. Indeed, this period even saw a revival of Sumerian religious literature. In Egypt, temples continued to be built in the Egyptian style, their walls decorated with hieroglyphic texts. Large numbers of papyri written in Egyptian script have survived from the Hellenistic era, besides those in Greek. Native authors who wrote about the history and culture of their own peoples in the Greek language betray a certain national pride *vis-à-vis* their conquerors. Such feelings are for example evident in the works of the Egyptian Manetho (see p. 14) and the Babylonian Berossus and in the writings of Flavius Josephus from Judea, who lived in the early Roman imperial age (37–*c.* AD 100).

There was very little merging of Near Eastern and Greek cultures into a new, Hellenistic culture. Greek and Near Eastern architectural styles were for example to be found side by side. The same holds for the scenes that were painted on the walls of Egyptian tombs. Sometimes a building or a wall painting shows elements of both styles, but they are then usually not combined

FIGURE 11.3 The dying Gaul—a typical example of Hellenistic sculpture: third century BC

Notes. The Gauls and Celts are topics of heated debate (pp. 238–41). Who were they and where did they live? In the works of Greek authors the term "Celts" is often used to collectively refer to all the peoples who lived north of Marseille. Some scholars now believe that the Celts came from northeastern France and southern Germany—the area of the archaeological La Tène culture. After 500 BC their territory must have gradually spread over the whole of Gaul, northwestern Spain, the Alps, the Po valley, Bohemia, and the British Isles (but whether they were indeed occupied by Celts was open to doubt even in antiquity).The people we call Gauls lived in the Po valley, France, and the adjacent German Rhineland and Belgium. In 279 tribes of "Celts" migrated from central Europe into Greece and Asia Minor. They settled in central Anatolia, where they had to put up many fights against the surrounding Hellenistic kingdoms. Those people were referred to as Galatians. The kings of Pergamum (in northwest Asia Minor) won great fame in their battles against them.

into a harmonious ensemble. This cultural division must also be borne in mind in the following discussions of the religion, philosophy, and science of these civilizations.

Greek religion

In the Greek world, the ancient myths about the Homeric deities had already been criticized in the Classical period; new ways of thinking had emerged that propagated more sublime conceptions of the gods and encouraged a more personal religious experience. We have previously mentioned for example the religious views of Xenophanes (see p. 80) and Plato (see p. 114) and the personal devotion of the initiates of the mysteries of Demeter at Eleusis. These trends continued in the Hellenistic era. More and more Greeks began to lose faith in the ancient Olympian gods. That is not to say that they became less religious or that the existence of the deities was widely denied. All the new Greek cities for example chose one of the Olympian gods as their patron deity, just like the *poleis* of the Greek homeland had done. And the Greek gods were honored in the gymnasia. Nevertheless we get the impression that the gods acquired a more universal character. This is particularly true of the supreme god Zeus, who was sublimed into a general divine power in philosophical works. The declining faith in the Olympian pantheon is also apparent from the worship of the abstractions Fate and Fortune as personalized goddesses. In the past, Fate had been regarded as an impersonal, arbitrary power over which even the gods had no control.

The contacts with the Near East had a profound influence on the Greeks' religious thought and practice. The Greeks started to identify their own gods with foreign gods (e.g., Zeus with other supreme gods such as the Syrian god of the sky Baal Shamen, the Egyptian Amon, the Babylonian Marduk, and even the God of Israel). But the Greeks also included new gods in their pantheon, the best-known examples being the gods of the Egyptians. The cult of the Egyptian goddess Isis, for example, became quite widespread in the Hellenistic world and later also in the Roman world. The goddess was, however, greatly Hellenized to make her acceptable to the Greeks. This is clearly apparent from the way in which she is portrayed in the visual arts and from the hymns that were dedicated to her. She was on a higher level than the Greek deities. She was even believed to be more powerful than Fate. Here we see a clear example of a trend toward henotheism. In Egypt, Isis remained the same Egyptian deity she had always been and people continued to worship her in the usual Egyptian manner. There was consequently a difference between the Egyptian and the Greek Isis cult.

The declining influence of the ancient gods is also apparent from the appearance of the ruler cult. The ruler was regarded as a god who moved among mortals, as a savior and a benefactor. In a hymn to Demetrius Poliorcetes, the "Besieger" who had freed Athens from the Macedonian garrison in 307, he and his father, Antigonus the One-Eyed, are honored as divine saviors. The hymn explicitly states that Demetrius succeeded where the other gods had failed. What is rather odd is that in this same hymn he is referred to as a son of Poseidon. This spontaneously emerged ruler cult, which became particularly popular in the Greek cities on the west coast of Asia Minor, differed from the

FIGURE 11.4 Sculpture of Poseidon, the god of the sea, from the island of Melos: second century BC state cults that the Seleucid and Ptolemaic kings instituted after some time, first for their deceased predecessors and later also for themselves and their wives.

Another way in which people sought security was by turning to mystery religions. Although cults like that of Eleusis had already existed for several centuries (see p. 79), mystery cults, revolving around Greek or Near Eastern deities (see p. 259), became far more widespread in the Hellenistic and Roman periods.

FIGURE 11.5 Fragment of a mummy shroud from Thebes: Roman imperial age, second century AD

Notes. The deceased is represented in a Roman style. His head is surrounded by a halo. The halo motif has a long history of use. It is to be found on Greek vases and Etruscan mirrors from the fifth century BC, but became particularly popular in the Roman imperial age. First it was used only for gods and heroes, later also for emperors, notables, and the deceased. In Christian art only Christ was originally represented with a halo; later on, the Virgin Mary and other important saints and also angels were shown with haloes.

To the right of the deceased is a mummified Osiris. Part of the sun boat and Re-Harakhte (Re-Horus of the Horizon), represented with a falcon's head and the solar disk, are visible on his chest.

A final example of Near Eastern influences on the West that should be mentioned here is that of Babylonian astrology. The Greeks and Romans copied the Babylonians in naming planets after deities. The Greeks called the Babylonian planet Marduk "Zeus," while the Romans later named it "Jupiter." Likewise, Ishtar became Aphrodite and Venus, respectively. "Chaldean" astrologers were renowned for their art of divination. Their influence is still noticeable today.

Near Eastern religions

In the cities and temples of the ancient Near East, Oriental deities continued to be worshipped with little evidence of Greek influences. Cult practices, prayers, and temples all retained their traditional forms and the kings encouraged these cults. Kings and officials would regularly visit the Temple of Marduk in Babylon to make offerings to the gods. The New Year's Feast was still celebrated and the kings sometimes participated in the celebrations. The rites practiced in Babylon are known to us from copies of ancient texts from the Seleucid era. In Egypt, the kings respected the cult of the Egyptian god Ptah and the holy bull Apis at Memphis. The Jewish temple worship at Jerusalem likewise continued, in spite of a certain degree of Hellenization of the priestly elite (see below).

It was Asia Minor that felt the influence of Greece the most. Inscriptions found in that region show that the native languages were increasingly supplanted by Greek. As the west coast of Asia Minor had been Greek for many centuries, this is not all that surprising. However, in Asia Minor, too, the deities who were awarded Greek names often remained Near Eastern in character. Syrian religion became more Greek when Antioch was made a capital of the Seleucid kingdom. The degree of Hellenization differed from one area to another, depending on the impact of the Greeks' presence. Sometimes the opposite would happen and Greeks would start to worship Near Eastern deities. Generally speaking, however, the religious practices of the Greeks and those of the Near Eastern natives remained distinctly separate.

Philosophy

The fact that most Greeks became subject to large Greco-Macedonian empires and the subsequent decline of the role of the Greek city state (*polis*) as an independent political unit are also reflected in Greek philosophy. Man was regarded more as a world citizen (a "cosmo-politan") than as a *polis* citizen. A consequence of this was that philosophers began to see man more as an individual than as a member of a citizen body. Attention shifted to man's personal responsibilities and personal ethics and to the question of how an individual can achieve happiness.

The principal schools of thought outside the Academy and the Lyceum, which still existed, were those of the Stoics, the Epicureans, and the Cynics. The Stoics (so called after the Stoa, a colonnade in Athens where Zeno, the founder of this school of thought, taught his pupils) maintained that the cosmos was governed by a rational divine power, which permeated every aspect of the cosmos. This power, which was referred to as *logos* (word, reason), but also as *theos* (god), controlled everything; something of this divine power resided in man, too. All things had their own purpose and their own place in the natural order. Man therefore had to accept whatever happened to him in life with "Stoic" equanimity and he had to "live according to nature." He was to free himself of strong emotions, he was to be self-sufficient, and was to allow himself to be governed entirely by his reason, which most closely resembled the ordering power governing nature. "Freedom" to the Stoics meant freedom from anxiety, which was superior to the old notion of political freedom enjoyed by a *polis*. The Stoics' doctrines opened up paths for the diffusion of Babylonian astrology, which was based on the assumption that there is a direct relation between the cosmos and life on earth. It was probably with good reason that a Stoic school of philosophy was established in Babylon in the 140s BC.

Epicurus regarded pleasure as the highest ideal. This, he believed, was to be attained not in a dissolute life of partying, but by freeing oneself from one's passions and fears. He therefore condemned magic, superstition, and fear of the gods, which terrorized people's lives. Like Democritus, Epicurus believed that everything consisted of atoms (see p. 80), but the movement of those atoms was in his opinion not governed by a controlling spirit, but by chance. That is also the main reason why all that man could aspire to was personal happiness.

The Cynics (dog-like, living like dogs) reacted against the contemporary conventional way of life. They taught that man must be entirely self-sufficient. The happiest man is he who can make do without anything. The Cynics saw little point in intellectual education. In their opinion the most virtuous man automatically made the best king; such a person did not require any education as he already knew how to rule his kingdom. The Cynics, including the school's founder Diogenes of Sinope, traveled around the Greek cities, begging for their living and giving moralizing speeches at markets.

Science

In the Hellenistic era a distinction arose between philosophy and the sciences. The sciences flourished in Alexandria in particular. They were greatly encouraged by Ptolemy I, who founded the "Museum" in that city—a center of scientific learning that also contained a library. Among the most famous scholars who worked there were Aristarchus of Samos, who propounded the theory that the sun was at the center of the universe, Eratosthenes of Cyrene, who calculated the earth's circumference, and Archimedes of Syracuse, renowned for the law of hydrostatics named after him and for his designs for military machines. Philologists made critical editions of Greek works which, partly on account of their critical note, became "classics" in their time. Medical science, for which Hippocrates had laid the foundations in the fifth century, also flourished and enjoyed great popularity. Many cities appointed doctors, whom they paid to provide medical treatment.

As far as we know, the philosophers and scientists mentioned above were all of Greek origin, with the exception of Zeno, who was a Semitic scholar from Cyprus. Their theories were hence essentially Greek. The greatest scholars in the field of astronomy were, however, to be found in Egypt and Babylon. Astronomical observations were recorded in cuneiform script in Babylonia until the first century AD. Aristotle had these observations sent to him during Alexander's life. Astronomical works written in the Persian era were translated into Greek. In Hellenistic Babylon, astronomy underwent a scientific revolution and Babylonian knowledge was used in Alexandria.

The Jews in the Hellenistic era

In the days of the Persian empire, after thousands of exiled Jews had returned from Babylonia, Judah had developed into a small temple state within the large satrapy known as "Beyond the River" (see Map 4.3, p. 42). After the conquests of Alexander the Great this state first came under Ptolemaic rule. Around 200 Antiochus III incorporated it in his Seleucid kingdom. There were, however, also large numbers of Jews living outside Judah. For a start, quite a few had remained in Babylon; many others had gone to Egypt, to serve in the Egyptian army or for other reasons. Alexandria had a very large Jewish community. These Jews are said to have lived "in the Diaspora" (*diaspora* being the Greek word for dispersal).

The Jews, too, of course became acquainted with Greek civilization, and some Jewish thinkers, especially in Alexandria, were greatly influenced by it. Many of the Jews in Alexandria could speak only Greek. For their benefit a Greek translation was made of the Old Testament (the *Septuaginta*). Jerusalem also underwent Greek influences. A gymnasium was built in the city and some citizens (even the high priests Jason and Menelaos) adopted Greek customs. But neither the Ptolemaic nor the Seleucid rulers ever tried to convert the Jews to the Hellenistic way of life.

In 168 BC the Jews rose against the Seleucids, when Antiochus IV Epiphanes invaded Egypt and the Romans forced him to retreat. A group of Jews in Jerusalem felt that this was a good moment to cast off the Seleucid yoke. Jason, a high priest dismissed by Antiochus, tried to regain his office. However, Antiochus soon suppressed the revolt and garrisoned Syrian soldiers near Jerusalem. For the benefit of those soldiers he installed a cult object dedicated to the Syrian god Baal Shamen (the "Lord of the Heavens," Zeus Olympios to the Greeks) in the temple. Jewish customs such as the observance of the Sabbath were banned and pigs (unclean animals according to Jewish law) were to be sacrificed in the temple. To

FIGURE 11.6 Statuette representing Isis: Roman period, second century AD

Notes. In the Ptolemaic and Roman periods Isis was identified with Thermoutis, the snake goddess of fertility and harvest. This is an example of a hybrid work of art. It features Egyptian symbols (the crown of Isis), the face and body are represented in a typically Greek manner, and the snake is again an Egyptian motif.

orthodox monotheistic Jews this was totally intolerable and a new uprising consequently broke out. This revolt was led by Judas Maccabaeus. As the power of the Seleucid dynasty gradually weakened in the incessant succession struggles that followed the death of Antiochus, the revolt was ultimately successful. In 152 the Maccabees claimed the offices of high priest and general from one of the pretenders to the throne. Ten years later Judah was granted exemption from taxation and acquired *de facto* independence following the disbandment of the Seleucid garrison. In 104 the Maccabees granted their leader the title of king (the Hasmonean dynasty). The Maccabees expanded Judah into a large kingdom and forced subject non-Jews to adopt Jewish customs, such as circumcision.

Our knowledge of this period we owe mainly to two Bible books, "I and II Maccabees," which are included in the *Septuaginta*, but not in the Hebrew Bible. The authors of the Books of Maccabees decried the Greek influences and Greek customs of the pre-Maccabean priests in Judah. In spite of this, the Hasmonean kings, too, were becoming more and more Hellenized; they chose Greek names for themselves and even called themselves "Phil-Hellene" (friendly to the Greeks). Within their kingdom they sought support sometimes among the rather aristocratic Sadducees, at other times among the Pharisees, who were more popular among the common people. The Sadducees were members of the old-established rich families of priests who had long since dominated the temple in Jerusalem, while the Pharisees were learned scholars specializing in Biblical law. The Sadducees accepted only the first five books of the Hebrew Bible (the *Thora*) as authoritative, the Pharisees the later ones (Prophets and Wisdom Literature), too, and also the oral tradition. The Sadducees focused on the temple in Jerusalem, whereas the Pharisees also traveled to other cities and villages to explain the Scriptures in synagogues.

The Hasmonean dynasty was weakened by internal succession struggles, in which the Romans ultimately intervened. In 63 the Romans incorporated Judea in the province of Syria. The Roman commander Pompey captured Jerusalem and sold many Jews on the slave markets. This led to the formation or intensification of a Jewish *diaspora* in several parts of the Roman empire and also in Rome itself.

THE IMPACT OF HELLENISTIC CULTURE IN THE PARTHIAN KINGDOM AND THE ROMAN EMPIRE

The Parthian kingdom originated in the Persian satrapy Parthia (see Map 4.3, p. 42), which is known to have already existed during the reign of Darius I. In the middle of the third century BC the Parni, a Scytho-Iranian tribe, invaded the satrapy, drove away the Greek satrap, who had then only just acquired independence, and founded a new dynasty. In the course of the third and second centuries BC the Parthians, as the Parni were now called, conquered Iran and Mesopotamia. The members of the Parthian dynasty considered themselves to be the heirs to the Persian empire; the Persians, however, regarded the Parthians as foreigners.

The Parthian kings soon started to call themselves "Phil-Hellene" on their coins to please the Greeks in their kingdom. The power of the Parthians was based on a strong cavalry, composed of Parthian nobles, but the kingdom lacked sufficient manpower and organizational expertise to form an effective administrative apparatus. It was hence not long before large numbers of vassal kingdoms emerged alongside the satrapies. At the same time, the Greek cities in the kingdom acquired considerable local autonomy.

The language used for official purposes was Greek, but in the first century AD the Parthian language (an Iranian language written in Aramaic script) became increasingly important and Greek culture was suppressed. A new Greco-Iranian style of architecture evolved, which found expression especially in the new cities. Some of these cities were built on the sites of former cities, such as Ctesiphon, the new capital which was built opposite Seleucia, and Hatra and Assur. According to Aramaic texts, the cult of the god Ashur continued or was revived in Assur. Buildings designed in the new Parthian style arose in Uruk and Babylon, too. The new and rebuilt cities attracted many Iranian, Aramaic, Arabic, and Jewish immigrants. Mesopotamia became a cauldron of foreign peoples and cultures. The ancient Sumero-Akkadian civilization, which had lived on in a language that had gone out of ordinary use a long time ago and whose last bulwarks Babylon and Uruk had suffered severe damage in the wars, was ultimately obliterated by all these foreign influences. This was, however, probably a long process, with the final blow occurring in the Neo-Persian era of the Sasanid dynasty (see p. 268).

The parts of the Hellenistic world that came under Roman sway continued to feel the influence of Greek culture for a long time yet. This was because the Romans themselves had already been assimilating elements of Greek culture for many centuries. The cultural traditions of the ancient Near East, however, gradually waned. In economic terms, Egypt faced hard times under the Romans. Large amounts of grain and other products such as gold from southern Egypt disappeared to Rome in the form of extortionate taxes. The Ptolemies had also imposed high taxes, but most of that money had been reinvested in the Egyptian economy. The native Egyptians reacted to the exploitation of the Greco-Roman elite rulers by adopting the Christian faith at a very early stage or by vehemently adhering to their own religion. The latter came to a definitive end when the Christian (East) Roman emperor Justinian closed the temple of Isis at Philae, the last heathen stronghold, shortly before AD 550.

CONCLUSION

Some historians claim that the Near Eastern world became entirely Hellenized after Alexander's conquests. That is not correct. Only the elite of the large cities became acquainted with Greek culture and adopted various elements of that culture. Nowhere in the Near East did Greek become the common spoken language, except in Asia Minor and in very large cities like Alexandria, where many Greeks lived together.

Something else that is often maintained is that Hellenistic civilization is a blend of Greek and Near Eastern elements. That is not correct either. What actually happened is that a combination of diverse factors moved Greek civilization into a new phase, in which it borrowed certain elements from the Near East. At the same time, the various cultures of the Near East assimilated Greek influences in varying degrees. We sometimes see this reflected in the art of these days in the form of hybrid works (see Figure 11.5). Juxtaposition is, however, a more apt characterization of the cultural situation than fusion.

PART III ROME

12 EARLY ROMAN HISTORY (753–265 BC)

THE WESTERN MEDITERRANEAN

The history of the civilization of the western Mediterranean differs from that of the ancient world further east.

In the third and second millennia BC there were in the West no highly civilized centers of the kind that were then to be found in Egypt, Western Asia, Crete, and Greece. For these two thousand years the western Mediterranean remained shrouded in the veils of prehistory. Only between 800 and 500 BC, that is, in the period coinciding with the Archaic period of Greek history and the era of the Assyrian, Babylonian, and Persian empires in Western Asia (pp. 36–44), did civilizations comparable with those of the East emerge in the western Mediterranean. They are the civilizations of the Etruscans in central Italy, the Carthaginians in North Africa (Tunisia), and the Greeks in the Greek colonies in southern Italy, Sicily, and southern Gaul (Map 12.1). The tribes living in the surroundings of these peoples were less civilized. We know only very little about their traditions and social organization.

The Etruscans

The Etruscans lived in city states that were associated in a loose federal organization. All cultural life and administrative affairs were concentrated in the urban centers of these city states; Etruscan civilization was very much an urban civilization. The Etruscan cities became quite wealthy thanks to the high workmanship of their craft products, especially their metalwork and pottery. Metals and metal objects from Etruria were important merchandise all over the Mediterranean.

The Etruscans were probably a class of aristocrats who ruled over the native Italian population. Their origins were already a matter of debate in antiquity. Some scholars claim that they originated in Italy itself; others believe that they came from Asia Minor. The latter maintain that the Etruscans' art of divination, which involved observing the flight of birds (Latin: *auspicia*) and studying the livers of sacrificed animals, was also practiced in Mesopotamia and Asia Minor (see p. 49), and that the few Etruscan words that have come down to us are reminiscent of

Rome and Latium

Carthaginian sphere of influence

Greeks

Etruscans

MAP 12.1 The (western) Mediterranean in the fifth and fourth centuries BC

languages spoken in Asia Minor. What we do know for certain is that these words are not Indo-European, whereas almost all the other languages that were spoken in Italy in these days did belong to the Indo-European family.

Etruscan civilization was a blend including Near Eastern, Italian, and Greek elements. The Greek elements reflect the influences of the Greek colonies that were founded in the western Mediterranean from the beginning of the Archaic period onwards (see pp. 179 and 117). Those influences extended to the other occupants of western Italy, too. Etruscan civilization reached its height in the seventh and sixth centuries BC. In that period the Etruscans had control over central Italy, large parts of the Po valley, and Campania in southern Italy (see Map 12.2). After 500 BC, however, the increasing competition of the Greeks (pp. 117–18) and the invasions of the Celts (Gauls) gradually undermined their power. Some time after 400 BC the Celts conquered the Po valley and repeatedly raided central Italy.

Carthage

Carthage was founded in the ninth or eighth century BC by colonists from the Phoenician city of Tyre (see p. 117). It was one of the military bases and trading posts that the Phoenicians founded along their shipping routes in the western Mediterranean (see Map 12.1; also see Map 9.1b, p. 71). When pressure from the Assyrians (p. 38) caused Tyre's power to decline, Carthage assumed control over the Phoenician network of trading posts and bases in the western

FIGURE 12.1   Etruscan tomb painting

Notes. The Etruscans buried their dead in *necropoleis* ("cities of the dead"). The tombs were beautifully decorated and the deceased were accompanied by a wide range of goods. Excavations in these *necropoleis* have taught us a good deal about the Etruscans.

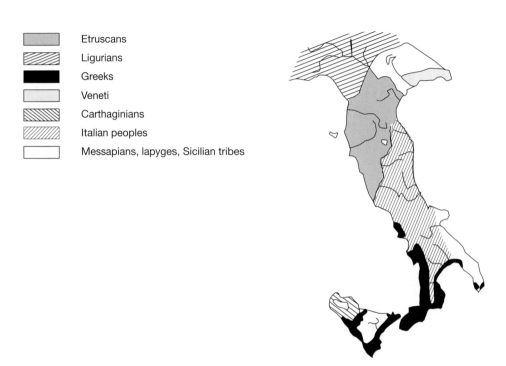

Etruscans
Ligurians
Greeks
Veneti
Carthaginians
Italian peoples
Messapians, Iapyges, Sicilian tribes

MAP 12.2 Peoples living in Italy, c. 600 BC

Mediterranean and founded a few new colonies herself, too. Those colonies, in North Africa, were essentially agricultural settlements.

Carthage was a prosperous city. Her wealth was partly based on her maritime trade in the western Mediterranean, the import of gold from Senegal and tin from Western Europe, and partly on her highly developed agricultural activities in her own African hinterland. The city's population was not large enough to enable her to man her mercantile ships, her war fleet, and her army all at the same time, and Carthage's wars were consequently fought predominantly with hired mercenaries, mostly from North Africa and Spain.

As far as shipping is concerned, Carthage held a near monopoly in the southwest Mediterranean and on the Atlantic Ocean between West Africa and the British Isles. To defend this position, she had established a network of fortified bases in western Sicily, Sardinia, North Africa, and Spain (see Map 12.1). Carthage was always prepared to engage in warfare whenever any of her bases were threatened. This was one of the causes of the constant wars between the Greeks and the Carthaginians in Sicily (pp. 117–18) and of the fierce battle between Carthage and Rome in the third century BC (pp. 168–72).

Carthage was governed by a class of large landowners and rich merchants that also included a few families which provided the army and navy commanders over several generations.

THE ORIGINS OF ROME

The first people to have settled at the site of what was later to become the city of Rome belonged to a tribe known as the Latins. They spoke Latin, an Indo-European language. The Latins probably arrived in Italy some time in the last centuries of the second millennium BC. From the tenth to the sixth century, Latium, which contained Rome, was characterized by a homogeneous culture attributed to the Latins that had a lot in common with the culture of the Etruscans.

According to Roman legend, Rome was founded in 753 BC by Romulus, who became the first king of Rome. From archaeological evidence we know that by that date there had for some time been settlements on the Palatine hill and a few other hills along the Tiber. Those settlements were in these early days apparently occupied by farmers who practiced fairly simple forms of agriculture, stock-keeping, and horticulture. It is nowadays often assumed that they were organized in family groups headed by "aristocratic" leaders—the *patres* ("fathers") of those groups.

The aforementioned hills lay in what was then the border region between Latium and Etruria; to the north of the Tiber lay the territory of the Etruscan city of Veii. The earliest Roman population was probably a mixture of Latins, Etruscans, and Sabines (a tribe that lived in the hills to the northeast of Rome).

FIGURE 12.2   The she-wolf that allegedly suckled Romulus and Remus: 480–470 BC

Notes. The figures of the twins, Romulus and Remus, are later additions (AD 1510). According to Roman legend, Romulus and Remus founded Rome. They were believed to have been born from a union of the god Mars with Rhea Silvia, the daughter of a Latin king. They were abandoned by a usurper, who deposed Rhea's father, and were kept alive by a she-wolf.

Towards 600 BC the influence of the Etruscans—and possibly also that of the Greeks—increased. It is only then that Rome grew into a true city, with a market surrounded by buildings and stone temples. After 600 Rome rapidly expanded into one of the largest cities in Italy. The city was favorably situated, in a fertile, relatively densely populated region, at the junction of an important road linking Etruria to the Greek and Etruscan settlements in Campania, a shipping route (the Tiber) and a road to the salt-pans at the coast (salt was an extremely important commodity in the ancient world).

Tradition has it that Rome was first ruled by seven kings (753–509 BC). The first four are largely legendary figures. Later Roman authors were to attribute many Roman institutions and customs to those kings to demonstrate their great antiquity and venerability. The last three kings, Tarquinius Priscus, Servius Tullius, and Tarquinius Superbus, ruled in the sixth century BC. They most probably came from Etruria.

FIGURE 12.3 "Brutus": third or second century BC

Notes. The sculpture is now on display in the Palazzo dei Conservatori in Rome. According to Roman tradition, L(ucius) Junius Brutus expelled the last king and established the republic (509 BC).

State and society in early Rome

Archaeological finds, such as the objects with which the deceased were buried, and evidence in the works of later Roman authors suggest that the population of Rome in her earliest days (seventh and sixth centuries BC) was already characterized by some degree of social differentiation. There was an upper layer of aristocratic families who owned a relatively large proportion of the available land, there was a class of well-to-do peasants, and below them was a class of poorer peasants. The farms were still almost all self-sufficient family units, but by now the stage of shepherds practicing small-scale crop cultivation was definitely a thing of the past. Craftsmen lived and worked in the city of Rome. On the basis of later evidence it is assumed that many of the peasants, even the more prosperous ones, were dependent on or protected by the aristocrats. Those peasants were called *clientes*, their aristocratic protectors *patroni*. The Latin word *clientes* means something like "dependants." The peasants and craftsmen who did not enjoy the patronage of the aristocrats were later to be referred to as "plebeians." The aristocrats themselves were "patricians." The *clientes*, on whom much of their power depended, were not classed as patricians. Only the members of the aristocratic families who claimed to descend from heroes of Roman legends and folk tales were patricians (*cf.* the *eupatridai* in Athens, p. 84).

From later evidence we know that the kings commanded the army, administered justice, and led the ceremonies for the state deities. As in other states in the ancient world, those were the main administrative tasks.

The kings enjoyed absolute power (Latin: *imperium*) that covered all the fields with which the state concerned itself. They were assisted and advised by the Senate, a council consisting of the heads of the aristocratic families, and they could summon a public assembly, the *Comitia Curiata*. This *Comitia Curiata* was the organ that formally conferred the *imperium* (supreme power involving the right to lead an army) on the kings and consequently sanctioned their position.

Here we find the same three kinds of state organs as in the Archaic Greek *poleis*: an executive authority, an aristocratic council, and a public assembly that had little effective power, but was nevertheless the body that sanctioned the executive authority.

The *Comitia Curiata* consisted of thirty *curiae*, which each had a vote. A *curia* consisted of a number of *gentes* (plural of *gens*), that is, clans, groups of families, who claimed to be linked by a common ancestor and who shared certain traditions. A gens was a group of several *familiae*. A *familia* was comparable with a Greek household in the Homeric era (see p. 66). It consisted of a husband and wife and their children (whether or not married), grandchildren, slaves, and *clientes*.

Within the family, the *pater familias*, the male head of the family, enjoyed absolute authority. He had power of life and death over his children and slaves. A woman married into her husband's family and on her wedding day she and her dowry passed under the authority of the *pater familias* of her husband's family.

The authority of the *pater familias* has been compared to that of the king. Just as the king enjoyed unrestricted authority over the affairs of the *res publica*, the Roman state, so the *pater familias* had absolute control over his *res privata*, his private household. And just as the king presided over the cult of the state gods, so the *pater familias* led the simple daily offerings and prayers to the household deities, the *Lares* and the *Penates*.

A note on Roman names

The organization in *gentes* and *familiae* was reflected in the names that the Romans were given. Each Roman had at least three names: a personal name (e.g., Publius, abbreviated to P.), a name denoting his *gens* (e.g., Cornelius, of the *gens* Cornelia), and one or more surnames, intended to distinguish the family within the *gens* (e.g., Scipio).

The army and the *Comitia Centuriata*

Originally, the *gentes* were not only groups of families united by strong religious and cultural traditions, but also military units. It is thought that the earliest Roman army was organized on this basis. The aristocrats, at the head of their *gentes*, presumably dominated the battlefields in those days (see pp. 66 and 73). It was probably in the sixth century that the Etruscans and the Romans started to fight in the same way as the contemporary Greeks, in a closed battle array of heavily armed infantrymen (a *phalanx*), surrounded by cavalrymen and lightly armed soldiers.

According to Roman tradition, the penultimate king, Servius Tullius (*c.* 578–535), adapted the organization of civilians to the changed fighting method and divided the civilians into property classes (see p. 84 on Solon).

The wealthiest citizens served in the cavalry. Their horses were provided by the state—a curious form of subsidizing of the rich (see p. 54). The members of this property group were called *equites* (plural of *eques*, "knight, horseman," after *equus*, the Latin word for horse). Almost all the patricians and a few wealthy plebeians belonged to this property group (and consequently to the cavalry). The wealthy peasants served as heavily armed infantrymen, the members of the lower classes as lightly armed soldiers. Propertyless citizens who could not afford to arm themselves did not serve in the army. This classification based on property was also employed in imposing property taxes (*tributum*) and in organizing a new public assembly, the *Comitia Centuriata*, which consequently had the same organization as the contemporary army. There were five property classes, which were each subdivided into *centuriae* (*centuria*—a unit of 100 men). Each *centuria* had one vote. The *centuriae*—and consequently the votes, too—were divided between the five property classes so that the first class with the cavalry could obtain a majority (see box on p. 163). They consequently pulled the strings at the *Comitia Centuriata*. The citizens without property (proletarians), who were excluded from the army organization, sat on this assembly in one added *centuria*. In other words, they collectively had one vote. We note the same direct relation between wealth, military importance, and political power as in some contemporary Greek *poleis* (see pp. 68–88; 107).

The *Comitia Centuriata* gradually superseded the *Comitia Curiata* in many respects, but the latter did continue to exist. We will return to the subject of the Roman popular assemblies at the end of this chapter (pp. 165–6).

THE EARLY REPUBLIC (509–265 BC)

State and society

Around 500 BC—the traditional date is 509—the era of the kings came to an end. Tradition has it that the Romans expelled their last king, Tarquinius Superbus, because they had had enough of his cruelty and arrogance, but it is more likely that the real reasons were the Romans' desire to break away from the Etruscan sphere of influence and rebellion of the nobles, in particular the patricians, against an increasingly powerful kingship. The last kings had focused ever more on the state and the citizenry as a whole, which must have undermined the power of the family groups and their leaders. We note the same development in Roman worship: Tarquinius Superbus commissioned the construction of a large temple on the Capitol hill (Map 12.5) for Jupiter, the supreme god of the collective Roman population. The temple was consecrated in 509, the year in which, according to Roman legend, the Romans put an end to monarchy. For the first fifty years after they had expelled the Etruscan king, the Roman aristocrats progressively directed their look away from Etruria and toward their tribal relatives, the Latins. Rome became an important member of the Latin League of city states. It is believed that the members of this League had shared a form of communal citizen rights, the "Latin rights," since the beginning of the fifth century. These Latin rights granted all the occupants of the League's member states the right to conduct trade with one another and to marry partners from all the member states.

When kingship was abolished in Rome the king's executive power was transferred to two annually elected magistrates, who were later, after 367, to be called "consuls." These magistrates shared the former king's *imperium* (see p. 147), but their power was restricted because they could check one another's acts by right of veto and because their term of office was limited to one year. After that year any dissatisfied citizen could file complaints against them if they so desired. The two ruling magistrates were assisted by two treasurers, or "quaestors," and like the kings before them, they turned to the Senate for advice in administrative affairs. As they usually followed the Senate's advice, the Senate had a powerful say in political affairs. The decisions of the popular assembly acquired the force of law only after they had been approved by the Senate.

The king's religious authority was passed on to the *rex* (king) *sacrorum* (of the *sacra*, the holy, sacred affairs) and the *pontifex maximus*, the president of the college of *pontifices* (the main college of priests). They were responsible for ensuring that the proper practices were observed when prayers and sacrifices were offered to the state gods to secure their favor.

Sometimes, in an emergency, for example when a war or a civil strife took a turn for the worse, the autocratic authority of the former kings would be temporarily restored. In such a situation the ruling magistrates could appoint a *dictator*, who was granted absolute power for six months.

After the fall of the last king the patricians dominated the political scene. It was they who furnished the magistrates and the senators; the *Comitia Centuriata* elected magistrates exclusively from the patriciate and new senators were almost always former magistrates (see below, p. 160). The patricians also provided the *pontifices* and the members of other important priesthoods. There were no true, separate priest castes; the priests were patricians who held the priesthood in addition to their secular offices.

The patricians also controlled every aspect of social and economic life: large numbers of peasants were their *clientes* or had been reduced to an even more dependent status by debts (debt bondage: see p. 85). The patricians were also the only members of society who were familiar with the unwritten laws and the ritual formulas with which pleadings had to be introduced.

However, it was not long before the patricians' powerful position was challenged by groups of dissatisfied plebeians.

The history of the Roman republic up to the third century BC is dominated by two lengthy historical processes:

1   the so-called "struggle of the orders" between the patricians and the plebeians;
2   the expansion of the Roman empire in peninsular Italy.

Roman expansion in Italy (509–265 BC)

The period 509–338 BC was characterized by endless struggles in central Italy between Rome, the Latins, the tribes who lived in the hills around Latium, and the southern Etruscan cities. They fought one another in constantly changing coalitions (see Map 12.3). The main issues of contention were the fertile land in the valleys and coastal plains and the control of the land trade routes between Etruria and Campania. The struggles dragged on for many years because the contending parties were one another's equals in military terms. In her wars against the hill tribes, Rome was usually assisted by the other members of the Latin League, but her battles against the Etruscans she fought largely by herself. In the early fourth century BC Rome managed to annex the southern part of Etruria (including the city of Veii, to the north of the Tiber). With this act Rome gained decisive ascendancy over the other Latin city states in terms of territory and manpower.

MAP 12.3 Rome and her allies, *c.* 350 BC

In the next fifty years Rome had to defend herself not only against the hill tribes, but also against the Latin cities, which were afraid that Rome would try to extend her sway over their territory, too, and against Celtic gangs, who repeatedly pillaged Italy after 400 (see p. 131). Etruria suffered the most from these Celtic raids. It could be said that, by weakening the Etruscan cities, the Celts helped to pave the way for Rome's expansion in Italy.

After 350 the process of expansion in Italy really got under way. In 338 Rome subjected the Latin cities and concluded treaties with the most important city states in Campania. That brought the most fertile and most densely populated regions of central Italy within Rome's sphere of influence and vastly expanded her military resources. Rome now dominated the Latin League's member states. The Latin citizen rights continued to exist: within Rome's territory the Latins remained equal to Roman citizens (and vice versa) in business transactions and marriage law. Latins who took up permanent residence in Rome and renounced the citizen rights of their own city state were entitled to full Roman citizenship.

After 326 a multiplicity of minor local and regional conflicts in different parts of Italy merged into a number of protracted coalition wars (326–290), which came to involve all the peoples in Italy. Rome emerged from these wars as the mistress of the whole of peninsular Italy, with the exception of the Greek cities in the south. Those cities were subjected in the years between 282 and 270, in spite of the help that they received from a general of the Macedonian school, king Pyrrhus of Epirus (see Maps 12.1, p. 142, and 13.1, p. 169). He helped the Greeks in southern Italy fight the Romans and assisted Syracuse in her battle against Carthage. In both wars he achieved spectacular successes. In 275, however, the Romans decisively defeated him at Beneventum (see Map 12.4). Rome entered into a series of individual alliances with the city states and tribes she subjected in Italy: they were made subordinate allies (= *socii*). These allies were

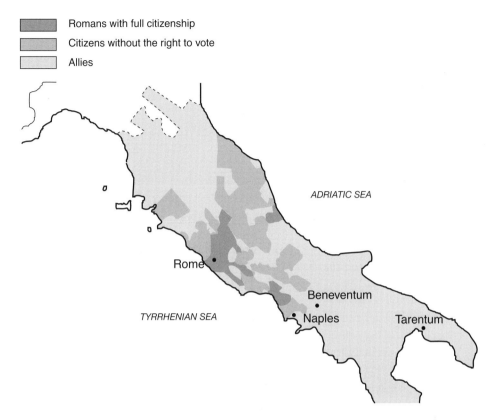

Romans with full citizenship

Citizens without the right to vote

Allies

ADRIATIC SEA

Rome

Beneventum

TYRRHENIAN SEA   Naples

Tarentum

MAP 12.4   Rome and her allies, 241 BC

obliged to supply troops for Rome's wars and to support Rome's foreign politics but they did not have to pay any tributes. They also retained their autonomy in internal affairs and their own citizen rights. They were not granted anything comparable with the Latin rights.

Colonization

Rome founded colonies in most of the lands she conquered. Her custom was to confiscate part of the territory of her subject opponents and to turn it into Roman public land, owned by the Roman state. On this public land (*ager publicus*), Rome settled Roman and Latin peasants with military experience and propertyless Romans and Latins. These colonies were called Latin colonies (*coloniae Latinae*), to distinguish them from the few small colonies that Rome had founded as military bases at strategic points throughout her territory (the *coloniae civium Romanorum*, "colonies of Roman citizens," *coloniae Romanae*—"Roman colonies" for short).

The Latin colonies lay scattered across Italy, usually on fertile soil at road junctions and other strategic points. They were not independent city states; although they enjoyed local autonomy, they were subject to Rome. The colonists were granted Latin rights, which meant that they were entitled to full Roman citizenship if they were ever to return to Rome. The colonists of the small *coloniae Romanae* retained their full Roman citizenship. The plots that the colonists were granted for their support varied in size from half a hectare to ten hectares. In addition to this land, they could also rent part of the land that had not been divided among the colonists. That land was usually exploited on a communal basis. The colonists were also allowed to rent public land. This land consequently became an extra source of income for the Roman treasury, on top of the property taxes.

The public land became a source of competition at an early stage in Roman history. Besides the Roman and Latin colonists, local Italian peasants and wealthy Roman and Italian landowners were all entitled to rent public land. The wealthy had their land tilled by slaves and seasonal workers, many of whom were small proprietors who supplemented their income with the wages of this seasonal work. According to some literary sources, as early as 367, Rome passed a law limiting the amount of public land that any one individual could hold, so as to reassure the poor Roman citizens.

This colonization policy was of great benefit to Rome. In the first place, she acquired a network of strategically based fortifications all over Italy and a means of solving internal conflicts in Rome and Latium by helping poor Roman and Latin citizens to start a new life under better conditions elsewhere. Secondly, the leasing of the public land meant extra income. Another great advantage of this policy was that it implied a considerable growth of Rome's military resources. This was because, if they came to possess sufficient land in a colony, citizens who had hitherto been excluded from the army on the grounds that they had no property (see p. 148) now came to belong to the property classes from which troops were recruited. In some respects (the fact that the colonies were not new city states, the social upgrading of poor citizens, the military strategic considerations underlying the colonization) the Latin and Roman colonies were more like the Athenian cleruchies of the fifth century BC than like the Greek colonies of the Archaic period (see pp. 72 and 93).

Municipia

Roman cities outside Rome that already existed and had not been founded as *coloniae* were called *municipia* (plural of *municipium*). Sometimes Rome would grant a subject city state with a culture and language akin to those of the Romans the status of a Roman city with local autonomy, as a reward for some service or for having voluntarily submitted to Rome's protection. The citizens of such city states had Roman citizen rights without the right to vote; some even enjoyed full Roman citizenship. This was another way in which Rome expanded her territory and her manpower resources.

Rome's colonization policy greatly encouraged the adaptation of the Italian peoples to the organization, language, and culture of the Romans. This process is called "Romanization." The notables who held the high offices in local government everywhere in Italy took the least time to adjust themselves to the Roman way of life. The vast majority of the Italian communities were governed by aristocratic or oligarchic landowning elites, just like Rome herself.

By around 265 BC Italy had become a patchwork of states and regions that stood in different relations to Rome and were bound to Rome in different ways (Map 12.4): the Roman heartland (with full Roman citizenship), the area of the former Latin city states and the *coloniae Latinae* with Latin rights, the *municipia* with citizen rights without the vote, and the allies, who had only

FIGURE 12.4   The Via Appia, the first paved Roman road in Italy

Notes. The Via Appia, which led from Rome to Campania and then on to Brundisium (present-day Brindisi), was started in 312 BC. The paved roads facilitated the rapid movement of troops. These roads and the network of *coloniae* served as means for preventing attacks by the tribes living in central and southern Italy and for the provisioning of Roman armies. Along the road, just outside Rome, lay large funerary monuments of distinguished Roman families.

their own local citizen rights. Rome's system worked well. The majority of the Italian city states and tribes loyally participated in her major wars in the period after 265 (p. 171) and played important parts in her expansionist campaigns in the third and second centuries BC. They never joined forces against Rome because their interests differed owing to the different terms of their alliances with Rome (Rome's "divide and rule" policy) and their different economic structures.

Alongside fairly primitive mountainous areas that were occupied mainly by traditional self-sufficient small farmers and shepherds such as Samnium (southeast of Rome), there were the economically far more developed regions and cities of Etruria and Campania and the Greek coastal towns with their commerce and shipping industry. The more developed areas established close ties with wealthy, powerful Romans far sooner than isolated mountainous areas.

The military character of Roman society

The wars that Rome fought in Italy in the fifth and fourth centuries BC were not as fierce as those which she waged on her enemies after 265, and were nothing like modern wars. They were essentially minor skirmishes and plunderings, which were fought only in the summer season (between March and November; seasonal wars). Only rarely did Rome engage in a pitched battle. Nevertheless, in these wars the Roman citizens came to regard warfare as an ordinary sideline and a lucrative, if hazardous, source of extra income, for it implied the possibility of acquiring booty and land (in the colonies). For the Roman elite, military fame was the chief status symbol, the best means of access to an honorable career in the state offices. Moreover, it was the elite, more than the rest of the population, who benefited from the booty. The many wars gave birth to a wealth of heroic tales and legends that were to influence Roman mentality for many centuries. Over and over again the Romans were exhorted to follow the examples set by their austere, valorous ancestors.

Even so, the Roman leaders felt the need to justify their wars. What they considered valid reasons for starting a war were an attack on Roman territory, aggression towards a Roman ally, violence committed against Roman ambassadors or other Romans in foreign areas and failure to pay damages or extradite individuals guilty of crimes. Warfare did not go against the Romans' religious principles. The Romans believed that they would be able to rely on the help of their gods in a war if that war was being fought for good reasons, if the Romans had prayed to their gods in the right manner and had made the required sacrifices, and if the gods had responded with good omens.

The Romans usually regarded their wars as a form of defense. Large, nearby states were soon seen as a threat and many Roman wars hence started as preventive actions (what we could call "forward defense") or as an act of support to small allies against great powers.

The struggle of the orders (c. 500–287 BC)

While Rome was engaged in her long struggle to extend her hegemony over Italy she also suffered a good deal of internal tension. As we have already seen above (p. 149), the patrician aristocracy had seized power in Rome after the fall of the last king, Tarquinius Superbus. But it was not long before the plebeians started to oppose their power.

The plebeians were not a clearly defined social group. There were rich plebeians, plebeians of moderate means, and poor plebeians, and the activities in which they engaged differed. The rich plebeians were large landowners who had arrived in Rome or had been incorporated into the Roman citizen body after the patricians had closed their ranks. The plebeians of moderate means comprised landowning farmers, who played important parts in Rome's military efforts, and merchants. The poor plebeians were small farmers, craftsmen, and day laborers (see p. 156, Figure 12.5).

The rich plebeians demanded to be admitted to the governing elite monopolized by the patricians, the poor plebeians wanted relaxation of the harsh debt laws (a debtor could be reduced to debt bondage; see p. 85 on Athens in Solon's days). All the plebeians—especially the poor ones—demanded that the main rules of the unwritten law be recorded in a written code, arbitrary acts of the patrician magistrates be checked, and the plebeians' assembly (*Concilium Plebis*) be recognized as an official popular assembly alongside the *Comitia Centuriata*.

Since the fall of the last king the *Comitia Curiata* had become an empty phrase. The plebeians assembled near a group of popular temples on the Aventine hill (Map 12.5); their assemblies were

MAP 12.5 The city of Rome in the republican era

Notes. The public assemblies usually convened in the Campus Martius (field of Mars). That is also where the armies were mustered. The temple of Jupiter was the main center of the cult of the state gods. Jupiter was the supreme god and the patron deity of Rome. The Regia was the house of the *rex sacrorum* (p. 149).

Vesta was the goddess of the domestic hearth. A fire burned near her temple, which was never allowed to go out. Her cult was administered by the Vestal Virgins, priestesses of high birth who were not allowed to marry.

All triumphal processions passed along the Via Sacra. The chariot races (popular games) were held in the Circus Maximus. *Emporium* = quaysides and warehouses.

led by *tribuni plebis* ("tribunes of the *plebs*") and *aediles* ("temple guards"). The *aediles* were originally the guards of the temples on the Aventine hill. The plebeians were in a powerful position because their middle ranks (mainly the landowning farmers) formed the backbone of the army: it was they who provided a large portion of the heavily armed infantry, the most important part of the armed forces. Without them, it was virtually impossible for Rome to form an army.

History of the struggle of the orders

During the many years that the so-called struggle of the orders was to last, the situation in Rome became quite critical on several occasions. This was in most cases the consequence of the poor plebeians' debt problems, which sharpened the social contrasts. When things got really bad and the entire plebeian body seceded from political life and refused to participate in Rome's military enterprises, the patricians made political concessions, after which the rebellion would die down. New wars would then temporarily distract attention from the internal problems and the subsequent division of booty and the settlement of poor citizens in colonies would ease a lot of the tension. This form of "social relief" proved effective, especially in the years between 350 and 270—the heydays of Rome's expansion in Italy. In 326 the problem of the debts was reduced by the abolition of debt bondage.

The most important political concessions that the patricians made to the plebeians were:

- **494 BC**: the recognition of the tribunes as the official champions of the plebeians. The tribunes of the *plebs* were elected annually (for a term of one year) in the *Concilium Plebis*. They became a kind of "anti-magistrates" as against the governing patrician magistrates. The latter were called consuls after 367. The tribunes had the right to intercede to prevent the implementation of what they considered arbitrary decisions of the patrician magistrates. They could for example veto measures that went against the interests of the *plebs* and they could prevent arbitrary arrests. They were also the presiding officers at the *Concilium Plebis*.

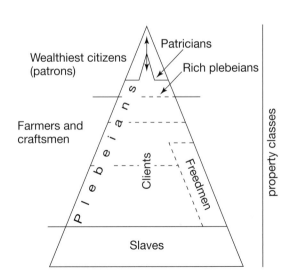

FIGURE 12.5
Social structure of the early republic

- **451 BC**: the first codification of a number of laws in the Twelve Tables. These laws consisted of a collection of concrete mandatory and prohibitory provisions and the penalties exacted if they should be violated ("if a person does this or that, then . . ."). Many of the penalties were based on the principle of an eye for an eye. Their main aim was probably to prevent blood feuds. These laws were of course rather primitive. Nevertheless, they were to form the basis for Roman civil law (see pp. 236–7). The introduction of this written legislation can be seen as a victory of the citizen body over the old system dominated by family groups in that it signified more state and less power of private family groups. Making justice and laws public reduced the power of leaders who had hitherto enjoyed the advantage of being the only ones who were familiar with the procedures and rules. From now onwards the rules (some of them at least) were more commonly accessible for consultation.
- **367 BC**: the *leges Liciniae Sextiae* ("Licinian-Sextian laws," so named after the two tribunes behind the laws, C. Licinius and L. Sextius, who had for years thwarted the election of magistrates as a means of coercion) admitted wealthy plebeians to the highest administrative office, which was from this year onwards called the consulship. It was decided that one of the two consuls was to be a plebeian, though this was to become standard practice only after 342 BC. Moreover, a new office was created: the praetorship. The consuls' main task was to command the armies, while the praetors (there was first only one, but a second was soon added) were to concern themselves mainly with the administration of justice. We will return to the matter of jurisdiction in Chapter 15 (pp. 236–7).

  It was probably in this same year that measures were taken to put an end to the concentration of public land in the hands of a small number of rich landowners (see p. 152).
- **287 BC**: the *Lex Hortensia* (so named after Q. Hortensius, who was appointed dictator to put an end to a "strike" of plebeians who seceded to the Janiculan hill): recognition of the *Concilium Plebis* as an official popular assembly. The decrees of this assembly (*plebiscita*) were recognized as having force of law (*lex*) and were binding on the whole Roman population (including the patricians, who did not attend this assembly). They did not require the Senate's sanction. From now onwards, the Senate only advised on legislative proposals before the assembly voted on them. Besides the *Concilium Plebis* there was another, similar meeting called a *Comitia Tributa*. This meeting was attended by both patricians and plebeians and was led by a magistrate with *imperium*, that is, a consul, praetor, or *aedilis curulis*. There were now two types of *aediles*: two patrician (*aediles curules*) and two plebeian (the latter had been officially recognized as magistrates, *cf.* p. 156). The *Concilium Plebis* was led by a tribune of the *plebs*. The assemblies were convened and opened by the presiding officer. It should be borne in mind that the *Comitia Centuriata*, *Comitia Tributa* and *Consilium Plebis* were assemblies intended for voting, not discussion. They were preceded by *contiones* (plural of *contio*), preliminary meetings in which magistrates expressed their opinions. These voting assemblies were usually held outside the town walls, on the field of Mars. Many *contiones* were held on the Forum, in the center of Rome (Map 12.5).

The *Comitia Tributa* and the *Concilium Plebis* were organized on the basis of districts instead of property classes (*cf.* p. 87 on Cleisthenes in Athens). Each district (*tribus*) had one vote. There were 35 *tribus* (four within the city and 31 outside the city).

The *Lex Hortensia* is taken to mark the end of the struggle of the orders. After the year of its introduction the contrasts between patricians and plebeians gradually faded, giving way to new social differences of a different kind.

THE INSTITUTIONS OF THE ROMAN REPUBLIC AT THE END OF THE STRUGGLE OF THE ORDERS

The magistrates

The magistrates embodied the Roman state. In the Athenian democracy the citizenry had embodied the state but in Rome this was not the case. New magistrates were elected every year and, as we have already seen (p. 148), their colleagues could stop their actions by a veto.

Within the sacred limits of the city of Rome (*pomerium*), the tribunes of the *plebs* had the right to veto the acts of their own colleagues and all the other magistrates. This right of veto was an important safeguard against arbitrary acts.

The magistrates were assisted in their tasks by small staffs of professional scribes, heralds, messengers, attendants, and wardens, but there was no true civil service in the modern sense. The scribes were mostly slaves and freedmen (released slaves). The magistrates could also appeal to groups of advisers—members of their own class who had acquired specific expertise, for example in the field of law or in military strategies and tactics. These groups of advisers (*consilia*) usually greatly influenced a magistrate's policy.

The most important magistrates have already been mentioned above; to summarize, they were:

- **Consuls** (two). The consuls were charged with military command, maintenance of public order and general administration. They were elected by the *Comitia Centuriata*.
- **Praetors** (two; after 241 four; after 80 BC eight). The praetors replaced the consuls whenever necessary and were in most cases responsible for the administration of justice in Rome. They were elected by the *Comitia Centuriata*.
- **Tribunes of the *plebs*** (ten). The tribunes had the right of veto and the right of intervention. They presided over the *Concilium Plebis*. The tribunes of the *plebs* had to be plebeians; this office was not open to patricians.
- **Aediles** (four in total, two patrician and two plebeian; see above). The *aediles* were charged with the maintenance of order in the markets and other police matters, fire-fighting, and the organization of the games in Rome (games involving wild animals or gladiators and chariot races). Organizing the games implied considerable personal investments on the part of the *aediles*. These investments were comparable with the liturgies in Athens (see p. 95).
- **Quaestors** (two; after 267 eight; after 80 BC twenty). Management of the state treasury.

The tribunes of the *plebs*, the *aediles*, and the quaestors were all elected by the *Comitia Tributa*. The office of **dictator**, a special office, has already been discussed on p. 149. Every five years the *Comitia Centuriata* elected two censors from among the former consuls, who were appointed for a term of one and a half years (which means that there were no censors for three and a half years). Their tasks were to select worthy new members to fill vacancies in the Senate (the Senate was to have 300 members), register all the citizens and divide them into property classes (see p. 148), commission the execution of public works, lease state contracts for supplying the armies, and farm the taxes. They had the right to remove unworthy senators from the Senate. Reasons for such removal could be poverty (e.g., insufficient landed property) and unworthy behavior. At the end of their term of office the censors offered a *lustrum*, an expiatory sacrifice, to the state gods to atone for the offences that the Romans had committed against them. The aim of this purification process was to ensure that the state gods would continue to bestow their favor on the Roman population (in the eyes of the Romans this was a prerequisite for future success).

The highest magistracies were the consulship and the praetorship. Only these offices had *imperium*, the full absolute authority of the chief executive magistrate and general (see p. 147). All the other magistrates—including the censors—had powers within their specific fields of activity but no complete authority covering all the fields with which the state concerned itself. The magistrates with *imperium* were recognizable by their special clothing and insignia. Out in the streets they were accompanied by *lictores*, the bearers of bundles of rods and axes, the so-called *fasces*. Within Rome's sacred city limits (the *pomerium*) the magistrates' *imperium* was curtailed by the citizens' right of appeal (see p. 166) and by the powers of the tribunes of the *plebs*, but outside the *pomerium* they enjoyed absolute *imperium*, limited only by their colleagues' right of veto. This *imperium* they exercised for example over their armies in the field.

Armed soldiers were not allowed to enter the *pomerium*; they first had to change into civilian clothing and lay down their weapons. An exception was made when a consul was granted permission to lead his army through the town on a triumphal procession, as an honorable conclusion to a successful campaign. Dressed in the official purple robes of the former kings, the consul would then lead his troops in parade to the Capitol (see Map 12.5), where the chief temples of the supreme god Jupiter and various other state gods stood. There he would donate part of his booty as a thank-offering.

The notables who were appointed to the state offices were to hold those offices in a traditional order, starting with the quaestorship. After their term of office as a quaestor they could become an *aedilis* or a tribune of the *plebs*, then a praetor, and finally a consul. Men who had been chosen to be quaestors were usually enrolled to the Senate by the censors. During their *cursus honorum* they were regularly a magistrate and a senator at the same time. This way all magistrates came to sit on the Senate. The offices of the *cursus honorum* did not immediately succeed one another. After holding one of the offices, a senator would be just a senator for an interval of at least one year. This was called the career of the honorary offices (*cursus honorum*). They were called "honorary offices" because the persons who held them were not paid for their services. That meant that they could only be held by the wealthy, who could spend all their time on the tasks those offices involved and could hire others to work for them on their estates. This is also the reason why censors regarded impoverished senators as unworthy and unsuitable for senatorship and the magistracies.

The Senate

The Senate was in effect the most important body of the Roman state. It included all the magistrates and ex-magistrates, because the censors tended to fill vacancies in the Senate with notables who had been appointed quaestor or *aedilis*. As a result, the Senate possessed a good deal of military, administrative, and diplomatic expertise and experience. The popular assemblies almost always followed the Senate's advice. The Senate had complete control over state finances and foreign politics. A consul or a praetor presided over the Senate, but the tribunes were also entitled to act as the presiding officers. The ex-consuls were allowed to speak first and they were consequently the effective rulers of the Roman republic, who almost always determined Rome's politics.

FIGURE 12.6 Artist's impression of the Senate in assembly

FIGURE 12.7   The Rostra (speaker's platform) on the Forum, Rome's central square

Notes. The *comitia* (voting assemblies) were rarely held on the Forum, but people did meet there to form and exchange opinions. Orators and politicians would address the population on such occasions. The Rostra was decorated with the beaks of ships captured in a victorious naval battle in the fourth century.

Nobiles, senators, and equites

The opening of the magistracies to the rich plebeians in 367 BC (see p. 157) led to the emergence of a new governing class. From now onwards a small circle of leading patrician families and rich plebeian families furnished all the praetors and consuls. Whenever a new consul or praetor was to be appointed, the *Comitia Centuriata* would always elect a member of one of these families. They were called the *nobiles* (nobles). These *nobiles* were the core of a wider circle of equally rich and distinguished senatorial families. This inner circle of nobles formed the actual oligarchic governing element within the Senate.

The senators (including the *nobiles*) in turn formed the active administrative part of the highest property class in Rome, that is, that of the knights (*equites*) (see p. 163). At the beginning of the third century there were probably some two thousand *equites*. There were more in the late republic, and by the beginning of the Christian era their number had grown to an impressive 20,000.

The senatorial families and the other *equites* provided the officers for all the army units. The highest officers were magistrates, the middle cadre (the military tribunes and the prefects of ally units) consisted of the senators' young sons and other *equites*. The majority of the next rank of junior officers, the centurions, came from the army's rank and file.

There was not much difference in wealth or lifestyle between the senators and the other members of the property class of the *equites* (below, we will refer to the members of this class simply as "knights" or "*equites*"). The senatorial and equestrian families were often related and knew each other well. The censors would almost always elect new senators from among the younger members of the rich, noble senatorial families who had acquired a good reputation and had behaved in a dignified manner in a series of campaigns and in Rome. In Rome, such wealthy young nobles could prove their abilities in one or two of the lower governing bodies that assisted the magistrates and were charged with specific tasks such as the minting of coins, road repair work, the maintenance of public order, and the administration of justice among the lower classes. (These governing bodies cannot be discussed in any further detail in this brief survey of ancient history.)

Occasionally a knight from a family that had not yet furnished any magistrates or senators managed to gain admittance to the *cursus honorum* by virtue of his remarkable military performance or excellent eloquence. The censors would then include him in the Senate. If such a person was ultimately appointed consul, he was called a *homo novus* (a "new man"). In the course of the third century the *nobiles* started to close ranks. After 200 only three or four "new men" managed to penetrate into the governing circles of the Roman republic.

FIGURE 12.8 A Roman noble with busts of his ancestors

Notes. For distinguished Roman families, ties with ancestors were very important. The busts representing the deceased ancestors were given honorary positions in their homes and were carried in procession at funerals. The Roman is wearing a toga, the official dress of Roman men.

Social composition of the Roman population

It's not so easy to present a reliable picture of the composition and social structure of the Roman population in the days of the early republic. The texts from which we must obtain the relevant information were all written later and are mixtures of historical and contemporary information. The box below attempts to represent the Roman social structure in those early days insofar as we are able to reconstruct it from our sources.

THE *COMITIA CENTURIATA*

In the early republic, the subdivision of the five property classes into centuries and the order of voting were as follows:

Class I

12 centuries of *equites* (cavalry)
80 centuries of heavily armed infantry
  (40 cs. of seniors, aged 46 and older, 40 cs. of juniors, aged 17–46)
6 centuries of *equites* (cavalry)

Class II

20 centuries of infantry
  (10 seniors and 10 juniors)

Class III

20 centuries of infantry
  (10 seniors and 10 juniors)

Class IV

20 centuries of infantry
  (10 seniors and 10 juniors)

Class V

30 centuries of infantry
  (15 seniors and 15 juniors)

Below this classification were five more centuries for those who were exempt from military service because they did not meet the lowest property qualification, including one century for unpropertied citizens (proletarians).

The top layer of society consisted of landed patricians and plebeians who after 367 BC together constituted the *nobiles*, the core of the Senate. The other senators ranked just below them. One step down were wealthy plebeians from Rome herself and other Roman communities, the great majority of whom lived off their landed property, like the senators. Along with the senators, the members of this elite constituted the highest property class, that of the knights (*equites*). Below them was a broad group of landed farmers who provided the most heavily armed soldiers. In the cities there were also merchants and owners of large workshops who were on a par with these farmers in terms of wealth. At the bottom—of the ranks of free men at least— were poor small farmers and proletarians. In rural areas they were farmers who owned at most a vegetable plot, a small field, and a few animals. They had to secure sufficient income to survive through wage labor in harvest seasons or as shepherds. Their holdings can be characterized as mixed small farms focusing on self-sufficiency. Surplus produce was sold at markets. Any farmer could try to lease state-owned or communal land in order to supplement his income with what he grew on it. There were substantial differences within the constantly growing group of unfree men (slaves), too. The Romans had quite a lot of slaves in the fourth century already. We have virtually no information on earlier times, but we may assume that they used slaves then, too. The great majority of the slaves worked at the farms or in mines and quarries and lived a very marginal existence. They were not allowed to marry officially or to own property and were subject to the absolute authority of their masters and mistresses. Male and female slaves performed household tasks in the houses of the wealthy. The Romans did at all times free slaves, for example in reward for creditable behavior or because a slave was redeemed or purchased his own freedom. The latter was a matter of trust. A master could for example release a technically well trained slave on the condition that he would then earn a specific sum through hard work to repay his master. Freed slaves had restricted citizen rights. They were not allowed to serve in the armies or hold public offices, but those restrictions did not hold for their descendents, who hence enjoyed full Roman citizenship. We will return to the matter of slavery in the next chapter (p. 180).

Large landowners hardly ever owned a single large ranch, but usually a fairly large farm where specialist slaves were assisted by free seasonal laborers at peak times, plus a few small farms around it, which were tended by tenant farmers, freed slaves, or slaves. From later times we know that Romans liked to spread risks. Landowners would for example preferably have farms on both sides of a mountain—that way they would always have a chance of at least one good harvest irrespective of the weather. Roman landowners also liked to have farms in different parts of the Roman heartland. In times of emergency small farmers had various survival strategies to fall back on. They could use up existing supplies, borrow money from relatives and friends, wealthier neighbors, or patrons, earn extra money with seasonal labor in areas with better circumstances, or reduce the size of their families by selling children or sometimes even killing or abandoning them. Many abandoned children were picked up by slave traders, who would teach them a trade and then sell them at a high price.

Although we don't know exactly how many occupants Rome had in the early republican era, she must have been one of the largest cities in Italy quite early on. Around 310 BC work began on the construction of the first large aqueduct in Rome, the *aqua Appia* (so named after the censor Appius Claudius who proposed its construction). The work was completed within a few years.

A second aqueduct, the *aqua Anio Vetus*, was to follow in the mid-third century. By then, the natural springs and rain-fed wells (water from the Tiber was considered second-rate) evidently no longer sufficed to meet the town population's need for drinking water. The aqueducts supplied good spring and river water from the hills in the hinterland. The city of Rome was populated by senators, knights, wealthy merchants, bankers, workshop owners of a certain standing who supplied products of high status, masses of common craftsmen with smaller workshops, day laborers working in transport or the building industry who provided all kinds of small services, and a growing quantity of slaves and freedmen. Slaves worked in workshops and the households of wealthy families and in public services. Many of them gained more experience and expertise in their everyday work than free day laborers. The best among them were released and constituted the lion's share of a group of specialist, well-trained craftsmen. Rome had already attracted many immigrants at an early stage, for example from the rural surroundings of Rome, Latium, and other parts of Italy.

In the course of the third and second centuries BC a disparity emerged between the senators and the knights. In 218 BC a law (the *Lex Claudia*) was passed forbidding senators to engage in trade, banking, and fiscal enterprises (tax farming). These sectors came to be controlled by a small group of rich *equites*. They set up large companies with vast staffs of specialized free men, slaves, and freedmen, which concluded contracts with the censors for supplying the armies, road construction, public works in the city of Rome, and tax collection. Whenever they collected a particular tax (e.g., a toll) or the taxes of a particular area, they would pay an advance sum to the state treasury, which they would then recover with profit from the taxable population. These knights were called *publicani*. The other knights remained landed gentry and continued to provide officers for the army as of old.

From the fourth century onwards the cavalry no longer consisted exclusively of members of the equestrian order. There were simply no longer enough knights to make up the entire cavalry. After 300 the cavalry included progressively more contingents supplied by allies in Italy and other areas.

The popular assemblies

After the struggle of the orders, Rome in effect had two popular assemblies: the *Comitia Centuriata* and the *Comitia Tributa* (or *Concilium Plebis*; see p. 157 on the *Lex Hortensia*). The *Comitia Curiata* had by this time long lost its political importance and met only to confirm the appointment of magistrates and priests, adoptions, and wills.

No discussions were held at the popular assemblies. The assemblies were actually voting meetings, means for consulting the citizens. The citizens had the opportunity to form opinions on political issues and decide how they would vote at informal meetings (*contiones*), where politicians could advocate their views.

The officer who presided over a popular assembly had a very powerful position. After putting an issue or a legislative proposal before the assembly, he would first inform the assembly of the Senate's advice (see p. 157 on the *Lex Hortensia*) and would then invite them to vote on the issue— that is, providing a tribune did not pronounce a veto. But that hardly ever occurred in the 150 years between the struggle of the orders and the civil strife of the late republic (from 133 BC).

The great majority of the tribunes of the *plebs* were *nobiles* themselves, who always followed the Senate's advice.

Things were no different at elections. The presiding officer would present the list of candidates set up by the consuls then in office, after which one of the candidates was elected. The *Comitia Centuriata* was always led by a magistrate with *imperium*, in other words a consul or—if both consuls were engaged in warfare—a praetor. The *Comitia Tributa* was led by a consul, a praetor, or a patrician *aedilis*, but only a tribune of the *plebs* could preside over the *Concilium Plebis*.

After 287 the citizens met as a *Comitia Centuriata* virtually exclusively for specific purposes, for example when a war was to be declared or a peace treaty was to be ratified or when new censors, consuls, or praetors were to be elected. All other issues and elections were left to the *Comitia Tributa* (or *Concilium Plebis*).

The terminology (knights, *centuria*—unit of 100 soldiers) reminds us of the army assembly which the *Comitia Centuriata* had once been, but that was a thing of the past. In the third and second centuries BC a *centuria* no longer had anything to do with an army company. It was, instead, a group of voters belonging to a particular property class. The *centuriae* of this popular assembly moreover differed in size. A *centuria* of propertyless citizens included thousands of members, whereas a *centuria* of the highest class was much smaller. At the *Comitia Centuriata*, the vote of the first *centuria* entitled to vote—always one from the first class—was of great importance, because the other *centuriae* would quite often follow its example. Then came the knights, then the rest of the first class, and then the other property classes. The voting was stopped when half plus one was reached. If the wealthy were in agreement, then the lower classes would of course not get to vote.

The citizens who met in a *Comitia Tributa* were organized according to the district in which they lived (*tribus*). Each district had one vote. In principle, the poor citizens had a greater influence at the Comitia Tributa than at the *Comitia Centuriata*, because within their *tribus* it was the power of their number that counted. In practice, until well into the second century BC, the *Comitia Tributa*, too, almost always followed the Senate's advice and abided by the presiding magistrate's opinion.

After 287 the *Comitia Tributa* also served as a court of appeal (in the fifth and fourth centuries BC appeal cases had been one of the responsibilities of the *Comitia Centuriata*). Appeal cases were brought before the *Comitia Tributa* by a consul or a tribune of the *plebs*. Only in the late republic (end of the second century and the first century BC) were separate courts with juries set up specifically for this purpose. But it was only very important cases that were tried by such jury courts. The vast majority of cases were handled by lower governing bodies (see p. 162), by jurors whom the praetors appointed per case, and by the magistrates who were responsible for the maintenance of public order.

An oligarchic government

The Roman republic had no constitution and few written laws. Only issues that had provoked dissension, for example in the struggle of the orders, were provided for by written laws. Otherwise all state procedures and acts were based on unwritten rules and political codes of conduct, which were honored by the governing class and respected by all the citizens. The Roman polity was essentially oligarchic. It was the *nobiles* who pulled the strings. They dominated the popular assemblies via their many clients, their personal relations, and the authority that they enjoyed among all classes. This authority they owed to a deep-rooted traditional respect for the old-established families and to their successful command in the great wars of the third and second centuries BC (see pp. 168–72). These wars had temporarily suppressed the growing feelings of discontent. Not only had they provided booty, they had also won the Romans great fame and had created strong feelings of solidarity among the Roman population *vis-à-vis* its enemies. The *nobiles,* moreover, respectfully protected the interests of the members of the highest property class, who dominated the *Comitia Centuriata* and were therefore very important for the *nobiles,* because it was the *Comitia Centuriata* that elected the consuls and the praetors.

Such considerations, private friendships, and vertical ties between clients and their patrons were of overriding importance in politics, far more so than political views or programs. There were consequently no political parties. *Ad hoc* coalitions of *nobiles* would form around particular issues or candidates at elections. Those *nobiles* would mobilize their networks of relations, friends, and clients to advance their interests or to help their favorite candidate win an election.

A new type of client

The patron–client relationship had changed somewhat since the beginning of Roman history (see p. 146). In the third, second, and first centuries BC (and in fact also in the imperial age), clients were essentially poor citizens who were generously assisted by their patron in times of hunger and hardship and who were supported by him if they became involved in a conflict (e.g., a legal matter or a business conflict). Freedmen were in this way protected by their former masters. In return, the clients supported their patron at elections and in political conflicts, they escorted him in public, and greeted him at his home at the break of day (on which occasion he would grant them a small sum of money or some food). A large group of clients was an important status symbol. When the clients greeted their patrons in the morning they could also ask them for advice, for example on business or legal matters.

Some demographic data

Rome never became a democracy comparable with that of Athens. In actual fact, the Roman citizenry had already become too large for a democracy by the third century BC. It is thought that about 265,000 male adults (of over 16 years of age) had Roman citizenship in 264 BC. That means that only a small proportion of the Roman citizens, mostly occupants of the city itself, could attend the popular assemblies on a regular basis.

In the 150 years preceding 264 BC Rome's citizenry had expanded tremendously. One of the causes of this was the incorporation of central Italian and southern Etruscan tribes and cities into the Roman citizen territory. Another was Rome's policy of granting citizen rights to children of mixed marriages (e.g., of a Roman citizen with a member of an Italian tribe), immigrants from Latium and the Latin colonies (see p. 151), and freed slaves. What's more, the Roman birth rate in these early days was probably still high in all classes, partly on account of the young age at which boys and girls married. Girls would sometimes marry when they were only thirteen years old.

13 FURTHER EXPANSION AND NEW SOCIAL TENSIONS (264–133 BC)

ROMAN EXPANSION BETWEEN 264 AND 121 BC

The Punic Wars

Contacts had existed between Rome and Carthage since the end of the sixth century BC. Carthage conducted trade with Italy and occasionally tried to fish in troubled waters. She had little to fear from Italy as long as the country remained divided. This changed around 270, however, when Rome acquired hegemony over the whole of peninsular Italy and came to represent a formidable power close to Carthage's sphere of trade and influence (see p. 144). Whereas Rome and Carthage had still fought side by side in the war against Pyrrhus in 282–275 (p. 150), after that time they began to distrust one another and to fear one another's might.

In 264 Rome became involved in a problem in Sicily. Since 289, a group of Campanian mercenaries who had settled at Messina after doing service for a tyrant in Syracuse had been enriching themselves as pirates. They were now hard-pressed by Syracuse, which intended to put an end to their piracy. The pirates enlisted the help of Carthage, Syracuse's traditional enemy, and Rome, Campania's "patron." Both powers responded to the appeal and consequently impinged on one another's sphere of influence. This led to the First Punic War (264–241; Punic–Phoenician–Carthaginian). Syracuse defected to Rome after the first year of the war.

This war was a protracted and severe struggle because both parties were well versed in military tactics and neither was prepared to give in to the other. After their first successful campaigns, the Romans contemplated conquering all Sicily, but Carthage was of course anxious to retain her bases on that island. Most battles were fought on land and at sea, on and off Sicily. The Romans finally won the war thanks to their superior power on land and because they built strong fleets, which also enabled them to defeat the Carthaginians at sea. In this war the Romans achieved supremacy over the seas around Italy. In building their naval forces, the Romans received much help from their maritime (Greek) allies along the coasts of southern Italy.

In 241 Sicily became Rome's first province. Instead of making the states on Sicily her allies, as she had done with the Italian tribes and cities, Rome placed all the states, with the exception of Syracuse, under a praetor's authority. She allowed them to retain local autonomy, however.

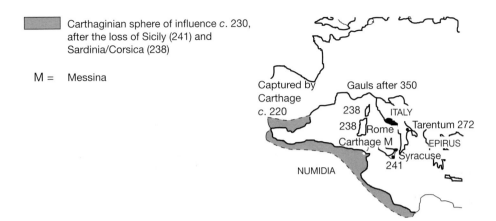

Carthaginian sphere of influence c. 230,
after the loss of Sicily (241) and
Sardinia/Corsica (238)

M =   Messina

Captured by
Carthage
c. 220

Gauls after 350

238

ITALY

238 Rome

Tarentum 272

Carthage M

EPIRUS

Syracuse

241

NUMIDIA

MAP 13.1   Roman expansion, c. 500–220 BC

The Roman Senate probably opted for this form of government because Sicily would be in the front line if any more wars should break out against Carthage. We may regard this as a form of military control in a war-threatened area. This was to prove an influential precedent: most of the territories that Rome conquered from this stage onwards were ultimately converted into provinces, even those that were not in any front-line position.

In the twenty years between 238 and 218, Rome took Sardinia and Corsica (238) and restored order on the Adriatic Sea (229), where pirates from Illyria (now Albania and part of former Yugoslavia) were causing havoc. The Romans also subjected the Gauls in the Po valley (222).

Carthage sought to compensate for the loss of Sicily, Sardinia, and Corsica by reinforcing her position in Spain. In the subsequent wars against the tribes living there, which lasted for many years, the Carthaginian army in Spain became one of the best-trained professional armies of that time. It consisted chiefly of Spanish and North African mercenaries.

In 218 a new struggle broke out between Rome and Carthage, the Second Punic War (218–201), which evolved into a coalition war with far-reaching consequences. It was one of the fiercest and most intensive wars in Roman history. The competent Carthaginian general Hannibal, who had commanded the Carthaginian army in Spain since 221, embarked on a spectacular campaign through southern Gaul and over the Alps into Italy, where he won the support of the Gauls in the Po valley, who had only just been defeated by Rome.

In the years 218–216 Hannibal gained major victories over the Romans and their Italian allies. The greatest was that which he won in the battle at Cannae (216), in which over 40,000 Roman and Italian soldiers were killed (see Map 13.2). Hannibal owed his success to his brilliant tactical maneuvers and his troops' great experience. After the battle at Cannae, Hannibal received support from a number of southern Italian states, which had lost faith in the Romans' chances of victory, and from Philip V (221–179), the king of Macedonia. Philip, too, was anxious to see the Romans defeated. He regarded Rome's intervention in the Illyrian piracy issue, just before he had come to power, as a prelude to an attempt to invade the Balkans—and they were his territory. Even Syracuse, Rome's ally in the previous war, sided with Carthage.

Each of these blocks represents a group of 30 cavalry

cavalry

Each of these blocks represents one *maniple* (2 *centuriae*).
A *centuria* of *hastati* or *principes* numbered about 60 men. A *centuria* of *triarii* numbered 30 men.

triarii

hastati or *principes*

velites (lightly armed soldiers) (40 per maniple)

vexillarii (the standard bearers; one per *centuria*)

centurions (one per *centuria*)

cavalry

triarii

principes

hastati

cavalry

FIGURE 13.1 Battle order of a Roman legion at the time of the Second Punic War (218–201 BC)

Notes. The commanders signaled their orders to the soldiers. They could for example order the maniples to increase or reduce the intervals between them or to form into a square. In the latter case the rear line (*triarii*) would turn round and march away from the middle line and the maniples of the middle line (*principes*) would march to the sides. The maniples could also form a closed front; the maniples of the *principes* would then fill the gaps between the maniples of the *hastati*. The commanders could also order their men to increase the distances between the three lines. And they could create a very wide front by ordering the *triarii* and *principes* to march left and right and align with the *hastati* in the middle. These possibilities made the Roman legions far more maneuverable than the Greek or Macedonian *phalanx*.

MAP 13.2 The expansion of the Roman empire between 218 and 120 BC

Notes. Immediately after the Second Punic War Rome became involved in the struggle for influence in Greece and started to consolidate and strengthen her positions in Spain.

The struggle over Greece proceeded as follows: in 200–197 Rome successfully fought Macedonia. In 196, after the Romans' victory, the Roman general Flamininus proclaimed the Greeks free and autonomous; Greece was not turned into a Roman province. The Romans regarded the Greeks as "clients" of the Roman people, who were allowed to govern themselves. They stood under the supervision of the Roman governor of Macedonia.

In 192 the Seleucid king Antiochus III (222–187) tried to acquire influence in Greece. That brought him into conflict with the Romans, who did not tolerate another "patron" in Greece besides themselves. In 188 Rome won the war. Antiochus had to retreat behind the Taurus mountains (Cilicia) and pay Rome a tribute of 15,000 talents (Appendix 2). His territories in Asia Minor were divided between Pergamum and Rhodes (Rome's allies).

In 171–168 the Romans definitively defeated Macedonia. The land was divided into four republics (Roman satellite states). After uprisings in Macedonia and Greece (149–146) the Senate turned Macedonia into a province.

Nevertheless, Carthage ultimately lost the war. The Romans mobilized all their manpower resources (see box on p. 206), including the troops of most of their Italian allies who, contrary to Hannibal's expectations, honored their alliances with Rome. One of the Romans' land forces successfully attacked the Carthaginians in Spain and in so doing undermined the basis of Hannibal's success (Hannibal obtained large parts of his troops and army supplies from Spain). As the Roman fleet commanded the seas around Italy, it was very difficult for the Carthaginians to provision Hannibal by sea. The Roman commanders meanwhile waged a war of attrition on Hannibal himself, in which they exhausted his troops. In a series of minor skirmishes and sieges they ultimately confined him to the toe of Italy. There, after some time, he found insufficient resources to maintain a large army. The weakness in Hannibal's strategy was logistics. Having no fixed, reliable source of provisions, he was too often forced to live "off the land" in Italy. The Romans on the contrary used an efficient system based on stocks of supplies, which proved most beneficial to them. In this war their main source of extra provisions was Etruria, which in those days abounded in surplus resources.

Around 205 the first signs of victory for the Romans began to appear. The Roman general P. Cornelius Scipio, who had driven the Carthaginians out of Spain between 210 and 205, crossed over to North Africa, where he won over new allies in Numidia, one of Carthage's neighbor states (see Map 13.1). In 202, in the great battle at Zama, he defeated Hannibal, who had been called back from Italy to defend his home town. In 201 Carthage made peace. The peace treaty compelled her to surrender all her outlying provinces and her war fleet to Rome and to pay an indemnity of 10,000 talents (Appendix 2, p. 300) in instalments. The Roman treasury was to benefit from those instalments for over forty years. Syracuse lost her status of a free ally and was reduced to the same rank as the other subject city states on Sicily.

This war established Rome as the greatest power in the Mediterranean.

Wars in Spain, the Po valley, and the Hellenistic East

After 201 the Romans engaged in a series of wars that started as sequels to the Second Punic War but eventually led to a tremendous expansion of Rome's sphere of influence. Rome came to be the capital of a vast empire (see Map 13.2).

Between 197 and 190 the Romans once again brought the Gauls in the Po valley under their control. The Gauls had already been subjected between 235 and 222, but in 218 they had rebelled against the Romans and had sided with the Carthaginians. The tribes in the interior of Spain were subjected in two protracted, difficult wars (197–178 and 154–133), which claimed many victims on both sides. The Romans then split up the Iberian peninsula into two Roman provinces. In the years 125–121 Rome also captured the strategic coastal strip between Italy and Spain, which she formed into the province of Transalpine Gaul (see Map 13.2).

The Po valley, southern Spain, and southern Gaul became important regions for Roman and Italian merchants and emigrants. Many Roman and Italian veterans remained here after their military service, while peasants from all over Italy flocked to these regions in search of a better livelihood.

In a series of brief, successful wars between 200 and 146 BC (see p. 171, the text accompanying Map 13.2) against Macedonia, the leagues of Greek states, and the Seleucid kingdom, Rome established her hegemony over the southern Balkans.

The Hellenistic kingdoms never joined forces against Rome. The Romans managed to win the wars against these kingdoms with comparative ease and rapidity thanks to the discord dividing their opponents, which enabled Rome to defeat them one by one. Rome, moreover, had the best-trained military manpower in the entire Mediterranean. In the Second Punic War and the wars that were to follow, a remarkably high percentage of the Romans and their Italian allies were under arms (see box on p. 206), gaining military experience. What's more, the Roman armies used more flexible and more efficient tactics against which the strategies of the armies of the Hellenistic kings were no match.

FIGURE 13.2
Boarding bridges used by the Romans during the First Punic War

Notes. In the First Punic War the Romans managed to gain naval supremacy over the Carthaginians' highly experienced naval forces by turning a naval battle into a "land" battle. This they did by lowering the illustrated boarding bridges, known as "crows," onto the Carthaginian ships so that they could cross over to conquer the Carthaginian ships. These crows, however, unbalanced the ships and many Roman ships were consequently wrecked in storms. The Romans therefore soon stopped using this device.

Below: cross-section through a double-deck war galley (a quadrireme). Each oar was pulled by two men. The rowers were propertyless citizens and men drawn from the cities of Rome's maritime allies.

Two forms of Roman expansion

In the first half of the second century BC the Roman Senate, which in this period still controlled foreign politics (see p. 160), maintained a different policy towards the West (Spain, the Po valley, Gaul) than towards the East and North Africa. All that Rome initially (in the first half of the second century BC) demanded from her conquered opponents in the East and North Africa was that they acknowledged Rome's hegemony and paid the requested tributes. These tributes filled the Roman treasury and effectively weakened the conquered states, as they consequently had less money to spend on mercenaries and fleets. Rome meanwhile enjoyed the material advantages of her victories and did not have to worry about establishing an administrative system in those distant regions and the difficulty of control that that would have entailed. Moreover, many Roman notables cherished a deep respect for Greek civilization, which they regarded as a superior sister culture. They felt that the Greeks deserved to retain their autonomy. Their attitude can be compared to that of the Assyrians towards Babylon (pp. 38–9).

In the East and in North Africa Rome pursued a divide-and-rule policy. Her aim was to weaken the powerful Hellenistic states (Macedonia and the Seleucid kingdom) and Carthage, and at the same time strengthen and support their weaker neighbors, such as Pergamum in Asia Minor and Numidia in North Africa. Ptolemaic Egypt played no part in international politics after 170. From that year onwards it was constantly torn apart by succession struggles and unrest. The only reason why Egypt retained its independence was that Rome did not incorporate it in her empire and did not allow any other state to assume control over it. This divide-and-rule policy was fairly successful in Asia Minor, but Greece and Macedonia remained restless. On four occasions between 200 and 146 Rome was forced to engage in wars in those areas (see Map 13.2). In 146 Rome had had enough and put an end to the unrest once and for all. She turned Macedonia into a province and placed it under a Roman governor, who also had to supervise the "free" states in Greece and forestall internecine warfare and social upheavals there. Out of frustration, a craving for booty, or as a warning to other cities she destroyed the Greek city of Corinth, which had been a center of anti-Roman activity since 149. The population was killed or sold into slavery. That same year Rome also liquidated the last remains of the Carthaginians' power in North Africa after Carthage had come into conflict with her neighbor Numidia, one of Rome's allies (Third Punic War, 149–146). Carthage was destroyed and her entire population was killed or sold into slavery. Her territory was turned into the province of Africa. In 133 BC the last king of the Attalids bequeathed the kingdom of Pergamum to Rome. In 129, after suppressing a revolt of mercenaries, slaves, and poor tenant farmers in the western half of the kingdom, the Romans turned that area into the province of Asia (see Map 13.2). The rest of the kingdom they left in the hands of local vassal rulers loyal to Rome.

Toward the West the Roman Senate pursued a different policy. The territories that the Romans conquered in the Po valley, Spain, and southern Gaul were immediately turned into Roman provinces. The Romans wished to establish permanent control over these areas. Situated immediately above peninsular Italy, the Po valley was strategically important, while Spain was a source of metals for the Romans: there were rich gold, silver, and other metal mines in the southern, eastern, and central parts of Spain (Andalusia and Castile). The occupants of the central and northwestern parts of the Iberian peninsula, however, did not readily submit to the yoke of Roman control and forced the Romans to engage in wars over and over again. The Romans were rarely able to use large armies in those areas owing to logistic problems. In the Spanish interior, transport usually had to take place by land and there were few surplus resources. It is also quite possible that the Senate was reluctant to invest money and effort in wars here. So the struggles continued for quite some time. What was also an important factor was the different political situation in these areas: besides states at a reasonable stage of development with urban traffic, there were also regions occupied by tribes that could not be classed as states, having not yet reached the same stage of urbanization and urban culture. In the case of these tribes it was impossible to conduct negotiations with a single king or council in order to arrive at binding agreements and secure their observance. In the central and northwestern parts of the Iberian peninsula in particular, rebellions broke out time and time again. In a series of harsh wars Rome slowly moved the boundaries of her empire further north and west, until in the end only the northwest corner of Spain was still free of Roman dominion (133 BC).

The decisive victories in North Africa (146) and Spain (134–133) were both won by a member of the Cornelius Scipio family, P. Cornelius Scipio Aemilianus. The Roman population hailed him as a great hero, but he never misused his popularity. He remained entirely loyal to his fellow-rulers in the Senate.

In the wars between 264 and 133 the Romans' traditional shifts in command proved a great disadvantage. In principle, the consuls (and praetors) could command their armies only during their one-year term of office. The exigencies of prolonged warfare, however, called for a new solution. In order to increase the number of commanders and to give capable generals the opportunity of remaining in command after their one-year term of office, the Senate created the "pro"-magistracy. "Pro" means "in the place of." A proconsul's *imperium* was actually that of a consul, but it was limited to his own army and his own battlefield. So a proconsul's *provincia*, his "sphere of influence," was limited in time, place, and duties. It ended when the Senate called him back or when the predetermined term of his command came to an end.

The administration of a province

In every new province they established, the Romans left the local administrative system as they had found it and placed a governor above it, to keep an eye on things. At first the governors were all praetors, but in the course of the second century BC the Senate started to appoint ex-consuls and ex-praetors as proconsuls and propraetors. The *provincia*, sphere of influence, of their *imperium* was limited to the district they were appointed to rule (which hence came to be called a *provincia*, "province"), their term of office usually to one or two years. A governor's main responsibilities were the defense of his province and the administration of justice. After some time, the governors came to share their judicial duties with the local rulers. The governors had a small staff of councilors (e.g., Romans and Italians who had gone to live in the province), scribes, and deputies, and were assisted by quaestors, who supervised expenditures and tax collection. The taxes were collected in cash or in kind by the local councils and were handed over to either the Roman governor or the agents of the *publicani* (see p. 165), who had already deposited an advance in Rome's treasury. The provincial quaestor received part of the money to cover the costs of the provincial government and any Roman troops stationed there. In effect, it was the governor's councilors who preserved the continuity of the provincial government, for they remained, whereas the governors were replaced every year or every two years. The governors would every year go on a tour of their province, always following a fixed route. This enabled their subjects to approach them with petitions or legal business when they visited their towns— after some time everyone knew when the governor would be visiting their area.

The lion's share of the day-to-day administrative work was done by the local rulers. For the bulk of the provincial population they represented the immediate authorities. In the western provinces the local rulers were aristocratic members of Gallic and Iberian tribes. In the eastern provinces they were mainly the councilors and magistrates of the Greek cities that had emerged all over the Near East in the Hellenistic era (see p. 127), but also local sovereigns, temple priests, and village chiefs.

The Romans encouraged an oligarchic form of government in the Greek cities. In Italy, the Roman Senate had found that well-organized councils of noble landowners constituted very effective local governments for the cities of Rome's allies, her colonies, and her *municipia* (see p. 152) and it therefore decided to extend this system to the provinces. The oligarchically bent rich in the Greek cities on their part usually accepted the Romans' sovereignty. They realized that a pro-Roman attitude would secure them a privileged position in local government and would safeguard their property. Under Rome's supervision the civil strife between the rich and the poor that had afflicted many Greek cities between 240 and 150 was suppressed.

In Italy, and also in the western and eastern provinces, the city councils that were responsible for local government gradually came to consist of wealthy notables who sat on the council for life and were appointed to the local administrative offices by the citizens of their city. The councils had between 100 and 600 members, depending on the size and population of the city and of the rural areas governed by that city.

Disadvantages of Roman control

In the second and first centuries BC most of Rome's provinces groaned under Rome's control. In their provinces, the governors, their staff and the *publicani* were able to take advantage of their positions to enrich themselves because Rome exercised very little control over their activities. The Romans' administrative system did not include provisions for checking on magistrates far away from Italy. Governors and their assistants "sold" the law and favored cities and individuals who gave them generous "gifts," while *publicani* employed greater profit margins than they were entitled to according to traditional standards. The provincial population also had to suffer the ruthless practices of Roman veterans and Italian merchants and slave traders. Italian merchants, for example, would with a Roman governor's cooperation extort low prices for the goods they purchased and charge exorbitant prices when they sold them. And the slave traders sold many former captives, rebels, and well-educated provincials into slavery in Italy or Sicily.

In 149 BC, after a number of serious scandals (in Spain), Rome decided to take measures against the governors' extortionist practices. A permanent jury court was established in Rome for the specific purpose of handling complaints of extortion in the provinces. The complaints were to be lodged by Roman notables acting as the "patrons" of the provinces. These patrons were chosen from among notables who, as a general in a war or a governor, had formed a special bond with their province, or who belonged to a family from which the Senate had chosen governors for a particular province for several generations. The jury consisted of senators.

NEW SOCIAL TENSIONS

The consequences of Rome's expansion

In the many years of Rome's expansion between 264 and 121 BC, vast quantities of money, goods, and slaves poured into Italy. Within two or three generations this led to major changes in the cities (especially Rome) and in rural areas. Increasing amounts of tributes and taxes flowed from the subjected territories into Rome's treasury, financing further expansionist campaigns. The *tributum*, the property tax that had burdened the Roman citizens in Italy, was no longer collected after 167 BC (see p. 62).

Grain was imported into Rome on a regular basis by sea from the fertile coastal plains of Sicily and North Africa (it was much cheaper and more efficient to transport bulk goods by water than overland, across Italy). The abundant availability of this staple foodstuff led to a tremendous increase in Rome's population as it attracted many occupants of rural areas to the city. Other foodstuffs were obtained from nearby Italian regions. Those regions focused more on cattle-keeping and the production of wine, olive oil, and fruit than on cereal cultivation. But cereal continued to be produced. The fairly large, more market-oriented farms in the surroundings of

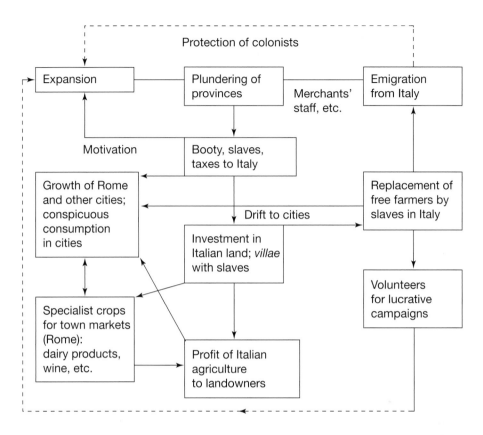

FIGURE 13.3   The consequences of Rome's expansion in the second century BC

Note. Villae are medium-sized plantations producing cash crops and foodstuffs for their own labor force.

Rome grew many different crops for the people who lived and worked at those estates and they also had a separate field or garden for a crop specifically intended for the market. Such farms were known as *villae*. They were usually owned by wealthy senators and knights and were tended by slaves who were at peak times assisted by seasonal workers from nearby villages. The latter were free small farmers, rural proletarians, or tenants of rich proprietors.

Most of the booty (slaves, money, and goods) fell into the hands of the rich and powerful. They spent vast amounts of money in Rome and had expensive country estates built for themselves, but most of their wealth they invested in land in Italy, especially in the immediate surroundings of Rome, on which they put slaves to work. Many *villae* consequently arose in fertile regions with good transport possibilities in the vicinity of Rome or other densely populated cities, where trained slaves produced the goods which would sell well in Rome and other cities. More and more of the public land in those regions thus came into the possession of the rich, who added it to their *villae*. This meant that the free farmers (landowning farmers, tenant farmers, and landowning farmers who leased extra land) were no longer able to exploit the public land and so lost a large portion of their income (see p. 152). Romans would give dowries to their daughters and bequeath equal parts of their land to their male heirs. So if a farmer had a large family his descendants could end up with very small parcels of land—too small for them to till without running into debts. Those who were forced to neglect their farms for the long periods that they had to spend in military service were even worse off. Many farmers eventually gave up, sold their private land, and migrated to the towns, in particular Rome. Others ran up debts, lost their land to their creditors, and joined the ranks of the tenants and day laborers who hired themselves out in the countryside and in Rome and other towns. This process took place especially in the easily accessible surroundings of Rome.

Yet other farmers emigrated to the Po valley, southern Spain, or southern Gaul, where they accelerated the process of Romanization. There were also farmers who, returning from a successful war with a share of the booty, were able to buy land or a good workshop or shop in a city. They, too, sometimes had a few slaves.

Similar changes took place among the Italian communities, especially those in southern Italy and Latium. As large parts of southern Italy had been devastated in the battle against Hannibal between 216 and 203 (see p. 172), the farmers in those regions were at an extra disadvantage. Many had run up debts because they had had to borrow money to rebuild their farms. Moreover, the communities in southern Italy that had sided with Hannibal after the battle at Cannae (216) had been forced to surrender their best land to Rome. That land had become Roman public land and had passed into the hands of wealthy investors. On this land arose not only *villae* of the type described above, but also large cattle ranches. Many southern Italians drifted to Rome or towns closer by in Italy, or to the Po valley, Spain, or southern Gaul. Rome, moreover, received a great influx of people from the Latin city states, who moved to the city so as to obtain full Roman citizenship (see p. 151).

The consequence of all this was that the urban and rural proletariat grew all over Italy, while the number of free farmers decreased. The social pattern became more complex. Beneath the top layer of senators, knights, and local notables in the Italian cities there were now merchants varying in wealth, gentlemen farmers with a few slaves, small-time free farmers adhering to old-fashioned farming practices, tenants (sometimes with a little land and a few animals of their own), proletarians (sometimes with their own vegetable plot), slaves, and freedmen. Indeed, tenants, too – and their number was probably increasing, considering that large landowners liked to spread risks: in the vicinity of their *villae* they usually had a few separate smaller mixed farms which were run by tenants, slaves, or freedmen (p. 177). The best chances of survival for old-fashioned farming villages dominated by landed free small farmers were in regions further away from Rome, in particular in remote areas without good transport possibilities, which were of little interest to wealthy Roman and Italian investors.

These developments probably had positive consequences for the Italian economy in that they meant that more, and more varied, crops were grown, which were often sold at good prices, but for the Roman state they were fairly serious. Usually, the bulk of the soldiers were recruited from among the citizens who could afford to arm themselves. The state treasury lacked the funds to equip entire armies. However, as the free landed peasantry declined, the number of citizens qualifying for recruitment decreased. The larger numbers of tenants and proletarians were of little use to the magistrates responsible for composing the armies as those citizens did not own enough to qualify for military service. The situation was aggravated by the fact that many (peasant) soldiers were killed on campaigns or stayed behind in conquered regions.

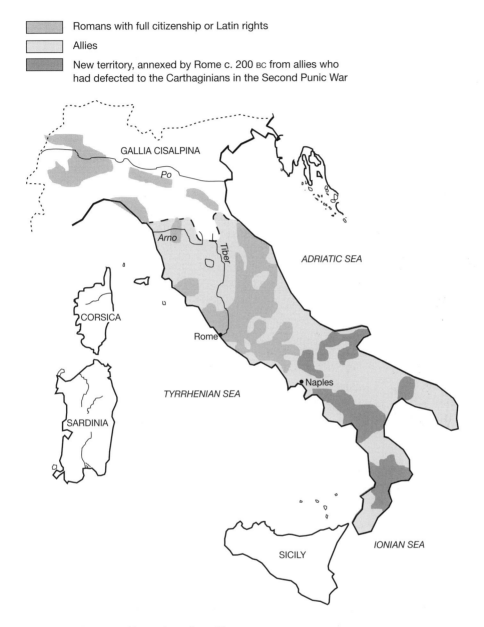

Romans with full citizenship or Latin rights

Allies

New territory, annexed by Rome c. 200 BC from allies who
had defected to the Carthaginians in the Second Punic War

MAP 13.3 Rome and her Italian allies, 91 BC

Note. This map clearly reflects the massive expansion of the citizen territory.

Some farmers more or less completely abandoned their farming way of life by volunteering
for—preferably lucrative—campaigns whenever they got the chance. They constituted the semi-
professional backbone of the Roman armies in the numerous wars of those days. They were of
great importance for Rome's expansion: experienced soldiers were invaluable.

Slavery in Italy and Sicily

In the third century BC there must already have been vast numbers of slaves in Italy and Sicily, partly because so many captives and other people subjected in the Punic Wars had been sold into slavery. It was, however, in the second century BC that slavery really expanded in Italy and Sicily. According to a plausible estimate, two million of the six million inhabitants of Italy were slaves at the height of this development, between 150 and 70. Those slaves were former war captives, deportees from subject regions, victims of pirates and slave traders, foundlings picked up by slave traders, poor people who had sold themselves and their children into slavery because they saw no other way out, and those who had been born into slavery. Slaves were the property of their masters; they were "instruments without a voice."

Large concentrations of slaves worked in the mines, in the quarries, and on the large estates that specialized in the cultivation of crops specifically intended for sale (cash crops). Many slaves were also employed in the workshops or did the dirty and heavy work in the public services in the cities and in the homes of the rich, as domestic personnel. Small-time farmers and craftsmen who were doing quite well for themselves had one or two slaves. Well-to-do farmers and urban entrepreneurs usually had more. There were great differences between the slaves themselves. A notable's well-educated domestic slave often enjoyed a position of trust as a secretary or a family tutor and stood a good chance of being released from slavery some day. The slave of a small-time farmer or craftsman was regarded more or less as a member of the family, but the

FIGURE 13.4 A slave chain

Notes. In rural areas slaves were sometimes chained together to prevent them from running away. Example of the tokens that some slaves wore around their necks. The tokens bore a text. This text reads: *Tene me ne fugia[m] et revoca me ad dom[i]nu[m] meu[m] Viventium in ar[e]a Callisti*—"Stop me from running away and return me to my master, Viventius, who lives in Callistus' court."

fate of the masses of slaves who worked in the mines and on the large agricultural estates was wretched. Even worse off were the slaves who were forced to perform as gladiators at the games; they had to fight one another to death in the arenas in Italy. Occasionally a slave would be released. For many slaves the chance of being freed from slavery was their only hope and a reason for working hard and not rising in revolt. As already mentioned above, freedmen were granted restricted Roman citizenship. They were not liable for military service and were not allowed to hold public offices. Their sons did enjoy full citizenship (see p. 167).

Slave revolts

Between 150 and 70, conditions in Italy and Sicily (and probably also in Asia Minor) became more conducive to slave revolts. The number of slaves increased tremendously within a relatively short space of time. The new slaves were set to work on the large estates in groups. Coming from the same areas, large groups of them spoke the same languages and could communicate with one another. They longingly recalled their days of freedom, whose memory was still fresh in their minds, and they were in a position to rise as a group. Around 134 and 104 BC, major slave revolts broke out on Sicily and in the years 133–129 slaves joined the uprisings in the former kingdom of Pergamum, in Asia Minor (see p. 174). The rebellious slaves were certainly not acting according to some international plan; as far as we know, they were not in contact with one another and had no communal reform program. They were not even motivated by a desire to abolish slavery. All they were interested in was regaining their own personal freedom. The greatest slave revolt that ever broke out in Italy occurred later, in 73–71 BC, under the leadership of Spartacus (see p. 196).

The slave revolts on Sicily were a serious problem for the population of Rome because Rome obtained much of her grain from Sicily. The Roman legions therefore made great efforts to firmly suppress those revolts.

Piracy

A side effect of the slave trade was piracy, which rapidly spread across the Mediterranean. Slaves were profitable merchandise for pirates. Since Rome had acquired supremacy over the Mediterranean and their own power had declined, the Hellenistic kingdoms were no longer able to secure the safety of the sea and the coasts. And as for Rome, the Roman Senate made no effort to curb piracy as the senators themselves stood to benefit by a good supply of slaves because they needed many for their estates. They were particularly interested in skilled workers from the well-developed Hellenistic world, to whom they could entrust the cultivation of their cash crops and domestic chores.

Some demographic data

The import of slaves and the influx of foreigners into Rome and the ports led to a considerable increase in the Italian population. In the first century BC Italy probably had some six million inhabitants. The number of Roman citizens also increased, largely as a result of the inflow of

Latins and foreigners into Rome (p. 178) and the release of slaves (see p. 181). Between 225 and 143 BC the number of adult male Roman citizens (above the age of 16) increased from about 300,000 to about 400,000. The percentage of traditional free landed peasants among those citizens, however, decreased (see the box on p. 206).

The city of Rome

The great numbers of former peasants, ex-soldiers reluctant to return to a farming existence after their military service, foreigners, slaves, and freedmen who flocked to Rome swelled the city's population. By the mid-second century BC already the need arose for a third aqueduct with a large capacity for conveying water to Rome. The construction of that aqueduct, the *aqua Marcia*, was completed in 144 BC. The newcomers found work in the building industry and transport or as craftsmen. The rich spent large sums of money in Rome. New occupational groups emerged, which satisfied the increasing demands of the wealthy public. The elite, impressed by the culture, level of learning, and luxurious conditions with which they became acquainted in the Hellenistic cities, strove to alter their own way of life accordingly. In Rome this led to a demand for teachers, artists, architects, doctors, secretaries, bankers, legal advisors, and manufacturers of luxury goods. Quite a few of the specialist craftsmen and intellectual professionals who met this demand were former slaves from the Hellenistic east who set themselves up in business after being released from slavery by their masters. Law was mainly the domain of notable Romans. Engaging in legal affairs was considered a respectable *métier* for a Roman gentleman, unlike professions in commerce or manual trades. Roman senators and *equites* would assist in litigation and provide magistrates with advice. In their capacity as patrons they also acted as advisors for their clients, who would consult them about all kinds of matters, for example when they came to greet them in the morning.

Inadequate organization

The Romans made very few efforts to adjust their public institutions to the altered conditions. They created a promagistracy (proconsulship and propraetorship, p. 175) and increased the number of praetors and quaestors (p. 158), but otherwise they did not extend the magisterial apparatus. Neither did the Romans establish a standing army along the frontiers of their empire to prevent or settle border conflicts. Many administrative matters were arranged via relations with important *nobiles*, whose patronage covered a wide range of interest groups in Rome, and entire cities and regions in Italy and the provinces. The traditional Roman way of thinking in terms of patron–client relationships extended to Rome's international relations. Rome saw herself as the patron of her allies and vassals in the Hellenistic world and the *nobiles* were the patrons of large groups of people, cities, and regions in the Roman empire.

The discrepancy that came to exist between the public sector and the vastly expanded private sector is also reflected in contemporary Roman law. Public law still amounted to little, comprising as it did only a few rules relating to the magistrates, the Senate, and the popular assemblies, but private law had grown tremendously (see p. 236). The public sector remained largely dependent on unwritten rules and customs.

A CHANGE IN MENTALITY

It is believed that the old Roman family ties (see p. 147), traditions, and customs lived on for a fairly long time in rural areas and in small cities, not only among the lower classes, but even among the political class that governed the Italian communities (see p. 152). In Rome itself (and perhaps also in some ports) a major change in mentality, however, took place in the second and first centuries BC. We don't know much about the lower classes, but we may assume that they, too, felt the impact of the spiritual disruption generally associated with the influx of large groups of newcomers into a city.

We are somewhat better informed about the ruling classes in Rome. In their public and private lives, the Roman notables slowly drifted away from the old Roman traditions. They surrounded themselves with ever more luxury and developed a more individualistic attitude. In theory, the old family ties and the power of the *pater familias* (see p. 147) still existed, but in practice they were gradually eroded. This is for example apparent from the opportunities that became accessible to women. Progressively fewer elite women married in the old-fashioned way, formally passing under the authority of the *pater familias* of their husbands' families. Less conventional forms of cohabitation emerged and divorce became quite common among the higher classes. Again we know very little about the situation in the lower classes; our sources provide virtually no information on this matter.

Greek influences

One of the most influential factors in the change in mentality among the Roman elite was the latter's increasing familiarity with the culture and lifestyle of the Hellenistic cities in the eastern provinces (and in southern Italy and Sicily). Roman notables acquired first-hand acquaintance with the Hellenistic world as governors and generals, and Greek doctors, secretaries, and teachers worked in their homes. Most of these Greeks were brought to Rome by Romans returning from the East or were imported as slaves. Others voluntarily settled in Rome or were sent there as envoys or hostages by their home towns. Among the latter was the Greek historian Polybius (c. 203–c. 120). He came to Rome as a hostage around 168 and later became a friend of the Cornelius Scipio family, one of the most distinguished families of *nobiles*. He wrote a history of Rome's expansion from 218 onwards, in which he also looked back on the 150 years that had preceded it. He attributed Rome's success to her balanced mixed constitution, which he considered a successful blend of the three elements of monarchy (the consuls), democracy (the popular assemblies), and aristocracy (the Senate).

Literature and other forms of amusement

The years around 200 BC saw the birth of a Roman literature that was largely modeled on Greek literature. Roman authors started to imitate Greek literary genres (epic, drama, histories, and scientific prose) in their own, Latin language. The earliest epic and historical works originated in the heroic age of the Second Punic War (218–201). Roman poets celebrated the valorous deeds of their people and Roman historians absolved Rome from guilt in the war.

The third century BC also witnessed the emergence of the Roman games that were to become so tremendously popular in later times—chariot racing and combat sports that took place in the *Circus Maximus*, a large elongated stadium at the foot of the Palatine hill, and gladiator fights in specially built timber settings or on the Forum at the center of Rome. Similar games were organized in Roman and Italian cities outside Rome. They were first held in Campania (the region around Naples) or Etruria, where they were originally funerary games, staged in honor of a deceased nobleman. Such games were definitely taking place in Rome in the third century BC, possibly even earlier. Gladiator fights were spectacles of male valor and triumph over death. The gladiators who emerged from the fights victorious had escaped death.

The Greek educational system (primary school, secondary education in literature, grammar and other subjects and higher rhetorical education; see p. 112) was introduced in Rome. Here it was usually bilingual—the pupils were taught both Greek and Latin.

Some Roman authors criticized the changes they saw around them. They interpreted the increasing luxury and the influence of the Greek way of life (clothing, athletics, luxury goods) in their circles as signs of moral decay. The increasing individualistic pursuit of private interests they saw as greed and evil ambition. Cato (234–149) is the best-known exponent of these feelings. He wrote about the Romans' virtuous and glorious ancestors and about agriculture, and vehemently criticized the growing Greek influences.

In one respect the decline of the former collective moral standards indeed implied a major threat. As Rome did not have an extensive legal system, much depended on a homogeneous acceptance of the unwritten laws that applied in politics. The disappearance of that homogeneity was to lead to much discord and uncertainty after 140 BC.

The change in mentality had consequences for foreign politics, too. Self-seeking individual *nobiles* increasingly set their own interests and glory before the wellbeing of the Roman state. At the same time, more groups came to have an interest in Rome's conquests. *Publicani* sought new areas for taxation, merchants ransacked the new additions to the empire for cheap merchandise, and other citizens saw the expansionist campaigns as ideal opportunities for acquiring booty with which to improve their economic position.

14 THE CENTURY OF THE CIVIL WARS (133–30 BC)

SERIOUS PROBLEMS AND DISCONTENT

In the second half of the second century BC the Roman republic was confronted with a number of serious problems which interacted with one another and created an unstable political climate.

The decline of the traditional free landed peasantry led to a shortage of recruits, because poorer citizens were not yet admitted to the army on a large scale. In the course of the second century BC the Roman government was on several occasions forced to reduce the minimum property requirement for service in the armies so as to be able to secure sufficient soldiers.

The poorer farmers, and in particular of course the rural proletarians, yearned for a redivision of the public land with themselves as the chief beneficiaries. Possession or lease of that land would imply better opportunities for them to earn an income (p. 152). At first, the urban proletariat in the rapidly expanding city of Rome still managed to find sufficient casual labor, for example in the building industry and in the harbors. But by 140 BC many of the major building projects had been completed and less booty, with which further projects could have been financed, was pouring into Rome. The lucrative wars in the East and North Africa were over after 146 and only the costly, bloody campaigns in Spain continued. In fact, the wars in Spain even reached a climax around 133. After 140, crop failures, transport problems, and the slave revolt in Sicily (see p. 181) moreover caused grain prices to rise. The charity that the rich patrons distributed among their clients was probably no longer adequate.

Feelings of discontent arose among the higher echelons of society, too. The *equites* ("knights") who operated as *publicani* (see p. 165) wanted more influence in administration and jurisdiction, especially in the permanent jury court that was established in 149 to handle cases of extortion in the provinces. If they were to be admitted to that jury they would be able to see to it that governors who were too lenient toward taxpayers in the provinces were punished.

A great threat to Rome was the growing resentment of her Italian allies. The Italians were not a homogeneous group. Some regions in Italy, such as Etruria and Campania, were on a par with Rome and Latium in terms of economic and cultural development. The notables living in those regions had by this time been in close contact with the Roman elite for quite some time and were in a position to communicate their wishes to the Senate and the magistrates. Other territories, such as Samnium (southeast of Rome) and other mountainous areas in the interior were more isolated and had far less contact with Rome. Regions with only few Latin *coloniae* were even more isolated. The people living in areas with a higher concentration of Latin colonies were more accustomed to the Latin language and Roman customs, standards, and legal rules. Coastal towns benefited from the flourishing trade with conquered regions and became quite prosperous. They formed a marked contrast with the many traditional farming communities living in the interior, which suffered the consequences of the trend among wealthy Romans and Italians to invest their money in land; they had thus come to monopolize the communal land (municipal and public land). It is assumed that by the end of the second century BC all Italian notables were well aware that, as Rome's allies, they had contributed as much to Rome's expansion as the Romans themselves, but they profited far less from the conquests. They had to pay their own soldiers, they received a smaller share of the booty, and they were precluded from holding offices in provincial administration and from operating as *publicani*. The Italians were also vexed by the Roman magistrates' ruthless behavior in Italy, against which they were far less capable of protecting themselves than Roman citizens. For the latter it was much easier to bring charges against a magistrate after his term of office. Some Italians began to long for full Roman citizenship, to make them equal to the Romans in every respect, but others—in particular the leaders of tribes adhering to a traditional way of life that had very little contact with Romans and Roman culture— wanted to break loose from Rome.

THE GRACCHI

Tiberius Gracchus

Tiberius Sempronius Gracchus was a *nobilis* from one of the most distinguished families in Rome. He was a brother-in-law of Scipio Aemilianus (see p. 174). His aim was to solve the shortage of recruits and at the same time improve the material position of the unpropertied citizens. In 133 BC, when he was a tribune of the *plebs*, he set up a bill reviving an old law possibly dating from 367 (see p. 152) that limited the amount of public land that any one individual could own or use (the maximum was 125 ha). The public land that would become available once this bill had been passed he intended to split up among the landless. His plan found great support among small peasants and rural proletarians, but met with fierce opposition among most senators, who regarded it as a threat to their investments in public land. They, moreover, saw Tiberius Gracchus as a potential autocrat, as they feared that he would use his popularity among the lower rural population to make a bid for power with their support. Some compared him to Greek tyrants of the past.

Tiberius Gracchus submitted his bill to the popular assembly (the *Concilium Plebis*; see p. 165), where it was passed against the will of the Senate. He saw to it that a fellow tribune who pronounced his veto after the bill had been read out (p. 156) was deposed. He became an even greater threat to the Senate when he stood for re-election as a tribune, for fear of prosecution for fabricated charges after his term of office, and started to interfere with the Senate's affairs (see p. 160). He tried to persuade the popular assembly to accept his proposal to use the treasures which Pergamum had bequeathed to Rome (p. 174) to finance his land program. But before he could realize his re-election he was murdered in public by a group of senators who saw his bid for re-election as a prelude to an attempt to gain absolute control. We may assume that they were also vexed by this interference in affairs which were traditionally the Senate's prerogative, that is, state finance and foreign politics.

After Tiberius' death his land scheme was nevertheless implemented, probably so as to prevent the risk of revolts among poor rural citizens or possibly because the Senate felt pressed by the need to solve the shortage of recruits.

The redivision of public land emphasized and intensified the Italians' resentment. Large amounts of public land were confiscated from Italian landholders and, as it was not so easy for them to appeal to a Roman judge, the lack of Roman citizenship was felt ever more acutely. After 129 the redistribution of public land gradually came to an end, but the Italians' discontent remained a burning issue.

Gaius Gracchus

Ten years after the death of his older brother, Gaius Sempronius Gracchus was elected tribune of the *plebs*. He was a great orator and a far more radical politician than his brother had been. Gaius was elected tribune of the *plebs* twice in succession (123 and 122 BC). His aims were to continue the redistribution of public land in Italy, solve the Italian problem, improve the existence of the proletariat in Rome, and settle landless citizens in a colony which he intended to found at the site of the former city of Carthage (which had been destroyed in 146; see p. 174). He also wanted to break the power of the *nobiles*, the traditional group of regents in the Senate. The senators who had opposed his brother (the majority in the Senate) distrusted Gaius even more and fiercely resisted his plans. They feared that such an overseas colony would evolve into a closed rank of private supporters for Gaius Gracchus, and his long term of office as tribune of the *plebs* also caused them much concern—this they saw as a prelude to a form of absolute power.

Gaius tried to break their resistance by securing the loyalty of different interest groups by granting them political favors. To this end he had the popular assembly (*Concilium Plebis*) pass various bills intended to enable him to achieve his political goals while at the same time accumulating a powerful backing. One of the new laws granted the *equites* the right to compose the juries that tried extortion cases (see p. 176). By arranging state subsidies for the purchase of grain he made the population of Rome happy with a fixed low wheat price. It was of course only the Roman citizens who benefited from this favor. Gaius also proposed to grant the Italians Roman citizenship, but that proposal was rejected. All the ranks of the Roman citizenry were against granting the Italians any more benefits of Rome's expansion than they already enjoyed.

In 121 Gaius Gracchus and some three thousand of his followers were murdered by the conservative senators and their backing of clients and political allies. Gaius' plans for the foundation of a colony in North Africa came to nothing, but all his other reforms were retained. The grain subsidies came to be a heavy burden on the state treasury.

Political consequences of the Gracchan reforms

The political struggle of 133–121 affected the elite's internal cohesion and undermined the old political codes of conduct. Violence had become a means for achieving political aims. Hostility grew between the senators and the *equites*. This development coincided with the emergence of a perceptible distinction between the two groups. In 129 the senators and the *equites* became two separate orders.

Political distinctions arose within the Senate itself, too. There was a group of senators who were of the opinion that reforms were necessary. These senators, who were known as *populares*, wanted the popular assembly to pass proposals for reforms, if necessary against the will of the senatorial majority. The *populares* were by no means all idealistic reformers. Many of them were only interested in strengthening their own position within the Roman elite. The word *populares* comes from *populus* (people). They were so called because they tried to realize their political aims via the popular assembly. But in the Senate the *optimates* were in the majority. They wanted things to remain as they were where possible. The word *optimates* is derived from *optimi* (the best). The *equites*, the Italian notables, and the lower classes in Rome did not steer a fixed course in the ensuing political struggles. In determining their political preferences they were usually guided by ties of patronage or concrete private interests. There were no political parties with a more or less fixed group of followers and an ideologically founded program.

MARIUS' MILITARY REFORMS

In the years 113–100 BC wars against the Numidians in North Africa, who, after being Rome's allies for a century, had now revolted, and troubles with migrating German tribes demanded Rome's full attention. It was in these years that Rome first collided with the Germans, in this case the Cimbri (from Jutland) and the Teutones (from central Germany), who had left their homelands in search of better occupation areas. Corruption scandals in North Africa and crushing defeats in the wars against the Germans brought discredit on the *nobiles*. The defeat at Arausio (now Orange, near the Rhone in southern France) in 105 was as disastrous for Rome as the defeat at Cannae in 216 had been.

The competent general Gaius Marius (157–86 BC), a "new man" from the equestrian order, who was elected consul six times between 107 and 100 (in defiance of the law banning the re-election of consuls; a testimony to the crisis of the republic and the voters' lack of confidence in the old rulers), reformed the army and brought the wars to a successful conclusion. He subjected his recruits to a gladiatorial training program, equipped them with better and more varied arms, and introduced more efficient fighting tactics. More so than in the past, Roman units were now given standard arms and equipment. Marius composed legions of six thousand (uniformly armed) men, organized into ten cohorts which could operate as independent units in a battle. This system afforded greater tactical possibilities than the former *phalanx* organization. Marius' system was to be retained, with only minor changes, until well into the imperial age. It was soon to prove its worth, for in 102 Marius defeated the Teutones in southern Gaul, and in 101 he routed the Cimbri in northern Italy.

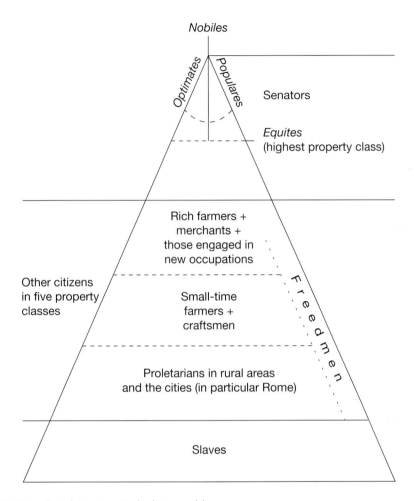

FIGURE 14.1   Social structure in the late republic

Another of Marius' reforms was the admission into the army of proletarian volunteers, who were armed by the state. This was the culmination of a development that had started in the second century BC, when progressively poorer citizens had been recruited. The old property qualification for service in the heavily armed forces had been increasingly often ignored after 218 (the outbreak of the Second Punic War) and in the second century BC the state had had to contribute more and more towards equipping the armies. The soldiers in effect became semi-professionals, who enlisted for the sake of improving their material position and were armed by the state. This, alongside Gaius Gracchus' grain subsidies, came to be the treasury's heaviest burden.

The new burdens on the state treasury prompted further imperialistic campaigns: Rome went in search of fresh areas on which she would be able to levy taxes. So yet another incentive to expansion was added to those already mentioned above, with respect to the changed mentality. Rome's imperialism increasingly became a matter of material benefit for the treasury, the notables, the *publicani*, the merchants, the soldiers, the populace in Rome, and everyone who profited

FIGURE 14.2 A Roman officer in the first century BC

indirectly from Rome's conquests. It was also boosted by the ambition and desire for prestige of the Roman leaders.

Marius and the other contemporary political leaders did not fix periods of service or arrange pensions for the new proletarian soldiers. The soldiers were simply discharged when a war was over, just as in the past. But the proletarian soldiers had no farm or anything else to fall back on and they became a political threat. Unpropertied citizens would volunteer for military service for the sake of improving their economic position and, after the war for which they had been enrolled was over, they desired a plot of land for their support or money with which to buy a workshop in Rome or another town, and a slave who would do most of the work for them. Subject to the availability of sufficient booty, discharged soldiers would at the end of a campaign regularly be rewarded with bonuses in the form of money, valuable goods, or slaves. The Senate, however, always tried to prevent the distribution of land among ex-soldiers. They were afraid that that would lead to the formation of military colonies, which would support their former commander as one man. The majority of the senators had previously opposed Gaius Gracchus' colonization plans for more or less the same reason. One of their greatest fears was a disturbance of the balance of power within the oligarchy. The generals were almost always important fellow senators who already had large numbers of clients and ramified networks of relations. If colonies of veterans should be added to those numbers, the generals would have a very powerful backing indeed.

Competent generals who won wars and were able to grant their soldiers booty and land would be in a position to use their soldiers as private support in political struggles providing they were—or appeared to be—fighting for a just cause: Roman soldiers had a lot of respect for laws and regulations. The generals moreover had to have good ties with their officers—the military tribunes, the prefects of the auxiliaries, and the centurions (see p. 162)—because they had a decisive influence on the troops. So smart generals would enrich their officers and offer them the prospect of rising to a higher social rank, for example by securing them a good position in the local government of a town in Italy.

FIGURE 14.3 The basis of power of important generals

Note. Period: the civil wars.

Dignitas: dignity; high status obtained through major achievements, especially military achievements.

Not indicated in this diagram is the continuing expansion of the Roman empire, its capital, and the retinues of the powerful politicans and generals.

Authors writing around the time of the civil wars complained about the unbridled greed and ambition of the powerful politicians; this figure illustrates their complaint.

The first signs heralding the armies' potential new political role already appeared in Marius' own time. In 103 and 100 BC serious conflicts broke out concerning the foundation of colonies for Marius' veterans who had fought in North Africa and against the Germans. Marius himself remained loyal toward the Senate and did not wish to use his troops as a political weapon, but a few radical *populares* amongst his followers were differently disposed. In their capacity as tribunes of the *plebs* they used violence to persuade the popular assembly to pass land and colonization bills. The consequence was that Marius' veterans were granted land in Tuscany, the Po valley, and North Africa. This affair widened the breach between the *optimates* and the *populares* within the Senate.

THE SOCIAL WAR (91–88 BC) AND THE FIRST CIVIL WAR (88–82 BC)

Citizenship for the Italian allies

Discontent had been smoldering amongst the Italian allies since the time of the Gracchi. In the years 100–91 BC attempts to arrive at a peaceful solution failed and in 91 BC most of the Italian allies took up arms. They established their own federal state, with a center of communal government in the interior of central Italy. In a short but savage war, known as the Social War (*socii* = allies), Rome managed to quickly win over Italian regions with close ties with the Romans, such as Etruria, by making concessions: those regions were the first to be granted Roman citizenship. Rome then won the war in military terms, but did not want to alienate herself from the other Italian allies for good. And so, after 88, she admitted the Italians to the Roman citizenry and recorded them as citizens. The number of adult male Roman citizens consequently increased from about 400,000 in 88 BC to 1.03 million in 83 BC. The Italian contingents were abolished; from this point onwards Italian soldiers served in the Roman legions and wealthy Italians qualified for admission to the Roman knighthood.

Italy came to consist of self-governing communities of Roman citizens. They were governed by oligarchic town councils and the local magistrates they produced. These local oligarchies consisted of large landowners with estates and farms outside the town walls, some of whom also owned property in more remote parts of Italy. On the basis of parallel developments in later times, for example in towns in the provinces on the Iberian peninsula, we assume that the occupants of the Italian communities now enjoyed two types of citizenship: Roman and local. The differences that had previously existed between individual parts of the Italian peninsula (p. 186) remained, but they did gradually become less pronounced. The terms *colonia* and *municipium* (pp. 151–4) now referred to communities of Roman citizens in Italy that differed from one another in terms of the privileges they enjoyed. A *colonia* was generally assumed to rank higher in status than a *municipium*. The latter term lost its former specific meaning and came to stand for a Roman town with its surrounding land. Another term that was more commonly used to refer to an urban settlement with surrounding land was *civitas*. This term was also used for towns and comparable centers of occupation with surrounding land in the western and northern provinces and in the Greek-speaking eastern parts of the empire. The English word "city" and the French *cité* both come from *civitas*. The local rulers of Greek-speaking towns often still used the old Greek term *polis*; this came to stand for something rather like what we would term a municipality (town + surrounding land) today.

The Romanization of Italy, which had started many years earlier (*c.* 300 BC), was greatly accelerated by this development. It went hand in hand with the spread of urbanization, even in fairly isolated areas with a traditional way of life. Italy evolved into a country full of small and medium-sized cities with impressive centers modeled on Hellenistic examples (see p. 121, Figure 11.1), from which the surrounding rural areas were governed. Those rural areas contained the estates of local and Roman notables, which were worked by slaves and tenant farmers, and the farms of the remaining independent small landowning farmers.

In the fifty years that followed the Social War the Italian notables came to form a third order (known as *decuriones*), below the two higher orders of senators and knights. Just as new senators were occasionally chosen from the equestrian order, so too new knights were from time to time recruited from the Italian local elites.

The popular assemblies

Roman citizenship in effect came to be a legal concept, a set of private and civil rights. Its political dimension diminished because only a small percentage of the citizens still voted in the assemblies on a regular basis. Most Romans (old citizens) and Italians (new citizens) who lived outside Rome only went to vote when a patron drummed them up, to help him win an election or get a bill passed. And they were mostly wealthy citizens, who didn't have to work on the land or in a workshop.

Usually the popular assembly (in particular the *Comitia Tributa* or the *Concilium Plebis*) was dominated by a group of citizens living in Rome, who gave their votes to successful men who granted them donatives, organized games, and behaved in a popularist fashion. Such politicians would often use intermediates to influence groups of town dwellers, for example members of trade associations. Such associations were known as *collegia* (plural of *collegium*). The popular politicians used tribunes with whom they were friendly as their henchmen. The latter would see to it that the popular assembly passed bills and measures that were to the advantage of their "bosses." The tribunate became a vehicle of demagogic politics.

The First Civil War (88–82 BC)

The political tension that had been building up since the middle of the second century BC (see p. 185) ultimately exploded in civil wars. Conflicting interest groups rallied around generals who competed for power and used their troops as political weapons. They availed themselves of tribunes, clients, and wide networks of political and private relations in Rome, Italy, and the provinces. Via these networks the civil struggles in Rome were propagated to the furthest corners of the empire.

The First Civil War (88–82) broke out when the armies that had fought the Italians (91–88) were still in the field. Its cause was a conflict between the two most important generals and politicians of those days, the aforementioned Marius and L. Cornelius Sulla (138–78 BC), who had served under Marius in the wars against the Numidians and the Germans, and had been the most successful Roman commander in the Social War.

Marius and Sulla competed for the supreme command in a new foreign war, against Mithridates, king of Pontus from 120 to 64 BC. Pontus was a Hellenistic kingdom in the north of Asia Minor (Map 14.1) which the Romans had hitherto left alone.

Around 100 BC Mithridates had built up a powerful empire along the eastern shores of the Black Sea, from Pontus up to and including the Crimea. He saw the conflict between the Romans and the Italians as a good opportunity to attempt to reduce the Romans' influence in Asia Minor. At first, Mithridates received much support from the exploited natives in the Roman province of Asia and in Greece.

He initiated the war in 88 by killing Romans and Italians all over Asia. But when, soon after this act, Mithridates proved himself as much an oppressor as Rome had been, many natives, in particular the notables in the Greek cities, moved over to Rome again (see p. 175).

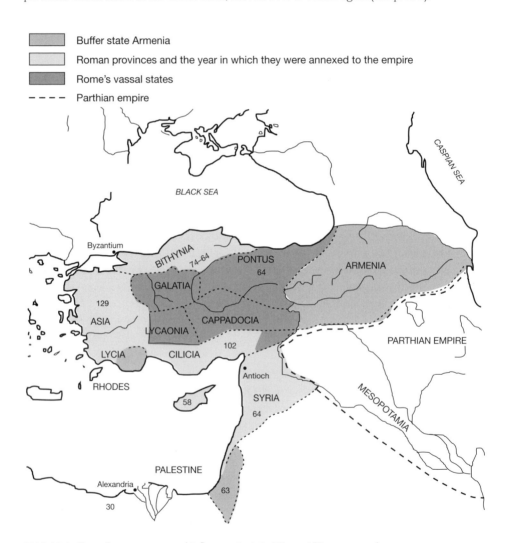

MAP 14.1 Rome's conquests and influence in Asia Minor, 133 BC onwards

The Senate granted Sulla, who had been elected consul for the year 88, the command against Mithridates. It was common practice for the Senate to allocate military command, for the Senate controlled foreign politics. But this time things went differently. A tribune who sympathized with Marius persuaded the popular assembly to transfer the command to Marius. The *populares* in the Senate, most of the knights who were active as *publicani* and bankers, the majority of the Italian elite, Marius' veterans, and the greater part of the urban proletariat in Rome supported Marius. The *publicani* in particular expected to gain more from him than from Sulla. Sulla was supported by many *optimates* with their private backing and the soldiers who had served under him in the Social War. He responded to this transfer in command by marching his army into Rome and occupying the city—an outrageous act!

Sulla then secured important magistracies for his chief supporters, resumed his command, and departed for the East. However, after he had left, in 87, Marius and his followers seized power in Rome and executed some of Sulla's followers. Marius was not to enjoy his triumph for very long, though, for he died shortly after (early 86).

In the years 88–84 Sulla won the war against Mithridates in Greece and western Asia Minor and returned to Italy with an experienced army that was completely devoted to him. Mithridates was allowed to retain his original kingdom in Pontus. Sulla would not allow himself the time to defeat him there too.

In the years 83–82 Sulla defeated the Marians in a fierce, bloody civil war in Italy. In 82 he had himself proclaimed *dictator*, without the traditional restriction to six months of office (see p. 149). He shamelessly enriched his soldiers and settled some 80,000 of his own and Marius' veterans on land in Italy which he confiscated from his political enemies and from communities that had chosen in favor of Marius. Sulla then began a reign of terror in which he is thought to have liquidated about a hundred senators, representing about one-third of this order, plus an assumed sixteen hundred knights, which may then have amounted to one-ninth of this group. The men who were deemed enemies of the state were publically identified, which is why such a reign of terror is commonly known as a "proscription." The victims' property was confiscated and fell to the state. Sulla's attempt to fill the state coffers by selling confiscated land caused the prices of land in Italy to plummet. Some of Sulla's henchmen, such as the distinguished senator M. Licinius Crassus, would buy chattels and estates at a low price and wait for the land prices to recover before selling them. This made Crassus the wealthiest senator in Rome.

Sulla introduced a series of new laws with which he hoped to restore stable government. Statutory rules started to take the place of unwritten standards of political conduct now that the consensus regarding such matters had disappeared within the elite (see p. 184). Sulla ejected the knights from the juries, but as a form of compensation he admitted three hundred knights who sympathized with him to the Senate. This raised the number of senators to six hundred and marked the definitive end of the Senate's internal cohesion. Sulla created five new permanent criminal courts that were to handle different kinds of offences. These courts were presided over by praetors. The tribunate was stripped of many of its powers. The persons who had held this office were, moreover, no longer allowed to stand for election to higher offices. By these measures Sulla hoped to dull the cutting edge of the populares' demagogic politics. In 79 Sulla voluntarily resigned. He died shortly after, in 78.

THE YEARS 79–49 BC

The thirty years between Sulla's resignation and the outbreak of the Second Civil War (49–45) witnessed the aggravation of the internal problems and a number of major wars. The powerful politicians in these years were Gnaeus Pompeius (Pompey, 106–48), Marcus Licinius Crassus (*c.* 112–53) and Gaius Julius Caesar (102–44). Pompey restored order in the Roman part of the Iberian peninsula and reorganized the province. The Romanization that had successfully begun in southern and eastern Spain in the second century gradually spread across the entire peninsula in the subsequent period, though northwestern Spain was to remain outside Rome's sphere of influence until the time of the emperor Augustus. Here, too, as in Italy, the process of Romanization went hand in hand with the emergence of Roman-style towns surrounded by rural areas that were governed by landowning elites living in the cities.

Italy remained restless. Sulla's attempts to solve the old social and political problems (see p. 195) had been unsuccessful and the civil war and Sulla's reign of terror had caused much suffering. Italy was full of discontented men seeking revenge and bankrupt veterans who had failed to make a living for themselves as farmers.

FIGURE 14.4
Gnaeus Pompeius (Pompey)
(106–48 BC)

Notes. Pompey started his career as an officer in his father's army in the Social War (91–88 BC). He then served as a junior commander in Sulla's army in Italy in 83, at the head of a private army that he had recruited from among his father's veterans. After that, he led campaigns into North Africa, Sicily, and Spain. Pompey did not pursue the usual *cursus honorum*; in 70 BC he achieved the consulship without having held a lower office, which was quite exceptional. After that year he was granted more extraordinary commands, first against the pirates (67) and later against Mithridates of Pontus (66–63). In 60 he allied himself with Caesar and Crassus. In 57 and 52 he was granted extraordinary powers to solve problems in Rome (grain supply, restoration of order). In 49–48 he was defeated by Caesar in the Second Civil War. In 48, having been devastatingly defeated by Caesar at Pharsalus in Greece, Pompey fled to Egypt, where he was treacherously murdered.

Spartacus' slave revolt (73–71 BC)

Crassus is best known for his suppression of the greatest slave revolt Italy had so far experienced. For two years tens of thousands of pillaging slaves had roamed Italy, led by the former gladiator Spartacus. They yearned for freedom and an acceptable economic position. Some of them wanted to return to their home countries. Their revolt was not motivated by any ideologically founded program (see p. 181). In 71 Crassus' legions repressed the slaves' revolt in a bloody battle.

After 71 no more major slave revolts broke out in Italy, Sicily, or the other provinces for over three centuries. Slaves were treated in a slightly better manner and there were no longer such large, homogeneous concentrations of them who, having been in Italy or Sicily for only a short time, still avidly recalled their days of freedom. The proportion of slaves who had been born into slavery and had hence never known a different life steadily increased. The slaves hoped to be released some day. Their hopes were not unfounded, for in Rome and elsewhere in Italy manumission became increasingly common; it served as a means of diverting discontent and as an incentive for encouraging slaves to work hard.

Pompey, Crassus, and Caesar

In 70 BC the two most important political magnates and generals of the time, Pompey and Crassus, were both elected consul. They undid the restrictions that Sulla had imposed on the tribunate. Pompey in particular was to benefit from this. On two occasions (67 and 66) tribunes with whom

FIGURE 14.5 According to an eighteenth-century illustrator, this is the mausoleum of Caecilia Metella

Notes. Caecilia Metella was the daughter of Q(uintus) Caecilius Metellus Creticus. She was married to a member of the Licinius Crassus family. The Caecilius Metellus family played an important part in Roman politics between 150 and 50 BC. The Licinii Crassi were also a powerful family. Such important families often intermarried for the purpose of strengthening their political positions. They also built large funerary monuments to emphasize their high status.

he was friendly succeeded in persuading the popular assembly (*Concilium Plebis*) to grant him important commands with powers that exceeded those of a consul and a proconsul and applied in several provinces (*imperium majus* = greater *imperium*). The majority of the Senate was of course very much against this.

Pompey abused his special powers to further strengthen his political position and expand his backing of soldiers and protégés in Italy and the provinces. He and his supporters almost came to constitute a state within the state. In 67 BC he acquired authority over all the coastal regions in the empire and within three months he did away with the pirates, who had evolved into an autonomous power and were ravaging many coastal areas. They had even established contacts with Mithridates, Spartacus, and Sertorius (Pompey's opponent in Spain). We have already seen above (p. 181) how they had managed to acquire such power.

In the years 66–64 BC Pompey settled accounts with Mithridates of Pontus, who had been at war with Rome again since 74 BC. In 64/63, acting on his own authority, Pompey reorganized Asia Minor into a system of Roman provinces and vassal kingdoms (see Map 14.1) and annexed Syria (the last remaining part of the Seleucid kingdom) and Judea to the Roman empire. Syria was turned into a province and the Jewish territory became a vassal state. That put an end to the independent Jewish kingdom of the Maccabees, which had existed since 142 BC (see p. 137). The Euphrates came to mark the border between the Roman empire and the kingdom of the Parthians, who ruled over Mesopotamia and Iran.

In the meantime, in Rome, Caesar had risen to power. After an adventurous start and several military expeditions to Asia Minor (82–73) he followed the usual *cursus honorum* (standard political career). A *popularis*, he continued along the course marked out by the Gracchi and the Marians. In a series of lawsuits he prosecuted many of Sulla's executioners and henchmen and openly admitted to his Marian sympathies. His generosity and popular behavior won him the favor of the lower classes in Rome, but his lavish lifestyle and generosity did plunge him into deep debt. In 61, while he was a governor in northern Spain, he won a war against the last free tribes in the northwest of that country (see Map 14.2). That granted him a substantial booty, which helped him pay off his debts. It also boosted his military reputation.

Crassus had started his career as Sulla's second-in-command, but had gradually gone over to the *populares*. He had become the champion of the *publicani*, who looked to him to defend their interests in the Senate. He also lent money to many senators—including Caesar—which granted him a lot of influence in the Senate.

The resentment against Pompey, Crassus, and Caesar's power grew among the *optimates* in the Senate. In 63 BC the Senate successfully crushed a conspiracy led by Lucius Sergius Catilina (Catiline), an impoverished patrician from a family that had for quite some time not provided any consuls. He had military experience and had been one of Sulla's henchmen and executioners. As a senator, he lacked authority in the Senate and that was one of the reasons why his desire to achieve the consulship remained unsatisfied in 65, 64, and again in 63. Out of rancour he organized a coalition of discontented parties all over Italy and established contacts with a rebellious tribe in southern Gaul (Pompey's opponents in Spain had formed similar combinations of dissident Romans and rebellious tribes; p. 196). The consul M(arcus) Tullius Cicero (106–43), a *homo novus* (new man) from the equestrian order who had made a successful career in politics thanks to his great rhetorical skills and the support of a number of important *nobiles* (including

Annexed to the Roman empire by Pompey and Caesar

The Roman empire in 62 BC

Caesar's campaigns against the Pompeians and the *optimates* in the second Civil War (x = places where battles were fought). Pompey fought battles at Dyrrachim (D) and Pharsalus (PH), where Caesar won. Pompey then fled to Egypt. Caesar followed him, restored order in Egypt in 47, and returned to Rome via Asia Minor. In passing, he defeated one of the sons of Mithridates of Pontus who had rebelled against Rome.

In 46 BC Caesar defeated the *optimates* in North Africa and in 45 he settled accounts with the army of Pompey's two sons in Spain. Pompey himself had been killed in Egypt in 48.

GT   *Gallia Transalpina*

GC   *Gallia Cisalpina*

MAP 14.2   The situation under Caesar and Pompey

Pompey), played an important part in this affair. He exposed Catiline's conspiracy to the Senate and the *Consilium Plebis* and crushed it with the assistance of some of Pompey's officers and *nobiles* with military experience. The Catiline conspiracy was to acquire great fame largely thanks to a particularly well-written treatise by the historian Sallust (p. 205) and the speeches that Cicero devoted to it, but in itself this affair was no serious threat to the Roman state.

FIGURE 14.6
M(arcus) Tullius Cicero (106–43 BC)

Notes. A great orator and prose writer who is particularly well-known for his speeches, rhetorical treatises, philosophical works, and letters. Cicero is regarded as one of the founders of written classical Latin.

Cicero often opposed the *populares*, but the *optimates* thought very little of him because of his low social origin. At first he supported Pompey, but after 60 BC he tried to steer a middle course between the different rulers and groups in the Senate.

The *optimates* thought that they would now also be able to put Pompey, Crassus, and Caesar in their places and obstructed all their aims and ambitions in the Senate. In 62, after Pompey's return to Rome, they successfully prevented a distribution of land amongst Pompey's veterans and refused to ratify Pompey's arrangements in the East.

The first Triumvirate

In 60 BC the three politicians privately agreed to assist one another in their political struggles. This agreement is known as "the first Triumvirate" (to distinguish it from the second, of 43 BC; see p. 204). Together, they secured the election of Caesar to the consulship in 59. With violence, and without consulting the Senate, Caesar persuaded the public assembly to pass a bill granting land to Pompey's veterans. As for himself, with the help of a sympathizing tribune he saw to it that the popular assembly voted him an important command in Gaul. Like Pompey before him, he used his command to pursue private ambitions. In the years 58–50 BC he conquered all of Gaul up to the Rhine. Caesar became one of the richest men in Rome and acquired a large backing of formerly pro-Marian families, Italian notables, knights, and senators. The successful Gallic campaign turned his army into the best-trained and most disciplined fighting machine of those days; his men were entirely devoted to him. Pompey's and Caesar's foreign adventures clearly reflect the consequences of the change in Rome's imperialist policy outlined above: the pursuit of private interests, power, and wealth of a small number of political magnates had become the chief motivation for expansion (see Figure 14.3 on p. 191).

Chaos in Rome

Rome was in these years the seat of fierce political struggles involving mob violence and political mock trials. There was progressively more scope for demagogues to manipulate the masses, because with every new generation the lower classes of citizens in Rome became more alienated from the old state institutions as the distance between them and the ruling *nobiles* increased.

One of the men who saw the masses in Rome as a vehicle for acquiring more power was the demagogue P(ublius) Clodius, a *nobilis* born into a patrician family. He left the patriciate so as to be able to become a plebeian tribune (see p. 156) and play politics via the popular assembly. Caesar helped him switch to the status of plebeian. Clodius found his greatest support among the *collegia*, associations of craftsmen which often doubled as neighborhood associations as many craftsmen tended to live in the same neighborhoods. From those *collegia* Clodius recruited a group of supporters who were willing to enforce his wishes with violence. In 58 he managed to persuade the popular assembly to acknowledge the *collegia* and convert the subsidizing of grain into the distribution of free wheat. He also got Cicero, his greatest enemy, exiled, but Pompey saw to it that he was recalled in 57. More bills were passed under Clodius' influence, but it would be beyond the scope of this account to discuss them all here. Better than any other Roman politician Clodius knew how to control politics through violence and by exploiting his demagogic skills. But his star soon began to wane. In 57 Pompey turned against him and unleashed a counterterror campaign on him. His rival Milo, one of Pompey's henchmen, gathered a backing of armed servants, most of whom were former gladiators.

Clodius' grain bill meanwhile had major consequences in the form of a massive influx into Rome of impoverished citizens from all over Italy and slaves who had been freed by their masters as they had become unprofitable (they were effectively written off as workers). In less than ten years the number of people receiving free wheat in Rome rose to about 320,000. To stem the chaos and street violence in Rome, the Senate granted Pompey special powers in 57 and 52 BC: in 57 to improve the supply of grain to Rome and in 52 (when he was appointed sole consul) to control the mob violence. Both tasks he successfully fulfilled. In 52 Clodius was killed by Milo's supporters, which led to a notorious lawsuit against Milo. Cicero defended him, but was unable to prevent his exile.

In the meantime Crassus disappeared from the scene. In 56, when the Triumvirate was renewed, he had had himself appointed to an important command against the Parthians at the eastern border of Syria (Caesar remained in Gaul and Pompey in Rome), but in 53 BC he lost the war against the Parthians, dying on the battlefield. The main reasons for his defeat were his failure to establish a logistic system adapted to the conditions of the dry region between the Parthian and Roman empires and his inability to cope with the Parthian cavalry's swift hit-and-run tactics.

In Rome, Pompey and the *optimates* started to grow closer to one another after 52, for fear of the rising star of Caesar, who was achieving great successes in Gaul, conquering one region after another. He even launched expeditions to Britain and Germany beyond the Rhine, but without any permanent results—both territories remained outside the empire. Conquered Gaul did not: from 50 BC onwards it belonged to the Roman empire. Until the time of the emperor Augustus (see the next chapter) there were two provinces in Gaul: the old province Gallia Narbonensis (in southern France), which had been added to the empire in 121 BC, and the new province Gallia Comata. The river Rhine became the latter's boundary in the north. In 50 Pompey and the *optimates* entered into a monstrous alliance with the intention of bringing about Caesar's downfall.

Many people in Rome began to yearn for restoration of order and peace, but without the abolishment of the existing state institutions. In 52–50 the orator, politician, and philosopher Cicero wrote two works on the state in imitation of Plato. In his opinion the solution to Rome's problems lay in concord between the higher orders (in particular the senators and knights) and a curtailment of the greed and ambition of the powerful. The existing polity should be turned into a mixed constitution (see p. 183 on Polybius), and the state should be ruled by senators who were well prepared for their tasks and who were selected for their virtues. Cicero still thought entirely in terms of the old city state, which was not surprising: nobody in Rome had yet come to realize that the organs of a city state were not suited to the administration of a large empire comprising a wide diversity of peoples and cultures and having a capital with around 800,000 inhabitants.

THE SECOND CIVIL WAR (49–45 BC) AND ITS AFTERMATH (44–30 BC)

The year 49 BC saw the outbreak of a civil war between Pompey and the *optimates* on the one hand and Caesar and his followers on the other. Caesar won this war in a series of daring and spectacular campaigns which, between 49 and 45 BC, took him to all the corners of the Roman empire (see Map 14.2). In passing, in 47 BC, he restored order in Egypt, which was then torn apart by succession struggles (p. 126). Caesar subsequently helped Cleopatra to ascend the throne as Egypt's queen. In 47 BC Caesar was appointed *dictator* and in 44 he was even made *dictator* for life. He appointed magistrates on his own authority and admitted his agents and henchmen into the Senate. At the time of his death, in 44 BC, the Senate had about one thousand members, the great majority of whom came from the traditional high orders. Authors with a traditional outlook accused Caesar of having admitted lowly upstarts to the Senate, but that's not correct. We actually know of only one or two senators who were at one time centurions in Caesar's army. Caesar was more lenient than Sulla; he spared the lives and wealth of most of his opponents.

Between his campaigns, he launched his program of reforms. He tightened the control of the governors in the provinces, limited the number of recipients of wheat in the city of Rome to 150,000, and settled about 40,000 veterans and tens of thousands of proletarians and freedmen from Rome in colonies, two of which were founded at the sites of the former cities of Carthage and Corinth, which had both been destroyed in 146 BC and were rebuilt as Roman cities.

Caesar governed the Roman empire like an absolute monarch. He had himself appointed *dictator* in 46, and in 44 *dictator* for life. That was the reason for his assassination, on 15 March

FIGURE 14.7 The Senate House, built in Caesar's time

Note. It was restored in late antiquity (during Diocletian's reign, AD 284–305).

44, by the *optimates* Marcus Junius Brutus and Gaius Cassius Longinus. But Caesar's murder did not lead to the restoration of the old regime, for after his death his adherents, supported by his soldiers, seized control in Rome. They were led by Marcus Antonius (Mark Antony, like Caesar consul in 44), Marcus Aemilius Lepidus, and Gaius Octavius, one of Caesar's young grandnephews (born in 63 BC), whom he had posthumously adopted as his son in his will (Caesar had no legitimate sons of his own; he did have an illegitimate son with Cleopatra). After his adoption, Octavius' full name became Gaius Julius Caesar Octavianus (Octavian). He illegally admitted veterans of Caesar into his private army. Brutus and Cassius fled to the eastern provinces.

When Caesar's inheritance brought Antony and Octavian into conflict with one another, the Caesarians' enemies seized their chance to build up military power. One of Pompey's sons (Sextus Pompeius) built a strong fleet and established himself on Sicily, from where he could obstruct the supply of grain to Rome (see p. 181). Brutus and Cassius composed an army in the eastern provinces. The Senate, which regarded Antony as the strongest party, supported Octavian in his struggle against Antony, legalized his army, and sent him on campaign (officially with

praetorian *imperium* under the consuls of 43 BC)
against Antony, who had illegally seized Gallia
Cisalpina as his province. Antony was beaten
at Mutina (Modena) in the Po valley, but the
consuls fell in battle. Octavian then demanded
appointment as consul, even though he was far
too young for that office. The senators, and in
particular Cicero, thought they would now be
able to get rid of Octavian, but had to yield and
the Caesarian leaders came to terms and
formed the Second Triumvirate. The three men
saw to it that the popular assembly granted
them dictatorial powers in Rome, Italy, and the
provinces. In the years 42–36 they then settled
scores with the *optimates* and Pompey junior in
a series of major battles at sea and on land and
a reign of terror. One of the victims was Cicero,
who had always been hostile to Antony, and was
of the opinion that Antony should have been
murdered along with Caesar in 44.

The greatest battle was fought in 42 at
Philippi, in Macedonia, where Antony (and
Octavian) decisively defeated Brutus and
Cassius. After this battle Lepidus ruled over
Africa and Antony over the eastern half of the
empire, while Octavian set about restoring order

FIGURE 14.8 G(aius) Julius Caesar (102–44 BC)

Note. An important politician, statesman, general,
and prose writer (he justified his behavior in Gaul and
in the Second Civil War in two books).

in Italy. In 41–40 Octavian ruthlessly confiscated land from eighteen selected communities in Italy, on which he settled almost 100,000
veterans who had fought for the Triumvirs and their opponents and whose services were now
no longer required. These confiscations, together with those during the reign of terror against
the Caesarians' opponents, were the greatest Italy had ever known. In 36 Octavian liquidated
Pompey's son and sidetracked Lepidus. Lepidus' troops defected to Octavian, who now had
control over the entire western half of the empire.

Since 42 Antony had been behaving like a Hellenistic absolute monarch in the East and had
started to work together with Cleopatra, the queen of Egypt. In 36 Antony suffered a costly defeat
against the Parthians, which made him dependent on subsidies granted by Cleopatra, in return
for which he had to comply with all her demands. Via Antony, Cleopatra hoped to gain control
over rich regions so as to be able to revive the faded glory of the Ptolemies (she was the last of
this dynasty to rule over Egypt).

In 33–32, in a shrewd propaganda campaign, Octavian managed to win the support of the
Caesarians and almost everyone else in Italy and the western provinces in his struggle against
Antony and Cleopatra's "Eastern despotism."

In 32 the Italian communities took an oath of allegiance to Octavian (the *coniuratio Italiae*). Octavian defeated Antony and Cleopatra in 31 BC in a naval battle off Actium (close to what is now Albania in the Balkans) and in 30 he conquered Egypt. Antony and Cleopatra committed suicide in Alexandria. Octavian then returned to Italy, where he used his copious Egyptian booty to *buy* land for the tens of thousands of superfluous soldiers. There was no longer any need for him to confiscate land for this purpose.

Octavian had brought the civil wars to an end and was the sole surviving ruler. He owed his victory to a group of faithful friends (among whom were Maecenas and Agrippa) who helped him in every respect and won his naval and land battles for him, to Caesar's soldiers, who regarded him as Caesar's own son, and to Caesar's agents and henchmen, who supported his enterprises financially and in any other way they could. At first, in the years following Caesar's death, Octavian was greatly dependent on the support of Caesar's followers, but he gradually gathered his own backing and an army of his own. But to acquire a permanent, stable position, Octavian had to seek the support of a wider circle (including, in particular, the notables), without however estranging his soldiers and the Caesarians.

Octavian set out from a good starting position: almost everyone was now prepared to accept a moderate form of monarchic rule if that would mean a definite end to the civil wars. The civil wars after 44 had caused much dismay. Never before had so many Roman soldiers been under arms and never before had so many men died in civil strife (see the box on p. 206).

THE FLOURISHING OF CULTURAL LIFE DURING THE CIVIL WARS

For the arts and humanities the period of the civil wars was by no means a period of decline. In fact, it was only now that Roman architecture and the visual arts came into bloom, partly as a result of the inspiration provided by Greek examples.

In the realm of literature, the fifty years between 80 and 30 BC were characterized by great productivity. Cicero wrote not only about the state, but also about rhetoric and (ethical) philosophy. From a whole range of Greek works he selected that which best suited his purpose, which he then remodeled into a work of his own. His speeches, which were often published in a polished form afterwards, were regarded as examples of pure classical Latin in later centuries, even after antiquity.

Caesar wrote long memoirs to justify his deeds in Gaul and his behavior in the Second Civil War. Roman poets, historians, and writers of scholarly prose texts produced works in imitation of Greek authors which have remained classics to this day. The best-known historian of this period is Sallust, one of Caesar's followers and an opponent of the *optimates*. Writing in the style of the Greek historian Thucydides (see p. 116), he discussed the war against the Numidian king Iugurtha (p. 188) and the Catiline conspiracy (p. 198).

In 55 BC Rome acquired her first stone theater. Its construction, on the field of Mars, was commissioned by Pompey. Adjoining it was a temple dedicated to the goddess Venus. Until then, the Romans had used timber theaters and temporary settings erected at venues such as the Forum at the center of town. Theaters were intended for musical performances and drama. Cicero tells us that the Circus Maximus—a hippodrome at the foot of the Palatine hill (see Map 12.5)—was

NUMBER OF CITIZENS UNDER ARMS

Year BC	Estimated number of adult male citizens	Size of the armies in the field (some figures are estimates)	% of the number of citizens
225 BC	300,000	52,000	17
213	260,000	75,000	29
203	235,000	60,000	26
193	266,000	53,000	20
183	315,000	48,000	15
173	314,000	44,000	14
163	383,000	33,000	9
153	374,000	30,000	8
143	400,000	44,000	11
133	381,000	37,000	10
123	(not known)	32,000	(not known)
113	(not known)	34,000	(not known)
103	400,000	50,000	13
93	*ditto*	52,000	13
83	1,030,000	143,000	14
73	*ditto*	171,000	17
63	*ditto*	120,000	12
53	*ditto*	121,000	12
43	1,480,000	240,000	16
33	1,600,000	250,000	16
23	1,800,000	156,000	9

Notes. We here observe the effects of the intensive Second Punic War (218–201 BC, p. 169), the granting of Roman citizenship to the Italians (p. 192) and the civil wars, which coincided with the continuing expansion of the Roman empire (pp. 193–205). These figures were inferred from data in the works of Roman historians and other ancient sources by P. A. Brunt and K. Hopkins. The 156,000 soldiers in 23 BC are Augustus' legionaries and guards. They had to be recruited from among citizens (p. 218).

used for racing, boxing, wrestling contests, and chariot racing, while the theaters were intended for singing and lyre and flute performances. Gladiatorial combats, in which the contestants—often several pairs at a time—were required to fight one another to death in duels, were in these days still held in temporary timber structures that were erected on the Forum and at other venues.

Rome of the first century BC has been compared to Pericles' classical Athens. And, indeed, we note the same convergence of money, talent, and a broad interested public. The money that was spent in Rome was one of the fruits of Rome's expansionist campaigns. The talent was drawn to Rome from every part of the Greek and Roman cultural world, the well-paying patrons of letters who were to be found in that city acting as magnets for artists and intellectuals. And the broad interested public consisted of the Roman elite, who customarily received a thorough grounding in rhetoric and literature—a tradition which the Romans had adopted since the second century BC in emulation of the Greeks (see pp. 112 and 184).

15 THE EARLY IMPERIAL AGE (27 BC–AD 193)

AUGUSTUS

Augustus' constitutional position and the real basis of his power

The struggles in Rome had left Octavian the sole surviving ruler in 30 BC. He was elected consul several years in succession and he also still enjoyed his triumviral powers. He was therefore legally entitled to remain in power. But more important than this legal basis were the support of the armies and the common acceptance of his position by all the social classes. They constituted the real basis of his power. Almost everyone accepted Octavian's leadership because he was the man who had finally put an end to the civil wars. This achievement had won Octavian powerful informal authority (*auctoritas*). In 28 BC Octavian announced on coins that he was giving the Romans back their laws and rights. The old political culture that had been the cause of so many struggles was dead and would never return. But Octavian was anxious to formalize his authority. He did not wish to remain dependent on the annual consular elections and on the dictatorial powers granted him in the days of the Second Triumvirate. The civil wars had cast a slur on those powers. And so, in a long process of trial and error, he searched for an alternative way of securing a more constitutional position that would be generally acceptable to the Romans. In the provinces, especially those in the eastern half of the empire, he was a monarch in his own right from the very start of his sole reign.

The settlement of 27 BC: different types of provinces

In 27 BC Octavian laid down his powers and restored the government to the Senate and the popular assembly. They then granted him the name Augustus (majestic, he who has been promoted to greater power) and proconsular *imperium* in the three provinces where most of the troops were stationed: Gaul, Spain, and Syria. Until 23 BC he was, moreover, re-elected consul every year. In his three provinces Augustus was actually a proconsul, but he governed them through deputies (*legati*) with propraetorial *imperium* (*legati Augusti propraetore*). These deputies were responsible for governing these provinces and commanding any military forces stationed there. They came from the senatorial order.

FIGURE 15.1   Augustus (27 BC–AD 14)

They were assisted in their tasks by procurators from the equestrian order, who supervised expenditures and tax collection. They arranged resources for the military forces that were stationed or in action in or near their provinces. The taxes that were collected in their province in kind or in money they spent directly on soldiers or governmental tasks. That way the collected coins and resources did not have to be transported to Rome and from there on to other destinations. Fairly unproductive frontier provinces would obtain resources from nearby provinces lying more in the interior that did not have to maintain large armies themselves.

Syria, Gaul, and Hispania Tarraconensis (the northern half of the Iberian peninsula) were in 27 BC "imperial provinces." The other provinces used to be called "senatorial provinces." This term is open to debate. Many scholars nowadays refer to these provinces as "provinces of the people" or "public provinces." The latter term is adopted here. As in the past, the public provinces were governed by proconsuls, who were appointed every year or every two years and were assisted by quaestors. The tasks and responsibilities of a procurator in an imperial province were similar to those of a quaestor in a public province. The proconsuls of the public provinces were former praetors (in the smaller public provinces) or ex-consuls (in the larger ones). The title of propraetor went out of use in the public provinces; all their governors were then called "proconsul." Apart from such peculiarities in appointment policies, the difference between imperial and public provinces is no longer considered all that relevant. After 23 BC (see below) the emperor had supreme power in both types of provinces. More important was the difference between provinces with and without substantial armed forces. The provinces with fairly large armies lay at the frontiers and were controlled by the emperor, not the Senate and the people. The new provinces that were annexed to the empire under Augustus became imperial provinces.

Governors, procurators, and quaestors were paid a salary. The governor of Asia or Africa earned the impressive sum of 1 million sesterces a year, but then that was the highest rank attainable in the official career.

Egypt, which had been incorporated in the Roman empire in 30 BC, was an imperial province of a special category, as it was considered the emperor's private domain. Egypt was under stricter control than the other provinces. Powerful armed forces were stationed near Alexandria. The men who were appointed governors in Egypt came from the equestrian order; they were called *praefecti Aegypti*, "prefects of Egypt." The governorship of Egypt came to be one of the highest posts open to knights (see p. 216). Senators were not allowed to travel to Egypt without the emperor's permission. The reason for this must have been that the emperor considered a knight he had appointed himself more trustworthy than a senator with a long tradition of politically independent action behind him. In their long careers, senators held a wide variety of posts in which they took decisions independently, and they still recalled the days of the proud Senate of the republican era. Egypt also differed from the other provinces because the Romans had retained the bureaucratic system they had found there. In the other provinces the governors (*legati* and proconsuls) supervised the local municipal authorities (see p. 175), which took care of most day-to-day administration. In Egypt the governor was the head of a stratified civil service of district leaders and local rulers. We should, however, not overemphasize the differences between Egypt and the other provinces—most differences were differences in terminology rather than content. In Egypt there were for example also landed local notables in cities and large villages who did a lot of the day-to-day administration. In AD 200 the differences were to become even more blurred. Just like other provinces, Egypt then acquired municipalities with town councils and magistrates. Egypt did become an extremely important source of money for the imperial treasury. The Romans took over much of the sophisticated tax system that the Ptolemies had established in Egypt and used large parts of Egypt's surplus grain to help feed the city of Rome and provision Roman armies and fleets. The grain that was not needed to feed the Egyptian population was taken to Alexandria, from where it was either shipped to Rome or important military sectors, or sold to traders. The latter would also transport part of the grain to Rome, to sell it there. There was indeed quite a demand for this commercial grain in Rome as the city's occupants did not all qualify for the free wheat distributions—that was the prerogative of Roman citizens. Rome also imported grain from other parts of North Africa (what are now Algeria, Tunisia, and Libya) and from Sicily, which had served as Rome's granary since the mid-third century BC, and other areas that happened to have surplus supplies. Other important imports were olive oil from southern Spain and North Africa, gold from Spain and Egypt, and silver and other metals from Spain. The transport of all those goods was entirely in the hands of private entrepreneurs. The regular transport by sea from Egypt, Spain, and North Africa to Rome led to an impressive permanent transport and trading system in the republican era. In Alexandria, Tarraco, Cartagena, Cadiz, and the ports of North Africa and along the usual sailing routes merchants would always be able to find a ship destined for Rome and they would use the same routes in the opposite direction. The new city of Carthage that Caesar founded in North Africa evolved into a major port.

Egypt, Spain, Gaul, and Syria were of particular importance for the imperial government. Gaul was largely responsible for maintaining the large armies stationed along the Rhine as protection against the Germans. Spain produced essential resources and in these days it also accommodated a large army that was engaged in subjecting the northwestern part of the peninsula that had so far managed to remain outside Rome's sphere of influence. Syria was the only area along the eastern frontier with a fairly substantial Roman army. Until AD 73 there were only vassal states with their own small armies here, and Syria, as it were, served as Rome's bridgehead against the Parthian empire. The cities along the Syrian coasts were, moreover, the destinations of wealthy caravans from the East, bearing Indian, Iranian, Mesopotamian, and even Chinese products (the silk route, which still existed in the Middle Ages). The customs and taxes imposed on those caravans were major sources of income for the Roman treasury and for the cities along the caravan routes.

Egypt, too, was the final destination of major trade routes. Ships transporting products such as pepper and fragrances from Arabia, East Africa, and southern India would dock at the ports along the Red Sea. Pepper was becoming increasingly popular for seasoning meals and fragrances were used every day in the cults of the gods all over the Roman empire.

The southern and western parts of Asia Minor and North Africa, moreover, contained wealthy, fertile regions which were major sources of food, resources, and money in the form of taxes. They also had important ports, but no large armies. Virtually no troops were stationed in Asia, and Africa and Numidia had only one legion and a few auxiliaries along the boundary of the desert. Those areas the emperor could entrust to the Senate. Italy was not a province. The emperor, the highest magistrates and prefects in Rome and the Senate supervised the self-governing communities of Italy to varying degrees and administered the city of Rome. Rome and Italy did not pay the common taxes that were levied in the provinces. The free population of Rome and Italy consisted largely of Roman citizens, who only paid a 5 percent tax on inheritances and a 1 percent sales tax.

We have started to use the term "emperor." The word "emperor" comes from the Latin *imperator*, meaning "commander-in-chief." This was a title given to a general after an important victory. The general would add this title to his name. Imperator was also one of Octavian's names. At first, the Roman emperors were informally referred to by the popular name "Caesar," after Julius Caesar. The German word *Kaiser* and the Russian word *tsar* are both derived from it. At some time in the late imperial age "Caesar" became the official title of the heir to the throne. The Romans of the first centuries of the imperial age also used the title *princeps* (first citizen; English "prince"), which was not an official term, but rather a form of address. The word principate, which is often used to refer to the Roman monarchy as it was in the first two centuries of the imperial age, is derived from this.

The settlements of 23 and 19 BC

Augustus saw that his monopolization of one of the consulships meant that fewer senators could achieve this office, which was still the highest honorary office open to a senator. He realized that he would need other powers to regularize his position. In 23 BC the Senate and the popular assembly granted Augustus tribunician power for life; he did not become an actual plebeian tribune, but he did enjoy the authority and formal power associated with that post. He also acquired supreme control over the governors of the public provinces (he of course already had supreme control over his deputies in his imperial provinces). So he enjoyed *imperium proconsulare maius*, "greater proconsular *imperium*," for which Pompey had provided the precedent (see p. 198).

This *tribunicia potestas* (tribunician power) and the *imperium proconsulare* (proconsular power), which had been granted him in 27 and which was extended in 23, were to remain the legal, official basis of imperial power until the late imperial age. The Senate (also on behalf of the people)

FIGURE 15.2 Funerary monument of Gaius and Lucius Caesar next to one of Augustus' triumphal arches

Notes. Augustus hoped that Gaius, the oldest of the two, would succeed him. Both brothers, however, died at an early age (Lucius in AD 2 and Gaius in AD 4). Augustus was ultimately succeeded by his step-son Tiberius, the son of his wife Livia from a former marriage, whom he had made the heir to his empire by adopting him as his son. Tiberius ruled from AD 14 until 37.

Next to the funerary monument is one of Augustus' triumphal arches. The monuments are in St Rémy-en-Provence.

conferred these powers upon each new emperor. This conferment of powers was in fact tantamount to an official proclamation of a new ruler.

In 19 BC Augustus received the most important consular powers (with the exception of those relating to a consul's ceremonial duties) for life without actually having to hold the consulship. He had already been performing the tasks of a censor since 28 BC; as we have already seen, they comprised filling vacancies in the Senate and the equestrian order, conducting censuses, concluding contracts for tax collection, and commissioning the construction and maintenance of public works.

Thus Augustus clothed his control in a combination of constitutional powers derived from traditional offices, which entitled him to legally exercise direct authority in all areas of government. This made it easier for the senators and other traditionally minded Romans to accept Augustus' regime. His political system was rooted in the old republican institutions—in theory at least.

Changes in the administration

In practice, however, major changes took place behind this façade. Augustus assumed control over jurisdiction in appeal cases (see pp. 166 and 237) and acquired supremacy over foreign politics and public finance because the Senate meekly accepted everything he proposed. The powers granted him in 27 and 23 BC had given him control over the governors in the provinces. For the occupants of those provinces this was probably a favorable development, because Augustus kept the governors and tax collectors under surveillance, restricting their opportunities to exploit the provincials.

Local provincial notables remained responsible for collecting the direct taxes; they were placed under the supervision of procurators (in the imperial provinces) and quaestors (in the public provinces). The *publicani* continued to levy the indirect taxes (customs and duties).

These new conditions led to a busy correspondence between the emperor and his governors (or procurators), and to an intensive traffic of embassies to and from Rome. Governors would ask for advice, cities (in Italy and the provinces) would regularly request privileges and favors, and individuals with Roman citizenship would file complaints or refer cases to the emperor. The cities' requests were conveyed by delegates who visited the emperor in person, which implied a substantial financial burden for their municipalities. Private persons were also allowed to ask the emperor for a favor or—providing they enjoyed Roman citizenship—present a case to him (a form of appeal). They, too, would then have to travel to the emperor to address him in person. It is nowadays assumed that this system of communication evolved from old forms of patronage. In the republican era clients would call on their patrons at the break of day to greet them, and they could use that opportunity to ask their patrons for favors or advice, also concerning legal matters. In very much the same way people in later times would ask the empire's "superpatron"—the emperor—for advice and favors, again in a personal—face to face—encounter. The emperors had their answers to petitions (rescripts), their judgments in lawsuits and the legal advice they were asked to give displayed in public at the center of Rome so that the parties could make copies of them. The emperor's advice in lawsuits acquired decisive power, also in subsequent comparable cases, and the emperor's decisions on requested favors and conflicts that were presented to him for arbitration were copied in Rome, and inscribed in stone plaques and displayed at home. Imperial letters and answers to requests had the force of law.

In handling cases the emperor would seek the advice of a council of experienced senators and knights—the *consilium principis* ("advisory council of the princeps")—and consult notables who specialized in legal affairs. The emperor was soon no longer able to deal with all this work personally, and so the first imperial secretariats were established. All petitions were from then on to be submitted to the secretariats, which also carried out the written part of the work involved in handling cases. During Augustus' reign the secretariats were staffed by the emperor's private slaves, led by experienced freedmen. The emperor Claudius (41–54) extended the secretariats' services and granted the freedmen a lot of power—this to the great annoyance of many senators. Emperor Hadrian (117–138) made it his policy to place the secretariats under the leadership of experienced knights, for example intellectuals capable of writing good letters or administrators with legal and financial experience. Some of Hadrian's predecessors had incidentally already done this, too.

The emperor also acquired his own financial sector, separate from the old public treasury, which had always been controlled by the Senate. That public treasury was called the *aerarium*. Its management was transferred from the quaestors to experienced ex-praetors. In the course of his reign, Augustus appropriated more and more control over the *aerarium*. The financial resources available to the emperor besides his private funds were the funds of the imperial provinces: the *fisci* (plural of *fiscus*), which were managed by the procurators. These *fisci* were fed by the taxes levied in the imperial provinces. They were used to pay the soldiers in those provinces and cover other regional public expenditures. So the procurators were actually the armies' paymasters general. The main taxes in the provinces were the indirect taxes (customs, duties) and a direct tax based on landed property and on the produce of the land (it comprised a fixed percentage of the roughly estimated yield). There were also poll taxes. Taxes were paid not only in cash, but also in kind, the goods being used in nearby areas, for example to provision an army (p. 210). The emperor's private resources grew rapidly, largely because families anxious to win the emperor's favor would bequeath money and property to him and because the emperor confiscated goods of the individuals he convicted. The imperial properties were managed by the emperor's freedmen.

The emperor acquired decisive influence over the careers of the senators and knights. Around 5 BC this influence was formalized. The emperor was allowed to nominate candidates for all the important offices and those candidates were almost always elected. Candidates who had not been nominated or commended by the emperor stood little chance of achieving the most important magistracies. The emperor could of course appoint whomever he liked in his own provinces and services.

The emperor's trusted advisors, united in his *Consilium Principis*, acquired considerable executive influence. The *Consilium Principis* was to some extent comparable with the advisory committees of the republican magistrates and governors (see pp. 158, 175), only it was far more important. It was this council, and no longer the Senate, that prepared the emperor's decisions and discussed matters of policy and jurisdiction. Nowadays some scholars maintain that this *consilium* was not a fixed, permanent body, but a series of *ad hoc* advisory panels consisting of varying people, though they would be chosen from more or less the same group of high magistrates, juridical advisors, military men, and other experienced senators and *equites* (= knights).

The Senate and the popular assemblies

The importance of the popular assemblies declined substantially under Augustus. Hardly anybody attended them any more. After Augustus they convened only rarely. The last popular assembly seems to have taken place under the emperor Nerva (AD 96–98), but this is disputed.

The Senate ostensibly acquired more power. Senatorial decrees came to be as binding as laws and imperial edicts. Under Augustus, laws (Latin: *leges*, plural of *lex*) passed by popular assemblies were quite rare. In actual fact, laws were now created by imperial statements of a general nature (edicts), imperial orders to governors, imperial letters, judgments and advice, senatorial decisions (*Senatus consulta*), and answers from emperors (and governors) to petitions. Senatorial decisions were, however, almost always preceded by a letter from the emperor or by his speeches in the Senate, which they merely confirmed.

Augustus' successor, Tiberius (AD 14–37), transferred the responsibility of electing magistrates from the popular assemblies to the Senate.

In practice, the Senate was guided in all things by the emperor's wishes: the Senate's decisions were almost always based on imperial proposals or letters. The senators knew very well how things were really run and were aware that their prospects of promotion depended on the emperor's goodwill. The Senate's real importance lay in the fact that it consisted of the wealthiest Roman landowners with the most experience in higher administration and in military command: a combination of economic power and indispensable scarce knowledge. The Senate moreover represented legality. Until AD 282 a ruler was the legal emperor only after the Senate had conferred upon him the combination of powers which Augustus had first acquired.

FIGURE 15.3 A luxury glass goblet

The higher orders: senators and *equites* (= knights)

Augustus fixed property qualifications for admission to the senatorial and equestrian orders. In the past, the censors had also employed more or less traditional prosperity criteria, but now they were officially fixed. Only persons who had at least one million sesterces stood a chance of being admitted to the senatorial order; the property qualification for admission to the equestrian order was fixed at 400,000 sesterces (see Appendix 2 on Greek and Roman money, p. 300). Usually about 80 to 90 percent of the property of the members of these orders consisted of land. The rest comprised houses, bank balances, moveable property, and slaves. In these days, an estate of average quality yielded a profit of about 6 percent. That meant that a senator had an annual income of at least 60,000 sesterces. We get a good idea of how much that was when we compare it with a legionary's annual pay, which amounted to 225 denari (900 sesterces) in the first century of the imperial age.

Under Augustus (and his successors until the third century) the senators continued to hold the most important administrative offices. They still followed the old *cursus honorum* (see pp. 158–9), but all kinds of new posts emerged between the old honorary offices. After completing the praetorship, a senator could for example be appointed to a post with the treasury (the *aerarium*), to the office of legion commander, to that of *legatus Augusti propraetore* in a small imperial province, or to that of proconsul in a small senatorial province. The next office after the consulship was no longer the censorship (there were no longer any censors besides the emperor), but a governor's post in one of the large senatorial or imperial provinces or the office of *praefectus urbi* (prefect of the city, the mayor of Rome)—a post that had been created in AD 6. The most prestigious offices for senators were governorship of Asia (the western part of Asia Minor) and Africa (more or less what is now Tunisia) and prefecture of Rome, with a second consulate to confirm their status.

Some of the old honorary offices, such as the aedileship and the tribunate of the plebs, became honorable sinecures. The work formerly done by the magistrates who held those posts became the responsibility of the imperial services. The quaestors worked in the public provinces or in or near Rome, the praetors still played a role in jurisdiction in Rome and were partly responsible for organizing the games in that city, while the consuls had mainly ceremonial and representative tasks in Rome. In the provinces senators had a lot to do: they had to command legions and travel round their province according to a fixed route to handle cases and receive petitions in towns.

In Augustus' time the knights acquired an important position in administration. They furnished the army officers and could make themselves useful in the imperial provinces as procurators. After their service in those provinces they stood a chance of being appointed to one of the important administrative offices which Augustus created and reserved specifically for knights, namely those of prefect of one of the two fleets that Augustus had based in Italy (at Ravenna and Misenum), prefect of the grain supplies in Rome, prefect of Egypt (see p. 210), and prefect of the praetorian guard (*praefectus praetorio*), the imperial bodyguard, which was permanently quartered outside Rome from Tiberius' reign onwards. The prefect of this guard came to be the second most powerful man in the empire, after the emperor.

The *decuriones*

In the course of the first century BC the local notables of the Italian communities and of Roman cities outside Italy started to constitute a kind of third order, that of the *decuriones*, also known as *curiales* (the members of the *curia*, the council house). The members of this order avidly supported Augustus as they benefited from his regime, for Augustus greatly improved their prospects of social advancement. The vacancies that had arisen in the Senate due to the civil wars and the dying out of the old families he filled not only with knights, but also with Italian notables. They governed their cities fairly autonomously: Italy was not a province under a governor's authority; it fell directly under the emperor, the highest magistrates in Rome and the Senate.

In areas outside Italy that were rapidly Romanizing, such as southern Gaul and parts of Spain, or where new colonies were founded for discharged soldiers arose municipalities in which Latin was the official language and which were governed as towns in Italy. Their ruling elites came to belong to the rank of *decuriones* and eventually had the opportunity to rise to the equestrian order and even the Senate, but that was not until long after Augustus' time.

The city of Rome

Under Augustus Rome was a city with around 800,000 occupants. It is believed that up to 40 percent of the population consisted of slaves and freedmen. As in the late republican era, Rome attracted many migrants, especially Greek-speaking people from the eastern half of the empire. She also accommodated many Syrians and Jews. It is assumed that the death rate exceeded the birth rate and that the only way in which the city could remain large was by attracting immigrants from Italy and the provinces.

Augustus took comparatively good care of Rome. He divided the city into districts and appointed district leaders to oversee them. In AD 6 he established a body of seven thousand night watchmen (known as *vigiles*), which also served as the city's fire brigade. He created a police force of four thousand men (the four urban cohorts, the *cohortes urbanae*). This put an end to political violence in Rome. The night watchmen were recruited from freedmen and were commanded by an equestrian prefect. The urban cohorts were led by the senatorial *praefectus urbi*—i.e., the urban prefect (see above). This office was also introduced in AD 6. The urban prefecture came to be a very influential post. The urban prefect was the head of Rome's administration, but he also played an important part in the administration of justice and the maintenance of order in Italy, as a kind of arbitrator above the self-governing municipalities in that area.

Augustus improved the distribution of free wheat and got his helper and friend Agrippa to manage the town's waterworks. The latter created a properly trained team for maintaining the water pipes and had existing aqueducts repaired and new ones built. Some of the emperors who succeeded Augustus, in particular Claudius (41–54) and Trajan (98–117), improved Rome's waterworks, for example by commissioning the construction of new aqueducts. Those same two emperors also improved the grain supply to Rome by building harbors at Ostia to the southwest of Rome.

Rome was not the only city to build aqueducts in the imperial age. Famous remains of aqueducts can still be admired at Segovia (Spain) and at Nîmes in southern France, spanning the river Gard (the *Pont du Gard*).

Augustus had more than eighty temples restored and a few new ones built. By the time of his death, Rome was a city of marble. He also completed Caesar's Forum and commissioned the construction of a square of his own, the Forum of Augustus. In 29 BC Rome also acquired her first stone amphitheater, a stadium for games featuring wild animals and gladiators (theaters were intended for musical performances and drama; see p. 111). This amphitheater was destroyed by fire under Nero, which gave Vespasian the opportunity to erect a spectacular new amphitheater: the Colosseum. An amphitheater is so named because the rows of seats are arranged around (*amphi* in Greek) a central area intended for performances. A Roman theater had a stage for performances at one end, with an acoustic wall behind it (Figure 10.10 on p. 111).

The army

The control over the armies, which were almost all stationed in the imperial provinces, Augustus reserved for himself. He also saw to it that the Senate granted all important military commands to his relatives and friends, so as to prevent the emergence of new military commanders from outside his own circle.

Augustus established a standing army of about 300,000 professional soldiers. One half consisted of legions of six thousand men (recruited from Roman citizens), the other of auxiliaries (*auxilia*—recruited from provincials). There were also naval forces; the two largest fleets were based at Ravenna and Misenum (at the Gulf of Pozzuoli in southern Italy). The auxiliaries comprised squadrons of cavalry and cohorts of six hundred or one thousand infantry. The legions were commanded by senators, the lower officers came from the equestrian order. As in the past, the majority of the centurions in the legions (see p. 162) still came from the army's rank and file, though more and more young knights and sons of *decuriones* would apply for these offices as a prelude to a military career.

Augustus also created an imperial bodyguard (the praetorian guard) of about nine thousand men led by an equestrian prefect, which he quartered in camps in Italy. This guard was responsible for guarding and defending the emperor, the capital, and Italy. The guard prefect (*praefectus praetorio*) was a powerful man. Several guard prefects had a decisive influence on the appointment of new emperors after Augustus. This powerful position they owed to the fact that they commanded the largest military force in the vicinity of the capital (and the emperor's court) after Tiberius permanently stationed the guard near Rome. The urban troops of Rome—the town cohorts and night watchmen—have already been mentioned above.

Augustus fixed good terms of service for his soldiers and made provisions for their retirement. Praetorians did sixteen years' service, legionaries served for twenty years, and auxiliaries for twenty-five years. When they were discharged, the soldiers were granted a plot of land or a sum of money. The auxiliaries also received Roman citizenship. Soldiers were not allowed to have a wife, but they could have a mistress outside the camp. On their discharge they could legally marry their mistress and officially acknowledge their children. Their wives and children then acquired Roman citizenship too (if they did not already have it).

Augustus paid his soldiers' retirement bonuses from his private resources at first, but in AD 6 he established a special treasury for this purpose (the *aerarium militare*), which was maintained out of a 5 percent death duty levied on legacies of Roman citizens exceeding 100,000 sesterces and a 1 percent sales tax.

The pay scales employed in the armed forces differed tremendously. Officers and junior officers received many times the amounts paid to ordinary soldiers (until AD 83 a legionary's pay was 225 *denarii*; after that, it was 300 *denarii* per year).

Ideal and religious aspects of emperorship

Emperor worship

Augustus succeeded amazingly well in neutralizing the sharp distinctions created by the civil wars and incorporating the different social groups into his political system. He made it impossible for anyone outside his own circle to acquire a powerful military position; he granted the knights access to the administrative offices; he gave Italian aristocrats the chance to rise to the equestrian order and the Senate, and he arranged good terms of service and pensions for his soldiers, which created a bond between the army and the emperor. Everyone in the empire benefited from the restored peace.

Augustus wanted to be neither an Eastern despot, a master of slaves, nor a military dictator. He wished to be seen as a father and a benefactor, who respected the old state institutions, the citizens' private rights, and the traditional privileges of the higher orders. Augustus presented his reign as a new epoch of success, peace, prosperity, and plenty after the sufferings caused by the civil wars. He propagated the revival of the traditional rites and ceremonies for the state gods and of the old strict code of conduct, which (in his eyes) had assured the greatness of Rome. As vehicles in his "propaganda," Augustus used the visual arts, legends and representations on coins, and inscriptions in well-frequented places. All his successors did the same and elaborated on the slogans introduced in Augustus' time.

During Augustus' reign emperorship already began to acquire religious traits. The emperor cult emerged in the eastern provinces, whose occupants had become accustomed to worshipping their kings in the Hellenistic era (see pp. 132–3). From there it gradually spread across the whole empire. It played a prominent part in the military camps in particular, where it was employed as a means of binding the soldiers to the emperors.

Latin literature in the Augustan era

Echoes of Augustus' "propaganda" are to be found in the Latin literature of his reign. This period is regarded as the golden age of Latin literature. The emperor and his friends (especially Maecenas) financially supported good poets and prose writers and organized private gatherings at which writers were invited to read from their works. Many a creative mind and knowledgeable literature lover would meet at these gatherings.

Some of the literary works that were written in these days have continued to exert an influence on European literature into our times. Among these works is the *Aeneid*, an epic inspired by the works of the Greek poet Homer (see p. 65), which the poet Virgil (70–19 BC) wrote towards the end of his life. It recounts the adventures of the Trojan hero Aeneas on his way to Italy after the Greeks had destroyed his home town Troy. According to Roman legend, Roman history began with Aeneas: he was believed to have been the founder of the Julio-Claudian dynasty, the family of Julius Caesar and his adopted son Augustus. Another well-known writer from this period is Horace (65–8 BC), who won fame with his odes, satires, and verse epistles. One of those epistles is the *Ars poetica*, a work discussing literature, which had a profound impact on European literature. It owes much to one of Aristotle's works (see pp. 115–16). Livy (59 BC–AD 17) wrote a history of Rome from its beginnings down to his own times. He believed that Rome would regain her former greatness if the Romans were to revive the virtues of their ancestors.

Latin literature continued to flower for some time after Augustus. One of the most famous authors of the period around AD 100 is the historian Tacitus (*c.* AD 55–120). He wrote about the emperors who ruled between AD 14 and 96, about the Germans and about Britain. Tacitus was of the opinion that a monarchy was the only possible form of government, but he criticized its shortcomings and regretted the loss of the republican freedom.

FIGURE 15.4 Part of the relief on the Altar of Peace consecrated by Augustus in 9 BC, showing the imperial family

Notes. Various "propagandistic" scenes were represented on the Ara Pacis: Mars, a procession of the Senate and the people of Rome, the *dea Roma* (divine personification of Rome) seated on weapons, the goddess Italia (personification) surrounded by plenty, the imperial family attending a sacrificial ceremony and Aeneas, the legendary founder of the Julio-Claudian dynasty.

The scenes were intended to link the old-established Julio-Claudian dynasty, Augustus' family, with prosperity, presented as the consequence of military success, and Augustus' dynasty, the Senate, and the people with the restored piety towards the state gods.

Augustus' conquests

Augustus' officers conquered the northwest of Spain, the Alps, and the Danubian plain, which had not yet been brought under Roman control (see Map 15.1). Between 15 BC and AD 9 several new imperial provinces were established to the south of the Danube. Augustus' aim was to expand his empire to the Elbe in the northwest, but he was unable to conquer Germany. In AD 9 the Germans inflicted a severe defeat on the Romans in the Teutoburg forest, north of the present city of Osnabrück. After a number of punitive expeditions, Augustus' successor, Tiberius (14–37), decided that subjecting Germany would cost more than it was worth.

In 20 BC Augustus diplomatically worked out a *modus vivendi* with the Parthians: Armenia was to become a buffer state in which Rome and Parthia were to share influence. Augustus readily entrusted important campaigns and diplomatic enterprises to his loyal friends and relatives. The most important of these were Agrippa, the husband of his daughter Julia (see Appendix 3, p. 301), and his stepsons Tiberius (who was emperor from 14 until 37) and Drusus. Tiberius played an important part in the conquest of the Danubian regions. Drusus gathered laurels in the Rhine-Meuse delta and in western Germany between 12 and 9 BC, the year in which he died. His son Germanicus commanded the fighting there from AD 13 until 17.

The end of Augustus' reign was also the end of the era of Rome's major conquests. The Roman empire entered a new phase. Up to 146 BC the Roman empire had primarily aimed at hegemony (see p. 173). After that date there followed a transitional period in which Rome, evidently desiring a more direct form of control, began to govern increasingly more regions as provinces. By the time of the Late Republic and Augustus' reign the Roman empire had become a territorial empire with clearly defined frontiers, containing provinces and vassal states. The latter were to be found mainly in the east. Some scholars believe that Augustus made a determined effort to establish natural, easily defensible frontiers, but this is something we don't know for sure; how well were the Romans of those days acquainted with the geography of Europe and Asia Minor? It may well be that Rome's expansion simply ended where it became too much of an effort or too non-beneficial to continue it. Under Augustus, Roman imperialism may have been partly motivated by propagandistic interests. Military achievements and a good reputation on a battlefield were excellent means for an emperor to impress his people and make himself popular in his armies. Augustus propagated the new expansionist campaigns launched during his reign as the successful consequence of the restoration of concord and the revival of the old Roman virtues of piety and valor. Contemporary authors began to praise the Romans as the nation most suited to subjecting and governing peoples in the surrounding world.

After Augustus, new expansionist campaigns alternated with periods of consolidation. Tiberius (14–37) put an end to the efforts to subject Germany. Nero (54–68) had no interest in military expansion whatsoever, Vespasian (69–79) reinforced Rome's military presence in the East (in 73), but made no further conquests, and his son Domitian (81–96) was forced to engage in difficult border wars against tribes pushing forward from Dacia (more or less what is now Romania). Hadrian (117–138) resolutely opted for consolidation and even returned some recently conquered areas in Mesopotamia to the Parthians. His successor Antoninus Pius (138–161) ruled his empire in peace, hardly ever leaving Rome. Other emperors, such as Claudius (41–54) and Trajan (98–117), added new territories to the empire (see Map 15.2) for the sake of winning their

MAP 15.1
The Roman empire
under the emperor
Augustus

Note. Grey: Vassal states.

MAP 15.2
The Roman empire
under the emperor
Trajan (98–117)

Notes. Some vassal states
had been reduced to
provinces since Augustus'
reign. Vespasian (69–79)
had for example created
such provinces in the east
in 73 and Domitian (81–96)
established the provinces
of Germania Inferior and
Superior (Lower and Upper
Germany along the Rhine).
Trajan conquered Dacia
(present-day Romania),
part of Arabia to the east
of the Jordan, and parts of
Mesopotamia (in the
Roman–Parthian war of
114–117). His successor
Hadrian (117–138) returned
the conquered areas in
Mesopotamia to the
Parthians. Britannia was
subjected between AD 42
and 84. Scotland and
Ireland stayed outside the
empire.

soldiers' esteem, securing a frontier, or annexing areas where they expected to find great wealth or mineral resources. The Rhine, the Danube, the Euphrates, and the Sahara came to mark the empire's definitive borders. In 200 the Roman empire reached its largest expanse, extending from the Irish Sea in the west into Mesopotamia in the east and from the Danube and Romania in the north to the Sahara desert in the south.

THE EARLY IMPERIAL AGE AFTER AUGUSTUS (AD 14–193)

Wars and rebellions

For the greater part of the first two centuries of the principate (27 BC–AD 161) the Roman empire was hardly ever forced to engage in severe wars at several frontiers simultaneously, which meant that it was able to keep all its enemies outside its borders and could maintain peace and order throughout the empire. The armies remained stationed in permanent camps, forts, and fleet bases along the frontiers and in Italy. In some regions, for example near Strasbourg and in the East, were a few large concentrations of soldiers stationed more inland, a little further from the frontier (see Map 15.3, p. 238). The Romans endeavored to maintain a buffer zone in the regions across the Rhine and the Danube and tried to play tribes living there off against one another. For a long time they were quite successful. For the first two hundred years of the imperial age no major wars broke out along more than one of the northern frontiers at a time. That period did see a few dangerous wars in individual frontier regions. In 69–70, for example, the Batavi, who lived in the region traversed by the Rhine, the Waal, and the Meuse (the Netherlands), revolted against the Roman empire just when it was divided by succession struggles. The year 69 is known as "the year of the four emperors." Nero, the last emperor of the Julio-Claudian dynasty, had died without appointing a successor, and four rival pretenders to the throne were fighting one another at the head of their armies.

In the years between 42 and 84 Britain was annexed to the Roman empire (see Map 15.2). The emperor Claudius (41–54) launched the first campaigns to Britain for the sake of winning military fame. But he did not succeed in establishing permanent control over Britain, for border conflicts and rebellions were to break out intermittently until 84, when the country was finally pacified.

During the reign of the emperor Domitian (81–96) the empire was alternately threatened by tribes in the regions along the Rhine and the Danube. To raise his soldiers' morale Domitian increased their pay from 225 to 300 denarii per year in 83. With this act Domitian, an emperor with little military experience, made himself popular among his troops. It was the emperor Trajan (98–117) who set things right in the aforementioned regions: in a series of major campaigns (*c.* 101–106) he subdued Dacia (present-day Romania), which had been the greatest hotbed of raids and resistance in the years before 96. In 106 he also annexed Arabia and turned it into a province (more or less coinciding with what are now southern Syria and Jordan).

A state of armed peace was maintained along the eastern Parthian frontier, which on several occasions was disturbed by wars over the buffer state Armenia (*c.* 55–65, 114–117, 161–166). But those wars were largely ineffective: the *status quo* that had been reached under Augustus was preserved until the end of the second century.

FIGURE 15.5   Gaius Caesar (Caligula)

Notes. A grandson of Agrippa and Augustus' daughter Julia, Caligula ruled from AD 37 until 41.

Fierce Jewish revolts broke out a few times in the southeastern corner of the empire. The Jews in Palestine rose in revolt in 66–73 and 132–136 and those in Cyrenaica and Egypt and on Cyprus, and ultimately those in Palestine, too, in 115–117. The latter revolt was a desperate response to increasing discrimination. The aim of the Jews in the first major uprising (66–73) was to found a new powerful Jewish state. Their aim was the same in 132–136.

The first two Jewish revolts (66–73 and 115–117) caused the Romans quite a few problems, as they coincided with other wars. The Jewish war of 66–73 coincided with a revolt in Britain, the Batavian uprising, and the internal strife in the year of the four emperors. In 69 the threat to the Roman empire became acute. However, the emperor Vespasian (69–79) solved all the problems. He eliminated the last other pretender to the throne and quelled the rebellions. In 70 his son Titus razed Jerusalem to the ground. The last stand of the Jewish resistance was concentrated in two strong fortresses, Masada and Machaerus, to the west and east of the Dead Sea, and it took the Romans several years to crush it, succeeding only in 73 BC. "Masada" became a symbol of determination for Zionist Jews in the nineteenth and twentieth centuries.

In the last Jewish revolt (132–136) the Jews were led by Bar Kokhba, who passed himself off as the Messiah, the savior of the people of Israel. After suppressing this rebellion, the emperor Hadrian (117–138) banned the Jews from Jerusalem. He turned the city into a colony for Roman veterans and called it Aelia Capitolina (Hadrian's *gens* name was Aelius). The cause of this revolt is a matter of dispute. In some sources it is attributed to the foundation of Aelia Capitolina and a ban on circumcision. Hadrian is in those sources portrayed as a second Antiochus Epiphanes, who had provoked the revolt of the Maccabees (see p. 136). But those measures may also have been a consequence of the revolt.

Emperorship and the problem of the emperor's succession

Thanks to Augustus' efforts, the monarchy rested on sound foundations. Augustus had secured the acceptance of imperial rulership by the higher orders, he had created strong ties between the emperor and his armies, and he had secured control over state finances (the *aerarium*, *fisci*, and the emperor's private funds) and influence over the election of the highest officials.

The emperors' vast private resources enabled them to act as the chief benefactors in the empire, in particular in the capital Rome (bread and circuses!). The emperors gradually took over a large part of the patronage of Rome's population from the senators and deprived them of the possibility of using their clients as weapons in political conflicts. The senators' power came to rest exclusively on their private estates (and the people living on them). The poor in Rome were no longer solely dependent on their elite patrons, but could now also look to their emperor as a "superpatron."

The emperors also had ties with the local elites in Italy and the provinces, who took care of a large share of the day-to-day municipal administration and constituted the local authorities for the greater part of the empire's population. The Roman empire of the early imperial age was an empire of cities from which landed notables governed the surrounding countryside. Above these municipal authorities were the provincial authorities and the central government. This stratified system was reflected in social relations, too, with the imperial aristocracy of senators and *equites* ranking higher than the local elites. The emperor came to supplant the senators in informal relations with local notables, too. Ties between senators and local notables now had political

FIGURE 15.6 Agrippina

FIGURE 15.7 Claudius (AD 41–54)

Notes. Claudius was the youngest son of Drusus, Tiberius' brother. Drusus had died at an early age, in 9 BC. Claudius, then, was a grandson of Augustus' wife Livia; Tiberius and Drusus were her sons from her previous marriage to Tib(erius) Claudius Nero, a *nobilis*. Claudius conquered Britain, expanded the imperial secretariats, created a new harbor at Portus, to the west of Rome, and was the first emperor to admit Romanized Gallic nobles with Roman citizenship into the Senate. In the last years of his life he was greatly influenced by his wife Agrippina, a granddaughter of Julia (the daughter of Augustus) and Agrippa. She persuaded Claudius to adopt her son Nero and make him his successor, even though Claudius had a son of his own.

influence only if there happened to be a vacuum at the top of the administrative system, for example in times of succession struggles.

The emperor's "job" essentially comprised commanding the armies in wartime, administering justice, nominating and appointing officials at all levels, and responding to the problems presented to him (petitions of cities and private persons, questions of governors, etc.). In our eyes this may seem a somewhat passive form of government, but in those days, with economic insight and means of communication being as they were, it was virtually the only form possible.

THE EMPERORS OF THE ROMAN EMPIRE IN THE FIRST AND SECOND CENTURIES AD

The following emperors ruled between AD 14 and 193:

The Julio-Claudian house

Tiberius	14–37	
Caligula	37–41	
Claudius	41–54	
Nero	54–68	
	68–69	

These emperors were all related to Augustus or his wife Livia. In 68–69, the "year of the four emperors," four pretenders struggled for power after the murder of Nero, who had died without an heir. Those pretenders were Galba (68–69), Otho (69), Vitellius (69), and Vespasian (69–79). The latter emerged from the struggle victorious and founded a new dynasty—that of the Flavian emperors (69–96). They are known as Flavians after Vespasian's *gens* name; his full name was T(itus) Flavius Vespasianus:

The Flavian house and the adoptive emperors

Vespasian	69–79	
Titus	79–81	
Domitian	81–96	
Nerva	96–98	
Trajan	98–117	
Hadrian	117–138	
Antoninus Pius	138–161	
Marcus Aurelius	161–180	

Having behaved like a tyrant, Domitian was killed in 96, and left behind no heir. The Senate appointed an elderly senator, Nerva, and shortly after chose a successor who was popular among the soldiers. That was M(arcus) Ulpius Trajanus (Trajan). Nerva was the first in a series of emperors known as the adoptive emperors because they adopted their successors. The series ended with Marcus Aurelius (161–180), who had a son of his own to whom he bequeathed his throne (Commodus, 180–192).

Notes. Antoninus Pius appointed two successors, who first ruled as colleagues—Marcus Aurelius and Lucius Verus (161–169). After the latter's death Marcus Aurelius became the sole emperor. In 192 his son Commodus, who had been behaving as a superhuman despot, was murdered. The years between 193 and 197 saw a series of civil wars, from which L(ucius) Septimius Severus emerged victorious (193–211). He founded the Severan dynasty (193–235).

A difficult problem from Augustus' reign onwards was the issue of succession (see the box on p. 229 and Appendix 3, p. 301). The reigning emperor had to prevent the risk of the armies, which had the greatest effective power, pushing forward their own favored candidates after his death. That would mean a revival of the civil wars in the form of succession struggles. Hereditary succession within one imperial family was a good solution, because the soldiers could relate far better to the person of the emperor and to his family than to the government's abstract laws and rules. If for example a lack of sons precluded hereditary succession (daughters were not eligible for appointment to the throne in the Roman empire), the reigning emperor could choose a man who was popular with the troops and acceptable to the Senate for adoption as his son. The problem of selecting the most suitable candidate was then solved through hereditary succession via adoption. In Roman society adoption had always been a frequently used and commonly accepted means of securing a family's continued existence or of enhancing it with new competent members.

Augustus himself was the first emperor to adopt a successor, namely his stepson Tiberius, who reigned from AD 14 to 37 (Augustus had no sons of his own; see Appendix 3, p. 301). The emperors who ruled between 96 and 161 also adopted successors. By coincidence, none of those emperors had any sons of their own. Most of the later emperors modeled their conduct on Augustus' example and respected the members of the higher orders, in particular the senators. They tried to act as the protectors and benefactors of citizens, and not as the masters of slaves.

Some emperors on the contrary behaved like absolute despots, such as Caligula (37–41), Nero (54–68), Domitian (81–96), and Commodus (180–192). Domitian even insisted on being addressed as "master and god" (*dominus et deus*). Those emperors had a poor relationship with the Senate and were all killed by conspiracies of senators and other high officials. Oddly enough, the main cause of the antipathy that they aroused was their behavior—in administrative matters and their election policy these emperors acted very much the same as the other emperors. But behavior was an important issue in Roman society. The common people in Rome would for example closely watch their emperor's behavior at the games (which the emperors were supposed to enjoy, like good fathers who were pleased to see their "children" having a good time).

Developments in administration after Augustus

The political system that Augustus had so carefully constructed during his long reign was to endure for another two centuries after his death, with only a few minor changes.

The most important of those changes was the expansion of bureaucracy in administration. The local rulers (*decuriones* or *curiales*) passed on more and more tasks and decisions to the governors and the emperors, especially in the fields of criminal justice and security. This greatly increased the workload of the imperial secretariats and the governors' bureaux (*officia*). The quaestors and procurators in the provinces had to concern themselves ever more with jurisdiction in fiscal matters. The provincial bureaux recruited extra personnel from the administrative staffs of the nearby armies. The secretariats in Rome sometimes did the same, but they employed predominantly rhetorically and/or legally trained intellectuals. Many a legal advisor (see pp. 182 and 236) and graduate of the schools of rhetoric was appointed to a post in the imperial bureaux, especially after the latter had acquired an official status under Hadrian (117–138).

FIGURE 15.8 Nero

Notes. The son of Agrippina and the adopted son of Claudius, Nero ruled from AD 54 until 68. Having little knowledge of military and financial affairs he left his governmental tasks to servants and friends so that he could concentrate on his favorite pastime: music. He adored all forms of Greek culture.

In Julio-Claudian times the bureaux were still staffed predominantly with slaves, supervised by freedmen (who enjoyed a great deal of influence), but by the second century their staffs already included a large proportion of intellectuals of free birth. The emperor Hadrian also replaced the freedmen at the head of the imperial bureaux by knights.

The staff responsible for the emperor's private estates also expanded, because the emperor accumulated ever more land through inheritance or confiscation (see p. 214). The imperial estates were amongst the most rapidly expanding landed properties in the empire. They included mines, quarries, and workshops and were spread across many parts of the empire. The large group of slaves, freedmen, and free citizens who worked on the imperial estates had their own hierarchical system. In some provinces they constituted a separate social group, the *Caesariani* (the emperor's men). Together with the staff of the imperial bureaux they formed the *familia Caesaris*. In the provinces they were important men, just like the officers, centurions, and other military men who performed tasks in provincial administration for the governors, for example as bailiffs or members of arrest teams.

This expansion of bureaucracy led to a steadily growing stream of post. In the imperial age the Roman empire had a well-organized public post and messages system. All the corners of the empire were connected by a vast network of paved roads, along which were inns where the couriers could exchange their horses or carriages on presentation of a special pass. The expense of maintaining the roads, inns, and means of transport fell on the local authorities. This implied a considerable burden on their financial resources, especially in poor regions.

The spread of Roman citizenship

In the first two centuries AD Roman citizenship gradually spread through more and more provinces. Every year, thousands of veteran auxiliaries (and their families) and many wives and children of discharged legionaries acquired Roman citizenship in the frontier provinces (see p. 218). The number of Roman citizens in the frontier regions around the military camps and in the cities in their hinterlands consequently rapidly multiplied. Such new Roman citizens retained their local rights and thus enjoyed two kinds of citizenship: Roman and local.

By the end of the second century, several legions (which had to consist of Roman citizens) were recruiting almost all their troops from their own hinterlands. Roman citizenship also spread rapidly amongst the elite in the Romanized cities in the west and in the Greek cities in the east. The emperors would sometimes enfranchise entire cities or regions that had become so Romanized that there was very little difference between them and Italian cities or regions. We will return to the Romanization of the western provinces on pp. 238–41.

Changes in the higher orders

The local elites in the Romanized cities in the west and Greek cities in the eastern half of the empire came to belong to the order of *decuriones* (or *curiales*), like their Italian fellows. And like their Italian fellows, they too then stood a chance of climbing the social ladder.

When the time came for an emperor to fill vacancies in the Senate, he would always select young members of senatorial families and members of the equestrian order who enjoyed his favor,

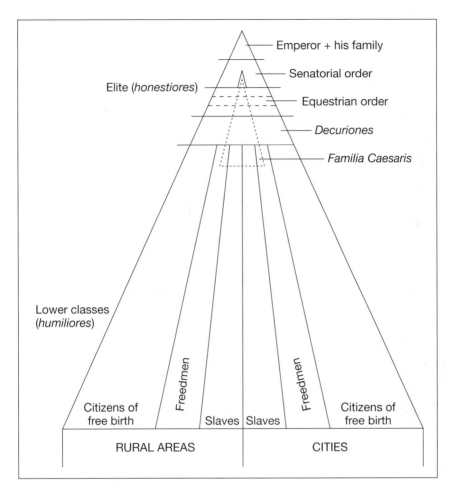

Emperor + his family

Senatorial order

Elite (*honestiores*)

Equestrian order

Decuriones

Familia Caesaris

Lower classes
(*humiliores*)

Freedmen

Freedmen

Citizens of
free birth

Slaves | Slaves

Citizens of
free birth

RURAL AREAS | CITIES

FIGURE 15.9   Social structure in the early imperial age
Source: After G. Alföldy

who had impressed him with their competence, or who had contacts among his circles. Augustus had brought the number of senators back to six hundred again. Over the years, many a senator was removed from the Senate because he or his family had fallen into disfavor with the emperor, suffered severe financial losses (there was a property qualification for admission to the Senate!), or lost lawsuits. Moreover, quite a few old senatorial families died out. Consequently vacancies regularly occurred for "new men" in the Senate. The vast majority of these vacancies were filled with knights.

The expansion of bureaucracy led to a corresponding expansion of the equestrian order. Ever more successful junior officers, intellectuals, and *decuriones* managed to acquire positions in the imperial services, from where they could with relative ease rise to the equestrian order, because the emperor would often admit competent members of those services to that order. So the expansion of bureaucracy can be said to have improved the aforementioned groups' chances

FIGURE 15.10 Hadrian (AD 117–138)

Notes. Hadrian was a major reformer in the fields of administration and the codification of law. He visited most of the empire's provinces in person. Hadrian put an end to the expansionist politics of his predecessor Trajan and set about consolidating and strengthening the frontiers instead. He was a great admirer of Greek culture. He is here shown with a beard, as also worn by contemporary Greek philosophers.

of social advancement. Some very wealthy provincial notables even managed to gain admission to the Senate. Usually the process of social advancement would span a few generations: a father would be granted Roman citizenship, his son would make his mark in the army and would rise to the equestrian order as an officer, after which his grandson would be admitted to the Senate after following a successful career in the offices that were accessible to knights.

The first notables from Spain and southern Gaul were included in the Senate under the emperor Tiberius. They were descendants of Roman emigrants. The emperor Claudius admitted the first real Gallic nobles to the Senate (AD 47). After that this development gained momentum. In the second century large numbers of notables from the Romanized and Hellenized interior provinces (southern and eastern Spain, Gaul, North Africa, Sicily, Greece, southern and western Asia Minor, Syria, and the Hellenistic cities in Egypt) were admitted to the Senate. An even greater number of notables and intellectuals from these regions rose to the equestrian order. Even military men from the northern and eastern frontier regions managed to gain admission to this order.

By AD 200 an aristocracy of service (an aristocracy serving in an administrative machinery) had emerged throughout the empire. It comprised three ranks (senators, knights, and *decuriones*) and shared a common Latin-Greek elite culture and a common spiritual baggage of popular moralistic notions absorbed from a wide diversity of Hellenistic philosophical schools. The language of this elite was Greek in the eastern half of the empire and Latin in the west. Of great importance to this elite was the literary culture (Greek: *paideia*) with which they were brought up. It was this which distinguished them most from the masses who still spoke their original languages or vernaculars. Anyone who lacked *paideia*, who could not speak pure, civilized Latin and/or Greek and who could not quote passages from the works of classical authors did not really belong to the upper ten. Even if he was rich and powerful, he would always give himself away and prove himself a parvenu. On the other hand, anyone who did not belong to this elite but nevertheless had *paideia* did stand a chance of climbing the social ladder. The literary elite culture was more or less the same all over the empire. From Gaul to Syria it encompassed a thorough grounding in Latin and Greek written rhetoric (in the eastern half of the empire virtually exclusively Greek; in the west only Latin or both Greek and Latin) and familiarity with classical literature. Also important were etiquette and knowledge of a code of conduct based on the instructions and recommendations of popular philosophers. Only a small group of students at the schools of philosophy (e.g., those of Athens, pp. 115–16 and 134–5) actually studied philosophy as a science.

FIGURE 15.11 School scene

Notes. The pupils are holding their scrolls. Until in late antiquity the scroll (of papyrus) was the most common form of book. The texts were written on the scrolls in columns. The reader unwound the scrolls as he read the columns. The scrolls were not easy to read. The individual words were not separated by gaps and there was no punctuation. Scrolls were costly because each scroll had to be written by hand. Some book sellers would dictate a text to thirty or more slaves at a time. That enabled them to produce several scrolls simultaneously.

Such book sellers were to be found only in large cities in the more developed provinces.

The educational system that the Romans had borrowed from the Greeks in the second century BC (see p. 184) spread across all the western provinces in the imperial age. In the Greek-speaking cities in the Hellenistic eastern provinces it had of course existed for several centuries already. This educational system was the vehicle by which the elite propagated their literary culture.

From time to time even the son of a former slave managed to rise to a high social position. A case in point is the emperor Pertinax, who ruled Rome for three months in AD 193. He was the son of a freedman who had been a private teacher as a slave and had established his own school when he was released from slavery. A senator (a relative of his father's former master) secured Pertinax a post as an army officer just around the time when serious border conflicts broke out in the east (c. 161–166) and along the Danube (c. 165–180). Pertinax proved his worth, was admitted to the equestrian order, and ultimately became a senator after a long career in equestrian offices. Around 180 he was a highly esteemed general and advisor of the emperor Marcus Aurelius (161–180). When the latter's successor Commodus (180–192) was killed by a court conspiracy before he had appointed a successor, Pertinax was placed on the throne.

However, such a career was very rare; generally speaking it was only in exceptional circumstances, such as a serious war, that a man of such humble birth could rise so high.

ROMAN LAW

All Roman citizens throughout the empire were protected by Roman law. Roman law, which was an original Roman achievement, had a profound influence on Western legal systems.

Roman law was formalistic. The Roman legal system revolved around the letter of the law and depended upon strict adherence to definitions and prescribed forms. There was for instance one rule for sale (which involved money), another for barter.

Roman law was essentially private law (including most criminal law), which had evolved in the practice of jurisdiction, legal advice, and jurisprudence and was hence not necessarily derived from legislation. We have already seen above (p. 182) that public law was relatively poorly developed. From the early republican era onwards the sources of law were enactments (the *leges* of the *Comitia Centuriata* and the *Comitia Tributa* and the *plebiscita* of the *Concilium Plebis*, p. 157), judgments, precedents, the *mos maiorum* (customary law), the commentaries of legal advisors, and the praetors' edicts. In the imperial age senatorial decisions and imperial letters, edicts and rescripts (= answers to petitions) gained force of law.

In the republican period it was the praetor who dismissed or allowed a claim. If he decided a claim was admissible, he would approach a *iudex* (sworn judge) or several *iudices* and draft written instructions specifying what definitions and rules would apply to the case. There were no public prosecutors. Bringing a defendant before the court was not the government's responsibility. Anyone wishing to lodge a complaint against an individual had to bring that individual before the praetor and the *iudex* himself. The *iudex* (or *iudices*) delivered judgment. At the beginning of their year of office, the praetors proclaimed what kinds of trials and procedures they would allow. This was known as the praetor's edict. In practice, a praetor would usually take over the greater part of his predecessor's proclamation, sometimes after slight adaptations. This led to the formation of a constantly expanding collection of edicts, adapted to practical requirements. Under the emperor Hadrian (AD 117–138) the jurist Julianus completed and systemized this collection. Nothing more was added to it after that.

A praetor usually based his proclamation on the advice provided by his private council of legal experts, his *consilium* (see pp. 158 and 175). These legal experts were Roman notables who studied law out of interest and gave free legal advice to magistrates and other individuals seeking their opinion on a point of law, including their own clients. They interpreted issues of customary law, legislation, and case law (judgments and cases). When someone came to seek their opinion they would provide their advice in public, so that everyone would be able to hear it and learn from it. Their written commentaries constituted one of the principal sources of private law. The various sources of private law were ordered and systematized on several occasions in the imperial age—first of all under the emperor Hadrian and again later, at the beginning of the third century and in the late imperial age. In the sixth century the sources were codified in the *Corpus Iuris Civilis* of Justinian (who was the emperor of the Eastern Roman empire from 527 until 565). This work comprised a textbook (the *Institutiones*), the legal advisors' interpretations of private law (the *Digesta*), and the imperial decrees (the *Codex*). The textbook was based on a similar work from Hadrian's time; it is still used as a guide to jurisprudence today.

In Rome, citizens could appeal to a higher court. In the republican era they could appeal to the popular assembly via a tribune of the *plebs*. Around the end of the second century BC the popular assembly delegated the task of hearing appeal cases to separate courts of justice. In the imperial age appeal cases became the emperor's responsibility. Many other legal cases from all over the empire were also referred to the emperor. The administration of justice came to be one of his most time-consuming tasks. To assist them in this task, the emperors therefore increasingly called in the help of others, for example the *praefectus urbi* (Rome's town prefect), the guard prefect, and, from Hadrian's time onwards, the emperor's deputies in Italy. In the first quarter of the third century AD, the time of classical Roman jurisprudence, the post of guard prefect was held by experienced military men, but also competent legal advisors.

The Romans had separate courts for different kinds of offences. The first of these courts was that which was established in 149 BC to handle extortion cases. Another five permanent criminal courts were instituted under Sulla (*c.* 80 BC; e.g., for cases of poisoning, embezzlement, and violence). The courts were presided over by praetors. In the imperial age there were courts-martial in the military camps.

In Rome and Italy the administration of justice in the imperial age was hence in the hands of the praetors' sworn judges, the six special courts, Rome's town prefect, the guard prefect, and the emperor. Local councilors administered justice at a lower level. In the provinces, the administration of justice was the responsibility of the local rulers (lowest level), the governors, and—for appeal cases, which prerogative was reserved for Roman citizens—the emperor.

There were also several lower colleges, which functioned only in the city of Rome, but they fall outside the scope of this book (see p. 162).

Much distinction was made between the different social classes in the administration of justice. Slaves, for example, unlike members of higher classes, could be tortured during interrogations. In the course of the imperial age Roman law increasingly discriminated between the members of the three highest orders (senators, knights, and *decuriones*), who were referred to as *honestiores*, and those of the lower classes, the *humiliores*.

THE WESTERN AND EASTERN PROVINCES

The western provinces

The Celts

Most of the western provinces were occupied by Celtic tribes and by peoples who were very much influenced by the Celts. Who the Celts were and where they lived is a topic of discussion. Even in antiquity itself there were for example authors who did not class the occupants of the British Isles as Celts. People who had migrated from Celtic areas to Galatia (central Asia Minor) and the northwestern part of the Iberian peninsula may have become alienated from their cultural roots and no longer identifiable as Celts. Greek and Roman authors may moreover have used the term "Celts" as a kind of collective noun. The Greeks for example referred to Germans as

MAP 15.3   Areas occupied by the Celts and the Germans before the Roman expansion

"Celts." Here, we assume that the term "Celts" refers to the people who in the Roman period lived on the British Isles and in Gaul, northwestern Spain, the Po valley, southern Germany, the Alps, Bohemia, and Galatia—in other words, the area largely coinciding with the distribution area of what archaeologists have identified as the "La Tène culture." We will use the term "Gauls" to refer to the occupants of what are now France, Belgium, the Rhineland, northwestern Switzerland, and the Po valley.

In terms of material culture and technology the Celts were not much inferior to the Greeks and the Romans. The Celtic occupants of the region between the Rhine and the Meuse (approximately what is now Luxembourg) and of Bohemia, for example, were talented iron craftsmen. What the Celts lacked, however, was an efficient military and political structure designed for long-term warfare. Celtic warriors were renowned for their personal valor, but they were poorly organized. The Celtic tribes probably consisted of groups of relatives (also referred to as "clans" in Ireland) that were led by aristocrats (see p. 145, on Rome's early history). To our knowledge, the lower peasantry was dependent on those nobles. A nobleman often had a personal retinue of warriors, who had voluntarily allied themselves with him. In times of war, the warriors' assembly would appoint one of the aristocrats as king.

Important centers in a Celtic tribe's occupation area were the *oppida* (plural of *oppidum*), or hillforts. They lay on easily defensible hilltops and had a small number of fixed inhabitants, but they were designed to serve as places of refuge for all the occupants of the surrounding areas with their goods and chattels in times of war. Inside these *oppida* were workshops and sanctuaries.

When Gaul came under Roman control, cities based on Roman (and Greek) models took the place of many of the *oppida*. As peace then reigned throughout the empire, there was no need for the cities to be fortified; many had a spacious layout and were situated in valleys. These cities evolved into *foci* of Roman culture and served as the administrative centers of the surrounding rural areas. Together with those surrounding areas they constituted communities that resembled Italian and Greek city states. The country folk living outside the cities adhered to their old customs and traditions

FIGURE 15.12 A Celt dressed in a hooded cape, breeches, and leggings

Note. Probably a member of the tribe that lived near Trier (the Treveri).

and continued to use their own languages for a long time. Celtic dialects continued to be spoken in rural areas in the western provinces through to the end of antiquity and even after. The old ties of dependence between the rural population and the notables lived on more or less unchanged (though sometimes Roman names were used to describe them).

The tribal noblemen flocked to the new cities and were quickly Romanized. The nobles joined the rank of *decuriones* and when that group was after some time granted full Roman citizenship they could become officers in the Roman army. Together with enfranchised rich immigrants from other provinces and veteran junior officers of the frontier armies, they came to constitute the elite of the new communities. We have already seen above that members of this elite started to be admitted to the equestrian order and the Senate in the mid-first century AD (p. 234). The urban councils in the western provinces were usually quite small (most had thirty to a hundred members) and were very oligarchic. Once the new elite had firmly established itself, its families monopolized the council for many generations. Only when one of those families was degraded or promoted to a higher class or when a family died out did a new family stand a chance of being admitted to the council.

Like the Italian cities, the cities in Gaul and Spain had theaters (for plays), amphitheaters (for gladiatorial and animal fights), and gymnasia, where people could practice athletics or attend lessons in Latin and Greek rhetoric.

Gaul in particular had been exposed to Greek influence for many centuries already. Much of this influence came from Massilia (Marseilles), the colony that the Greeks had founded in southern Gaul around 600 BC. In the imperial period Massilia was a center of Greek rhetorical education.

We don't know much about the Celts' religion or traditions because their myths, legends, and heroic songs were passed on orally. Celtic gods that resembled Roman deities were given Roman names in the imperial age, but retained their native character. The Druids held a special position in Celtic society. They were a kind of "medicine men," sages who were familiar with the

FIGURE 15.13 *Oppida*, pre-Roman hill forts

FIGURE 15.14   The Roman settlement of Namur

Notes. The settlement lay at the junction of the Sambre and the Meuse rivers. To the northwest of the settlement lay the former *oppidum.*

FIGURE 15.15   Gateway of an *oppidum*

secret incantations and rites which the Celts believed had power over the lives of human beings and cattle and the success of crops.

The western half of the empire also included the North African provinces Africa, Numidia, and Mauretania. These provinces were dotted with small towns, whose populations also included peasants. The higher classes had become Romanized as a result of the large-scale immigration of Romans from Italy (which started under Marius and Caesar; see pp. 192 and 202), but the lower classes had continued to use their own Berber and Punic (= Phoenician = Carthaginian) languages. In the first century AD the *decuriones* of the North African cities were given access to the equestrian order and in the second century the first of their ranks were admitted to the Senate.

In the first two centuries of the imperial age the western half of the empire enjoyed unprecedented peace and prosperity. Conditions in Italy began to stagnate somewhat in the second century, although it remained a prosperous and productive area, but Gaul, Spain, and North Africa now reached the height of their prosperity. After 161 the Roman empire was faced with more problems (see the next chapter), but they were not to culminate in a crisis until in the course of the third century. Large areas continued to prosper.

The eastern half of the empire

The Greeks in the Roman empire

The period from 30 BC until AD 230 was characterized by fairly peaceful and prosperous conditions in the eastern provinces, too. The most prosperous period in these parts was around the middle of the second century, but things continued to go well until about 230, apart from a few problems during the reign of Marcus Aurelius (161–180), when parts of the empire were afflicted by epidemics that the Roman armies brought back from the East, where they had successfully penetrated deep into the Parthian empire.

The Roman empire had had control over a large part of the Hellenistic world since the second century BC; the histories of Rome, Greece, Egypt, and the Levant had merged into the history of the Roman empire. But that had not meant the end of the Greek and Near Eastern civilizations. They had lived on under the Roman control, just like the civilization of Hellenistic Mesopotamia had endured under the sway of the Parthians (see p. 137). This is clearly apparent from the history of the cities. The Greek cities and their territories (some of which had once been independent city states) had retained local autonomy and their traditional institutions. The same holds for the Near Eastern cities, although many of those cities increasingly acquired a Greek character, largely as a result of the Hellenization of their elite inhabitants. The Greek cities in Parthia likewise retained their Greek character for a long time (see p. 138).

The Greek-speaking eastern half of the empire experienced a period of unrest and impoverishment in the second and first centuries BC. The Romans ruthlessly exploited those regions and took away thousands of educated people to serve as their slaves. Moreover, many of the battles of the Roman civil wars were fought in those regions.

FIGURE 15.16 A wounded Amazon: Greek copy (second century AD) of a Classical Greek sculpture

Notes. The Greeks of the Roman imperial age turned to Classical examples for inspiration in literature, philosophy and architecture, and also in sculpture.

Amazons were mythical female warriors. According to Greek legends they fought battles with Heracles, the Athenians, and the Greeks who besieged Troy (see p. 65 on Homer and the "Iliad").

In the Greek cities the Romans promoted an oligarchic form of government. They put an end to the civil struggles that had afflicted the cities for so many years (see pp. 128–9). After this, discord was to resurge within the Greek cities only during the Roman civil wars, when conflicts broke out between protégés of contending Roman generals or when rebels used their support of one of the struggling Roman parties as a cover-up for their own private pursuits.

FIGURE 15.17 Representation of Greek games: during Roman times athletics, chariot races, wrestling, and boxing spread across all the countries of the eastern Mediterranean and also to the West

Notes. Professional sportsmen would travel from city to city to participate in the games. Sometimes they were paid handsome fees.

The period from 30 BC until the end of the first century AD was a time of recovery, which was followed by an era of prosperity and cultural revival in the second and early third centuries. The notables who governed the Greek cities acted as benefactors and competed with one another and with notables in other cities in embellishing city gates, streets, and squares, and in arranging donatives and public entertainments. For the elite this aspect of their city was an important status symbol.

The period AD 70–230 saw major literary achievements in the Greek language, especially in certain sciences and rhetoric. These were the days of the doctor Galen (c. 129–210) and the geographer Ptolemy (mid-second century), who had a profound influence on later Western European science. In this period, too, itinerant orators attracted great crowds of people to the theaters with their show speeches on moralistic and historical themes. The Persian wars of 490–479 BC were particularly popular themes. Contemporary Greek culture adulated the magnificent achievements of Greece's classical past of the fifth and fourth centuries BC. The Greek-speaking public was familiar with those achievements and greatly enjoyed the variations on historical topics presented by the orators in their show speeches.

Most educated Greeks resigned themselves to Roman dominion and appreciated the positive aspects of the Roman imperial system. In their eyes there was a good symbiosis between the Romans, who were the best fighters and rulers and kept the barbarians outside the borders of the empire, and the Greeks, who had the most refined culture in the empire. They did not really look upon the Romans as a foreign people. Greeks and Romans tended to regard one another as kindred peoples.

The Greek-speaking elite appreciated the Romans' policies of enfranchizing the occupants of the provinces who shared in the Greek literary culture and giving Greek-speaking notables the chance to be admitted to the Senate and the equestrian order (see p. 234).

Most senators from the eastern half of the empire were descendants of (former) Hellenistic kings, Italian and Roman emigrants, local aristocrats, or Greek intellectuals. A good stepping-stone to the imperial aristocracy of senators and knights was a post in the provincial assemblies of the imperial cult. In all the provinces, both east and west, local notables periodically convened in provincial councils to worship the emperor and discuss matters of communal interest.

AGRICULTURE, TRADE, AND CRAFTS

The lower classes

Between 80 and 90 percent of the population of the Roman empire was involved in the production, processing, and transport of agricultural produce. Farm work was heavy and not very productive. Everything had to be done by hand—no mechanical aids were yet available. Crop yield ratios were low, except in areas where the soil was extremely fertile. This was the case for example in the Nile Delta, in the volcanic parts of southern Italy and Sicily, and in some valleys and coastal plains in North Africa. Egypt, Sicily, and North Africa were the granaries of the capital, Rome.

In the Mediterranean parts of the empire, stock-keeping was practiced at farms (where the cattle was kept in byres, orchards, and stubble fields) and by transhumant herders who moved their livestock to and fro between summer and winter pastures. The summer pastures were often in the hills and the mountains.

In the first two centuries of the imperial age the peasants and the landowners benefited from the peaceful conditions prevailing throughout the empire. Buildings and crops suffered little devastation through warfare. Most major building projects and the public entertainments and charity that were provided in the cities were financed by the regular, high profits that the landowners, who governed the cities, made on the produce of their land. In this way means were transferred from the countryside to the cities via the purses of the landowners.

A large proportion of the city dwellers were craftsmen. They sold their products to farmers who visited the town markets, members of the local elite, and the foreigners who were drawn to the towns by cultural manifestations, games, and religious festivals. The craftsmen were self-employed; they ran their businesses together with their relatives, one or two slaves and occasionally a day laborer at peak times. There were only few large workshops employing more than ten slaves. The craftsmen were united in trade guilds (*collegia*), which enjoyed the patronage of the local elite. Unlike in the city of Rome in the late republican era, they had no political power. They could not formulate their own regulations either, so they cannot be compared with the guilds of later times. *Collegia* had mainly social and religious functions. The vast majority of the craftsmen lived a very sober life, but they were not paupers. The paupers in the cities were the day laborers, the beggars, the tramps, and the invalids. They were usually dependent on the charity of the rich.

A wide variety of groups worked in the rural areas. In Italy, for example, large and medium-sized farms were often managed by a large landowner's steward, for instance a freedman who lived at the central farmstead. He would supervise a number of trained slaves for specific tasks and at peak times also free day laborers from nearby villages (small-time free peasants, tenant farmers, or day laborers with a small plot of land of their own who were largely dependent on this work for their survival). Around the central farmstead were smaller mixed farms where tenants, freedmen, or slaves lived and worked. They were required to regularly hand over fixed amounts of produce or money to their lord or his steward. Wealthy landowners liked to spread risks and usually owned estates in different parts of Italy or in several provinces. As already explained above, the emperors were the largest landowners, with domains in Italy and several provinces.

There were great differences between the rural areas of individual provinces where the social and economic conditions of former days still prevailed. In Egypt and the Levant little had changed in terms of social conditions since the Hellenistic era and earlier times; in Italy and some parts of Greece much use was still made of slaves and in the rural areas in Gaul, too, many of the social conditions of former days still remained (see p. 239). A comparatively large proportion of the occupants of the rural parts of the frontier regions behind the Rhine and the Danube were small-time landowning farmers. In those regions the difference in wealth between tribal aristocrats and farmers was probably not as great as that between landowners and farmers in Gaul, Spain, and Italy. There were different types of farms, using different farming methods and employing different types of staff.

Mixed farming aimed at self-sufficiency of the farm owners and tenant farmers prevailed in isolated, relatively under-developed regions. Estates in those regions often consisted of a central farmstead surrounded by tenant farms. In fertile regions with good means of transport to city markets there were often many medium-sized and large farms that specialized in the cultivation

FIGURE 15.18a   A street lined with shops in a small Roman town

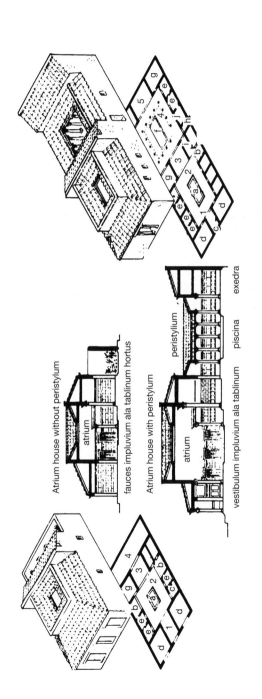

FIGURE 15.18b Plan and elevation of typical Roman houses

Notes.

Atrium house without a *peristylium*:
1. *fauces* (entrance passage)
2. *atrium* (hall)
3. *tablinum* (reception room)
4. *hortus* (garden)
a. *impluvium* (shallow catchwater basin)
b. *ala* (recess)
c. *vestibulum* (entrance court)
d. *taberna* (shop)
e. *cubiculum* (bedroom)

Atrium house with a *peristylium*:
1. *fauces*
2. *atrium*
3. *tablinum*
4. *peristylium*
5. *exedra* (open fronted garden room)

a. *impluvium* (shallow catchwater basin)
b. *ala* (recess)
c. *vestibulum* (entrance court)
d. *taberna* (shop)
e. *cubiculum* (bedroom)
f. *piscina* (basin)
g. *triclinium* (dining room)
h. *posticum* (back exit)
i. *andron* (corridor)
j. *culina* (kitchen)

Atrium house without peristylium

fauces impluvium ala tablinum hortus

atrium

Atrium house with peristylium

peristylium

atrium

vestibulum impluvium ala tablinum   piscina   exedra

FIGURE 15.18c   Street scene in a large Roman city

Notes. The tall, storeyed buildings which increasingly dominated the aspect of streets in Rome in the late republican era had no chimneys and no running water. Their occupants washed at the public baths or at other communal water sources and cooked on braziers, which also served as sources of heat during cold times of the year. On the ground floor there were usually workshops and cafés or restaurants. The living areas were on the floors above. There were also luxury apartment buildings with far better facilities.

Men lived mostly out in the streets. They ate at cheap restaurants (soup kitchens) and hung around in places where they hoped to find work. Those who had a business themselves were to be found in their workshops. Slaves worked all day, from early in the morning until late at night. In those days without mass media, information about what was going on elsewhere was picked up in the streets and squares, from travelers and the like. The rich lived in large houses laid out on one floor around a central garden and in luxurious apartments. They did not always reside in separate quarters. Many houses of the rich were to be found between other buildings.

of specific cash crops and employed trained slaves. Between these estates and specialized farms were tenant farms and the farms of small landowners. The small-time free peasants (both tenants and landowners) and the day laborers in the rural areas and in nearby towns constituted a reservoir of labor that could be exploited for seasonal tasks at the large and medium-sized farms.

There was a complex legal structure: farm owners would for example lease an extra plot of land or fishing water alongside their own property; a tenant often possessed cattle of his own, and a slave who did not live on his master's estate would exploit a nearby small quarry for his own account. The free paupers in rural areas were day laborers, tramps, and unpropertied tenants. In some regions there was a form of sharecropping: the landowner would provide the land and the means of production, and the tenant would hand over a percentage—often fifty—of the produce of the land.

Debt was a serious problem (p. 178). Small-time peasants who ran up debts were usually soon reduced to the status of proletarian day laborers. If a debtor failed to pay his debts, his property fell to his creditor.

MAP 15.4 The *limes* of the lower Rhine, AD 47–260

Note: Limes—fortified frontier/zone of defense.

MAP 15.5 Agricultural and industrial products and roads in the Roman empire

Trade

Most trade by far was retail trade at local markets and in the streets where the workshops were. The workshops were also shops.

But long-distance trade was also relatively common, both by water (seas and rivers) and overland. The chief commodities were metals, artisanal products, and articles of high value that were fairly non-perishable and took up little room. Contemporary eulogists praised the possibility of safe travel throughout the Roman empire. The Roman fleets endeavored to suppress piracy and the local authorities (or the governors in cases of severe disorder) policed the land routes. Nevertheless, the Romans preferably traveled in convoys and caravans, because banditry was never entirely eradicated. The paved highways that criss-crossed the empire from frontier to frontier had been built primarily to facilitate the rapid movement of troops, but they had soon evolved into important trade arteries, too. To spread the risks, a merchant would almost always find a number of co-financiers to help finance his long-distance commercial enterprises. There was also some trade with regions beyond the frontiers. The distribution patterns of Roman products and coins give us a good impression of the distances covered by the foreign trade routes. They extended into Scandinavia, central Asia, India, Further India, Arabia, and East and West Africa. Cities situated at the transitions of caravan routes to sea routes became very wealthy. Good examples of such cities are Carthage in North Africa, Tarraco (Tarragona) in Spain, Massilia (Marseilles) and Arelate (Arles) in southern Gaul, Ephesus and Milete in Asia Minor, the Syrian coastal towns, and Alexandria in Egypt.

Work and status

The social class to which a Roman belonged was far more important for his status than the kind of work he did. A slave always remained at the bottom of the hierarchical system, even if he worked as a doctor or an artist. At the top of the system were the landowners, who did not have to support themselves with the fruits of their own hands and were at leisure to devote themselves

FIGURE 15.19 Paying tribute: relief from a funerary monument in the Moselle region

FIGURE 15.20 Roman shop-lined street from around the beginning of the second century AD

Notes. The shops were also workshops. Above a shop was a storage area and above that were three or four residential floors. The shops could be closed with shutters.

entirely to education, administration, and entertainment. Small-time traders and usurers enjoyed little respect. A small step above them were the craftsmen and above them were the small farmers. Farmers supplied material products and were more independent because they produced their own food.

Women in the Roman empire

We have little information on the women of the low social classes. Observations in classical literature suggest that agricultural and artisanal tasks were traditionally divided between the genders throughout the entire Roman world. Boys were trained in the male tasks by their fathers

FIGURE 15.21   River ship transporting casks of wine

or other male relatives, girls in the female tasks by their mothers or other female relatives. Women's tasks included spinning, weaving, looking after small stock, preserving foodstuffs, tending to the vegetable garden, caring for children, and all other domestic chores. The men did the physically heavy work such as ploughing and work that had to be done far from home.

In the circles of the Roman notables much had changed since the earliest days of Roman history (see p. 147). The elite's old family ties now existed in theory only. Loose alliances, which could easily be broken, had taken the place of marriage in the ancestral sense. Women would marry at an early age (of about 13 or 14). Men usually married when they were between 20 and 35. Divorce was fairly common. Most men who divorced their wives did so for opportunistic reasons, for example so as to be able to improve their position by marrying another woman, from a powerful and wealthy family. A woman was allowed to own property in her own right. That property, however, was managed by her husband or some other male relative. If a couple got divorced, the proper custom was for the man to return the woman's dowry to her.

Women of the higher classes supervised the male and female slaves in their domestic tasks and accompanied their husbands to banquets, the theater, the games and the temples, but they had no say in administrative or legal matters. They did often enjoy a good primary and secondary education. Girls from fairly wealthy families went to school, just like boys, and quite a few well-to-do Romans had private teachers who would educate their master's children, any young relatives living in the same house, and even the children of their slaves. These private teachers were educated slaves. Girls could go to school until they were given in marriage, which is why they never followed higher, rhetorical education—by the time they were old enough to follow that form of education they would have been married off, and marriage meant the end of their education. Children from lower social classes enjoyed no education, because schools were commercial enterprises and poor families simply didn't have the money to pay them. What girls learned at home or at school enabled them to participate in the everyday life of their social class in a civilized manner.

Something that still puzzles us is the low birth rates in the highest Roman classes (of senators and knights) in the imperial age. Senatorial and equestrian families died out one after the other. This has been attributed to a desire to limit the number of heirs by minimizing legitimate offspring.

FIGURE 15.22a Portrait of a Roman boy from the middle of the imperial age

FIGURE 15.22b   A Roman lady at her toilet

FIGURE 15.22c   A family enjoying a meal

A noble Roman woman had more freedom of movement and more rights (including the right to own property) than her Greek counterpart (*cf.* p. 103). This difference continued in the Roman imperial age, when the position of elite women in the eastern half of the empire largely followed the Greek pattern, while in the western half it was more in accordance with the Roman one. Things were different again in Celtic and German areas. Various Greek and Roman authors were amazed by the freedom of movement that women in those areas seemed to enjoy. But we shouldn't see things in too rosy a light: there, too, women will in practice most probably have been subordinate to and dependent on their menfolk, and will have had no political power and few rights of their own.

RELIGION

There was a vast multiplicity of religions and religious rites in the Roman empire. Every people, every city, every association and every family had its own cults, religious rites, and patron deities. And all over the empire were temples, sacred groves, and trees and objects in which local spirits were believed to reside. Deities were worshipped in several local variants and were by no means the same everywhere. Every region had its own means for divining the future and its own magic devices for warding off evil or invoking misfortune on enemies.

The vast majority of the religions were ritual religions, characterized by many deities. Most rites were intended to win the gods' favor; the idea was that a person who made an offering to a deity could claim a favor in return. Offerings and sacrifices, prayers, vows, and incantations accompanied all acts in public life, work, and private life.

The different peoples living in the empire often identified their own deities with those of other peoples. For example, a Greek visiting Syria and seeing a temple of a sky god or a storm god would call that god Zeus, like his own supreme god, who was originally also a sky god. A Roman would call that same god Jupiter.

The rites were sometimes related to myths, stories recounting the deeds of the gods. Those myths were not dogmas—they were not generally held to be true, so it did not matter if they did not agree with one another. Some myths overlapped one another or even contradicted one another. Philosophical theories were expected to be dogmatically logical and pure, but stories about gods were not. Many gods were in one way or another associated with the forces in nature which controlled every aspect of man's life.

Every people and every town had its own religious calendar indicating when offerings or sacrifices were to be made to the different deities and on what days their festivals were to be celebrated. People did not work on those days. Only the Jews had a fixed weekly day of rest (the Sabbath).

Roman gods and religious practices

The principal Roman gods were the supreme god Jupiter (the sky god, the head of the divine family, and the patron god of Rome), Juno (his wife), Minerva (the goddess of handicrafts, learning, and the arts), and Mars (the god of war and of vital force in spring). They were the protectors of the Roman state, the state gods. The Romans originally regarded their gods as powers which they could not represent visually, but in the fifth century BC, under the influence of the Greeks, they started to depict their principal gods as superhuman beings. In time, the Romans came to identify their gods with kindred Greek gods. Their gods retained their Roman names, but their appearance, their myths, their genealogy, and the patterns of their deeds gradually acquired many Greek elements.

In addition to their gods in the form of superhuman beings (for which the Greek term "anthropomorphic" is often used), the Romans had many other deities that were associated with specific acts, times, and places. At harvest time, for example, they would pray to gods of threshing, winnowing, storage, etc. Those gods were called *numina* (plural of *numen*).

The Romans believed that their undertakings would be unsuccessful if the (state) gods were enraged, but that little could go wrong if the gods were satisfied. In the latter case they were at "peace with the gods" (*pax deorum*). In order to retain that peace with the gods, the Romans always had to make the required sacrifices and recite the required prayer formulas in a painfully accurate manner. If the slightest mistake was made during a ceremony, the whole ceremony was repeated. Every five years the censors (and later the emperors) would organize a *lustrum*, an expiatory sacrifice on behalf of the entire Roman people. The Romans believed that they could infer the gods' disposition and the outcome of their own undertakings from certain omens, or signs, such as the flight of birds, the structure of the liver of a sacrificed animal, and oracles (see p. 141). On the eve of an important undertaking, the kings, and later the magistrates with *imperium* (and later

FIGURE 15.23 Reconstruction drawing showing the sanctuary of Lenus-Mars near Trier, one of the most important cities in the Roman Moselle region

still the emperors), would always endeavor to find out what the gods had in store for the Romans. A magistrate with *imperium* (or the emperor) had the right to take auspices (observe the flight of birds for divination purposes). In the imperial age the governors acted in accordance with the prophesies inferred from the emperor's auspices.

In the case of serious incidents and major disasters a special college of priests would consult the Sibylline Books, a collection of oracles named after the Sibyl, a legendary prophetess. She was believed to have resided in a cave near Cumae, in the Bay of Naples. None of these Sibylline Books has survived. We do know of texts known as Sibylline books of a Jewish and Christian signature dating from the first centuries BC and AD.

The Romans had several colleges of priests. The *pontifices* were responsible for the cult of the principal gods (see p. 149). There were also colleges with specific tasks (for example the inspection of the liver of a sacrificed animal). The priests were Roman notables who performed their priestly tasks alongside their secular tasks.

Like the Greeks, the Romans too believed in life after death. Both peoples thought that the souls of the deceased would enjoy peace in the underworld, providing their bodies had been properly buried. If a deceased had not been buried (or cremated), his shadow would roam around miserably, unable to find peace.

FIGURE 15.24 The Roman god Mars

Note. As the local deity Lenus showed affinities with Mars, he was identified with that god.

The introduction of foreign gods

During the long span of Roman history, the Romans admitted both Greek and Eastern deities into their pantheon. Some Greek gods became very popular in Rome, such as Hercules (Herakles in Greek). He was a demigod who fought evil in his Twelve Labors and made the world fit for human occupation. Aesculapius (Asklepios) was a god of healing and the Dioscuri (Castor and Pollux) had in the early days of Rome's history saved the city from her enemies, which earned them a temple on the Forum at the center of town.

Foreign gods were often admitted into the Roman pantheon in times of misfortune, following the advice of oracles or if the cult of the gods in question had become widespread among the Roman people. The cult of the fertility goddess Cybele of Asia Minor, for example, was introduced in Rome during the difficult Second Punic War and the worship of the Greek god Dionysus (the

FIGURE 15.25 Representation of the three gods of the Capitol in Rome: Jupiter (center), the principal state god of Rome, Juno, and Minerva

god of wine, intoxication, and ecstasy), who was also called Bacchus, became very popular in Rome after this war. Undesirable side effects of the Bacchus cult, which included public disorder, were forbidden on the Senate's decree in 186 BC. The Bacchus cult then became subject to strict regulations.

In the imperial age a number of Eastern religions spread throughout the Roman empire. Those religions were no longer restricted to a particular city or people. The most important were the cult of the Egyptian gods Isis and Osiris, the worship of the Persian god Mithras, the Cybele cult, and Christianity.

Like Hercules, Mithras was a heroic fighter of evil. Hercules and Mithras were very popular in the military camps. The cult of Mithras was confined to men.

The cult of Isis and Osiris was a mystery religion. Isis was a fertility goddess who, with the help of her heroic son Horus, managed to recover the body of her husband Osiris, who had been killed by the evil god Seth, and bring him back to life. Osiris then became the god of the underworld.

Initiates in Isis' mysteries participated in Osiris' resurrection. Mysteries were a combination of rites, purifications, formulas, and theatrical performances with a magical undertone. The Greeks had a mystery cult of their own, which they celebrated at Eleusis, near Athens, in the sanctuary of their fertility goddess Demeter. That explains why Isis was much less popular among the Greeks than among the occupants of Italy, North Africa, and Gaul.

The Roman authorities were for a long time suspicious of the Isis cult, which they did not accept until the second century AD. Usually, however, the Roman authorities were very tolerant toward foreign religions. All that they required was that Roman citizens were prepared to participate in the public ceremonies and to pray to the Roman state gods. They took action only in cases of public disorder (e.g., during the *Bacchanalia*, the celebrations in honor of Bacchus, in 186 BC). It was only with the Jews and the Christians that they came into serious conflict.

FIGURE 15.26 Bacchus (Dionysus) flanked by two reveling ecstatic creatures

Note. Bacchanalian scenes were very popular all over the Roman world.

The Christians

The Jews and the Christians acknowledged only one god and rejected all the other deities. In this respect they differed from followers of other religions who sometimes devoted extra attention to one god in particular, but without renouncing the other gods (*cf.* p. 50).

The Jews were an ancient people and they were recognizable as a nation. That is the reason why they, as a people, did not have to conform to the Roman state cult from Caesar's time onwards. The Roman authorities did, however, take action against the Jews (in particular in Rome) if they made too many converts amongst non-Jews or when tension smoldered in the Jewish communities (see p. 226).

Christianity was a fairly new religion, which was not an advantage in antiquity, when only things with a long history were seen as authoritative, having proven themselves over the centuries. Christianity began with the appearance of Jesus of Nazareth in Palestine, in particularly in Galilee (= northern Palestine) and Judea. Jesus was most probably born *c.* 5 BC during the reign of the vassal king Herod the Great, who died in 4 BC. His birth was dated too late due to a calculation error made by the sixth-century monk Dionysius Exiguus, who laid the foundations for the Christian calendar. Jesus died during the reign of the emperor Tiberius, probably in AD 29, when Pontius Pilatus (Pilate) was the prefect (*praefectus*) of Judea. An inscription proves that his title was prefect, and not procurator as formerly thought. Pilate held this post from 26 until 36 AD, which is an exceptionally long time; usually such a term of office would last only one or two years. Jesus came from a relatively simple background; his father was a carpenter in the small town of Nazareth in Galilee. In spite of his humble beginnings, Jesus became a famous teacher, who felt attracted to the schools of thought of the Pharisees and also to the ascetic groups of Essenes and to ascetes who lived in the desert near the Dead Sea. The Pharisees explained the holy scriptures in the synagogues of Judea and were not solely focused on the Temple in Jerusalem (p. 137). Unlike the Sadducees, they believed in the immortality of the soul and they acknowledged the authority of both the Laws of Moses and the other books of the Old Testament and the tradition of scholarship that had evolved in commentaries on the Laws of Moses. The Pharisee movement that Jesus embraced was against the military uprising against Rome and

FIGURE 15.27 Sarcophagus showing Christian scenes

Notes. Left: the snake in Paradise tempts Adam and Eve to eat the forbidden fruit. Center: the Good Shepherd (this was originally a pastoral rather than a Christian motif; Christian artists Christianized it into the "Good Shepherd"). Right: the three young men whom God saved from burning in the furnace.

the foundation of a new Jewish kingdom. The Pharisees' key concern was a morally correct way of life. Jesus' followers saw in him the son of God and proclaimed that he had been resurrected after his crucifixion. His death on the cross they saw as God's triumph over evil and as atonement for the sins of all people who accepted Jesus as their savior and redeemer, the Messiah. The first generation of Jesus' followers were convinced that their Lord (Jesus) would soon return to earth, to do away with the old world and establish a new, heavenly earth. During the latter days of the reign of the emperor Tiberius and under Caligula (37–41) and Claudius (41–54) they began to convert people to their faith. At first their converts were all sympathizing Jews, but very soon they also began to include non-Jews who had felt attracted to the Jewish religion. In organizational terms, most Christian communities followed the example of Jewish communities and their custom of meeting one another at designated venues—for the Jews that was their synagogues. Such Christian communities arose in Palestine, Syria, northern Mesopotamia, Egypt, and Asia Minor. Some of Jesus' followers played a leading role in the early spread of Christianity—they were the apostles. It is thought that the most successful apostles were Peter, the first leader of a Christian community in Rome herself, and Paul. Paul was a strong opponent of Christianity at first. He even participated in the persecution of the first Christian community in Jerusalem. Later, however, he converted to Christianity and started to preach the Gospel, first in Syria and later in Asia Minor, on Cyprus, and in the southern Balkans (Macedonia and Greece). He is thought to have visited those areas between about AD 36 and 56. In 56 he was arrested in Jerusalem and taken to Rome. A Roman citizen, he claimed his right to be tried in Rome, before the emperor. In AD 65 Peter and Paul were executed in Rome by order of the emperor Nero, during the first persecution of Christians to have taken place in Rome. Nero used the Christians in Rome as a scapegoat after the devastating fire of 64, which reduced large parts of the city to ashes. It was rumored that Nero himself was responsible for the fire, so he publically blamed the Christians instead.

Paul is an extremely interesting figure. He was a Jew who grew up in Tarsus in Cilicia, a flourishing commercial town in the southeast of what is now Turkey, which was dominated by a Greek-speaking elite. In Jerusalem he studied the holy scriptures of the Jews under the Pharisees, he enjoyed Roman citizenship, and he was familiar with classical and Hellenistic Greek literature. All in all he is an excellent example of a man with a multiple identity. He was Jewish, Greek, and Roman at the same time and embraced the Christian religion.

So Christianity was not restricted to one people for very long; it was not the religion of an ancient, identifiable nation. This aroused the Roman authorities' suspicion. The Christians' secluded life also made them suspect and the Roman authorities came to see the ecclesiastical organization as a state within the state, which, they feared, might conspire against Rome. Christians started to be persecuted in different places, by governors and local authorities whom the Christians had annoyed, or by mobs searching for scapegoats in times of adversity. The Christians were even persecuted by various emperors. As already mentioned above, in 64 Nero blamed the Christians for the devastating fire that reduced the greater part of Rome to ashes. On this occasion only the Christians in Rome were persecuted.

Christianity originated as a Jewish sect that was particularly popular amongst non-Jews who felt attracted to the Jewish religion or had converted to Judaism. A dispute regarding an issue of Jewish law was the reason for the separation from Judaism. Most Christians were against enforcing Jewish rules of life on the non-Jews amongst them. Moreover, Christian authors soon started to explicitly distance themselves from Judaism. Different theories abound concerning the definitive schism between Jews and Christians. Some scholars attribute it to the apostles Peter and Paul, because they began to relax the Jewish laws. The Christians continued to share their holy scriptures with the Jews: the Old Testament (= the Hebrew Bible). To that they added the writings of evangelists and apostles (the New Testament).

It was not long before the Jewish Christians were outnumbered and surpassed in influence by Christians from non-Jewish peoples. The leadership of the Christian communities came to rest with a group of Greek-speaking intellectuals and merchants. They financed the ceremonies, provided the funds for poor relief and furnished the bishops (Greek: *episkopoi*—overseers) and the presbyters (elders) of the Christian communities, which otherwise consisted largely of slaves, freedmen, women, and small tradesmen in the cities. In rural areas Christianity found few followers in its early days. The occupants of those areas did not experience the feelings of disorientation associated with migration to a city and continued to adhere to their ancient ancestral rites, which were closely linked with their farming existence.

Slaves and women probably felt attracted to Christianity because in God's eyes they were equal to the other faithful in the Christian communities and they shared equally in the Sacraments. Things were often quite different in other contemporary religions. In the Christian communities even a slave could become a presbyter or a bishop (but a woman could not).

The popularity of Christianity among merchants and intellectuals was probably attributable to the latent monotheism inherent in the common popular schools of philosophy. Moreover, the Christians' clear and simple moral code and the uncompromising nature of their faith appealed to groups who were tired of the endless conflicts between the various schools of ethical philosophy. The Christian faith demanded commitment and offered security.

Literate Christians defended their faith in writing against attacks from various directions. In rhetorical written Greek they engaged in polemics with Jewish rabbis, Greek philosophers, the Roman authorities, and semi-Christian sects that combined Christian concepts with ancient Near Eastern ideas and Greek philosophy. Around 200 a similar Latin Christian literature emerged in North Africa—the Christian community in Rome continued to use Greek until in the third century; in that city it was mostly Greek-speaking slaves, freedmen, and foreigners who were attracted to Christianity.

The Christian authors developed a Christian literature that was acceptable to all the literate faithful. They also laid the foundations for a systematic, philosophical–logical doctrine, which was authoritatively preached by the bishops. It was, however, preached in simple stories and rules which everybody could understand. The Christian elite thus served both the literate and the illiterate. In time, a fair amount of Greek philosophy crept into the Christian doctrine. By 200 there were already centers of Christian scholarship, in particular in Alexandria in Egypt.

We should not underestimate the consequences that embracing Christianity had for the daily life of the earliest Christians. The exclusive, monotheistic nature of Christianity meant that Christians were required to distance themselves from everything in which Roman gods played a role, and that was no simple demand: it implied renouncing the *collegia* (trade associations), the gymnasia, the army, and the games, all of which in one way or another involved Roman gods. Strict Christians did not hold offices in local or central administration and they did not do military service. Their faith forbade them to take human life and they realized that they would be forced to participate in the worship of the Roman state gods and the emperor cult in the military camps and in administrative functions. Christian ethics also differed substantially from common Greco-Roman morality. According to Greco-Roman ethics you were supposed to help your friends and harm your enemies. Jesus, however, taught his followers to love their enemies, too. And in the cities, wealthy benefactors would be lavishly honored with statues, honorary inscriptions, and seats of honor in the theaters, whereas according to Jesus, acts of goodness should be performed in modest silence.

Unlike the heathens, the Christians had clear views on life after death. Paradise awaited those who persevered in their faith and this knowledge gave them the strength to undergo torture. All this isolated consistent Christians, which certainly contributed toward the hatred against Christians and the associated persecutions.

By the end of the second century quite a few Christians were becoming more flexible. A fair number of the soldiers in the armies of those days, especially those along the eastern frontier and in North Africa, were Christians. And all Christians were prepared to pray for the emperor and the empire and to pay taxes; they were not rebels.

16 THE CRISIS OF THE THIRD CENTURY AD AND LATE ANTIQUITY

GROWING PRESSURES ON THE NORTHERN AND EASTERN FRONTIERS

The years 161–166 saw a major war between Rome and the Parthians, which was followed by violent invasions of German tribes in the middle Danube region (165–180). In the east, the Roman generals won an overwhelming victory, but the Roman army returning from Mesopotamia brought back a plague, which claimed many victims in the Roman empire. A few years later, *c.* 170, the Germans managed to penetrate into Italy. For the first time since the days of Marius foreign invaders crossed the Alps. It cost the emperor Marcus Aurelius (161–180) great difficulty to expel the Germans and restore Roman control in the frontier region. It is assumed that populations declined in the areas where the wars were fought. The emperor Marcus Aurelius compensated for this by moving Germans to those areas.

The Romans' victory was, however, short-lived, for the third century, in particular the period from 235 to 282, was to see new wars against German tribes.

The Germans

During the period from 27 BC to AD 284 the German territory comprised Scandinavia to the west of Finland, northern and central Germany to the east of the Rhine and to the north of the Danube, the western part of Poland (the Weichsel area), and the greater part of what is now the Netherlands. It is not easy to say how far east their occupation area extended and where the transitions to the Celtic territories lay. Northern Switzerland, for example, was occupied by the Helvetians—a people with Celtic characteristics, but possibly also German ones. Similar problems arise in studies of the Netherlands and Belgium in the Roman period. The Frisians in the north, the Batavians in the southern part of the province of Gelderland, and the Canninefates in the area around the present towns of Leiden and Voorburg may be classed as Germans, whereas Celtic elements dominated in the southern part of the province of Limburg, the province of Zeeland, and Belgium. From time to time a Germanic elite may have dominated a Celtic substrate. This may have been the case in Batavian regions.

FIGURE 16.1 Marcus Aurelius (ruled AD 161–180), showing mercy on defeated opponents

Notes. Marcus Aurelius did not have a military background—until 161 he was more of an intellectual and a philosopher—but after initial defeats he nevertheless succeeded in halting the German invasions around 180. Later generations admired him for his energy and his self-sacrifice.

The German tribes were in many respects rather like the Celtic tribes (see p. 239). In the first place, they, too, were led by nobles who ruled over kinship groups and serfs and had a personal retinue of warriors. And like the Celts, they had warrior chieftains, elected by warriors' assemblies. The Germans lived in scattered settlements that consisted of a few large farms surrounded by a number of small huts. Agriculture and handicrafts were practiced by the free-born poor, dependent farm-hands, and women. The male members of the higher classes devoted themselves to warfare and hunting. In terms of material culture, however, the Germans were inferior to most Celtic tribes; they were also less prosperous. Around the beginning of the imperial age extensive trade contacts were established between the Romans and the Germans, via which goods and coins were distributed from the Roman empire as far as northeastern Germany and Scandinavia.

During the reigns of Caesar and Augustus the German nobles and their warriors were well trained and heavily armed, but their retainers from the lower classes had little more than a hardened wooden spear and a light shield. Those simple arms were nevertheless quite adequate for guerrilla warfare in the German forests and swamps. In the course of the imperial age the Germans borrowed much from the Romans' military organization. They for example borrowed the Romans' method of besieging cities and learned how to keep their armies together for long periods of time.

FIGURE 16.2 A German farmer plowing

By AD 69 the rebellious Batavians and their allies from free Germany had learned enough from the Romans to be able to force a Roman military base to surrender (Vetera, near Xanten in Germany). The Batavians had been able to observe the Romans' military tactics at close quarters as they had been living inside the Roman frontiers since *c.* 12 BC and had supplied many auxiliaries for the Roman armies. Nevertheless, the Romans should have taken the defeat at Vetera as an ominous portent (see p. 226).

We are poorly informed about the Germans' religion and literary tradition in this period because their myths, legends, and heroic songs were passed on orally.

Around 200, major changes took place in Germany. In the preceding 200 years the Goths had gradually moved from Scandinavia via the Weichsel area to the Crimean and the southern part of the Ukraine (the Ostrogoths) and Wallachia (the Visigoths). Around 238 they started to launch attacks on the Roman empire, which evolved into full-fledged wars that devastated the Roman provinces in the Balkans. It took the Romans many years, until 267–269, to rout the Goths, in battles fought in what is now Serbia.

Further west new alliances and federations of German tribes emerged, such as the Franks in the lower Rhine area and the Alamanni in the angle between the Rhine and the Danube. A few conflicts broke out along these frontiers in the first half of the third century, but they were only local disputes. Between 253 and 282, however, the Roman empire was confronted with massive invasions in these regions, too. The Roman armies had great difficulty restoring order along these frontiers and vast areas were laid waste in the confrontations with the Germans. The Germans' greatest feat was a major invasion of Gaul in 275–276.

Around 180, Germans started to settle in the northern frontier regions. This marked the beginning of a development which several centuries later was to result in the Germanization of areas in northern Gaul and to the south of the Danube. The Roman emperors did nothing to stop this development; some even encouraged it for the various advantages it implied: ravaged regions would be returned to cultivation and their populations would be able to pay taxes again, the German pressure on the frontiers would decrease, and the new occupants of the empire would furnish good recruits for the Roman armies.

The Sasanid empire

In 226 the rebellious Persians defeated their Parthian oppressors and assumed control over the Parthian empire. This new empire, which was ruled by the Sasanids, lasted until about 640, when it was unable to withstand the advancing Arabs.

Parthia had been an empire of practically autonomous provinces, with an upper class of warriors that sponged off the rest of the population. The new Sasanid empire was a centralist, bureaucratic state with high, efficiently collected taxes and—partly thanks to those taxes—a large, strong army. The heavily armed, armored cavalry was particularly formidable. The stirrup and the type of knight known to us from the Middle Ages were probably introduced in Persia.

The revival of Persian power went hand in hand with an aggressive form of nationalism, both in foreign politics and in religious and cultural life. According to contemporary Roman and Greek authors, the Persian kings of the third century aimed to conquer the eastern provinces of the Roman empire in order to recover Cyrus' empire. It is not entirely certain whether this was indeed their aim. What we do know for sure is that they made persistent efforts to conquer buffer states such as Armenia and Hatra (central Mesopotamia) and a series of fortified towns along the Euphrates that had once been Palmyrian and had come under Roman control in the second century. Those fortifications were important to the Romans because they lay along the caravan route from Syria to the Persian Gulf. The Romans also wanted to use them to store provisions for their armies, so that they would whenever necessary be able to quickly march from there to southern Mesopotamia—one of the heartlands of the Parthian—and later Persian—empire.

The years between 230 and 283 consequently saw a series of major wars between the Romans and the Persians, in which the Romans had the greatest difficulty holding their own. In

260 the Persians even managed to capture the emperor Valerian (253–260). It was not until under Diocletian (284–305), in the years 296–299, that the Roman armies won victories that caused the Persians to postpone further campaigns. By then the Romans had gained definitive control over most of the fortresses along the middle Euphrates, and had maintained their control over northern Mesopotamia and Armenia. The Arab city of Hatra—situated between the Roman and Persian spheres of influence in central Mesopotamia—had at the end of the second century AD fought Septimius Severus to a standstill, but went over to the Romans' side under the emperor Severus Alexander (ruled 222–235) and was destroyed by the Persians around 240.

The Persians regarded their Zoroastrianism (see p. 44) as a superior religion, and despised the religions of the minorities in their empire (e.g., those of the Greeks, the Jews, and the Babylonians). The Persians very soon destroyed several cities with a rich tradition: Hatra and Assur in Mesopotamia and Dura-Europos along the Euphrates. This implied the death of the almost four-thousand-year-old Sumero-Akkadian civilization and religion, although the Babylonian gods were to live on for some time as demons in various religious sects. The Greek culture that had been introduced here by Alexander the Great and his successors and that had been highly respected by the Parthians also gradually declined. The Greek cities and Greek quarters lost their privileges. This heralded the end of the Hellenistic era in these regions.

INTERNAL INSTABILITY IN THE ROMAN EMPIRE

The growing pressures on the frontiers exposed a whole range of weaknesses in the Roman system.

Military problems

The wars against the Germans and the Parthians (and after 226 the Persians) showed that the superiority that the Roman armies had enjoyed for so many centuries in the face of most of their enemies was no longer a matter of course. Over the years, those enemies had learned much from the Romans, whereas the military prowess of the Roman soldiers had suffered a decline. In the years after AD 83 the soldiers' pay was probably insufficiently raised. Their pay may even have lost some of its purchasing power, which will have induced the emperor Septimius Severus (ruled 193–211) to raise the soldiers' pay again. Since the spread of Roman citizenship throughout the frontier regions (see p. 232), from which ever more troops had to be recruited, the number of men who enlisted in order to acquire Roman citizenship had probably decreased considerably. From the works of contemporary Greek and Latin authors we get the impression that only the poorest and men who were not welcome anywhere else now voluntarily enlisted in the armies. Those authors claim that the soldiers did not shrink from terrorizing their own people whenever their material position was threatened. The higher officers still came from the senatorial and equestrian orders. Quite a few of those notables lacked the necessary military experience to be able to take effective action in a full-fledged war. In that respect they were surpassed by equestrian officers who had risen from the army's rank and file; they had been promoted to the equestrian order precisely on account of their military capabilities.

Army units that had spent a long time in particular frontier areas had developed strong regional ties and interests. Most of the soldiers came from the areas in which those armies were stationed (see p. 232). The consequence of this was that when an emperor paid insufficient attention to a threatened frontier, the troops on that frontier would proclaim their own general emperor, under the illusion that their new emperor would secure more resources and armed forces for their sector. In the third century several major wars consequently resulted in usurpations and succession struggles.

Structural defects

After two centuries of peace the Roman empire was no longer capable of coping with a more or less permanent state of war. The higher orders had lost much of their military prowess. The taxation system was too simple and too rigid to furnish the resources required to meet the high extra costs of defense. And there were no longer any extra sources of income in the form of the booty and tributes that had partly financed Rome's conquests in the second and first centuries BC.

All over the empire were countless indefensible unfortified cities. The busy trade was entirely geared to peaceful and reasonably safe conditions. There were very few reserves. Instead of productively investing the profits of their surpluses, the notables had squandered them on ostentatious buildings, popular entertainments, and cultural manifestations. And now they were suffering the consequences, for they were having to spend vast amounts on the upkeep of those buildings and on the gymnasia they had instituted and the games and other forms of entertainment they had introduced. They also had to support increasing numbers of poor seasonal laborers in periods when there was no demand for their labor. The lower classes had undoubtedly increased in number in the almost two hundred years of peace between 30 BC and AD 160 and many of their members were attracted to cities where public entertainments were provided.

In the course of the first and second centuries, wealth became increasingly disproportionately distributed, which ultimately resulted in a concentration of property in the hands of a small number of wealthy citizens. They grew richer and richer through inheritances and the purchase of land. This was the case in Italy in particular.

THE SEVERI (193–235)

Septimius Severus (193–211)

In 193 Septimius Severus, a Roman of North African origin, became emperor. In 193 he was the governor of Pannonia, where he had a strong army at his disposal. The period from 193 to 197 was a time of civil war and external warfare. After Commodus' demise Pertinax came to power. An excellent, experienced man, he nonetheless displeased the praetorian guard by not giving them the donatives they wanted, and was for that reason killed after a reign of about three months. The praetorians sold the throne to the highest bidder—Didius Julianus, who after a reign of even less than three months was beaten and eliminated by Severus and the army that he had brought along from the middle Danube. Severus discharged the praetorians, created a new guard from his own soldiers from Pannonia and went east to fight another pretender to the throne, Pescennius Niger, who lost the battle and his life. After a war against the Parthians and the Arabian fortified town of Hatra (195), Severus returned to Rome. In 197 he conquered and killed his last opponent, Albinus, the governor of Britain, in a battle at Lugdunum (Lyons), after which he went east again and won a war against the Parthians (199). He never succeeded in conquering Hatra. Septimius Severus, it is now believed, was not a military man originally, but a legal expert—a man with a keen interest in juridical and administrative matters.

Septimius Severus realized that he would have to expand and improve his army. He was also acutely aware of the fact that, not being a military man, he would have to offer his soldiers something extra to win their loyalty and attract good recruits. He created three new legions,

FIGURE 16.3 Septimius Severus (ruled AD 193–211)

greatly raised his soldiers' pay, and improved their fringe benefits. From this point onwards legionaries were to be paid 450 instead of 300 *denarii* a year, soldiers were allowed to marry, they were paid more extra allowances in cash and kind, and they were granted a plot of land in their own frontier region. Unfortunately, this further strengthened their allegiance to their local communities.

Septimius Severus made it easier for experienced junior officers to rise to higher officer posts and gave the knights more influence in administrative matters. His aims in increasing the soldiers' chances of social advancement were to make military service more attractive and to expand his army. However, his measures created unsolvable financial problems. The cost of defense increased explosively (one of the causes being the 50 percent raise in the soldiers' pay). These financial problems were to hound all the subsequent Roman emperors.

Septimius Severus and his son Caracalla (ruled 211–217) managed to find money in several ways. They cut the weight and metal content of the gold and silver coins while attempting to artificially preserve their purchasing power. They instituted legal proceedings designed to result in the confiscation of the property of helpers who fell into disgrace, such as Severus' praetorian prefect Plautianus in 205, and of rich senators whom they disliked or who had sided against them in the civil struggle of 193–197. These confiscations greatly expanded the imperial domains in Italy and several provinces. The staff that administered the imperial domains and belonged to the *familia Caesaris* (see p. 232) consequently became larger and more important. Furthermore, in 199 Septimius Severus acquired a rich booty in a successful campaign against the Parthians. In this war he also annexed a new province ("Mesopotamia"—northern Mesopotamia). The Roman empire then reached its greatest extent.

Roman citizenship for all free inhabitants of the empire

In 212 Caracalla granted all free inhabitants of the empire Roman citizenship. The contemporary historian Cassius Dio, a senator from the Greek-speaking elite of Nicaea, a town in northwestern Asia Minor, suggests that Caracalla's act was motivated by fiscal considerations. In the imperial age, Roman citizenship did not exempt the occupants of the provinces from paying direct taxes. In Italy, the old heartland of the empire, no property taxes had been collected since 167 BC, but in the provinces everybody had to pay direct taxes, except for a small group of citizens and communities to whom one of the emperors had granted special exemption. Exemption from taxation was one of the greatest privileges one could receive from an emperor. There were, however, also taxes that were imposed specifically on citizens, both in Italy and in the provinces, such as the 5 percent inheritance tax introduced by Augustus (see p. 219). So, on balance, this massive enfranchisement was fiscally advantageous for the state.

In 213 and 215 Caracalla paid barbarian tribes on the northern frontier sums of money to dissuade them from invading the empire; that was cheaper than engaging in warfare. This redemption policy had incidentally been applied before and was to remain popular until the end of the imperial age.

The last emperor of the Severan dynasty, Severus Alexander (ruled 222–235), tried to save money by pursuing a consistent peace policy that entailed negotiating with the enemy for as long as possible. He also cut back on incidental grants and donatives.

FIGURE 16.4 Caracalla (ruled AD 211–217)

In spite of all the problems, the Severan era was in most provinces a reasonably prosperous period, in which the cities continued to flourish culturally. It did, however, sharpen the contrasts between rival social groups. The members of the traditional higher classes and the intellectuals in the imperial services feared the rise of military specialists from the rank and file of the army and despised the soldiers for their greed and lack of discipline. The populace of Rome was not favorably disposed towards the soldiers either. It probably realized that the emperors would not be able to spend as much on the people in Rome if they had to give more to the soldiers; less money would then remain for donatives and games in Rome. People in numerous towns all over the empire had difficulty paying the many taxes and regularly complained about this burden. These feelings created an unstable political climate.

THE SOLDIER EMPERORS (235–284)

In the years after 235 there was no longer an officially recognized dynasty and the empire was under the wavering control of a series of emperors who followed one another in rapid succession. Harsh wars in the east (against the Persians) and in the Balkans cost a lot of effort and involved the risk of usurpation (see pp. 269–70). Money was devaluating and problems remained unsolved. Even so, outside the war zones continuity prevailed in the period 235–249; in those parts there was not yet a crisis atmosphere.

After 249, however, everything went wrong. Wars broke out on all the frontiers (see p. 268) and the individual armies fought one another in constantly recurring struggles for power. Quite a few emperors and usurpers succeeded one another for more than three decades (until 284). The emperors who ruled between 235 and 284 are known as the "soldier emperors," because their power rested exclusively on their soldiers' might and because they acquired that power through military coups. All that the Senate and the civilian population could do was wait and see which general would emerge victorious from the successive struggles. From time to time the empire's unity even came under threat, when different emperors governed different parts of the empire.

Large parts of the empire were between 249 and 284 repeatedly devastated by warfare and paid hardly any taxes. In such regions the agricultural surpluses decreased and the entire empire was ravaged by famine and pestilence, especially the war-ridden regions. There, and in the adjacent areas, deserters, escaped slaves, bankrupt farmers, and other desperate men united in large gangs of robbers. Something similar had happened before, in the years after 180, following the emperor Marcus Aurelius' wars in the areas along the middle and upper Danube.

Trade declined owing to the unsafe conditions and the decreasing purchasing power. Numerous cities in the afflicted regions fell into ruin. Many municipal councilors got into financial straits, caught between the decreasing profits of their estates and the increasing demands of the armies, army provisioners, and tax collectors traveling through their areas. Moreover, they had to meet the costs of local defense (town walls, emergency militias).

The interaction of price increases (which occurred in particular from around AD 274 onwards), the debasement of the coins, and extra payments for the soldiers, who revolted against the decrease in their purchasing power, led to the collapse of the Roman monetary system in these years. The emperors were forced to meet all their soldiers' demands because they owed their position to them and needed the armies in the many wars. Requisitions exacted by soldiers became a common phenomenon in parts of the empire that were regularly visited by armies. In many cities, especially in such regions, the local elite had little money left to finance charity, the construction and upkeep of ostentatious buildings, cultural manifestations, and public entertainment. We may suspect that the wealthiest citizens, members of the higher ranking elite, managed to evade the increasing burdens. They were able to buy abandoned land at a low price.

Between 235 and 284 things were not as bad everywhere in the empire. Large areas (Britain, Spain, parts of Asia Minor, Sicily, parts of North Africa and Egypt) were spared the ravages wrought by war. Partly as a consequence of this, the provinces in Africa and Asia became comparatively more important parts of the empire. The Roman empire owed its continued existence in the third century and its slight recovery in the fourth century to the military successes

FIGURE 16.5
Gate in Aurelian's wall
(Aurelian ruled AD 270–275)

of the soldier emperors who ruled between 260 and 284 and to the reforms that were introduced by those emperors and were completed by Diocletian (ruled 284–305). One of the soldier emperors was Gallienus. From 253 until 260 he ruled the empire together with his father Valerian and from 260 until 268 he was the sole emperor, after his father had been captured by the Persians in a battle he lost in Mesopotamia in 260. In 260 Gallienus banned senators from serving as officers in the army. In his opinion those "gentlemen" lacked the necessary military expertise as they had spent such large parts of their careers engaged in entirely different tasks. He replaced them by experienced soldiers from the equestrian order who had served in the army throughout their professional lives. Gallienus also introduced a system of extra defense behind threatened frontiers. In the years around 255, when he was still ruling together with his father Valerian and was fighting the Franks along the Rhine, he started using mobile forces consisting largely of cavalry, which could move fast from one threatened area to another. Gallienus also created a "general staff" of equestrian generals experienced in warfare who had risen from the rank and file of the army. Most of the emperors who ruled between 268 and 284 came from this staff.

DIOCLETIAN (ruled 284–305)

Diocletian's reign saw the end of the crisis of the third century. The pressures on the frontiers gradually decreased and Diocletian managed to remain in control for twenty-one years. The incessant succession struggles appeared to have come to an end.

Diocletian tried to prevent a new crisis by introducing a sophisticated and varied program of reforms. He expanded and reorganized his army and improved the frontier defenses. He adopted Gallienus' idea of mobile field forces, strengthened many frontiers, increased the number of soldiers, and organized the armed forces in smaller units than the traditional legions. Diocletian's units were also called legions, but were much smaller than the legions of the principate.

To finance this increased military effort Diocletian introduced a new, more elaborate taxation system that was better adjusted to the taxpayers' ability to pay. From this point onwards a plot of land was taxed according to its extent, its quality, and the number of people that worked on it (see p. 214). Allowance was hence made for the land's productivity. Poll taxes were introduced in the cities. The existing taxes in kind were increased and the arbitrary requisitions that the troops had been exacting over the past years were regulated into a system of payments and services to the armies and the civil service. In 301 Diocletian also made an attempt to halt the price increases by issuing an edict fixing maximum prices, but that attempt was unsuccessful and so were the monetary reforms with which he tried to put an end to the devaluation of the coins.

To ensure that the land would remain productive, Diocletian bound the farmers to the soil. This was a major step towards the serfdom of the Middle Ages. The craftsmen in the cities he bound to their trades; from now onwards a craftsman's son had to succeed his father. Diocletian's aim was to prevent the craftsmen from giving up their trade so as to avoid paying the heavy taxes. The municipal councilors (*curiales*) had in the Roman empire always been financially responsible for levying the taxes for the Roman authorities, but Diocletian took things further. He bound the *curiales* to their social class and to their council to prevent them from shirking their responsibilities by enlisting in the army or seeking employment in one of the imperial services.

Further expansion of bureaucracy

The exigencies of the new conditions necessitated changes in the central and provincial administrations. The refined taxation system and the stricter collection of the taxes (in cash and kind) implied more work, also in inspections. Moreover, the central and provincial authorities had to take over ever more of the municipal magistrates' tasks. Those magistrates were no longer capable of meeting the costs involved in maintaining law and order (which was disrupted by robbers and roaming barbarians) and the upkeep of the public works and amenities, while simultaneously paying the (higher) taxes. In the third-century crisis the increasing burdens had brought many *curiales* in the war- and disease-stricken regions into financial difficulties. Their estates were devastated and their cities were ravaged by war and the plague. Nevertheless, they were still required to finance local defense (city walls, emergency militias) and the construction and repair of public works. On top of that they also had to pay the taxes and war requisitions. What's more, the urban magistrates all over the empire had already been heavily taxed at the end of the second century (see p. 270). Many local councils had seen their best and wealthiest members depart to the senatorial and equestrian governing elites, the army, and the imperial services. However, many of them did not disappear completely from their local communities; they continued to influence local politics and society and every now and then contributed to the upkeep of the urban amenities (games, gymnasia, means of transport, baths, waterworks), which had expanded considerably in two centuries of peace. At a local level there was now a progressive social differentiation between completely local *curiales* and townsmen who still had local ties, but had meanwhile risen to higher social and administrative levels. What had once been prestige-enhancing liberality had by the end of the second century become an expensive obligation, which the local notables tried to offload onto one another. From the late second century onwards it was difficult to find people who were willing to hold the municipal posts that involved expensive liturgies. Whereas wealthy notables had in the past been elected for these posts it now became necessary to assign them to them by turns. Towards the fourth century ever more *curiales* began to aspire to posts in the army or the imperial bureaucracy so as to be able to evade the burdens of local administration.

To ensure that the taxes were efficiently collected and to counterbalance the decline of local administration, Diocletian strengthened the central and provincial administrative machineries. He appointed more officials and split up large provinces into smaller units. This led to the formation of two or even three separate administrative levels in those provinces. Diocletian regrouped the provinces into dioceses. After Diocletian's reign those dioceses were grouped into four large prefectures (see Map 16.1). The extra staff was preferably recruited from nearby armies and to a lesser extent from among students of law and rhetoric and imperial freedmen. The imperial bureaucracy acquired a rather military character. Soldiers who rose from the rank and file of the army to the military and administrative middle cadres had good career prospects. Diocletian tried to keep the *curiales* out of the bureaucracy and the army for the reasons outlined above, but he was not always successful. The expanding army and bureaucracy both needed large numbers of people with organizational experience.

Diocletian also divided military and civil power. This was a rather revolutionary measure. Since the beginning of Roman history, military tasks, government, and the administration of justice had always been united in the powers of the kings, the magistrates with *imperium*, and the emperors (and their governors). Now, however, the military tasks were entrusted to separate frontier commanders (*duces* and *comites*, plurals of *dux* and *comes*, from which the English words "duke" and "count" are derived) and to the generals who served in the mobile armies. Governors of the now smaller provinces had to administer justice and raise taxes in cash and kind, combining the tasks of former governors and procurators or quaestors. Remarkably, Italy lost its privileged position under Diocletian and was divided into a number of common tax-paying provinces.

The Senate and the equestrian order

These high officers and most of his governors Diocletian recruited from the equestrian order. This meant that the senatorial class lost its privileged position in higher administration. The Roman Senate came to be an assembly of fabulously rich landowners who had no say in important administrative matters and had no access to high military offices. But it did retain its influence in Rome's city life. The Senate of the late imperial age (fourth and fifth centuries) has been described as Rome's "town council." As the emperors were constantly away on campaigns after 230 and were only rarely to be found in Rome, the Senate took over a large part of their function as benefactors in that city.

From Diocletian's reign onwards the equestrian order grew tremendously and became increasingly heterogeneous, ultimately disintegrating into a number of new classes bound to offices in the army and the bureaucracy.

Emperorship and the emperor's succession

Diocletian appointed one co-emperor and two junior emperors, so that each of the four major armies (those of the Rhine, the upper Danube, the lower Danube, and the eastern frontier) could be led by an emperor. The two senior emperors were both given the title "Augustus"; the junior emperors were called "Caesar." The latter (*Caesares*) were to succeed the former (*Augusti*). This, Diocletian, hoped, would prevent succession struggles (see p. 274). The four emperors did not reside in Rome, but (when they were not away on campaigns with their royal households) in Nicomedia, Milan, Sirmium, and Trier (see Map 16.1)—four strategically located centers from where they could quickly reach their frontiers.

MAP 16.1 The Roman empire at the time of Diocletian and Constantine the Great

Notes. The empire has suffered its first losses: Dacia (present-day Romania) and the angle between the Rhine and the Danube were lost in the years 260–270. The empire was divided into four prefectures, each of which was led by an emperor or a junior emperor and a praetorian prefect.

Diocletian searched for better ideological foundations for the emperorship, which he hoped would prevent usurpations in the future. He presented himself and his co-ruler Maximian (ruled 286–305) as emperors by the grace of the gods Jupiter and Hercules and he began to surround his court at Nicomedia with the pomp and ceremony of an Oriental absolute despot.

These measures were designed to make the emperor more powerful, but things worked out differently in practice. In the course of the late imperial age the emperors lost direct contact with the local authorities and the local frontier commanders. The court and the greater number of administrative levels created an unbridgeable distance between the provincial administrations and the central government. The development towards a more sublime form of emperorship founded in religious concepts had incidentally begun much earlier. Domitian had already showed such tendencies (p. 230) and the emperor Commodus (ruled 180–192) and his successors all tried to consolidate their power in this way. They propagated themselves as a popular god's favorite.

Diocletian abdicated in 305 and lived for another eleven years secluded in a large palace at Spalato (present-day Split in Croatia).

FIGURE 16.6 Diocletian and his co-emperors, represented in close concord

The persecutions of the Christians

The years between 250 and 311 saw a number of systematic persecutions of Christians all over the empire (250, 257–260, and 303–311). These persecutions were inaugurated by the emperors Decius (ruled 249–251) and Valerian (ruled 253–260) because the Christians refused to publicly worship the Roman state gods or to participate in the emperor cult. They were accused of having brought down the wrath of the gods on the Roman empire. In 260 Gallienus (ruled 253–260 together with his father Valerian, and as sole ruler from 260 to 268) put an end to the persecutions in an attempt to eliminate extra sources of unrest at the low point of the crisis. In the following forty years the number of Christians grew tremendously. Many people turned to the Christian communities for spiritual security and material support.

Within the Church arose a separate, hierarchical clergy, which led the Christian communities. Christendom increasingly began to resemble a state within the state. Diocletian (ruled 284–305) watched this development with growing suspicion and when, in 303, he felt things had gone too

FIGURE 16.7 Decius (ruled AD 249–251), one of the soldier emperors

Notes. Decius tried to save the empire by restoring discipline and the old piety towards Rome's state gods. This brought him into conflict with the Christians, who refused to participate in sacrifices to those gods (the consequence was a major general persecution of Christians in 250). In 251 Decius was killed in a battle against the Goths near the mouth of the Danube. The emperors of this period (235–260) had themselves portrayed in the style of the late republic (Fig. 14.6, p. 200), the time of Rome's great military successes.

far he instituted a major persecution. This persecution was to last for another six years after his abdication, until his successor Galerius, the *Augustus* of the east (ruled 305–311), halted it on his deathbed in 311.

CONSTANTINE THE GREAT (ruled 306–337)

Diocletian's attempt to solve the succession problem was not successful. In 306 Constantine, who was not a junior emperor (*Caesar*), was acclaimed emperor (*Augustus*) at York in Britain, where he had been assisting his father Constantius in some fighting. After Constantius' death the army there opted for Constantine. Having defeated his rival Maxentius at the Milvian Bridge (*Pons Milvius*) near Rome (AD 312), Constantine acquired control over the western half of the empire and in 324 he became sole emperor after defeating his co-emperor Licinius (ruled 312–324). Constantine governed the Roman empire as sole emperor from 324 until 337.

Constantine's conversion to Christianity

The victory at the Milvian Bridge is of great importance in world history for another reason, too: it induced Constantine to embrace Christianity. The accounts of what exactly happened vary. Most sources tell us that Constantine—hitherto an adherent of *Deus Sol Invictus*, the "Invincible

FIGURE 16.8a   The Imperial Baths in Trier, one of the capitals of the Roman empire in the fourth century

Notes. Baths were buildings with large rooms with heated floors and walls that contained swimming pools and basins of hot, tepid and cold water. They were surrounded by dressing rooms, sweating rooms, areas for sunbathing, playing fields and a shop-lined colonnade. In Rome and other large Roman cities the baths were important meeting places. Men and women usually bathed separately.

FIGURE 16.8b Back view of the Aula Palatina, Constantine's immense throne room and audience hall in Trier

Notes. The building is built entirely of brick. The structure's simple shape enhances its overwhelming spatial impression. The aula is 67 m long, 27.5 m wide and 30 m high.

Sun God"—had a vision in which he saw a sign of a cross appear above the sun and in a dream Christ urged him to paint this sign on his soldiers' shields. This Constantine did (in itself this is not surprising in a world in which omens were considered so important) and when he indeed won the battle he came to see the Christians' God as a powerful deity. When his military endeavors remained successful he continued to put his faith in that God, possibly without initially realizing the consequences of embracing a monotheistic religion. He for example remained the *pontifex maximus* of the Roman state gods for the rest of his life. He was not baptised until the end of his life, but that was not uncommon among Christians in those days.

Constantine did immediately start to favor the Christians. He returned the property that had been confiscated during the Diocletianic persecution to the Church, granted the clergy privileges, and commissioned the construction of churches. All this represented a daring move in a world which had only recently witnessed mass persecutions, in which the worship of state gods was essential for securing "peace with the gods" (*pax deorum*) and in which the Christians were still a minority.

With the aid of literate Christians Constantine created a different ideological foundation for his emperorship. He proclaimed himself emperor by the grace of the one universal God of the Christians. He ruled over the civilized Roman empire like God ruled over the cosmos. Almost all of the emperors who succeeded Constantine followed the course he had set out and adhered to the Christian faith.

Constantine soon started to interfere with the internal relations within the Church. Religious struggles had broken out concerning the Godhead of Christ. Arius, a prominent presbyter in Alexandria, proclaimed that Christ was God's creation, and could therefore not be the same being as God the Father. His teachings, known as Arianism, won a lot of support, which threatened the unity of Christendom. Constantine himself presided over the council of bishops that was to resolve the dispute. This council was held in 325, in Nicaea in northwest Asia Minor. It condemned the teachings of Arius and declared that Christ was *homo-ousios* ("of one substance") with the Father. The confession of faith that was formulated by this council eventually resulted in the Nicene Creed, which has applied for almost all Christians for many centuries.

Constantinople

Between 324 and 330 Constantine built a new capital, Constantinople, on the site of the old Greek colony Byzantium in the Bosporus. From that location the emperors could reach the most important frontiers quickly by land and by sea. Constantine established a court with a new, complex hierarchy there, which under his successors gradually became increasingly pompous.

He also introduced a new Senate, which was to function alongside the Roman Senate. The Senate of Constantinople was filled with Christian notables and officials, mostly from the eastern half of the empire. The Roman Senate became the bastion of the wealthy conservative landowners all over the empire, east and west, who did not convert to Christianity. The senators who resided in Rome on a permanent basis controlled that city's cultural and social life after the court was permanently moved elsewhere. Rome caused them a lot of problems; in late antiquity the city was a restless place where riots frequently broke out.

Constantine saw to it that the senators regained their influence in central administration. He wanted to make use of their capabilities and hoped that they would place their wealth entirely at the disposal of the state and the community. But he was disappointed. Like many high-ranking officers and officials, the senators started to regard their offices as private vehicles for further enriching themselves and for creating networks of clients within the bureaucracy.

The army

Constantine relied on a well-trained, mobile army which followed him everywhere and consisted largely of cavalry. The frontier troops had now well and truly become garrison troops.

Under Constantine, and more so under his successors, this mobile army contained a growing number of German mercenaries. They were good and cheap and the landowners and *curiales* relinquished only the weakest elements from their territories to the armies. They preferred to keep capable, well-trained men at work on their own estates. This they were able to do because Diocletian had bound the farmers to the soil. Landowners, moreover, had the alternative of paying money instead of supplying recruits. That money could be used to hire Germans. The army and the officers who rose from its ranks consequently included progressively more Germans. By around 400, generals of German origin had acquired decisive influence in the imperial court and administration.

Increased fiscal burdens and the monetary system

Constantine and his immediate successors greatly expanded their bureaucracy and their domestic staff, they commissioned many building projects, and raised the military budget even further. Constantine increased the fiscal burdens by introducing new taxes and raising existing ones. Particularly notorious were the taxes he levied on workshops, which impoverished many a craftsman. In some provinces Constantine tightened the landowners' grip on their tenants so as to ensure that the workers in rural areas, on whose shoulders rested the greater part of the tax burden, would stay put. This was the second step towards the serfdom of the Middle Ages (Diocletian had already taken the first, see p. 276). This measure was particularly necessary in the west, in areas where the high taxes were forcing farmers to abandon their farms and chattels and flee to the cities.

In spite of his high expenses, Constantine managed to stabilize the monetary system to some extent. He introduced a new gold coin, the *solidus*, which was to remain the basic currency of the Byzantine empire and Western Europe up to the era of the Crusades.

FIGURE 16.9 A gold coin showing emperor Constantine the Great (ruled AD 306–337)

Notes. Constantine tried to reorganise the Roman monetary system after the chaos of the third century. The silver and copper money remained poor and unstable, but Constantine did introduce a new stable gold coin, the *solidus*.

THE ROMAN EMPIRE AFTER CONSTANTINE

The hundred and fifty years following Constantine's reign can be seen as a transitional period, the incubation period of the Middle Ages. The four most important features of this period were widening of the breach between the eastern and western halves of the empire, the decline of many cities, continuing Christianization of the empire and renewed pressure on the frontiers.

Major wars were fought between the Romans and the Persians between 336 and 364, and the second half of the fourth century saw the beginning of massive German migrations. Many Germans and steppe tribes from the area to the east of Germany moved into the

Roman empire. It was long believed that the migrations were prompted by population pressure in German areas and invasions of the Huns, who were advancing from Siberia into Europe, driving many peoples ahead of them. The Huns were Mongolian horsemen with impressive warrior qualities. They migrated westwards in the fourth century. In the mid-fourth century there was an Ostrogothic kingdom between the rivers Don and Dnieper, which was destroyed by the advancing Huns in 370. In the first half of the fifth century the Huns' empire extended from Hungary to the Ukraine.

It is nowadays more generally assumed that many Germans migrated into the Roman empire because life there seemed more appealing, and that they left behind a vacuum that was filled by other tribes—Slavic peoples and Huns. Something that is not disputed is that many Germans were for some time in the fifth century under heavy pressure from the Huns.

East and West

The eastern and western halves of the Roman empire had always differed substantially. The eastern half had been urbanized for much longer and more intensively than the western half; it had a long tradition of well-organized Greek and Phoenician city states and Asian and Hellenistic kingdoms. Large parts of the western half were urbanized only after the arrival of the Romans. The east was also richer than the west. Rome actually lived off the wealth of the eastern half of her empire, in particular Egypt. There was a cultural difference, too: the language of the elite was Greek in the east and Latin in the west.

In the fourth and fifth centuries the two halves of the empire drifted away from one another. After Constantine's death in 337, the western and eastern halves were constantly governed by separate emperors, first from Constantine's own house (until 363) and then from other dynasties (see Appendix 3, p. 304). These emperors in effect became increasingly distinct rulers of the Western and Eastern Roman empires, with separate administrations. After 395 there were no longer any emperors who ruled over the entire empire, although the pretense of a single, unified Roman empire was always maintained. The consequences were serious: the armies of the two halves that had hitherto helped one another when necessary were now far more reluctant to come to each other's aid. Some scholars see this as an important cause of the decline of the Western Roman empire.

The Western court usually resided in Milan or Ravenna, in Italy. In the east Constantinople was the capital. Constantinople grew rapidly and monopolized the grain surpluses of Egypt, Asia Minor, and the Crimean. Rome had to make do with the surpluses of North Africa and Sicily, while the capitals in northern Italy were fed by the farmers in the Po valley. Ephesus, the largest city in Asia Minor, halfway along the west coast, lost a lot to Constantinople and entered a phase of stagnation and decline.

The cities in the eastern half of the empire managed to hold out reasonably well. The old urban elites, the military cadre and the higher personnel of the imperial bureaux evolved into a loyal "aristocracy of service." In spite of continuous theological disputes, Christianity and the ecclesiastical hierarchy were unifying elements in this part of the empire. In the fifth century, warfare and migrations caused much less devastation in the Asian provinces and Egypt than in the west and the Balkans. In this century the Persians were preoccupied with their enemies

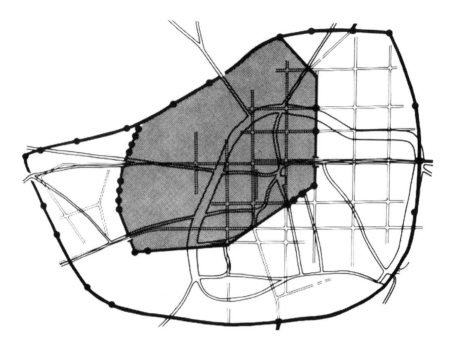

FIGURE 16.10a (*above*)
The city of Tongeren in Belgium, showing the walled area until AD 275 and the later urban area

Notes. The Roman empire weakened from the third century onwards and was threatened from outside. The towns depopulated as people drifted to rural areas and to the larger cities. Newly built fortifications always enclosed smaller areas than did their predecessors.

FIGURE 16.10b (*right*)
Maastricht in its Roman heyday and the fourth-century *castellum* (dark shading) in which the remaining population lived

along their northeastern frontiers. The Germans did not spread any further than the Balkans; the heavily fortified city of Constantinople cut off their routes to Asia Minor.

Many cities in the west went into decline. The German commanders and the landed elite of high officials and senators began to operate on their own authority, taking progressively less notice of the emperor. With a series of constantly repeated edicts the emperors tried to keep the farmers on their land and the craftsmen in their workshops, but their efforts were in vain. In the fifth century the revenues of the central government in the Western empire decreased progressively and it became increasingly difficult to defend the frontiers from the intensifying pressure of the Germans and the Huns.

The *curiales* who governed the cities were under great strain. They had to pay for the upkeep of the public works and the urban amenities out of their own pockets and they were financially responsible for levying the taxes (see p. 276). The wealthiest and smartest *curiales* managed to find ways of evading the emperors' edicts and escaping to the civil service, the army, and the Church (as bishops). More and more farmers, oppressed by the excessively high burden of the taxes imposed by the city magistrates, placed themselves under the patronage of powerful landowners with estates in their neighborhood, who held high offices in the army or central government. These powerful men took progressively less notice of the *curiales* in the cities. Their *villae* (estates) became "enclaves" in the city governments' territories, which were governed by the landowners themselves and in which the city magistrates were unable to interfere. These *villae* grew larger and larger and acquired their own workshops and armies and their own financial circuits. They evolved into almost independent economic units. Many farmers and craftsmen settled at the *villae* of the rich and powerful, seeking refuge against plundering enemies, bandits, and the *curiales*' tax collectors. After some time, however, the farmers working at the *villae* were as badly oppressed as the farmers who had remained independent and were squeezed dry by the *curiales*. In the fifth century major farmers' revolts consequently broke out in Gaul, and all over the empire escaped farmers swelled the gangs of robbers.

Many cities in the western half of the empire suffered a severe decline. Their markets lost important groups of customers from rural areas because the *villae* evolved into almost self-sufficient households with their own workshops and because pauperization continued unabated in afflicted regions in the fifth century (*cf.* p. 274). The town councils saw their best and wealthiest members depart, received progressively less tax, and were unable to pay for the upkeep of the public amenities in their towns. Sometimes local landowners and/or Christian bishops had to assume responsibility for the remnants of a community and take over its administration. The cities did continue to exist as built-up areas, often well into the Middle Ages.

In the western half of the empire, in particular in Gaul, Britain, the Rhineland, and the Danubian regions, this process went much further than in the eastern half, North Africa, and parts of Spain and Italy.

In the east and North Africa more rich people continued to live in the cities, which more successfully managed to retain their economic functions. Spain and Italy occupied an intermediate position. The large imperial residences (such as Trier, Ravenna, and Milan in the west), the city of Rome and the other cities that were important for the government held out reasonably well. With their offices of the central and provincial administrative machineries, law courts, and imperial workshops, these cities attracted flocks of people of all classes who were anxious to make a career in the emperor's service. Rome was no longer the main imperial capital, but remained a very large city and a symbol of Roman continuity. Decay, however, set in in the fifth century, and even more so in the sixth.

THE CHRISTIAN EMPIRE

After 312–313 many people converted to Christianity for pragmatic reasons. In the eastern half of the empire and here and there in the west, Christianity became the prevailing religion. Its churches were led by a hierarchical clergy. The Christian communities lost some of their independence and gradually grew into regional groups, led by the bishops of Rome (Italy and the other Western European parts of the empire), Carthage (North Africa), Alexandria (Egypt), Constantinople (the Balkans and Asia Minor), Jerusalem, and Antioch (Syria). The Christians in the Persian empire were led by the bishops of Edessa and Seleucia.

In the Persian empire the Christians always remained a despised minority, like the Jews. In the following discussion we will restrict ourselves to Christendom in the Roman empire.

The common people, unlike the clergy, were no longer required to abide by the old strict rules. Now that the empire was led by Christian emperors and was increasingly identified with Christendom, laymen (non-clergy) were allowed to engage in warfare and participate in administration. The bishops became important figures in the cities. Constantine made them responsible for part of the administration of justice.

The financial resources of the Church grew rapidly. Many Christians bequeathed estates to the Christian communities and Constantine granted the churches and bishops exemption from various burdensome taxes and services. The Christians in turn gave the emperor a new ideology: according to the Church Father Eusebius (c. 260–340), the author of the first History of the Church (*Historia Ecclesiastica*), God controlled the cosmos and the world and the emperor ruled over the Roman empire as God's counterpart on earth. So everything was now reduced to one: one God, one Church, one emperor, and one Christian empire, with a promising new future ahead of it.

But not all Christians identified the empire with Christendom. Some continued to reject the empire as an earthly evil. Others adhered to the old Christian belief that the emperors' wars were less important than the spiritual struggle against the devil and his forces of evil. The fourth century saw the appearance of hermits, ascetics, and monks who denied themselves all worldly goods so as to be able to devote themselves entirely to prayer, which they regarded as a weapon in that spiritual struggle. They did not think highly of the heritage of the Classical era (art, literature). Other Christians, on the contrary, borrowed much from Classical philosophy and science and imitated ancient Greek and Latin authors in their works. They created a Christian variant of Classical culture. The fourth and early fifth centuries were the days of the great Church Fathers. Their works have remained authoritative in Christian churches into our times.

The best-known Church Father is St Augustine (354–429), the bishop of Hippo in North Africa. To him, the Roman empire was of only relative significance. Far more important was the City of God, the kingdom of heaven, which would one day come on earth. Second in importance was the church militant on earth. The church militant existed in the evil earthly world and

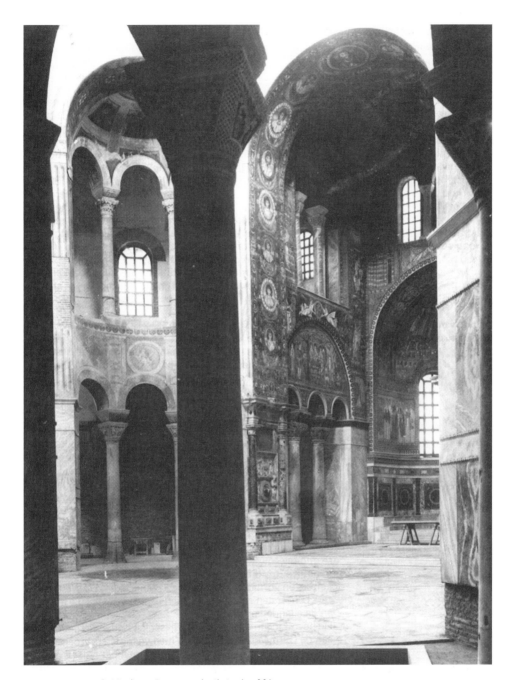

FIGURE 16.11   St Vitale at Ravenna, built in the fifth century AD

Notes. The fifth century AD produced several outstanding works of Christian art. Ravenna was the chief residence of the last Western Roman emperors.

foreshadowed and reflected the church triumphant in heaven and in the future world. Here, we find Plato's world of forms (see p. 114) combined with the Christian message.

The western half of the empire remained predominantly pagan in late antiquity. In the east and North Africa non-Christian religions lived on only in remote rural areas and among Greek intellectuals and notables in the cities, who cherished the Classical Greek literary culture as an alternative religion. They felt attracted to a new form of Platonism that had originated around the middle of the third century in the circles of the philosopher Plotinus, who worked in Rome. This Neo-Platonism was concerned not with politics, but with personal spiritual experiences. It had a mystical slant (the sudden acquisition, after long study, of knowledge of higher reality, in a moment of "enlightenment").

The only non-Christian emperor of the time, Julian (ruled 361–363), felt attracted to this school of philosophy. He made one last attempt to turn back the clock and undo the victory of Christianity. He also tried to revert to the political regime of the second century AD. But Julian's "pagan reaction" was short-lived because he ruled for only two years—in 363 he was killed during a major campaign against the Persians.

In 380 the emperor Theodosius the Great (ruled 379–395) and his co-emperor Gratian (ruled 375–383, the emperor in the west) published an edict confirming the Nicene Creed (new disputes had broken out concerning the creed's interpretation). "Catholic" Christianity was now the favorite religion of the emperors, but this did not mean the death of Arianism—Wulfila, the missionary who preached the Gospel to the Goths, was Arian, and so Arianism became the Goths' Christianity, strengthening their identity in their struggle against the Roman empire.

In 391 Theodosius ordered the closure of all pagan temples and banned all pagan cults. In that same year, following the bishop's suggestion, a group of Christians led by hermits destroyed the beautiful large temple complex of Isis and Serapis in Alexandria, believing they were doing a good deed by crushing a dwelling of evil spirits. These measures did not lead to the definitive triumph of Christianity either; that was not to take place until during the reign of the emperor Justinian in the sixth century.

The end of the Roman empire in the west

In the latter days of his government, after a series of indecisive battles, Constantine the Great had made peace with the Visigoths (see p. 268), who were then still living in Wallachia. This peace lasted for 35 years, until 376, when the Visigoths began to invade the Roman part of the Balkans. In 378 they won a major victory over the Eastern emperor Valens at Hadrianople (see Map 16.2). They then forced the Romans to grant them permission to settle inside the frontiers of the Roman empire as a self-governing tribe. They settled in the Balkans, in what is now Bulgaria.

In 406 a large group of western German tribes crossed the Rhine and exacted similar treaties. Like the Visigoths, they promised to supply troops and pay taxes in return. Frankish tribes settled in northern Gaul and Burgundian ones in eastern Gaul. It was not long before the Roman government lost all authority in those areas.

A few years after they had settled in the Balkans a dispute with the Roman authorities over the imposed taxes prompted the Visigoths to migrate again. Under their leader Alaric they crossed the Balkans, invaded Italy, and sacked Rome in 410—an act that shocked the entire

MAP 16.2 The German migrations and the fall of the Western Roman empire in the fifth century AD

Roman world. It was a shock to pagans and many Christians alike—Rome had not been sacked by a foreign nation since the invasion of the Gauls 800 years before. The Visigoths then settled in southwestern Gaul and northern Spain. In 419 they established a kingdom near Toulouse in southern Gaul.

In 370 the Ostrogoths lost their kingdom in south Russia (p. 285) and in the fifth century they were under the sway of the Huns, who allowed them to move to what are now Hungary and Slavonia, but when the kingdom of the Huns declined and vanished in the second half of the fifth century the Ostrogoths freed themselves. In 493 they invaded Italy, where Roman emperorship had come to an end in 476, when a German general, Odoacer, assumed control and had himself proclaimed king of the Germans in Italy. He did accept the supremacy of the Eastern Roman emperor, but the latter refused to acknowledge Odoacer. Odoacer's kingdom did not last long: in 493 it fell to the Ostrogoths led by Theodoric (ruled 493–526). So there was an Ostrogothic kingdom in Italy in the first half of the sixth century.

From the fourth century onwards Britain was meanwhile confronted with raids of Angles, Saxons, and Jutes from northwestern Germany and Jutland. The Roman troops left Britain in the early fifth century (409). In the mid-fifth century the Saxons and their allies began to settle on the island.

Between 429 and 439 the Vandals, led by Gaiseric, conquered North Africa and put an end to the food supplies to Rome, causing serious problems in that city. In 455 the Vandals raided Rome, forcing her into a long period of decline and depopulation. By the late Middle Ages, Rome was no longer a large city.

In the course of the fifth century the German tribes in the empire took progressively less notice of the Western Roman emperors and established their own, independent kingdoms. After the first years of the fifth century the Western Roman emperors governed an empire that had shrunk to Italy and the surrounding islands, until the final blow came in 476.

The population of the western provinces readily accepted the Germans' control. The new masters demanded less tax than the Roman emperors had done and they took over the political systems as they found them. The Germans had moreover been influenced by Roman culture for quite some time. The large landowners started to work together with the German aristocracy and powerful Roman dynasties began to arrange marriages with members of the German elite. Some German tribes had converted to the Arian form of Christianity even before they settled in the Roman empire. The conversion to "Catholic" Christianity of the Frank Clovis, who had around 500 established a large Frankish kingdom in former Gaul, had far-reaching consequences for the history of Europe and the influence of Rome.

The Eastern Roman (now usually called Byzantine) empire endured throughout the Middle Ages. In the sixth century the Eastern Roman emperor Justinian (ruled 527–565) managed to reconquer Italy, North Africa, and southern Spain, but invasions by the Longobards—a Germanic tribe—into Italy, incursions by tribes from the Eurasian steppe and Slavonic peoples into the Balkans—both in the decades after 565—and the Arab conquests after 632 reduced the Estern empire to Asia Minor, Greece, Sicily, and the coast of southern Italy. Byzantine outposts in southern Spain that had been conquered in the mid-sixth century were after a few decades reconquered by the Visigothic kings of the Iberian peninsula.

Justinian is worth mentioning for other achievements besides his military successes. He collected the Roman laws into the *Corpus Iuris Civilis* and adapted them to his own time (see p. 237). Justinian is also the emperor who finally closed the last pagan temples, including that of Isis at Philae in Egypt. The same fate befell the schools of philosophy in Athens (including Plato's Academy) in 529.

In 1453, after further territorial losses in the west (Italy) and the east (to the Turks, who swept across Asia Minor after 1060), the Byzantine empire ultimately fell to the Turks, who that year captured the capital Constantinople.

The Byzantine empire was a Christian state, with a Greek elite culture, a Roman law code and a Roman administrative system, and a pompous court characteristic of late antiquity. It was in this empire that the Greek Orthodox form of Christianity came into full bloom. The Byzantine empire had a profound cultural influence on late medieval Italy, the Arabian and Turkish states, and the Slavic peoples in eastern and southeastern Europe.

EPILOGUE

The end of the ancient world

Marking the end of the ancient world, and in so doing justifying the end of this book, is actually an impossible task. Antiquity is usually taken to end around 500. But why?

For a start, any periodization is an artificial abstraction. The beginning of a new period in history is rarely acknowledged as such at the time itself; people in the Middle Ages did not see the time they were living in as a new era in history. It was not until the Renaissance that people began to realize that "Middle Ages" separated their time from antiquity. Periodization is a useful tool for helping historians arrive at a better understanding of the past. When we say that the ancient world came to an end around such and such a date, that means that present-day historians see that date as marking the beginning of a new period of great changes and a transition to a different kind of society. Being a tool specifically developed by historians to help them in their studies, periodization is arbitrary. This is indeed evident from the fact that many different dates have over the years been suggested for the end of antiquity. One of the reasons for this is that historians are reluctant to accept a fixed definition of what specifically characterizes the ancient world. The matter is rarely discussed, and different historians tend to find different aspects specifically characteristic of antiquity.

Some historians focus on the political aspect, and take the decline of the Roman empire to mark the end of antiquity. In actual fact, however, the definitive demise of the Roman empire did not occur until 1453, when the Turks captured Constantinople. By then the "empire" had shrunk to a small area around Constantinople. Another development whose impact was at least as influential was the rise of Islam and the political power of the Arabs, who in the seventh century conquered Syria, Palestine, and Egypt and put an end to the Neo-Persian empire. Then there's the Western Roman empire. In 476 the last emperor was deposed there but, as we have seen above, the fiction of the unity of the empire lived on, and in the sixth century Justinian managed to restore a large part of the empire. By then the Western Roman empire had long lost most of its former power and included German kingdoms: kingdoms of the Visigoths around what are now Toulouse and Toledo, a Vandal kingdom in North Africa, and a little later a Frankish kingdom in northern France. The fiction of the Western Roman empire was, however, prolonged by the empire of Charlemagne (800) and the "Holy Roman Empire of the German Nation" that Napoleon abolished in 1806, while the rulers of Austria continued to use the title of emperor until 1918.

The Eastern Roman empire also lived on in theory: Moscow became the "Third Rome" after Constantinople and its rulers were called *tsars*—a title derived from *caesar*—until the last tsar was murdered in 1917. Viewed from this perspective we could say that antiquity lasted until 1917/18. The fiction of the Roman empire incidentally had a profound influence—both the German emperors and the Russian tsars invested a lot of energy in capturing Rome and Constantinople, respectively. The emperor Frederic Barbarossa (Roman emperor from 1155 until 1190 who was crowned in Rome) introduced the Roman law of Justinian's *corpus iuris* in his empire (though in actual fact with little success).

Another aspect that is considered to be of paramount importance with respect to the end of antiquity is the triumph of Christianity. That did indeed represent a tremendously important social and cultural turning point. It caused drastic changes in every aspect of public life. People adopted a critical view of ancient traditions; many elements of those traditions were seen to be worthless and after some time they gradually disappeared. This fate befell temples, academies, games, and books—they were replaced by churches, monasteries, popes, and new books. Christian standards and values differ essentially from pagan ones. But again we can quote different dates for the definitive turning point: 312, the year of Constantine's conversion; 391, when Theodosius banned all pagan cults; 529, when Justinian ordered the closure of Plato's Academy in Athens. What's more, there's no denying the fact that Christianity is entirely a product of the ancient world: Jesus Christ lived during the reigns of the emperors Augustus and Tiberius (*c.* 5 BC–*c.* AD 29) and was a follower of the Jewish faith, which was many centuries older. Christianity, moreover, absorbed quite a lot of the Greek body of thought. For the last centuries of its existence the Roman empire was a Christian empire. As far as the east is concerned, the decline of Christianity following the triumph of Islam in western Asia and North Africa is ironically also a major turning point.

Another cultural aspect that can be considered in this context is language. In the West, Latin ceased to be a spoken language around 500; it lived on into the nineteenth and twentieth centuries only as the language of scholars and the Church. And Greek lost ground everywhere except in the Eastern Roman, Byzantine empire. Augustine was barely familiar with the language. In the East, Arabic became the *lingua franca*, putting an end to the dominance of Greek and Aramaic.

Other important aspects, to conclude, are socioeconomic factors. The fifth century AD was a period of crisis, though mainly in the West. The schism between East and West caused increasing impoverishment in the West, which was dependent on the wealth of the East. On the preceding pages it has been explained how the cities sank into poverty and urban life languished. The city of Rome is often assumed to have had a million inhabitants in its heydays (though lower estimates have also been suggested; we prefer 800,000), but by the Middle Ages there were only a few thousand. Many other cities faced the same fate. The next city in Western Europe to have a population of a million was London in 1800. But this line of reasoning is very Western Europe focused; the European Middle Ages were quite exceptional—Constantinople remained a large city, the Chinese city Hang-Chou had a population of between five and seven million in the thirteenth century, and Baghdad was likewise a flourishing metropolis in the ninth century.

We could go on for quite some time. But is there any sense in such a discussion if we don't first decide how we are to define "the ancient world"? May we actually use a single term to refer to almost four thousand years of history in an area as large as the entire Mediterranean, which saw the birth of such highly diverse civilizations? That would seem to be impossible. What we can say is that a combination of conditions throughout almost the entire Mediterranean, close contacts, and especially the emergence of the Roman empire led to a form of cultural unity. It is this constellation that was broken, and that was the consequence of many different factors. The gradual dismantling of the Roman empire and the political, cultural, social, and economic changes that that implied can be seen to represent a transitional period between antiquity and the Middle Ages, which lasted from around 400 until around 650, with the turning point occurring slightly earlier in the West than in the East. The German kingdoms initially borrowed quite a lot from the legacy of the Romans (Latin as their administrative language, an adjusted form of Roman law), but the influences soon became watered down. In the East the break was more radical, with the Arabs and Islam conquering the greater part of the Byzantine empire and the entire Sasanid empire at a formidable speed in the mid-seventh century.

What we should bear in mind is that no break is ever absolute. Most aspects of everyday life simply continued as before. Classical Latin and Greek books continued to be read and reread and new ones were written. The Christian Church continued to exist. The Koran is inconceivable without the Bible and classical literature. Many aspects of ancient culture were rediscovered in later times, sometimes with an Arab veneer. The ancient philosopher Aristotle made his way back to Western Europe via the Arabs, who translated his works into Arabic.

Most elements of the ancient civilizations have, however, disappeared for good. Modern democracy did not originate in Athens, but in medieval parliament, and modern drama did not originate in Greek tragedy, but in medieval plays—original medieval creations. But the tragedies of antiquity have been rediscovered and are being performed again, often in a reinterpreted form. This is known as the "reception of ancient culture." And in this way the ancient world will always remain the "cradle of European and Islamic civilizations."

PART IV APPENDICES

1   GREEK AND ROMAN NAMES

The Greeks had a first name and also mentioned their father's name. In the Athenian democracy the father's name was replaced by an indication of the *deme* to which the citizen belonged. But in practice the father's name continued to be used, too.

The Romans had three names: a personal name, a name denoting their *gens*, and a surname to distinguish the family within that *gens*. The personal name was often abbreviated in writing: A. = Aulus, C. = Gaius, Cn. = Gnaeus, L. = Lucius, M. = Marcus, P. = Publius, Q. = Quintus, S. = Sextus, T. = Titus, and Tib. = Tiberius. Caesar, for example, was officially called C. Julius Caesar. When a man was adopted, he would add his new family's *gens* name and surname to his personal name and add an extra surname to his full new name. This extra surname was derived from his original *gens* name. When C. Octavius was adopted as Caesar's son in the latter's will, he came to be called Gaius Julius Caesar Octavianus. The full names of some of the Romans mentioned in this book are listed below:

> P. Cornelius Scipio Africanus (an extra surname based on his victory over the Carthaginians in North Africa in 202 BC)
>
> M. Porcius Cato
>
> Tib. and C. Sempronius Gracchus
>
> C. Marius (his surname is never used)
>
> L. Cornelius Sulla
>
> M. Licinius Crassus
>
> Cn. Pompeius (his father bore the surname Strabo, but that was always omitted in the case of Pompey)

We have sometimes used only one or two of the names, for the sake of brevity (e.g., Caesar, Tib. Gracchus).

In this book we have used the Latin spelling for all Greek and Roman names. This has for a long time been the customary way of writing such names in English-speaking countries.

2 GREEK AND ROMAN MONEY

The following coins were used in Classical Athens:

> 1 talent = 6,000 drachmas (silver)
> 1 mina = 100 drachmas
> 1 drachma = 6 obols
> 1 drachma (coin) weighed 4.31 g (Attic standard)

There were also coins worth four drachmas (silver teradrachmas).

In Pericles' time one drachma was a substantial wage for one day's work. Citizens who attended the meetings of the Council of Five Hundred or a lawsuit at a popular court were paid two obols. The talent and the *mina* were units of account.

The following coins were used in the early Roman empire:

> 1 *aureus* = 25 *denarii* (an *aureus* was a gold coin weighing 7.72 g; *denarii* were of silver)
> 1 *denarius* (3.80 g) = 4 sesterces (brass coins)
> 1 sesterce = 4 *asses* (= 2 *dupondii*) (copper coins)

During the reign of Augustus a *denarius* weighed 3.80 g and contained 3.65 g of silver; by the time of the reign of Decius (25) the coin weighed 3.10 g and contained only 1 gram of silver—a mark of debasement of the coinage.

Around AD 60 an inhabitant of Rome, which was then an expensive city, could live on a monthly allowance of five *modii* (= 45 liters) of grain and five *denari*. A legionary was in those days paid 225 *denarii* per year. That sum was sufficient to cover his cost of living. Legionaries were not particularly well paid, but they certainly did not belong to the ranks of the minimum wage earners.

See http://www.livius.org/w/weights/weights.html.

3   THE ROMAN EMPERORS

THE JULIO-CLAUDIAN DYNASTY

Augustus	27 BC–AD 14
Tiberius	AD 14–37
Caligula	37–41
Claudius	41–54
Nero	54–68

"Julio" refers to the fact that they all descended from C. Julius Caesar Augustus, as he was called after 27 BC. Augustus himself had only one daughter, Julia. Caligula and Nero were her descendants. Augustus' last wife (not Julia's mother) was called Livia. She had previously been married to Tib. Claudius Nero (Claudius was his *gens* name, Nero his surname). Her sons from this previous marriage were Tiberius and Drusus (Tib. Claudius Nero and M. Claudius Nero Drusus; Drusus was the surname of Livia's father, T. Livius Drusus). The emperor Claudius was a descendant of that second son, Drusus.

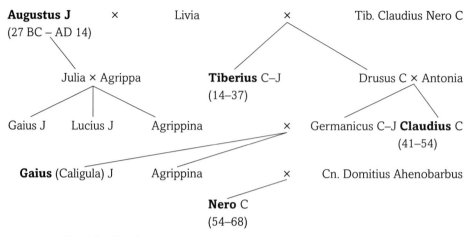

FIGURE A.1 The Julio-Claudian dynasty
Notes: J = Julii
        C = Claudii

Tiberius (14–37) became a Julius by adoption but Claudius remained a member of the Claudian family and therefore we speak of the Julio-Claudian dynasty.

Agrippa: one of Augustus' important generals, who worked together with him from 44 until 13 BC. He died in 12 BC. Augustus adopted his sons Gaius and Lucius, who both died while they were still young, in AD 4 and 2, respectively.

Germanicus: an important general in the wars against the Germans in AD 13–17; Tiberius' adopted son (and hence a Julius) and his appointed successor. He died at an early age in AD 19.

Nero: adopted by Claudius, even though the latter had a son of his own (Britannicus). But Nero was a matrilineal relative of Augustus and could hence claim a more distinguished descent.

> 68–69 was the year of the four emperors: Galba
>   Otho
>   Vitellius
>   Vespasian (T. Flavius Vespasianus) 69–79

THE FLAVIAN DYNASTY

The Flavian dynasty began with Vespasian and his two sons ruled after him:

| Titus | 79–81 |
| Domitian | 81–96 |

After the murder of Domitian, followed a series of emperors who all adopted their successors:

Nerva	96–98
Trajan	98–117
Hadrian	117–138
Antoninus Pius	138–161 (161–9 with Lucius Verus)
Marcus Aurelius	161–180

Marcus Aurelius was succeeded by his son Commodus, 180–192. After the latter's death a struggle for power ensued, which ultimately resulted in a temporary distribution of power in 193. First the empire was governed by Pertinax and Didius Julianus successively, after which Pescennius Niger ruled over Syria, Clodius Albinus over the northwest, and Septimius Severus over the rest of the empire. Niger was soon eliminated, but Albinus remained in control alongside Septimius Severus until 197. Then Septimius Severus was sole emperor until 211.

The following emperors reigned from 211 to 235:

Caracalla	211–217
Macrinus	217–218
Elagabalus	218–222
Severus Alexander	222–235

THE SOLDIER EMPERORS

The soldier emperors who ruled during the crisis of the third century:

Maximinus Thrax	235–238
Gordian I and II	238
Gordian III	238–244
Philippus Arabs	244–249
Decius	249–251
Trebonianus Gallus	251–253
Valerian	253–260

Gallienus ruled as co-emperor with his father Valerian from 253 until 260 and as sole emperor from 260 until 268. Then:

Claudius Gothicus	268–270
Aurelian	270–275
Tacitus	275–276
Probus	276–282
Carus and his two sons (Carinus and Numerian)	282–284

The above survey includes only the emperors who may to some extent be regarded as official emperors of the entire empire. The numerous pretenders have been omitted.

THE LATE IMPERIAL AGE

Diocletian and his co-emperor Maximian (Milan) and the junior emperors Galerius (East) and Constantius Chlorus (Trier) ruled from 284 to 305 (Diocletian 284–305; Maximian 286–305; Constantius 293–306, and Galerius 293–311). After 305 Galerius became the most important emperor in the East.

Then the dynasty of Constantius Chlorus came to power:

Constantine the Great	306–337
Constantius II	337–361 (until 350 together with Constans)
Julian	361–363

The emperors who reigned from 363:

Jovian	363–364
Valentinian I (western half)	364–375 and
Valens (eastern half)	364–378

Gratian (the son of Valentinian I; 375–383 in the western half), together with Theodosius I (379–394 in the eastern half; in his last year, 394–395, he was sole emperor of the entire empire). They were succeeded by Arcadius (395–408) and Theodosius II (408–450) in the east and by Honorius (395–423) in the west.

SELECT BIBLIOGRAPHY

WORKS OF GENERAL COVERAGE

Barraclough, G., ed., *The Times Atlas of World History*, 4th edn, London, 1996.

Barrington Atlas of the Greek and Roman World, edited by R.J.A. Talbert, Princeton NJ, 2000.

Barton, T., *Ancient Astrology*, London/New York, 1994.

Biers, W.R., *Art, Artefacts and Chronology in Classical Archaeology*, 2nd edn, London/New York, 1995.

Blakely, S., *Myth, Ritual, and Metallurgy in Ancient Greece and Recent Africa*, Cambridge, 2006.

Boardman, J. *et al. The Oxford History of the Classical World*, Oxford, 1988.

Borgeaud, Ph., *Mother of the Gods: From Cybele to the Virgin Mary*, translated into English by L. Hochroth, Baltimore MD/London, 2004.

Bremen, R. van, *The Limits of Participation. Women and Civic Life in the Greek East in the Hellenistic and Roman Periods*, Amsterdam, 1996.

Bremer, J.M., Th.J.P. van den Hout and R. Peters (eds), *Hidden Futures. Death and Immortality in Ancient Egypt, Anatolia, the Classical, Biblical and Arabic Islamic World*, Amsterdam, 1994.

Burkert, W., *Ancient Mystery Cults*, London, 1987.

Cambridge Ancient History, volumes *I – XIV*, 3rd/2nd edn., Cambridge, 1970–2005.

Cameron, A., *History as Text. The Writing of Ancient History*, London/Chapel Hill NC, 1989.

Casson, L., *Travel in the Ancient World*, 2nd edn, Baltimore MD, 1994.

Chaniotis, A., *War in the Ancient World. A Social and Cultural History*, Oxford, 2005.

Chaniotis, A. and P. Ducrey (eds) *Army and Power in the Ancient World*, Stuttgart, 2002.

Connolly, P. and H. Dodge, *The Ancient City. Life in Classical Athens and Rome*, Oxford, 1998.

Crawford, M.H. (ed.), *Sources for Ancient History*, Cambridge, 1983.

Cunliffe, B., *Greeks, Romans and Barbarians. Spheres of Interaction*, London, 1988.

——, *Prehistoric Europe: An Illustrated History*, Oxford, 1997.

Dalby, A., *Food in the Ancient World from A to Z*, London/New York, 2003.

Dickie, M.W., *Magic and Magicians in the Greco-Roman World*, London/New York, 2001.

Dodd, D.B. and Chr.A. Faraone (eds), *Initiation in Ancient Rituals and Narratives. New Critical Perspectives*, London/New York 2003

Easterling, P.E., *et al., The Cambridge History of Classical Literature I: Greek Literature*, Cambridge, 1982–1989.

Elsner, J. and I. Rutherford (eds), *Seeing the Gods. Pilgrimage in Graeco-Roman and Early Christian Antiquity*, Oxford 2005.

Fantham, E., *et al.*, *Women in the Classical World. Image and Text*, Oxford, 1994.

Finley, M.I., *Politics in the Ancient World*, Cambridge, 1983.

——, *Ancient History. Evidence and Models*, London, 1985.

——, *Ancient Slavery and Modern Ideology*, Princeton NJ, 1998 (new expanded edition).

——, *The Ancient Economy*, London, 1999 (updated edition).

Fornara, C.W., *The Nature of History in Ancient Greece and Rome*, Berkeley CA, 1983.

Garlan, Y., *War in the Ancient World. A Social History*, London, 1975.

Garnsey, P.D.A., *Non-slave Labour in the Graeco-Roman World*, Cambridge, 1980.

——, *Ideas of Slavery from Aristotle to Augustine*, Cambridge, 1996.

——, *Food and Society in Classical Antiquity*, Cambridge, 1999.

—— and C.R. Whittaker, *Trade and Famine in Classical Antiquity*, Cambridge, 1983.

Golden, M., *Sport in the Ancient World from A to Z*, London/New York, 2004.

Grant, M., *A Guide to the Ancient World: A Dictionary of Classical Names*, New York, 1986.

——, *Greek and Roman Historians. Information and Misinformation*, London/New York, 1995.

Grmek, M.D., *Diseases in the Ancient World*, Baltimore MD/London, 1989.

Gruen, E.S. (ed.), *Cultural Borrowings and Ethnic Appropriations in Antiquity*, Stuttgart, 2005.

Haring B. and R. de Maaijer (eds), *Landless and Hungry? Access to Land in Early and Traditional Societies*, Leiden, 1998.

Harris, D.R., *The Origins and Spread of Agriculture and Pastoralism in Eurasia*, London, 1996.

Harris, W.V., *Ancient Literacy*, Cambridge MA, 1989.

Hedrick, Ch.W., *Ancient History. Monuments and Documents*, Oxford, 2006.

Hekster, O.J. and R. Fowler (eds), *Imaginary Kings: Royal Images in the Ancient Near East, Greece and Rome*, Stuttgart, 2005.

Hooff, A.J.L. van, *From Autothanasia to Suicide*, London, 1990.

Hope V.M. and E. Marshall, *Death and Disease in the Ancient City*, London, 2000.

Horden, P. and N. Purcell, *The Corrupting Sea: A Study of Mediterranean History*, Oxford/Malden MA, 2000.

Howgego, Chr., *Ancient History from Coins*, Oxford/London/New York, 1995.

Hubbard, Th.K. (ed), *Homosexuality in Greece and Rome. A Sourcebook of Basic Documents*, Berkeley/Los Angeles/London, 2003.

Johnston, S.I., *Religions of the Ancient World. A Guide*, Cambridge MA/London, 2004.

Kallendorf, C.W., (ed.), *A Companion to the Classical Tradition*, Oxford/Malden MA, 2007.

Kleywegt, M., *Ancient Youth. The Ambiguity of Youth and the Absence of Adolescence in Greco-Roman Society*, Amsterdam, 1991.

Kyle, D.G., *Sport and Spectacle in the Ancient World*, Oxford, 2007.

Landels, J.G., *Engineering in the Ancient World*, 2nd edn, Berkeley/Los Angeles/London, 2000.

Lefkowitz, M.R. and M.B. Fant, *Women's Life in Greece and Rome*, 3rd edn, London, 2005.

Lendon, J.E., *Soldiers and Ghosts. A History of Battle in Classical Antiquity*, London/New Haven CT, 2005.

Lincoln, B., *Theorizing Myth. Narrative, Ideology and Scholarship*, Chicago ILL/London, 1999.

Lo Cascio, E. and D.W. Rathbone (eds), *Production and Public Powers in Classical Antiquity*, Cambridge, 2000.

Long, Ch.R., *The Twelve Gods of Greece and Rome*, Leiden, 1987.

Luck, G., *Ancient Pathways and Hidden Pursuits. Religion, Morals and Magic in the Ancient World*, Ann Arbor MI, 2000.

MacHardy, F. and E. Marshall (eds), *Women's Influence on Classical Civilization*, London/New York, 2004.

Marrou, H.I., *A History of Education in Antiquity*, New York, 1964.

Mattingly, D.J. and J. Salmon (eds), *Economies beyond Agriculture in the Classical World*, London/New York, 2001.

Meijer, F.J., *Greece, Rome and the Sea*, London, 1986.

Michailidou, A., *Weight and Value in Precoinage Societies*, Athens/Paris, 2005.

Morford, M.P.O. and R.J. Lenardon, *Classical Mythology*, 8th edn, Oxford, 2007.

Morley, N., *Theories, Models and Concepts in Ancient History*, London/New York, 2004.

Naiden, F.S., *Ancient Supplication*, Oxford, 2006.

Nelson, M., *The Barbarian's Beverage. A History of Beer in Ancient Europe*, London/New York, 2005.

Owens, E.J., *The City in the Greek and Roman World*, London, 1991.

Pomeroy, S.B., *Goddesses, Whores, Wives and Slaves: Women in Classical Antiquity*, New York, 1976.

Porter, B.N. (ed.), *One God or Many? Concepts of Divinity in the Ancient World*, Casco Bay ME, 2000.

Reynolds, L.D. and N.G. Wilson, *Scribes and Scholars. A Guide to the Transmission of Greek and Latin Literature*, 3rd edn, Oxford, 1991.

Rich, J. and A. Wallace-Hadrill (eds), *City and Country in the Ancient World*, London, 1991.

Roller, D.W., *Through the Pillars of Herakles. Greco-Roman Exploration of the Atlantic*, London/New York, 2006.

Rosen, R.M. and I. Sluiter (eds), *City, Countryside and the Spacial Organization of Value in Classical Antiquity*, Leiden/Boston MA, 2006.

Rougé, J., *Ships and Fleets of the Ancient Mediterranean*, New York, 1981.

Rowe, Chr. and M. Schofield (eds), *The Cambridge History of Greek and Roman Political Thought*, Cambridge, 2000.

Scheidel, W. and S. von Reden (eds), *The Ancient Economy*, Edinburgh, 2002

Scheidel, W., I.M. Morris and R.P. Saller, *The Cambridge Economic History of the Greco-Roman World*, Cambridge, 2007.

Segal, R.A., *Myth. A Very Short Introduction*, Oxford, 2004.

Seters, J. van, *In Search of History. Historiography in the Ancient World and the Origins of Biblical History*, Winona Lake IN, 1996.

Skinner, M.B., *Sexuality in Greek and Roman Culture*, Oxford/Malden MA/Carlton, Vict., 2005.

Stavrianopoulou, E. (ed.), *Ritual and Communication in the Graeco-Roman World*, Liège, 2006.

Too, Y.L. (ed.), *Education in Greek and Roman Antiquity*, Leiden/Boston MA, 2001.

Versnel, H.S., *Faith, Hope and Worship. Aspects of Religious Mentality in the Ancient World*, Leiden, 1981.

Versnel, H.S., *Ter unus. Isis, Dionysos, Hermes. Three Studies in Henotheism*, Leiden, 1990.

Veyne, P., *Bread and Circuses. Historical Sociology and Political Pluralism*, Harmondsworth, 1990.

Wallace-Hadrill, A. (ed.), *Patronage in Ancient Society*, London, 1988.

West, M.L., *Indo-European Poetry and Myth*, Oxford, 2007.

White, K.D., *Greek and Roman Technology*, New York, 1984.

Wikander, O. (ed.), *Handbook of Ancient Water Technology*, Leiden/Boston MA, 2000.

Woodford, S., *Cambridge Introduction to the History of Art. Greece and Rome*, Cambridge, 1982.

Woodman, A.J., *Rhetoric in Classical Histiography*, London, 1988.

Yoffee, N., *Myths of the Archaic State. Evolution of the Earliest Cities, States, and Civilizations*, Cambridge, 2005.

Younger, J.G., *Sex in the Ancient World from A to Z*, London/New York, 2005.

THE ANCIENT NEAR EAST TO ALEXANDER THE GREAT

Achaemenid History I–, Leiden, 1987–.

Ackroyd, P.R., *Israel under Babylonia and Persia*, London, 1975.

Algaze, G., *The Uruk World System. The Dynamics of Expansion of Early Mesopotamian Civilization*, 2nd edn, Chicago IL, 2005.

Aubet, M.E., *The Phoenicians and the West. Politics, Colonies and Trade*, 2nd edn, Cambridge, 2001.

Baines, J., *Visual and Written Culture in Ancient Egypt*, Oxford, 2007.

Baines, J. and J. Málek, *Cultural Atlas of Ancient Egypt*, Oxford, 1980.

Baker, H.D.and M. Jursa (eds), *Approaching the Babylonian Economy*, Münster, 2005.

Beaulieu, P.A., *The Reign of Nabonidus, King of Babylon 556–539 BC*, New Haven CT, 1989.

Ben-Tor, A. (ed.) *The Archaeology of Ancient Israel*, New Haven CT/Jerusalem, 1992.

Bottero, J. *et al.*, *Everyday Life in Ancient Mesopotamia*, translated into English by A. Nevill, Edinburgh, 2001.

Bowman, A.K. and E. Rogan, *Agriculture in Egypt from Pharaonic to Modern Times*, Oxford, 1999.

Briant, P., *From Cyrus to Alexander. A History of the Persian Empire*, Winona Lake, IN, 2002.

Brinkman, J.A., *A Political History of Post-Kassite Babylonia 1158–722 BC*, Rome, 1968.

——, *Prelude to Empire. Babylonian Society and Politics, 747–626 BC*, Philadelphia PA, 1984.

Brosius, M., *Women in Ancient Persia, 559–331 BC*, Oxford, 1996.

Brown, J.P., *Israel and Hellas I–III*, Berlin/New York, 1995–2001.

Bryce, T., *Life and Society in the Hittite World*, Oxford, 2002.

——, *Letters of the Great Kings of the Ancient Near East. The Royal Correspondence of the Late Bronze Age*, London/New York, 2003.

——, *The Kingdom of the Hittites*, 2nd edn, Oxford, 2005.

Burkert, W., *Babylon, Memphis, Persepolis. Eastern Contexts of Greek Culture*, Cambridge MA/London, 2004.

Burns, R., *Damascus. A History*, London/New York, 2005.

Chavalas, M.-W. (ed.), *The Ancient Near East. Historical Sources in Translation*, Oxford, 2006.

Cogan, M., *Imperialism and Religion, Assyria, Judah and Israel in the Eighth and Seventh Century BCE*, Missoula MT, 1974.

Coogan, M.D., *The Old Testament. A Historical and Literary Introduction to the Hebrew Scriptures*, Oxford, 2006.

Crawford, H., *Sumer and the Sumerians*, 2nd edn, Cambridge, 2004.

Dalley, S., (ed.), *The Legacy of Mesopotamia*, Oxford, 1998.

Feldman, L.H., *Jew and Gentile in the Ancient World*, Princeton NJ, 1993.

Finkelstein, I. and N.A. Silberman, *The Bible Unearthed. Archaeology's New Vision of Ancient Israel and the Origin of its Sacred Texts*, New York, 2001.

Frame, G., *Babylonia 689–627 BC. A Political History*, Leiden/Istanbul, 1992.

George, A., *The Epic of Gilgamesh. The Babylonian Epic Poem and Other Texts in Akkadian and Sumerian*, translated and with commentary, London, 1999.

Grant, M., *History of Ancient Israel*, London, 1984.

Grimal, P., *A History of Ancient Egypt*, Oxford, 1992.

Harden, D.B., *The Phoenicians*, 2nd edn, Harmondsworth, 1980.

Hornung, E., *Conceptions of God in Ancient Egypt. The One and the Many*, London, 1983.

Hudson, M. and B.A. Levine (eds), *Urbanization and Land Ownership in the Ancient Near East*, Cambridge MA, 1999.

Hudson, M. and M. van de Mieroop (eds), *Debt and Economic Renewal in the Ancient Near East*, Bethesda MD, 2002.

Jacobsen, T., *The Treasures of Darkness. A History of Mesopotamian Religion*, New Haven CT, 1976.

James, T.G.H., *An Introduction to Ancient Egypt*, 2nd edn, London, 1983.

Kemp, B.J., *Ancient Egypt. Anatomy of a Civilization*, 2nd edn, London/New York, 2006.

Knapp, A.B., *The History and Culture of Western Asia and Egypt*, Chicago IL, 1988.

Kuhrt, A., *The Ancient Near East c. 3000–330 BC*, London, 1995.

Lambert, W.G., *Babylonian Wisdom Literature*, Oxford, 1960/Winona Lake IN, 1996.

Lanfranchi, G.B., M. Roaf and R. Rollinger (eds), *Continuity of Empire? Assyria, Media, Persia*, Padova, 2003.

Larsen, M.T., *The Conquest of Assyria. Excavations in an Antique Land*, London, 1996.

Leick, G., *The Babylonians: An Introduction*, London/New York, 2003.

Lichtheim, M., *Ancient Egyptian Literature. A Book of Readings*, three vols., Berkeley/Los Angeles/London, 1973–1980.

Lipschits, O. and M. Oeming (eds), *Judah and the Judaeans in the Persian Period*, Winona Lake IN, 2006.

Liverani, M., *Prestige and Interest. International Relations in the Near East ca. 1600–1100 BC*, Padua, 1990.

Maisels, C.K., *The Near East: Archaeology in the "Cradle of Civilisation"*, London/New York, 1993.

Mieroop, M. van de, *The Ancient Mesopotamian City*, Oxford, 1999.

——, *King Hammurabi of Babylon. A Biography*, Oxford, 2005.

——, *A History of the Ancient Near East ca. 3000–323 BC*, 2nd edn, Oxford, 2007.

Miller, J.M. and J.H. Hayes, *A History of Ancient Israel and Judah*, 2nd edn, London, 2006.

Montserrat, D., *Akhenaten. History, Fantasy and Ancient Egypt*, London, 2000.

Nissen, H.J., *The Early History of the Ancient Near East 9000–2000 BC*, Chicago IL, 1988.

——, *Archaic Bookkeeping: Early Writing and Techniques of Economic Administration in the Ancient Near East*, Chicago IL, 1993.

Oates, J., *Babylon*, London, 1979.

Oppenheim, A.L., *Ancient Mesopotamia. Portrait of a Dead Civilization*, 2nd edn, Chicago IL, 1977.

Pastor, J., *Land and Economy in Ancient Palestine*, London, 1997.

Pitard, W.T., *Ancient Damascus. A Historical Study of the Syrian City-state from Earliest Times until its Fall to the Assyrians in 732 BCE*, Winona Lake IN, 1987.

Pollock, S., *Ancient Mesopotamia*, Cambridge, 1999.

Postgate, J.N., *Early Mesopotamia. Society and Economy at the Dawn of History*, London, 1992.

Powell, M.A. (ed.), *Labor in the Ancient Near East*, New Haven CT, 1987.

Redford, D.B., *Egypt, Canaan and Israel in Ancient Times*, Princeton NJ, 1992.

Roaf, M., *Cultural Atlas of Mesopotamia and the Ancient Near East*, 4th edn, New York, 2000.

Robins, G., *Women in Ancient Egypt*, London, 1993.

Rochberg, F., *The Heavenly Writing. Divination, Horoscopy, and Astronomy in Mesopotamian Culture*, Cambridge, 2004.

Sack, R.H., *Images of Nebuchadnezzar. The Emergence of a Legend*, Selinsgrove/London/Toronto, 1991.

Sandars, N.K., *The Sea Peoples. Warriors of the Ancient Mediterranean*, 2nd edn, London, 1985.

Sasson, J.M. (ed.), *Civilizations of the Ancient Near East*, four vols, 2nd edn, Peabody MA, 2000.

Silverman, D.P. and D. O'Connor (eds), *Ancient Egyptian Kingship*, Leiden, 1995.

Smith, M., *Palestinian Parties and Politics that Shaped the Old Testament*, 2nd edn, London, 1987.

Snell, D.C. (ed.), *A Companion to the Ancient Near East*, Oxford/Malden MA, 2005.

Soden, W. von, *The Ancient Orient. An Introduction of the Study of the Ancient Near East*, Grand Rapids MI/Leominster, 1994.

State Archives of Assyria, Vol I–, Helsinki, 1987–.

Taylor, J.H., *Death and the Afterlife in Ancient Egypt*, London, 2001.

Toorn, K. van der, *Family Religion in Babylonia, Syria and Israel. Continuity and Change in the Forms of Religious Life*, Leiden, 1996.

——, *Scribal Culture and the Making of the Hebrew Bible*, Cambridge MA/London, 2007.

Toorn, K. van der, B. Becking and P.W. van der Horst, *Dictionary of Deities and Demons*, Leiden, 1995.

Trigger, B.G., *et al.*, *Ancient Egypt. A Social History*, Cambridge, 1983.

Waerzeggers, C., The Babylonian revolts against Xerxes and the "End of Archives," *Archiv für Orientforschung* 50, 2003/4, 150–173.

Weiss, H., *The Origins of Cities in Dry-farming Syria and Mesopotamia in the Third Millennium BC*, Guilford CT, 1986.

Wiesehöfer, J., *Ancient Persia from 550 BC to 650 AD*, London/New York, 2001.

Wilhelm, G., *The Hurrians*, Warminster, 1989.

Wilkinson, T.J., *Archaeological Landscapes of the Near East*, Tucson AZ, 2003.

Wilson, R.R., *Prophecy and Society in Ancient Israel*, Philadelphia PA, 1980.

Wiseman, D.J., *Nebuchadnezzar and Babylon*, Oxford, 1985.

THE GREEKS

Albinus, L., *The House of Hades. Studies in Ancient Greek Eschatology*, Aarhus, 2000.

Austin, M.M. and P. Vidal-Naquet, *Economic and Social History of Ancient Greece*, London, 1977.

Barringer, J.M., *The Hunt in Ancient Greece*, Baltimore MD/London, 2001.

Boardman, J., (ed.), *The Oxford History of Greece and the Hellenistic World*, 2nd edn, Oxford, 2001.

Bremmer, J.N., *Greek Religion*, 2nd edn, Oxford, 1999.

Burkert, W., *Greek Religion*, Cambridge MA, 1985.

Buxton, R. (ed.), *Oxford Readings in Greek Religion*, Oxford, 2000.

Calame, C., *Myth and History in Ancient Greece. The Symbolic Creation of a Colony*, translated into English by D.W. Berman, Princeton NJ, 2003.

—— (ed.), *The Cambridge Illustrated History of Ancient Greece*, Cambridge, 1998.

Cartledge, P., *The Greeks. A Portrait of Self and Others*, 2nd edn, Oxford, 2002.

Cohen, E.E., *The Athenian Nation*, 2nd edn, Princeton NJ, 2003.

Coleman, J.E. and C.A. Walz (eds), *Greeks and Barbarians. Essays on the Interaction between Greeks and Non-Greeks in Antiquity and the Consequences for Eurocentrism*, Bethesda, MD, 1997.

Cook, B.F., *Greek Inscriptions*, London, 1987.

Cosmopoulos, M.B. (ed.), *Greek Mysteries. The Archaeology and Ritual of Ancient Greek Secret Cults*, London/New York, 2003.

Dillon, M., *Pilgrims and Pilgrimage in Ancient Greece*, London/New York, 1997.

Dodds, E.R., *The Greeks and the Irrational*, 2nd edn, Berkeley/Los Angeles/London, 1973.

Easterling, P.E. and J.V. Muir (eds), *Greek Religion and Society*, Cambridge, 1985.

Easterling, P.E., *et al.*, *The Cambridge History of Classical Literature*, I: *Greek Literature*, Cambridge, 1989.

Farenga, V., *Citizen and Self in Ancient Greece. Individuals performing Justice and the Law*, Cambridge, 2006.

Finley, M.I., *Ancient Sicily*, 2nd edn, London, 1979.

Flacelière, R., *Love in Ancient Greece*, translated into English by J. Cleugh, 3rd edn, Westport CT, 1977.

Foxhall, L. and P. Cartledge (eds), *Money, Labour and Land in Ancient Greece*, London, 2000.

Freeman, C., *The Greek Achievement. The Foundation of the Western World*, Harmondsworth, 2000.

Garland, R., *The Greek Way of Death*, London, 1985.

——, *The Greek Way of Life from Conception to Old Age*, London, 1990.

Goldhill, S. and R. Osborne (eds), *Rethinking Revolutions through Ancient Greece*, Cambridge, 2006.

Greaves, A.M., *Miletos. A History*, London/New York, 2002.

Hall, E., *Inventing the Barbarian*, Oxford, 1989.

Hall, J.M., *Ethnic Identity in Greek Antiquity*, Cambridge, 2000.

——, *Hellenicity between Ethnicity and Culture*, Chicago IL/London, 2002.

Hall Sternberg, R., *Tragedy Offstage. Suffering and Sympathy in Ancient Athens*, Austin TX, 2006.

Hansen, M.H., *Polis and City-State. An Ancient Greek Concept and its Modern Equivalent*, Copenhagen, 1998.

——, *Studies in the Population of Aigina, Athens and Eretria*, Copenhagen, 2006.

Hard, R., *The Routledge Handbook of Greek Mythology*, London/New York, 2004.

Harrison, Th. (ed.), *Greeks and Barbarians*, Edinburgh, 2002.

Hornblower, S., *The Greek World 479–323 BC*, 3rd edn, London/New York, 2002.

Humphreys, S.C., *The Strangeness of Gods. Historical Perspectives on the Interpretation of Athenian Religion*, Oxford, 2004.

Isager, S. and J.E. Skydsgaard, *Ancient Greek Agriculture. An Introduction*, London, 1992.

Kendrick Pritchett, W., *The Greek State at War I–II*, Berkeley CA, 1974–1991.

——, *Athenian Calendars and Ekklesias*, Amsterdam, 2001.

Lancellotti, M.G., *Attis. Between Myth and History: King, Priest and God*, Leiden/Boston MA, 2002.

Larson, J., *Greek Nymphs. Myth, Cult and Lore*, Oxford, 2001.

Lordkipanidze, O., *Phasis. The River and City in Colchis*, Stuttgart, 2000.

Luce, T.J., *The Greek Historians*, London, 1997.

MacGlew, J.F., *Tyranny and Political Culture in Ancient Greece*, Ithaca NY/London, 1993.

Malkin, I. (ed.), *Ancient Perceptions of Greek Ethnicity*, London/Cambridge MA, 2001.

Mikalson, J.D., *Athenian Popular Religion*, Chapel Hill NC/London, 1983.

——, *Ancient Greek Religion*, Oxford/Malden MA, 2005.

Newby, Z., *Greek Athletics in the Roman World. Victory and Virtue*, Oxford, 2005.

Parker, R., *Athenian Religion. A History*, Oxford, 1997.

Patterson, C.B., *The Family in Greek History*, London/Cambridge MA, 2001.

Phillips, E.D., *Aspects of Greek Medicine*, London, 1987.

Price, S.R.F., *Religions of the Ancient Greeks*, Cambridge, 1999.

Reden, S. von, *Exchange in Ancient Greece*, London, 2003.

Reed, C.M., *Maritime Traders in the Ancient Greek World*, Cambridge, 2003.

Rich, J. and G. Shipley (eds), *War and Society in the Greek World*, London, 1993.

Sallares, R., *The Ecology of the Ancient Greek World*, Ithaca NY/London, 1991.

Sansone, D., *Ancient Greek Civilisation*, Oxford/Malden MA/Carlton, Vict., 2004.

Sealey, R., *The Justice of the Greeks*, Ann Arbor MI, 1994.

Sowerby, R., *The Greeks. An Introduction to their Culture*, London/New York, 1995.

Ste. Croix, G.E.M. de, *The Class-Struggle in the Ancient Greek World*, Ithaca/New York/London, 1981.

Thomas, R., *Literacy and Orality in Ancient Greece*, Cambridge, 1992.

Vernant, J.-P., *Myth and Society in Ancient Greece*, 2nd edn, New York, 1988.

Wees, H. van, *Greek Warfare. Myths and Realities*, London, 2004.

West, M.L., *Early Greek Philosophy and the Orient*, Oxford, 1971.

Young, D.C., *A Brief History of the Olympic Games*, Oxford/Malden MA, 2004.

Zelnick-Abramovitz, R., *Not Wholly Free. The Concept of Manumission and the Status of Manumitted Slaves in the Ancient Greek World*, Leiden/Boston MA, 2005.

ARCHAIC AND CLASSICAL GREECE

Andrewes, A., *The Greek Tyrants*, 4th edn, London, 1980.

Blok, J.H. and A.P.M.H. Lardinois (eds), *Solon of Athens. New Historical and Philological Approaches*, Leiden/Boston MA, 2006.

Boardman, J., *The Greeks Overseas. Their Early Colonies and Trade*, 2nd edn, London, 1980.

Boedeker, D. and K.A. Raaflaub (eds), *Democracy, Empire and the Arts in Fifth-century Athens*, London/Cambridge MA, 2001.

Borza, E.N., *In the Shadow of Olympus. The Emergence of Macedon*, 2nd edn, Princeton NJ, 1991.

Brock, R. and S. Hodkinson (eds), *Alternatives to Athens. Varieties of Political Organization and Community in Ancient Greece*, Oxford, 2000.

Buck, R.J., *Boiotia and the Boiotian League 432–371 BC*, Edmonton, 1994.

Cartledge, P., *Sparta and Lakonia. A Regional History 1300–362 BC*, 2nd edn, London/New York, 2002.

——, P. Millett and S. Todd (eds), *Nomos. Essays in Athenian Law, Politics and Society*, Cambridge, 1990.

Chadwick, J., *The Mycenaean World*, Cambridge, 1976.

Connor, W.R., *The New Politicians of Fifth-century Athens*, Princeton NJ, 1971.

Crielaard, J.P. (ed.), *Homeric Questions*, Amsterdam, 1995.

——, *The Euboeans Overseas. Long-distance Contacts and Colonization as Status Activities in Early Iron Age Greece*, Amsterdam, 1996.

Demand, N., *Birth, Death and Motherhood in Classical Greece*, Baltimore MD/London, 1994.

Descoeudres, J.-P., *Greek Colonists and Native Populations*, Oxford, 1990.

Dickinson, O.T.P.K., *The Aegean Bronze Age*, Cambridge, 1994.

Ducat, J., *Spartan Education. Youth and Society in the Classical Period*, translated into English by E. Stafford, P.J. Shaw and A. Powell, Swansea, 2006.

Ellis, W., *Alcibiades*, London, 1989.

Erskine, A., *Troy between Greece and Rome. Local Tradition and Imperial Power*, Oxford, 2001.

Farrar, C., *The Origins of Democratic Thinking. The Invention of Politics in Classical Athens*, Cambridge, 1988.

Finkelberg, M., *Greeks and Pre-Greeks. Aegean Prehistory and Greek Heroic Tradition*, Cambridge, 2005.

Fornara, C.W. and L.J. Samons II, *Athens from Cleisthenes to Pericles*, Berkeley/Los Angeles/London, 1991.

Gagarin, M. and P. Woodruff, *Early Greek Political Thought from Homer to the Sophists*, Cambridge, 1995.

Gardner, R., *Law and Society in Classical Athens*, London, 1987.

Garland, R., *The Piraeus from the Fifth to the First Century BC*, London, 2001.

Gould, J., *Herodotus*, Bristol, 2000.

Graham, A.J., *Collected Papers on Greek Colonization*, Leiden/Boston MA, 2001.

Hall, J.M., *A History of the Archaic Greek World, ca. 1200–479 BC*, Oxford, 2007.

Hammond, N.G.L., *Philip of Macedon*, London, 1994.

Hansen, M.H., *Demography and Democracy. The Number of Athenian Citizens in the Fourth Century BC*, Gjellerup, 1986.

——, *The Athenian Democracy in the Age of Demosthenes*, 2nd edn, Oxford, 1993.

——, *Polis. An Introduction to the Ancient Greek City-state*, Oxford, 2006.

——, *The Shotgun Method. The Demography of the Ancient City-state Culture*, Columbia, MI/London, 2006.

——, *Hoplites. The Classical Greek Battle Experience*, 2nd edn, London/New York, 1993.

Hanson, V.D., *The Western Way of War: Infantry Battle in Classical Greece*, 2nd edn, Berkeley/Los Angeles/London, 2000.

Harris, E.M., *Democracy and the Rule of Law in Classical Athens*, Cambridge, 2006.

Herman, G., *Morality and Behaviour in Democratic Athens. A Social History*, Cambridge, 2006.

Hodkinson, S., *Property and Wealth in Classical Sparta*, London/Swansea, 2000.

—— and A. Powell (eds), *Sparta and War*, Swansea, 2006.

Hopper, R.J., *Trade and Industry in Classical Greece*, London, 1979.

Hornblower, S., *Thucydides*, Baltimore MD, 1987.

Hunter, V. and J. Edmondson (eds), *Law and Social Status in Classical Athens*, Oxford, 2000.

Jones, A.H.M., *The Athenian Democracy*, 2nd edn, Oxford, 1978.

Jones, N.F., *Rural Athens under the Democracy*, Philadelphia NJ, 2004.

Kinzl, K.H. (ed.), *A Companion to the Classical Greek World*, Oxford, 2006.

Lang, M., *The Athenian Citizen. Democracy in the Athenian Agora*, 2nd edn, Princeton NJ/Oxford, 2004.

Lavelle, B.M., *Fame, Money and Power. The Rise of Peisistratos and "Democratic" Tyranny at Athens*, Ann Arbor MI, 2005.

Lazenby, J.F., *The Peloponnesian War. A Military Study*, London/New York, 2004.

Lintott, A.W., *Violence, Civil Strife and Revolution in the Classical City 750–330 BC*, London, 1982.

Littman, R.J., *The Greek Experiment. Imperialism and Social Conflict 800–400 BC*, London, 1974.

Lloyd, G.E.R., *The Revolutions of Wisdom. Studies in the Claims and Practice of Early Greek Science*, Berkeley/Los Angeles/London, 1989.

Low, P., *Interstate Relations in Classical Greece. Morality and Power*, Cambridge, 2007.

Luraghi, N. (ed.), *The Historian's Craft in the Age of Herodotus*, Oxford, 2001.

Meiggs, R., *The Athenian Empire*, Oxford, 1979.

Miller, M.C., *Athens and Persia in the Fifth Century BC. A Study in Cultural Receptivity*, Cambridge, 1997.

Mitchell, L. and P.J. Rhodes (eds), *The Development of the Polis in Archaic Greece*, London, 1997.

Möller, A., *Naukratis. Trade in Archaic Greece*, Oxford, 2000.

Morris, I.M., *Burial and Ancient Society. The Rise of the Greek City-state*, Cambridge, 1987.

——, *Classical Greece. Ancient Histories and Modern Archaeologies*, Cambridge, 1995.

—— and B. Powell (eds), *A New Companion to Homer*, Leiden/Boston MA, 1997.

Munn, M., *The School of History. Athens in the Age of Socrates*, Berkeley/Los Angeles/London, 2000.

Murray, O., *Early Greece*, London, 1980.

—— and S.R.F. Price, *The Greek City from Homer to Alexander*, Oxford, 1991.

Nielsen, Th.H., *Arkadia and its poleis in the Archaic and Classical Periods*, Göttingen, 2002.

Ober, J., *Mass and Élite in Democratic Athens: Rhetoric, Ideology, and the Power of the People*, Princeton NJ, 1989.

——, *Political Dissent in Democratic Athens. Intellectual Critics of Popular Rule*, Princeton NJ/Oxford, 2002.

Osborne, R., *Greece in the Making 1200–479 BC*, London/New York, 1996.

—— and B. Cunliffe (eds), *Mediterranean Urbanization 800–600 BC*, Oxford, 2005.

Parker, R., *Miasma. Pollution and Purification in Early Greek Religion*, 2nd edn, Oxford, 1996.

Powell, A., *Athens and Sparta: Constructing Greek Political and Social History from 478 BC*, London/Portland OR, 1988.

Raaflaub, K.A., J. Ober and R.W. Wallace (eds), *Origins of Democracy in Ancient Greece*, Berkeley/Los Angeles/London, 2007.

Rhodes, P.J., *A History of the Classical Greek World, 478–323 BC*, Oxford, 2005.

——, *The Greek City-states. A Source Book*, 2nd edn, Cambridge, 2007.

Ridgway, D., *The First Western Greeks*, Cambridge, 1992.

Roberts, J.T., *Athens on Trial. The Anti-democratic Tradition in Western Thought*, Princeton NJ, 1994.

Robinson, E.W., *The First Democracies. Early Popular Government outside Athens*, Stuttgart, 1997.

—— (ed.), *Ancient Greek Democracy. Readings and Sources*, Oxford/Malden MA, 2004.

Rosenzweig, R., *Worshipping Aphrodite. Art and Cult in Classical Athens*, Ann Arbor MI, 2004.

Salmon, J.B., *Wealthy Corinth. A History of the City to 338 BC*, Oxford, 1984.

Samons II, L.J., *Empire of the Owl. Athenian Imperial Finance*, Stuttgart, 2000.

Sancisi-Weerdenburg, H. (ed.), *Peisistratos and the Tyranny. A Reappraisal of the Evidence*, Amsterdam, 2000.

Sanders, L.J., *Dionysius I of Syracuse and Greek Tyranny*, London, 1987.

Sinclair, R.K., *Democracy and Participation in Athens*, Cambridge, 1988.

Snodgrass, A.M., *Archaic Greece. The Age of Experiment*, London, 1980.

Ste. Croix, G.E.M. de, *The Origins of the Peloponnesian War*, London, 1972.

Stockton, D., *The Classical Athenian Democracy*, Oxford, 1990.

Thomas, C.G. and C. Conant, *Citadel to City State. The Transformation of Greece, 1200–700 BC*, Bloomington IN/Indianapolis IN, 1999.

Thorley, J., *Athenian Democracy*, 2nd edn, London/New York, 2004.

Walker, K.G., *Archaic Eretria. A Political and Social History from the Earliest Times to 490 BC*, London/New York, 2004.

Wallinga, H.T., *Xerxes' Greek Adventure: The Naval Perspective*, Leiden/Boston MA, 2005.

Webster, T.B.L., *Athenian Culture and Society*, London, 1973.

Wees, H. van, *Status Warriors. War, Violence and Society in Homer and History*, Amsterdam, 1992.

West, M.L., *Early Greek Philosophy and the Orient*, Oxford, 1971.

Whitby, M. (ed.), *Sparta*, Edinburgh, 2002.

Whitley, J., *Style and Society in Dark Age Greece. The Changing Face of a Pre-literate Society 1100–700 BC*, Cambridge, 1991.

THE HELLENISTIC WORLD

Allen, R.E., *The Attalid Kingdom. A Constitutional History*, Oxford, 1983.

Aperghis, G.G., *The Seleukid Royal Economy. The Finances and Financial Administration of the Seleukid Empire*, Cambridge, 2004.

Archibald, Z.H. *et al.* (eds), *Hellenistic Economies*, London/New York, 2001.

—— (ed.), *Making, Moving and Managing. The New World of Ancient Economies 323–31 BC*, Oxford, 2005.

Austin, M.M., *The Hellenistic World from Alexander to the Roman Conquest. A Selection of Ancient Sources in Translation*, 2nd edn, Cambridge, 2006.

Bagnall, R.S. and P. Derow (eds), *The Hellenistic Period. Historical Sources in Translation*, 2nd edn, Oxford, 2004.

Berthold, R.N., *Rhodes in the Hellenistic Age*, Ithaca NY/London, 1984.

Bickerman, E.J., *The Jews in the Greek Age*, Cambridge, 1988.

Bilde, P. *et al.* (eds), *Religion and Religious Practice in the Seleucid Kingdom*, Aarhus, 1990.

——, *Ethnicity in Hellenistic Egypt*, Aarhus, 1992.

——, *Centre and Periphery in the Hellenistic World*, Aarhus, 1993.

——, *Aspects of Hellenistic Kingship*, Aarhus, 1996.

Billows, R.A., *Antigonos the One-Eyed and the Creation of the Hellenistic State*, Berkeley/Los Angeles/London, 1990.

——, *Kings and Colonists. Aspects of Macedonian Imperialism*, Leiden, 1995.

Bosworth, A.B., *Conquest and Empire. The Reign of Alexander the Great*, Cambridge, 1988.

——, *Alexander and the East*, Oxford, 1996.

—— and E.J. Baynham (eds), *Alexander the Great in Fact and Fiction*, Oxford, 2000.

——, *The Legacy of Alexander. Politics, Warfare and Propaganda under the Successors*, Oxford, 2002.

Boiy, T., *Late Achaemenid and Hellenistic Babylon*, Leuven, 2004.

Bugh, G.R. (ed.), *The Cambridge Companion to the Hellenistic World*, Cambridge, 2006.

Bulloch, A.W. and E.S. Gruen (eds), *Images and Ideologies. Self-definition in the Hellenistic World*, Berkeley/Los Angeles/London, 1993.

Carney, E., *Olympias: Mother of Alexander the Great*, London/New York, 2006.

Cartledge, P. and A. Spawforth, *Hellenistic and Roman Sparta. A Tale of two Cities*, London/2nd edn, New York, 2002.

Chamoux, F., *Hellenistic Civilisation*, translated into English by M. Roussel, Oxford/MaldenMA/Berlin/Melbourne, 2003.

Chaniotis, A., *War in the Hellenistic World. A Social and Cultural History*, Oxford, Malden MA, 2005.

Clarysse, W. and D.J. Thompson, *Counting the People in Hellenistic Egypt I–II*, Cambridge, 2006.

Cohen, G.M., *The Seleucid Colonies. Studies in Founding Administration and Organization*, Wiesbaden, 1978.

Cribiore, R., *Gymnastics of the Mind. Greek Education in Hellenistic and Roman Egypt*, Princeton NJ/Oxford, 2001.

Dignas, B., *Economy of the Sacred in Hellenistic and Roman Asia Minor*, Oxford, 2002.

Downey, G., *A History of Antioch in Syria. From Seleucus to the Arab Conquest*, 2nd edn, Princeton NJ, 1974.

Ellis, W.M., *Ptolemy of Egypt*, London/New York, 1994.

Engels, D.W., *Alexander the Great and the Logistics of the Macedonian Army*, Berkeley/Los Angeles/London, 1978.

Erskine, A.E., (ed.), *A Companion to the Hellenistic World*, Oxford/Malden MA, 2005.

Fraser, P., *Ptolemaic Alexandria I–III*, Oxford, 1972–1984.

Geller, M.J., H. Maehler and A.D.E. Lewis (eds), *Legal Documents of the Hellenistic World*, London, 1995.

Goudriaan, K., *Ethnicity in Ptolemaic Egypt*, Amsterdam, 1988.

Grainger, J.D., *Seleukos Nikator. Constructing a Hellenistic Kingdom*, London/New York, 1990.

——, *The Cities of Seleukid Syria*, Oxford, 1990.

——, *Hellenistic Phoenicia*, Oxford, 1991.

——, *The Roman War of Antiochos the Great*, Leiden/Boston MA, 2002.

Green, P., *Alexander to Actium. The Historical Evolution of the Hellenistic Age*, Berkeley/Los Angeles/London, 1993.

Gruen, E.S., *The Hellenistic World and the Coming of Rome I–II*, Berkeley/Los Angeles/London, 1984.

Heckel, W., *Who is Who in the Age of Alexander the Great? Prosopography of Alexander's Empire*, Oxford, 2006.

Heckel, W., and J.C. Yardley, *Alexander the Great. Historical Texts in Translation*, Oxford/Malden MA/Carlton, Vict., 2004.

Hölbl, G., *A History of the Ptolemaic Empire*, translated into English by T. Saavedra, London/New York, 2001.

Holt, F.L., *Into the Land of Bones. Alexander the Great in Afghanistan*, Berkeley/Los Angeles/London, 2005.

Jones, A.H.M., *The Greek City from Alexander to Justinian*, 3rd edn, Oxford, 1971.

Koester, H., *History, Culture and Religion of the Hellenistic Age: Introduction to the New Testament*, 2nd edn, Berlin/New York, 1995.

Kuhrt, A. and A.N. Sherwin-White (eds), *Hellenism in the East*, London, 1987.

Kuhrt, A. and A.N. Sherwin-White, *From Samarkhand to Sardis. A New Approach to the Seleucid Empire*, Berkeley/Los Angeles/London, 1993.

Lane Fox, R., *Alexander the Great*, 5th edn, London, 1997.

Lewis, N., *Greeks in Ptolemaic Egypt*, Oxford, 1986.

Ma, J., *Antiochos III and the Cities of Western Asia Minor*, Oxford, 1999.

Manning, J.G., *Land and Power in Ptolemaic Egypt: The Structure of Tenure*, Cambridge, 2003.

Momigliano, A., *Alien Wisdom. The Limits of Hellenization*, Cambridge, 1975.

Ogden, D. (ed.), *The Hellenistic World. New Perspectives*, London, 2002.

Roisman, J. (ed.), *Brill's Companion to Alexander the Great*, Leiden/Boston, 2003.

Rostovtzeff, M.I., *The Social and Economic History of the Hellenistic World I–III*, 3rd edn, Oxford, 1986.

Shipley, G., *The World after Alexander, 323–30 BC*, London, 2000.

Sidky, H., *The Greek Kingdom of Bactria*, London, 2000.

Spek, R.J. van der, The Theatre of Babylon in Cuneiform, in: W.H. van Soldt, *et al.* (eds), *Veenhof Anniversary Volume. Studies presented to Klaas R. Veenhof on the Occasion of his Sixty-Fifth Birthday*, Leiden, 2001, 445–456.

——, Darius III, Alexander the Great and Babylonian Scholarship, in: *Achaemenid History* XIII, Leiden, 2003, 289–346.

——, Palace, Temple and Market in Seleucid Babylonia, in: V. Chankowski and F. Duyrat (eds), *Le roi et l'économie. Autonomies locales et structures royales dans l'économie de l'empire séleucide*, Topoi, Suppl. 6, Paris, 2005, 303–332.

——, How to Measure Prosperity? The Case of Hellenistic Babylonia, in: R. Descat (ed.), *Approches de l'économie hellénistique*. Entretiens d'archéologie et d'histoire 7, St-Bertrand-de-Comminges, 2005, 287–310.

——, Ethnic segregation in Hellenistic Babylon, in: W.H. van Soldt (ed.), *Ethnicity in Ancient Mesopotamia*, Leiden, 2005, 393–408.

——, The Size and Significance of the Babylonian Temples under the Successors, in: P. Briant and F. Joannès, *La transition entre l'empire achéménide et les royaumes hellénistiques*, Persika 9, Paris, 2006, 261–307.

——, Seleukiden, Seleukidenreich [Seleucids, Seleucid Empire], in: *Reallexikon der Assyriologie*, forthcoming in English.

——, *Commodity Prices from Babylon (385–61 BC)*, http://www.iisg.nl/hpw/data.html#babylon.

—— and I.L. Finkel, *Babylonian Chronicles of the Hellenistic Period*, www.livius.org > Babyl. Chronicles, forthcoming in print.

Tarn, W.W. and G.T. Griffith, *Hellenistic Civilisation*, 3rd edn, London, 1975.

Thomas, C.G., *Alexander the Great in his World*, Oxford, 2007.

Walbank, F.W., *The Hellenistic World*, 3rd edn, London, 1992.

Whitehouse, J., *Cleopatras*, London/New York, 2001.

Wolski, J., *The Seleucids. The Decline and Fall of their Empire*, KrakSeleucids.Worthington, I. (ed.), *Alexander the Great. A Reader*, London/New York, 2003.

ROME

Adkins, L. and R.A., *Dictionary of Roman Religion*, Oxford, 2001.

Aldrete, G.S., *Floods of the Tiber in Ancient Rome*, Baltimore, 2007.

Alföldy, G., *The Social History of Rome*, Baltimore MD/London, 1988.

Allen, J., *Hostages and Hostage-taking in the Roman Empire*, Cambridge, 2006.

Ando, C. and J.Rüpke (eds), *Religion and Law in Classical and Christian Rome*, Stuttgart, 2006.

Andreau, J., *Banking and Business in the Roman World*, Cambridge, 1999.

Atkins, M. and R. Osborne (eds), *Poverty in the Roman World*, Cambridge, 2006.

Aubert, J.J., *Business Managers in Ancient Rome. A Social and Economic Study of Institores, 200 BC–AD 250*, Leiden/Boston MA, 1994.

Aufstieg und Niedergang der Römischen Welt [= Rise and Decline of the Roman World], edited by H. Temporini, and W. Haase, I 1–4 (Roman Republic); II 1–37 (Principate), Berlin/New York, 1972–1998.

Balsdon, J.P.V.D., *Romans and Aliens*, London/Chapel Hill NC, 1979.

Barton, I.M. (ed.), *Roman Public Buildings*, Exeter, 1989.

Bauman, R.A., *Crime and Punishment in Ancient Rome*, London/New York, 1996.

Beard, W.M., J. North and S.R.F. Price, *Religions of Rome, vol.1, A History; vol. 2, A Sourcebook*, Cambridge, 1998.

Beard, W.M. *et al.* (eds), *Literacy in the Roman World*, Ann Arbor MI, 1991.

Bishop, M.C. and J.C.N. Coulston, *Roman Military Equipment. From the Punic Wars to the Fall of Rome*, 2nd edn, Oxford, 2006.

Boatwright, M.T., D.J. Gargola and R.J.A. Talbert, *A Brief History of the Romans*, Oxford, 2006.

Bonner, S.F., *Education in Ancient Rome*, London, 1977.

Bowersock, G.W., *Fiction as History. Nero to Julian*, Berkeley/Los Angeles/London, 1994.

Bradley, K.R., *Discovering the Roman Family. Studies in Roman Social History*, Oxford, 1991.

——, *Slavery and Society at Rome*, Cambridge, 1994.

Bremmer, J.N. and N. Horsfall (eds), *Roman Myth and Mythography*, 2nd edn, Groningen, 2005.

Bruun, Chr., *The Water Supply of Ancient Rome. A Study of Roman Imperial Administration*, Helsinki, 1991.

Buchanan, D., *Roman Sport and Entertainment*, London, 1976.

Burns, Th.S., *Rome and the Barbarians, 100 BC–AD 400*, Baltimore/London, 2003.

Carlsen, J., *The Rise and Fall of a Roman Noble Family: The Domitii Ahenobarbi 196 BC–AD 68*, Odense, 2006.

Champion, C.B. (ed.), *Roman Imperialism: Readings and Sources*, Oxford, 2004.

Clarke, J.R., *Art in the Lives of Ordinary Romans. Visual Representation and Non-elite Viewers in Italy, 100 BC–AD 315*, Berkeley/Los Angeles/London, 2003.

Cokayne, K., *Experiencing Old Age in Ancient Rome*, London/New York, 2003.

Cooley, A.E. and M.G.L. Cooley, *Pompeii. A Sourcebook*, London/New York, 2004.

Cornell, T.J. and K. Lomas (eds), *Urban Society in Roman Italy*, London, 1995.

Dalby, A., *Empire of Pleasures. Luxury and Indulgence in the Roman World*, London/New York, 2000.

D'Ambia, E., *Roman Women*, Cambridge, 2007.

D'Arms, J.H., *Commerce and Social Standing in Ancient Rome*, Cambridge MA, 1981.

Davies, R.W., D. Breeze and V.A. Maxfield (eds), *Service in the Roman Army*, Edinburgh, 1989.

Dench, E., *Romulus' Asylum. Roman Identities from the Age of Alexander to the Age of Hadrian*, Oxford, 2005.

Dixon, S., *The Roman Mother*, London, 1990.

Drinkwater, J.F., *Roman Gaul. The Three Provinces, 58 BC–AD260*, London, 1983.

Dunbabin, K.M.D., *The Roman Banquet. Images of Conviviality*, Cambridge, 2003.

Duncan-Jones, R., *Structure and Scale in the Roman Economy*, Cambridge, 1990.

Dupont, F., *Daily Life in Ancient Rome*, Oxford, 1992.

Dyson, S.L., *Community and Society in Roman Italy*, Baltimore, 1992.

Edwards, C. and G. Woolf (eds), *Rome the Cosmopolis*, Cambridge, 2003.

Eilers, C., *Roman Patrons of Greek Cities*, Oxford, 2002.

Elsner, J., *Roman Eyes. Visuality and Subjectivity in Art and Text*, Princeton NJ/Oxford, 2007.

Erdkamp, P.P.M. (ed.), *The Roman Army and the Economy*, Amsterdam 2002.

——, *The Grain Market in the Roman Empire. A Social, Political and Economic Study*, Cambridge, 2005.

——, (ed.), *The Blackwell Companion to the Roman Army*, Oxford/Malden MA, 2007.

Ferris, I.M., *Enemies of Rome. Barbarians through Roman Eyes*, Phoenix Mill, 2000.

Flower, H.I., *The Art of Forgetting. Disgrace and Oblivion in Roman Political Culture*, Chapel Hill NC, 2006.

Fraschetti, A. (ed.), *Roman Women*, translated into English by L. Lappin, Chicago/London, 2001.

Futrell, A., *Blood in the Arena. The Spectacle of Roman Power*, Austin TX, 2000.

Gardner, J.F., *Women in Roman Law and Society*, 2nd edn, London/New York, 1990.

——, *Being a Roman Citizen*, London/New York, 1993.

Garnsey, P.D.A. and R.P. Saller, *The Roman Empire. Economy, Society and Culture*, London, 1987.

George, M. (ed.), *The Roman Family in the Empire. Rome, Italy and Beyond*, Oxford, 2005.

Gold, B.K. and J.F. Donahue, *Roman Dining*, Baltimore, 2005.

Goldsworthy, A.K., *The Roman Army at War, 100 BC–AD 200*, Oxford, 1996.

Goodman, P.J., *The Roman City and its Periphery. From Rome to Gaul*, London/New York, 2007.

Gowing, A.M., *Empire and Memory. The Representation of the Roman Republic in Imperial Culture*, Cambridge, 2005.

Griffin, J., *Latin Poets and Roman Life*, 2nd edn, Bristol, 1994.

Habinek, Th.N., *The Politics of Latin Literature. Writing, Identity and Empire in Ancient Rome*, Princeton NJ, 1998.

——, *The World of Roman Song from Ritualized Speech to Social Order*, Baltimore/London, 2005.

Harl, K., *Coinage in the Roman Economy*, Baltimore/London, 1996.

Hemelrijk, E.A., Matrona docta. *Educated Women in the Roman Elite from Cornelia to Julia Domna*, 2nd edn, London/New York, 2004.

Jackson, R., *Doctors and Diseases in the Roman Empire*, London, 1988.

Jones, A.H.M., *The Criminal Courts of the Roman Republic and Principate*, Oxford, 1972.

Jones, P. and K. Sidwell, *The World of Rome. An Introduction to Roman Culture*, Cambridge, 1997.

Jongman, W., *The Economy and Society of Pompeii*, Amsterdam, 1988.

Keay, S.J., *Roman Spain*, London, 1988.

Kehoe, D.P., *Investment, Profit and Tenancy. The Jurists and the Roman Agrarian Economy*, Ann Arbor MI, 1997.

Keppie, L., *The Making of the Roman Army. From Republic to Empire*, 2nd edn, London/New York, 1998.

——, *Legions and Veterans. Roman Army Papers 1971–2000*, Stuttgart, 2000.

——, *Understanding Roman Inscriptions*, London/New York, 2001.

King, C.E. and D.G. Wigg (eds), *Coin Finds and Coin Use in the Roman World*, Berlin, 1996.

Kleijn, G. de, *The Water Supply of Ancient Rome. City Area, Water, and Population*, Amsterdam, 2001.

Kyle, D.G., *Spectacles of Death in Ancient Rome*, 2nd edn, London/New York, 2001.

Lendon, J.E., *Empire of Honour. The Art of Government in the Roman World*, Oxford, 1997.

Lennox Manton, E., *Roman North Africa*, London, 1988.

Ligt, L. de, *Fairs and Markets in the Roman Empire*, Cambridge, 1993.

Lomas, K. and T. Cornell (eds), *Bread and Circuses. Euergetism and Municipal Patronage in Roman Italy*, London/New York, 2003.

Lott, J.B., *The Neighbourhoods of Augustan Rome*, Cambridge, 2004.

MacKay, Chr.S., *Ancient Rome. A Political and Military History*, Cambridge, 2004.

Morley, N., *Metropolis and Hinterland. The City of Rome and the Italian Economy, 200 BC–AD 200*, Cambridge, 1996.

Mouritsen, H., *Elections, Magistrates and Municipal Elite: Studies in Pompeian Epigraphy*, Rome, 1988.

Neeve, P.W. de, *Colonus. Private Farm-tenancy in Roman Italy during the Republic and the Early Principate*, Amsterdam, 1984.

Nippel, W., *Public Order in Ancient Rome*, Cambridge, 1995.

North, J., *Roman Religion*, Oxford, 2000.

Noy, D., *Foreigners at Rome: Citizens and Strangers*, London/New York, 2000.

Ogilvie, R.M., *The Romans and Their Gods*, 2nd edn, London, 1986.

Parkin, T.G., *Demography and Roman Society*, Baltimore MD, 1992.

——, *Old Age in the Roman World. A Cultural and Social History*, Baltimore MD/London, 2003.

Proceedings of the workshops of the international network Impact of Empire (Roman Empire, 200 BC–AD 476): vol. 1 edited by L. de Blois, *Administration, Prosopography and Appointment Policies in the Roman Empire*, Amsterdam, 2001;

——, vol. 2 edited by L. de Blois and J. Rich, *The Transformation of Economic Life under the Roman Empire*, Amsterdam, 2002;

——, vol. 3 edited by L. de Blois, P.P.M. Erdkamp, O.J. Hekster, G. de Kleijn and S.T.A.M. Mols, *The Representation and Perception of Roman Imperial Power*, Amsterdam, 2003;

——, vol. 4 edited by L. de Ligt, E.A. Hemelrijk and H.W. Singor, *Roman Rule and Civic Life: Local and Regional Perspectives*, Amsterdam, 2004;

——, vol. 5 edited by L. de Blois, P. Funke and J. Hahn, *The Impact of Imperial Rome on Religions, Ritual and Religious Life in the Roman Empire*, Leiden/Boston, 2006;

——, vol. 6 edited by L. de Blois and E. Lo Cascio, *The Impact of the Roman Army (200 BC–AD 476): Economic, Social, Political, Religious and Cultural Aspects*, Leiden/Boston, 2007;

——, vol. 7 edited by O.J. Hekster, G. de Kleijn, and D. Slootjes, *Crises and the Roman Empire*, Leiden/Boston, 2007.

Rawson, B., *Family in Ancient Rome*, London, 1992.

——, *Marriage, Divorce and Children in Ancient Rome*, Oxford/New York/Canberra, 1991.

Rich, J. and G. Shipley, *War and Society in the Roman World*, London, 1995.

Richardson, J.S., *The Roman Provincial Administration 227 BC–AD 117*, Basingstoke, 1976.

——, *Hispaniae. Spain and the Development of Roman Imperialism, 218–82 BC*, Cambridge, 1986.

——, *The Romans in Spain*, Oxford, 1996.

Rickman, G., *The Corn-supply of Ancient Rome*, Oxford, 1980.

Robinson, O.F., *Ancient Rome. City Planning and Administration*, London/New York, 1992.

——, *The Criminal Law of Ancient Rome*, London/Baltimore, 1995.

Rostovtzeff, M.I., *Social and Economic History of the Roman Empire*, 2nd edn, Oxford, 1957.

Roth, J.P., *The Logistics of the Roman Army at War (264 BC–AD 235)*, Leiden/Boston, 1999.

Rüpke, J. (ed.), *A Companion to Roman Religion*, Oxford/Malden MA, 2007.

Saller, R.P., *Patriarchy, Property and Death in the Roman Family*, Cambridge, 1994.

Scheidel, W. (ed.), *Debating Roman Demography*, Leiden/Boston, 2001.

Sirks, A.J.B., *Food for Rome. The Legal Structure of the Transportation and Processing of Supplies for the Imperial Distributions in Rome and Constantinople*, Amsterdam, 1991.

Smith, C.J., *The Roman Clan. The* gens *from Ancient Ideology to Modern Anthropology*, Cambridge, 2006.

Spurr, M.S., *Arable Cultivation in Roman Italy*, c. *200 BC–AD 100*, London, 1986.

Stambaugh, J.E., *The Ancient Roman City*, Baltimore MD, 1988.

Toner, J.P., *Leisure and Ancient Rome*, Cambridge, 1995.

Treggiari, S., *Roman Social History*, London/New York, 2002.

Versnel, H.S., *Triumphus. An Inquiry into the Origin, Development and Meaning of the Roman Triumph*, Leiden, 1970.

Veyne, P., *From Pagan Rome to Byzantium. A History of Private Life*, Cambridge MA, 1987.

Wacher, J., *The Roman World*, London/New York, 1987.

Wallace-Hadrill, A., *To Live as a Roman. Houses and Society in Pompeii and Herculaneum*, Princeton NJ, 1994.

Wardman, A., *Rome's Debt to Greece*, London, 1976.

Warrior, V.M., *Roman Religion*, Cambridge, 2006.

White, K.D., *Roman Farming*, London, 1970.

Wildfang, R.L., *Rome's Vestal Virgins*, London/New York, 2006.

Wiseman, T.P., *The Myths of Rome*, Exeter, 2004.

Woolf, G., *Becoming Roman. The Origins of Provincial Civilization in Gaul*, Cambridge, 1998.

—— (ed.), *Cambridge Illustrated History of the Roman World*, Cambridge, 2003.

Woolliscroft, D.J., *Roman Military Signalling*, Stroud, 2001.

ETRUSCANS, EARLY ROME AND THE ROMAN REPUBLIC

Alföldi, A., *Early Rome and the Latins*, Ann Arbor MI, 1965.

Badian, E., *Roman Imperialism in the Late Republic*, Ithaca NY/London, 1971.

Beard, W.M. and M.H. Crawford, *Rome in the Late Republic: Problems and Interpretations*, 2nd edn, London, 1999.

Blois, L. de, *The Roman Army and Politics in the First Century BC*, Amsterdam, 1987.

Bradley, G., *Ancient Umbria. State, Culture and Identity in Central Italy from the Iron Age to the Augustan Era*, Oxford, 2000.

Bradley, K.R., *Slavery and Rebellion in the Roman World 140–70 BC*, 2nd edn, Bloomington IN, 1998.

Brennan, T.C., *The Praetorship in the Roman Republic* I–II, Oxford, 2000.

Brunt, P.A., *Social Conflicts in the Roman Republic*, 2nd edn, London, 1978.

——, *Italian Manpower*, 2nd edn, Oxford, 1987.

——, *The Fall of the Roman Republic*, Oxford, 1988.

Canfora, L., *Julius Caesar. The People's Dictator*, translated into English by M. Hill and K. Windle, Edinburgh, 2007.

Cornell, T.J., *The Beginnings of Rome. Italy and Rome from the Bronze Age to the Punic Wars, c. 1000–264 BC*, London, 1995.

Crawford, M.H., *Coinage and Money under the Roman Republic. Italy and the Mediterranean Economy*, London, 1985.

Eckstein, A.M., *Mediterranean Anarchy. Interstate War and the Rise of Rome*, Berkeley/Los Angeles/London, 2006.

Erdkamp, P.P.M., *Hunger and the Sword. Warfare and Food Supply in Roman Republican Wars (264–30 BC)*, Amsterdam, 1998.

Evans, R.J., *Caius Marius. A Political Biography*, Pretoria, 1994.

——, *Questioning Reputations. Essays on Nine Roman Republican Politicians*, Pretoria, 2003.

Flower, H.I. (ed.), *The Cambridge Companion to the Roman Republic*, Cambridge, 2004.

Forsythe, G., *A Critical History of Early Rome. From Prehistory to the First Punic War*, Berkeley/Los Angeles/London, 2005.

Gabba, E., *Republican Rome. The Army and the Allies*, Oxford, 1976.

Gruen, E.S., *The Last Generation of the Roman Republic*, 2nd edn, Berkeley/Los Angeles/London, 1995.

Habicht, Chr., *Cicero the Politician*, Baltimore, 1990.

Harris, W.V., *War and Imperialism in Republican Rome 327–70 BC*, 2nd edn, Oxford, 1985.

Haynes, S., *Etruscan Civilization. A Cultural History*, London, 2000.

Hopkins, K., *Conquerors and Slaves: Sociological Studies in Roman History*, 2nd edn, Cambridge, 1981.

Hoyos, D., *Hannibal's Dynasty. Power and Politics in the Western Mediterranean, 247–183 BC*, London/New York, 2005.

Huzar, E.G., *Mark Antony*, London, 1978.

Kamm, A., *Julius Caesar: A Life*, London/New York, 2006.

Keaveney, A., *Sulla, the Last Republican*, London, 1986.

——, *Rome and the Unification of Italy*, London, 1987.

——, *The Army in the Roman Revolution*, London/New York, 2007.

Kelly, G.P., *A History of Exile in the Roman Republic*, Cambridge, 2006.

Kleiner, D.E.E., *Cleopatra and Rome*, London/Cambridge MA, 2005.

Lazenby, J.F., *Hannibal's War. A Military History of the Second Punic War*, London, 1978.

——, *The First Punic War: A Military History*, London, 1996.

Lintott, A.W., *The Constitution of the Roman Republic*, Oxford, 1999.

Lomas, K., *Rome and the Western Greeks. Conquest and Acculturation in Southern Italy*, London, 1993.

MacNamara, E., *The Etruscans*, Cambridge MA/London, 1991.

Millar, F.G.B., *The Crowd in Rome in the Late Republic*, 2nd edn, Ann Arbor MI, 2002.

Mitchell, Th.N., *Cicero. The Senior Statesman*, New Haven/London, 1991.

Mouritsen, H., *Plebs and Politics in the Late Roman Republic*, Cambridge, 2001.

Neeve, P.W. de, *Peasants in Peril. Location and Economy in Italy in the Second Century BC*, Amsterdam, 1984.

Nicolet, C., *The World of the Citizen in Republican Rome*, Berkeley/Los Angeles/London, 1980.

Ogilvie, R.M., *Early Rome and the Etruscans*, 3rd edn, London, 1983.

Osgood, J., *Caesar's Legacy. Civil War and the Emergence of the Roman Empire*, Cambridge, 2006.

Pallottino, M., *The Etruscans*, Harmondsworth, 1976.

Raaflaub, K.A., *Social Struggles in Archaic Rome: New Perspectives on the Conflict of the Orders*, 2nd edn, Oxford, 2005.

Ridgway, D., *The World of the Early Etruscans*, Göteborg, 2002.

Rosenstein, N., *Rome at War. Farms, Families and Death in the Middle Republic*, Chapel Hill NC/London, 2004.

Rosenstein, N. and R. Morstein-Marx (eds), *A Companion to the Roman Republic*, Oxford, 2006.

Scullard, H.H., *From the Gracchi to Nero. A History of Rome from 133 BC to AD 68*, 3rd edn, London, 1970.

——, *Festivals and Ceremonies of the Roman Republic*, London, 1981.

——, *A History of the Roman World 753–146 BC*, 4th edn, London/New York, 1991.

Shotter, D., *The Fall of the Roman Republic*, 2nd edn, London/New York, 2005.

Stockton, D., *The Gracchi*, Oxford, 1979.

Syme, R., *The Roman Revolution*, Oxford, 1967, revised edition.

Tatum, M.J., *The Patrician Tribune: Publius Clodius Pulcher*, Chapel Hill NC/London, 1999.

Taylor, L.R., *Roman Voting Assemblies: From the Hannibalic War to the Dictatorship of Caesar*, 2nd edn, Ann Arbor MI, 1990.

Thomson de Grummond, N., *Etruscan Myth, Sacred History, and Legend*, Philadelphia, 2006.

Tingay, G., *Julius Caesar*, Cambridge, 1991.

Vanderbroeck, P.J.J., *Popular Leadership and Collective Behavior in the Late Roman Republic, c. 80–50 BC*, Amsterdam, 1987.

Verboven, K., *The Economy of Friends. Economic Aspects of* Amicitia *and Patronage in the Late Republic*, Brussels, 2002.

Wiedemann, Th.E.J., *Cicero and the End of the Roman Republic*, Bristol, 1994.

Williams, J.H.C., *Beyond the Rubicon. Romans and Gauls in Republican Italy*, Oxford, 2001.

Wiseman, T.P., *New Men in the Roman Senate, 139 BC–AD 14*, Oxford, 1971.

Wood, N., *Cicero's Social and Political Thought*, Berkeley/Los Angeles/London, 1988.

Yakobson, A., *Elections and Electioneering in Rome. A Study in the Political System of the Late Republic*, Stuttgart, 1999.

Yarrow, L.M., *Historiography at the End of the Republic. Provincial Perspectives on Roman Rule*, Oxford, 2006.

Yavetz, Z., *Julius Caesar and his Public Image*, Ithaca NY/London, 1983.

IMPERIAL ROME

Alföldy, G., B. Dobson and W. Eck, *Kaiser, Heer und Gesellschaft in der Römischen Kaiserzeit*, Stuttgart 2000 (a majority of the contributions in English).

Anderson, G., *Sage, Saint and Sophist. Holy Men and their Associates in the Early Roman Empire*, London/New York, 1994.

Ando, C., *Imperial Ideology and Provincial Loyalty in the Roman Empire*, Berkeley/Los Angeles/London, 2000.

Baharal, D., *Victory of Propaganda: The Dynastic Aspect of the Imperial Propaganda of the Severi. The Literary and Archaeological Evidence, AD 193–235*, Oxford, 1996.

Ball, W., *Rome in the East. The Transformation of an Empire*, London, 2000.

Banaji, J., *Agrarian Change in Late Antiquity. Gold, Labour and Aristocratic Dominance*, Oxford, 2001.

Barnes, T.D., *The New Empire of Diocletian and Constantine*, London, 1982.

Barrett, A.A., *Caligula. The Corruption of Power*, London, 1989.

Bennett, J., *Trajan, Optimus Princeps*, 2nd edn, London/New York, 2001.

Birley, A.R., *Septimius Severus. The African Emperor*, 2nd edn, London, 1988.

——, *Marcus Aurelius*, 2nd edn, London, 1991.

——, *Hadrian. The Restless Emperor*, London/New York, 1997.

——, *The Roman Government of Britain*, Oxford, 2005.

Blois, L. de, *The Policy of the Emperor Gallienus*, Leiden, 1976.

——, The Onset of Crisis in the First Half of the Third Century *AD*, in: K.-P. Johne *et al.* (eds). *Deleto paene imperio Romano. Transformationsprozesse des Römischen Reiches im 3. Jahrhundert und ihre Rezeption in der Neuzeit*, Stuttgart 2006, 25–36.

——, J.A.E. Bons, A.H.M. Kessels and D.M. Schenkeveld (eds), *The Statesman in Plutarch's Works, Volume I (Plutarch's Statesman and his Aftermath: Political, Philosophical and Literary Aspects); Volume II (The Statesman in Plutarch's Greek and Roman Lives)*, Leiden/Boston, 2004–2005.

Boatwright, M.T., *Hadrian and the Cities of the Roman Empire*, Princeton NJ, 2000.

Bowersock, G.W., *Greek Sophists in the Roman Empire*, Oxford, 1969.

——, *Julian the Apostate*, London/Cambridge MA, 1978.

——, *Hellenism in Late Antiquity*, Cambridge/Ann Arbor MI, 1990.

——, *Fiction as History. Nero to Julian*, Berkeley/Los Angeles/London, 1994.

——, *Martyrdom and Rome*, Cambridge, 1995.

—— and P. Brown, *Late Antiquity. A Guide to the Postclassical World*, Cambridge MA, 1999.

Braund, D.C., *Augustus to Nero: A Sourcebook on Roman History, 31 BC–AD 68*, London, 1985.

——, *Ruling Roman Britain. Kings, Queens, Governors and Emperors from Julius Caesar to Agricola*, London/New York, 1996.

Brown, P., *The World of Late Antiquity*, London, 1971.

——, *Society and the Holy in Late Antiquity*, London, 1982.

——, *The Body and Society. Men, Women and Sexual Renunciation in Early Christianity*, New York, 1988/London, 1990.

Burns, J., *Great Women of Imperial Rome. Mothers and Wives of the Caesars*, London/New York, 2007.

Burrell, B., *Neokoroi. Greek Cities and Roman Emperors*, Leiden/Boston, 2004.

Cameron, A(lan), *Bread and Circuses. The Roman Emperor and his People*, London, 1973.

Cameron, A(veril), *The Mediterranean World in Late Antiquity*, London/New York, 1993.

Campbell, J.B., *The Emperor and the Roman Army 31 BC–AD 235*, Oxford, 1984.

——, *The Roman Army, 31 BC–AD 337: A Sourcebook*, London/New York, 1996.

Caner, D., *Wandering, Begging Monks. Spiritual Authority and the Promotion of Monasticism n Late Antiquity*, Berkeley/Los Angeles/London, 2002.

Carlsen, J., P. Oersted and J. Skydsgaard (eds), *Landuse in the Roman Empire*, Rome, 1994.

Carson, R.A.G., *Coins of the Roman Empire*, London/New York, 1989.

Chadwick, H., *The Early Church*, Harmondsworth, 1993 (revised edition).

Champlin, E., *Nero*, London/Cambridge MA, 2003.

Christie, N. and S.T. Loseby (eds), *Towns in Transition. Urban Evolution in Late Antiquity and the Early Middle Ages*, Aldershot, 1996.

Clark, G., *Christianity and Roman Society*, Cambridge, 2004.

Curran, J.R., *Pagan City and Christian Capital. Rome in the Fourth Century*, Oxford, 2000.

Donfried, K.P. and P. Richardson, *Judaism and Christianity in First-century Rome*, Grand Rapids MI/Cambridge, 1998.

Drijvers, J.W. and J.W. Watt (eds), *Portraits of Spiritual Authority. Religious Power in Early Christianity, Byzantium and the Christian Orient*, Leiden/Boston MA, 1999.

Drinkwater, J.F., *The Gallic Empire: Separatism and Continuity in the North-western Provinces of the Roman Empire AD 260–274*, Stuttgart, 1987.

——, *Fifth Century Gaul: A Crisis of Identity?*, Cambridge, 1994.

Duncan-Jones, R., *Money and Government in the Roman Empire*, Cambridge, 1994.

Eck, W., *The Age of Augustus*, translated into English by D.L. Schneider, Oxford, 2003.

Edwards, M. (ed.), *Constantine and Christendom. Translated Texts for Historians* 39, Liverpool, 2003.

Elsner, J., *Reflections of Nero. Culture, History and Representation*, Chapel Hill NC, 1994.

——, *Imperial Rome and Christian Triumph. The Art of the Roman Empire AD 100–450*, Oxford, 1998.

Elton, H., *Warfare in Roman Europe AD 350–425*, Oxford, 1996.

——, *Frontiers of the Roman Empire*, London, 1996.

Errington, R.M., *Roman Imperial Policy from Julian to Theodosius*, Chapel Hill NC, 2006.

Esmonde Cleary, A.S., *The Ending of Roman Britain*, 2nd edn, London/New York, 2000.

Evans, J.A.S., *The Age of Justinian. The Circumstances of Imperial Power*, London, 1996.

Fantham, E., *Julia Augusti. The Emperor's Daughter*, London/New York, 2006.

Fishwick, D., *The Imperial Cult in the Latin West*, Leiden/Boston, 2002–2005.

Flinterman, J.J., *Power, Paideia and Pythagoreanism. Greek Identity, Conceptions of the Relationship between Philosophers and Monarchs and Political Ideas in Philostratus' Life of Apollonius*, Amsterdam, 1995.

Frakes, R.M. and E. de Palma Digeser (eds), *Religious Identity in Late Antiquity*, Toronto, 2006.

Franklin, J.L., Pompeiis difficile est. *Studies in the Political Life of Imperial Pompeii*, Ann Arbor MI, 2001.

Frend, W.H.C., *Martyrdom and Persecution in the Early Church*, Oxford/Garden City NY, 1965.

——, *The Rise of Christianity. The Early Christians in the First Six Centuries*, 2nd edn, London, 1986.

——, *Orthodoxy, Paganism and Dissent in the Early Christian Centuries*, Aldershot, 2002.

Galinski, K., *The Cambridge Companion to the Age of Augustus*, Cambridge, 2005.

Gardner, I. and S.N.C. Lieu, *Manichaean Texts from the Roman Empire*, Cambridge, 2004.

Ginsburg, J., *Representing Agrippina. Constructions of Female Power in the Early Roman Empire*, Oxford, 2006.

Gradel, I., *Emperor Worship and Roman Religion*, Oxford, 2002.

Grainger, J.D., *Nerva and the Roman Succession Crisis of AD 96–99*, London/New York, 2003.

Grant, M., *The Antonines. The Roman Empire in Transition*, London/New York, 1994.

Gregory, T.E., *A History of Byzantium*, Oxford/Malden MA, 2005.

Griffin, M.T., *Nero. The End of a Dynasty*, 2nd edn, London, 2001.

Grünewald, Th., *Bandits in the Roman Empire. Myth and Reality*, translated into English by J.F. Drinkwater, London/New York, 2004.

Haarer, F.K. and I. Anastasius, *Politics and Empire in the Late Roman World*, Cambridge, 2006.

Hannestad, N., *Roman Art and Imperial Policy*, 2nd edn, Aarhus, 1988.

Heather, P. and P.S. Barnwell, *Emperors, Prefects and Kings. The Roman West, 395–565*, London, 1992.

Heather, P., *The Fall of the Roman Empire*, London, 2006.

Hedrick, Ch.W. Jr., *History and Silence. Purge and Rehabilitation of Memory in Late Antiquity*, Austin TX, 2000.

Hekster, O.J., *Commodus. An Emperor at the Crossroads*, Amsterdam, 2002.

——, *Rome and her Empire, 193–284 AD*, Edinburgh, 2008.

Jones, A.H.M., *The Later Roman Empire, 284–602. A Social, Economic and Administrative Survey I–II*, Oxford, 1964.

——, *The Decline of the Ancient World*, 2nd edn, London/New York, 1975.

——, *Augustus*, 2nd edn, London, 1977.

Jones, B.W., *The Emperor Titus*, London, 1984.

Jones, C.P., *Plutarch and Rome*, Oxford, 1971.

——, *Culture and Society in Lucian*, Cambridge MA, 1986.

Jones Hall, L., *Roman Berytus. Beirut in Late Antiquity*, London/New York, 2004.

Kahlos, M., *Debate and Dialogue. Christian and Pagan Cultures c. 360–430*, Aldershot, 2007.

Kelly, Chr., *Ruling the Later Roman Empire*, London/Cambridge MA, 2004.

King, A. and M. Henig, *The Roman West in the Third Century*, Oxford, 1981.

Lane Fox, R., *Pagans and Christians in the Mediterranean World from the Second Century AD to the Conversion of Constantine*, Harmondsworth, 1986.

Laurence, R. and J. Berry, *Cultural Identity in the Roman Empire*, 2nd edn, London/New York, 2001.

——, *Pagans and Christians in Late Antiquity. A Sourcebook*, London/New York, 2000.

Lee, A.D., *War in Late Antiquity. A Social History*, Oxford/Malden MA, 2007.

Lenski, N. (ed.), *The Cambridge Companion to the Age of Constantine*, Cambridge, 2006.

Levene, D.P. and D.S. Nelis (eds), *Clio and the Poets. Augustan Poetry and the Traditions of Ancient Historiography*, Leiden/Boston MA, 2002.

Levick, B., *Claudius*, London, 1990.

——, *Vespasian*, London/New York, 1999.

——, *The Government of the Roman Empire. A Sourcebook*, 2nd edn, London/New York, 2000.

Lewit, T., *Agricultural Production in the Roman Economy AD 200–400*, Oxford, 1991.

——, *Villas, Farms and the Late Roman Rural Economy (third to fifth centuries AD)*, Oxford, 2004.

Liebeschuetz, J.H.G.W., *From Diocletian to the Arab Conquest: Change in the Late Roman Empire*, Aldershot, 1990.

——, *Decline and Fall of the Roman City*, Oxford, 2001.

——, *Decline and Change in Late Antiquity. Religion, Barbarians and their Historiography*, Aldershot/Burlington VT, 2006.

Lintott, A.W., *Imperium Romanum. Politics and Administration*, London/New York, 1993.

Maas, M. (ed.), *The Cambridge Companion to the Age of Justinian*, Cambridge, 2005.

MacMullen, R., *Enemies of the Roman Order. Treason, Unrest and Alienation in the Empire*, Cambridge MA, 1966.

——, *Soldier and Civilian in the Later Roman Empire*, Cambridge MA, 1967.

——, *Roman Social Relations, 50 BC to AD 284*, New Haven CT, 1974.

——, *Roman Government's Response to Crisis, AD 235–337*, New Haven CT/London, 1976.

——, *Paganism in the Roman Empire*, New Haven CT, 1981.

——, *Christianizing the Roman Empire AD 100–400*, New Haven CT, 1984.

——, *Constantine*, London, 1987.

——, *Changes in the Roman Empire. Essays in the Ordinary*, Princeton NJ, 1990.

——, *Paganism and Christianity, 100–425 CE: A Sourcebook*, Minneapolis MN, 1992.

——, *Romanization in the time of Augustus*, New Haven CT/London, 2000.

Malitz, J., *Nero*, translated into English by A. Brown, Oxford, 2005.

Mango, C. (ed.), *The Oxford History of Byzantium*, Oxford, 2002.

Meeks, W.A., *The First Urban Christians. The Social World of the Apostle Paul*, New Haven, 1983.

——, *The Origins of Christian Morality. The First Two Centuries*, New Haven CT, 1993.

Meijer, F.J., *Emperors Don't Die in Bed*, translated into English by S.J. Leinbach, London/New York, 2004.

Millar, F.G.B., *The Emperor in the Roman World (31 BC–AD 337)*, 2nd edn, Oxford, 1992.

——, *Rome, the Greek World and the East I–III*, Chapel Hill NC, 2002–2006.

——, *A Greek Roman Empire: Power and Belief under Theodosius II (408–450)*, Berkeley/Los Angeles/London, 2006.

—— and E. Segal, *Caesar Augustus. Seven Aspects*, Oxford, 1984.

Mitchell, S., *Anatolia: Land, Men and Gods in Asia Minor I (The Celts and the Impact of Roman Rule); II (The Rise of the Church)*, Oxford, 1993–1995.

——, *A History of the Later Roman Empire, AD 284–641*, Oxford/Malden MA, 2007.

Murison, Ch.L., *Galba, Otho and Vitellius. Careers and Controversies*, Hildesheim/New York, 1993.

Nicasie, M.J., *Twilight of Empire. The Roman Army from the Reign of Diocletian until the Battle of Adrianople*, Amsterdam, 1998.

Nijf, O.M. van, *The Civic World of Professional Associations in the Roman East*, Amsterdam, 1997.

Odahl, Ch.M., *Constantine and the Christian Empire*, 2nd edn, London/New York, 2004.

Patterson, J.R., *Landscapes and Cities. Rural Settlement and Civic Transformation in Early Imperial Italy*, Oxford, 2006.

Peachin, M., *Iudex vice Caesaris. Deputy Emperors and the Administration of Justice during the Principate*, Stuttgart, 1996.

Phang, S.E., *The Marriage of Roman Soldiers (13 BC–AD 235). Law and Family in the Imperial Army*, Leiden/Boston, 2001.

Pohlsander, H.A., *The Emperor Constantine*, London/New York, 2004.

Potter, D.S., *The Roman Empire at Bay, AD 180–395*, London/New York, 2004.

——, *A Companion to the Roman Empire*, Oxford, 2006.

Price, S.R.F., *Rituals and Power. The Roman Imperial Cult in Asia Minor*, Cambridge, 1986.

Raaflaub, K. and M. Toher, *Between Republic and Empire. Interpretations of Augustus and his Principate*, 2nd edn, Berkeley, 1993.

Ramage, E.S., *The Nature and Purpose of Augustus'* Res Gestae, Stuttgart, 1987.

Rapp, C., *Holy Bishops in Late Antiquity. The Nature of Christian Leadership in an Age of Transition*, Berkeley/Los Angeles/London, 2005.

Rich, J. (ed.), *The City in Late Antiquity*, 2nd edn, London/New York, 1996.

Ridley, R., *The Emperor's Retrospect. Augustus'* Res Gestae *in Epigraphy, Historiography and Commentary*, Leuven/Dudley MA, 2003.

Rives, J.B., *Religion in the Roman Empire*, Oxford, 2007.

Rohrbacher, D., *The Historians of Late Antiquity*, London/New York, 2002.

Roller, M.B., *Constructing Autocracy. Aristocrats and Emperors in Julio-Claudian Rome*, Princeton NJ/Oxford, 2001.

Rothaus, R.M., *Corinth, the First City of Greece. An Urban History of Late Antique Cult and Religion*, Leiden/Boston MA, 2000.

Rowe, G., *Princes and Political Cultures. The New Tiberian Senatorial Decrees*, Ann Arbor MI, 2002.

Roymans, N., *From the Sword to the Plough. Three Studies on the Earliest Romanization of Northern Gaul*, Amsterdam, 1996.

Russell, D.A., *Antonine Literature*, Oxford, 1990.

Saller, R.P., *Personal Patronage under the Early Empire*, Cambridge, 1982.

Salway, P., *A History of Roman Britain*, 2nd edn, Oxford, 1997.

Sarris, P., *Economy and Society in the Age of Justinian*, Cambridge, 2006.

Scheidel, W., *Measuring Sex, Age and Death in the Roman Empire. Explorations in Ancient Demography*, Ann Arbor MI, 1996.

Seager, R., *Tiberius*, 2nd edn, Oxford, 2005.

Selinger, R., *The Mid-third Century Persecutions of Decius and Valerian*, 3rd edn, Frankfurt am Main/New York/Oxford, 2004.

Shotter, D., *Tiberius Caesar*, 2nd edn, London/New York, 2004.

——, *Roman Britain*, 2nd edn, London/New York, 2004.

——, *Nero*, 2nd edn, London/New York, 2005.

——, *Augustus Caesar*, 2nd edn, London/New York, 2005.

Slootjes, D., *The Governor and his Subjects in the Later Roman Empire*, Leiden/Boston MA, 2006.

Sorensen, E., *Possession and Exorcism in the New Testament and Early Christianity*, Tübingen, 2002.

Swain, S.R., *Hellenism and Empire. Language, Classicism and Power in the Greek World AD 50–250*, Oxford, 1996.

—— and M. Edwards (eds), *Approaching Late Antiquity. The Transformation from Early to Late Empire*, Oxford, 2004.

Starr, Ch.G., *The Roman Empire 27 BC–AD 476. A Study in Survival*, Oxford, 1982.

——, *The Roman Imperial Navy 31 BC–AD 324*, 3rd edn, Chicago IL, 1993.

Tacoma, L.E., *Fragile Hierarchies. The Urban Elites of Third Century Roman Egypt*, Leiden/Boston MA, 2006.

Talbert, R.J.A., *The Senate of Imperial Rome*, Princeton NJ, 1984.

Tilburg, C. van, *Traffic and Congestion in the Roman Empire*, London/New York, 2007.

Tougher, S., *Julian the Apostate*, Edinburgh, 2007.

Vout, C., *Power and Eroticism in Imperial Rome*, Cambridge, 2007.

Watson, A., *Aurelian and the Third Century*, London/New York, 1999.

Webster, G. and H. Elton, *The Roman Imperial Army of the First and Second Centuries AD*, 3rd edn, Norman, 1998.

Wellesley, K., *The Year of the Four Emperors*, 3rd edn, London/New York, 2000.

Whittaker, C.R., *Rome and its Frontiers: The Dynamics of Empire*, London/New York, 2004.

Wiedemann, Th.E.J., *Adults and Children in the Roman Empire*, London/New York/New Haven, 1989.

——, *The Julio-Claudian Emperors*, Bristol, 1989.

——, *Emperors and Gladiators*, London/New York, 1992.

Whitby, M. and J. Streeter (eds), *De Ste. Croix, G.E.M., Christian Persecution, Martyrdom and Orthodoxy*, Oxford, 2006.

Wilkinson, S., *Caligula*, London/New York, 2005.

Williams, D., *The Reach of Rome: A History of the Roman Imperial Frontier, 1st to 5th centuries AD*, London, 1996.

Wilson, R.J.A., *Sicily under the Roman Empire. The Archaeology of a Roman Province, 36 BC–AD 565*, Warminster, 1990.

Wilson Trigg, J., *Origen. The Bible and Philosophy in the Third-century Church*, Atlanta, 1983.

Yavetz, Z., *Plebs and Princeps*, Oxford, 1969.

Zahariade, M., *Scythia minor. A History of a Later Roman Province (284–681)*, Amsterdam, 2006.

Zanker, P., *The Power of the Images in the Age of Augustus*, translated into English by A. Shapiro, Ann Arbor MI, 1988.

CELTS, GERMANS, AND TRIBES FROM THE EURASIAN STEPPE

Chadwick, N., *The Celts*, Harmondsworth, 1997.

Christensen, A.S., *Cassiodorus, Jordanes and the History of the Goths. Studies in a Migration Myth*, Copenhagen, 2002.

Drinkwater, J.F., *The Alamanni and Rome 213–496 (Caracalla to Clovis)*, Oxford, 2007.

Freeman, Ph., *War, Women and Druids. Eyewitness Reports and Early Accounts of the Ancient Celts*, Austin TX, 2002.

Green, M.P. (ed.), *The Celtic World*, London/New York, 1995.

Heather, P., *Goths and Romans, AD 332–489*, Oxford, 1991.

Heather, P., *The Goths*, Oxford, 2002.

Hutton, R., *The Pagan Religions of the Ancient British Isles. Their Nature and Legacy*, Oxford, 1991.

Rankin, H.D., *Celts and the Classical World*, London/New York, 1996.

Roymans, N., *Ethnic Identity and Imperial Power. The Batavians in the Early Roman Empire*, Amsterdam, 2004.

Roymans, N. and F. Theuws, *Images of the Past. Studies on Ancient Societies in North-western Europe*, Amsterdam, 1991.

Speidel, M.P., *Ancient Germanic Warriors. Warrior Styles from Trajan's Column to Icelandic Sagas*, London/New York, 2004.

Thompson, E.A. and P. Heather, *The Huns*, Oxford, 1996.

Todd, M., *The Early Germans*, Oxford, 1992.

Wolfram, H., *History of the Goths*, translated into English by Th.J. Dunlap, Berkeley/Los Angeles/London, 1988.

JEWS, EGYPT, AND THE NEAR EAST UNDER THE ROMANS

Alston, R., *Soldier and Society in Roman Egypt*, London/New York, 1995.

Avi-Yonah, M., *The Jews under Roman and Byzantine Rule: A Political History of Palestine from the Bar Kokhba War to the Arab Conquest*, Jerusalem, 1984.

Bagnall, R.S., *Egypt in Late Antiquity*, Princeton NJ, 1993.

——, and B.W. Frier, *The Demography of Roman Egypt*, Cambridge, 1994.

Barclay, J.M.G., *Jews in the Mediterranean Diaspora from Alexander to Trajan, 323 BCE–117 CE*, Edinburgh, 1996.

Belayche, N., *The Pagan Cults in Roman Palestine*, Tübingen, 2001.

Bowman, A.K., *Egypt after the Pharaohs, 332 BC–AD 642, from Alexander to the Arab Conquest*, 2nd edn, London, 1996.

Drijvers, J.W., *Cyril of Jerusalem: Bishop and City*, Leiden/Boston, 2004.

Edwards, D.R., *Religion and Power. Pagans, Jews and Christians in the Greek East*, Oxford, 1996.

Frankfurter, D., *Religion in Roman Egypt. Assimilation and Resistance*, Princeton NJ, 1998.

Goodman, M., *The Ruling Class of Judea. The Origins of the Jewish Revolt against Rome, AD 66–70*, Cambridge, 1987.

Gruen, E.S., *Outside the Promised Land. Diaspora: Jews amidst Greeks and Romans*, London/Cambridge MA, 2002.

Isaac, B., *The Limits of Empire. The Roman Army in the East*, Oxford, 1992.

Jong, J.H.M. de, *Emperors in Egypt. The Representation and Perception of Roman Imperial Power in Greek Papyrus Texts from Egypt, AD 193–284*, Nijmegen, 2006.

Kaizer, T., *The Religious Life of Palmyra. A Study of the Social Patterns of Worship in the Roman Period*, Stuttgart, 2002.

Levine, L.J., *The Synagogue in Late Antiquity*, Philadelphia, 1987.

Lewis, N., *Life in Egypt under Roman Rule*, Oxford, 1983.

——, *On Government and Law in Roman Egypt*, Atlanta, 1995.

Lieu, J., J. North and T. Rajak, *The Jews among Pagans and Christians*, London, 1992.

Meier, J.P., *A Marginal Jew. Rethinking the Historical Jesus*, New York, 1991/2001.

Mendels, D., *The Rise and Fall of Jewish Nationalism. Jewish and Christian Ethnicity in Ancient Palestine*, 2nd edn, Grand Rapids MI, 1997.

Millar, F.G.B., *The Roman Near East*, 4th edn, Cambridge MA, 2001.

Pollard, N., *Soldiers, Cities and Civilians in Roman Syria*, Ann Arbor MI, 2000.

Rajak, T., *The Jewish Dialogue with Greece and Rome. Studies in Cultural and Social Interaction*, Leiden/Boston, 2001.

Ross, S.K., *Roman Edessa. Politics and Culture on the Eastern Fringes of the Roman Empire, 114–242 CE*, London/New York, 2001.

Sartre, M., *The Middle East under Rome*, translated into English by C. Porter and E. Rawlings with J. Routier-Pucci, London/Cambridge MA, 2005.

Schäfer, P., *The History of the Jews in the Greco-Roman World*, London/New York, 2003.

Schürer, E., *History of the Jewish People in the Age of Jesus Christ 175 BC–AD 135*, 2nd edn, Edinburgh, 1973–1987.

Smallwood, E.M., *The Jews under Roman Rule*, 2nd edn, Leiden, 2001.

Sperber, D., *The City in Roman Palestine*, Oxford, 1998.

INDEX

f before a page number indicates a caption to a map or illustration
(d) = divinity